The Latter-day Saint
Experience in America

The Latter-day Saint Experience in America

Terryl L. Givens

To my friend and fellow student Basil. Best. Terryl Givens

The American Religious Experience
Philip Goff, Series Editor

Greenwood Press
Westport, Connecticut • London

Library of Congress Cataloging-in-Publication Data

Givens, Terryl.
    The Latter-day Saint experience in America / Terryl L. Givens.
      p. cm. — (The American religious experience)
    Includes bibliographical references and index.
    ISBN 0-313-32750-5 (alk. paper)
    1. Church of Jesus Christ of Latter-day Saints—History.   2. Mormon Church—
United States—History.   3. United States—Church history.   I. Title.
II. American religious experience (Greenwood Press (Westport, Conn.))
BX8611.G59   2004
289.3'32'09—dc22   2004054375

British Library Cataloguing in Publication Data is available.

Library of Congress Catalog Card Number: 2004054375
ISBN: 0-313-32750-5

First published in 2004

Greenwood Press, 88 Post Road West, Westport, CT 06881
An imprint of Greenwood Publishing Group, Inc.
www.greenwood.com

Printed in the United States of America

∞™

The paper used in this book complies with the
Permanent Paper Standard issued by the National
Information Standards Organization (Z39.48-1984).

10 9 8 7 6 5 4 3 2 1

To the memory of my father,
George W. Givens

Contents

Series Foreword

Philip Goff

Some years ago, Winthrop Hudson, a leading religious historian, began his survey book on religion in America with a description of a London street. "When Americans walk down the street of an English city," he wrote, "they will be reminded of home."[1]

Few would dispute that for many years this was the case. Multiple faith traditions in today's United States trace their roots to English lineage, most notably the Episcopal, Methodist, and Baptist churches. But that sort of literary device would not hold up under the pressure of today's diversity. Lutherans, Presbyterians, and Dutch Reformed adherents would balk at such oversimplification—and those are just a few among only the Protestant Christians. Add the voices of Jews, Eastern Orthodox, Muslims, Buddhists, and Irish, Italian, and Polish Catholics, and we would have a powerful chorus demanding their stories be told. And their stories do not begin on the streets of London.

Of course, Hudson knew that was the case. His point was not that all significant American religions began in England, but that, "with only a few exceptions, the varied religious groups of America have their roots abroad."[2] But clearly the "abroad" Hudson worked with was predominantly European, even if not entirely English. Today's scholarship has broadened that focus to include African, Asian, Central and South American, as well as Canadian and some "homegrown" traditions that are on their way to becoming worldwide faiths. If ever scholarship in American religion has reflected the lineage of its people, it is in the recent writings that have moved beyond conventional ideas of faith traditions to include non-Anglo peoples who, while often existing off the radar screen of the establishment, have nonetheless formed much of the marrow of American religious life.

Although our studies of American religion have expanded to include more migrating faith groups from more areas of the world, the basic question that divided historians early in the twentieth century remained: namely, are traditions of American life (religion, politics, economics, etc.) transplants from the Old World, or did something entirely new and unique form in the New World? That is, should we seek to comprehend America's present religious scene by understanding its roots? Or should we try to understand it by looking at its transformations?

Of course, the truth lies somewhere in between. One cannot understand present-day Methodists or Buddhists by knowing their Old World beginnings in England and China or Japan. Nor can one determine the transformations those faith traditions underwent in America without knowing a good deal about their Old World forms. The American experience, then, is one of constancy of tradition from one angle and continual revision from another. The fact that they may look, think, and sound different than their Old World forms does not negate the fact that they are still recognizably Methodist and Buddhist in their new contexts.

This book series is meant to introduce readers to the basic faith traditions that characterize religious life today by employing that continuum of constancy and change. Each volume traces its topic from its Old World beginnings (when it applies) to its present realities. In doing so, readers will see how many of the original beliefs and practices came to be, as well as how they transformed, remained nearly the same, or were complemented by new ones in the American environment. In some cases —African Americans and Mormons most clearly—the Old World proved important either implicitly or imaginatively rather than explicitly and literally. But even in these cases, development within the context of American culture is still central to the story.

To be sure, each author in this series employed various approaches in writing these books. History, sociology, even anthropology, all play their parts. Each volume, then, may have its idiosyncrasies, as the authors chose which approaches worked best at which moments for their respective topics. These variations of approach resemble the diversity of the groups themselves, as each interacted in various ways at different stages with American society.

Not only do these volumes introduce us to the roots and development of each faith group, they also provide helpful guides to readers who wish to know more about them. By supplying timelines and glossaries, the books give a deeper sense of beliefs, behaviors, and significant figures and moments in those religions. By offering resources for research—including published primary and secondary sources as well as helpful Web sites—the series presents a wealth of helpful information for formal and informal students of religion in America.

Clearly, this is a series conceived and published with the curious reader in mind. It is our hope that it will spur both a deeper understanding of the varieties of religious experience in the United States and better research in the country's many and always changing traditions.

Notes

1. Winthrop Hudson, *Religion in America*, 4th ed. (New York: Macmillan, 1987), 11.

2. Ibid., 11–12.

Olympic medals plaza, 2002 Salt Lake City Winter Olympics
(Photo credit Steve Greenwood. Copyright Greenwood Productions. Used by permission)

Introduction: What Is a Mormon?

These will be the Mormon Games. And as with Barcelona and
Sydney, the setting will linger in the collective memory long after
we have all forgotten who won the ice dancing. If it all goes well,
it will be Utah's triumph. That means a Mormon triumph.
—*The Guardian*, 21 January 2002

Founded in 1830 by twenty-four-year-old Vermont native Joseph
Smith, the Church of Jesus Christ of Latter-day Saints (the Mormon
Church) has risen from inauspicious beginnings to become a major American religious denomination and a contender to be the next world faith.
Initially distinguished by their belief in living prophets and additional
scriptures including the Book of Mormon, Latter-day Saints experienced
a difficult passage from forced exile in Utah to their contemporary position of respect and influence in American society. In some ways, the highly
publicized Olympic Games of 2002, dubbed the "Mormon Games" by the
media, signaled a dramatic arrival of sorts. A new respectability and the
double-edged sword of unprecedented media focus were both implicit in
Salt Lake's selection to be the host site, as recognized by the city's ex-
mayor: "The[se] Olympics," said Ted Wilson, "mean the refuge is over."[1]

The 2002 Winter Olympics were the Mormon games in several ways.
Latter-day Saint politician Mitt Romney headed the organizing committee.
The Tabernacle Choir performed four times. Ten to fifteen thousand LDS
members worked as volunteers, almost four thousand of them bilingual
returned missionaries serving as interpreters. One million visitors came to
the 2002 Olympics in Salt Lake City. Three billion more television viewers
watched awards ceremonies each night taking place in Olympic Medals
Plaza, with the soaring spires of the Salt Lake temple in the background.

Of the many stages in Mormonism's evolution, this was an especially
triumphant milestone. The granite blocks of the solid, stately temple still
embody much that is distinctively Mormon. Built by an impoverished and
exiled people, this Notre Dame of the West had no benefit of an established
economic base, no urban setting from which to draw its laborers, donors,
and appreciative pilgrims. Its fortress-like appearance evokes the memory

of a church long under siege for distinctive religious beliefs and unorthodox practices. This enduring symbol of Mormonism is crowded round with teeming businesses and a towering church headquarters, but looks no more disposed to yield ground to architectural newcomers than the church has to the forces of modernity. As if to suggest a symbolic accommodation between the church and secular society, those gilded spires adorn a temple that television—and the great American publicity machine—chose to exploit for its cinematographic beauty and its evocation of Mormon uprightness and respectability, even if they cannot penetrate the sacred inner chambers those spires crown.

The Salt Lake temple is one of a series of Mormon symbols: the Mormon Tabernacle Choir and Brigham Young University (BYU) football; golden plates and the angel Moroni; Joseph's martyrdom at Carthage; Brigham Young and all those wives. Mormonism is replete with symbols and trappings that have become American cultural icons. But Mormonism itself, like any complex cultural phenomenon, is easier to talk about and around than to penetrate or define adequately. The famous explorer Richard Burton was the most successful European in history at insinuating himself into the Arab cultures he studied, and was the first outsider to infiltrate the forbidden city of Harar in Somaliland, as well as Mecca and Medina. But even the intrepid Burton sensed that "there is in Mormondom, as in all other exclusive faiths, . . . an inner life into which I cannot flatter myself or deceive the reader with the idea of my having penetrated."[2]

Few who study Mormonism are satisfied to label it a simple religious denomination. Mormonism has also been called a culture, a global tribe, a religious tradition, the next world religion, and even "the clearest example to be found in our national history . . . of a native and indigenously developed ethnic minority."[3] Whether Mormons (or Latter-day Saints or LDS or Saints) really constitute a distinct ethnic group within American society may be disputed. But the mere suggestion is itself an indication of the failure of a term like *denomination* to characterize the group adequately. Certainly there is a denominational aspect to Mormon identity. Devout Mormons, or members of the Church of Jesus Christ of Latter-day Saints, are generally unanimous in assenting to a number of fundamental truth-claims. They believe in a supreme deity, God the Father. They revere his son, Jesus Christ, as Savior of the world. But they believe the Father and Son are separate and distinct corporeal beings, not members of a Trinity as defined by the church councils of Christian orthodoxy. (They also believe in the Holy Ghost, as a personage of spirit.) They believe in the Bible as the word of God ("as far as it is translated correctly"). But they also believe that the Book of Mormon is the word of God, on a par with—or even more reliable than—the Old and New Testaments. They believe in the patriarchs and prophets of old: Abraham, Moses, Jeremiah, and Isaiah. But they also believe in prophets of the current age or "dispensation": Joseph Smith, Brigham Young, and Gordon B. Hinckley.

One sociologist has noted that Mormons are like conservative Protestants in their rejection of the "new morality," are close to mainstream Protestants in their educational attainments, resemble Jews in their norms against interfaith marriage, and echo Catholics in their opposition to abortion.[4] In their belief system as a whole, more than one commentator insists they move as far beyond normative Christianity as Christianity did beyond Judaism.

However, defining Mormonism in terms of a common belief structure has two deficiencies. First, as we will see, Mormonism—at least in recent years—has come to encompass elements of shared heritage, social behaviors and attitudes, cultural vocabulary, lifestyle, worldview, and other factors that far transcend mere creedal statements. Second, many persons claim a Mormon identity, even as they reject those truth-claims most fundamental to historical Mormonism. Subscribing to a particular set of beliefs, in other words, appears to be neither a sufficient nor a necessary condition for inclusion in the worldwide community of Mormons. This study employs the term persuasively popularized by historian of religion Jan Shipps: Mormonism is neither a cult, nor a denomination, nor Catholic, nor Protestant, she writes, but a new "faith tradition." These words seem the best of those available, because they suggest the rootedness of Mormonism in a set of claims that ask for faithful assent; and indeed, to be a Mormon is still, for the most part, to be convinced of the truthfulness of a set of beliefs that, however they may overlap the creeds of Christianity, include as well a number of highly distinctive and highly unorthodox tenets. This is still the primary thrust of what it means to be a Mormon. At the same time, the movement has grown into a body of many millions, has acquired an identity bordering on ethnicity or cultural autonomy that transcends any set of doctrinal claims, and has shown itself capacious enough to accommodate varying types of affiliation, as the term *tradition* suggests. This is not to say that the LDS Church has acquired a theological laxness tolerant of dissent and heterodoxy. Far from it. It is to say, rather, that some members now feel an affinity to Mormonism, a historical or cultural or affective kinship, that may overshadow all theological identification, or may exist in the absence of any theological identification at all.

In the nineteenth century, popular representations of Mormonism both reflected and contributed to public perceptions that Mormons were distinctive in very visible, discernible, and generally unflattering ways. Novels and nickel weeklies depicted their speech as peculiar, their dress as odd, and their appearance as foreign, exotic, or most frequently, "oriental." One purportedly scientific report presented in 1861 described the Mormons as a new racial type that had evolved with remarkable rapidity. At the New Orleans Academy of Sciences, the audience heard the particulars:

> This condition is shown by . . . the large proportion of albuminous and gelatinous types of constitution, and by the striking uniformity in facial expression and in physical conformation of the younger portion of the community. . . . there is . . . an expression of countenance and a style of feature, which may be styled the Mormon expression and style; an expression compounded of sensuality, cunning, suspicion, and a smirking self-conceit. The yellow, sunken, cadaverous visage; the greenish-colored eyes; the thick, protuberant lips; the low forehead; the light, yellowish hair, and the lank, angular person, constitute an appearance so characteristic of the new race . . . as to distinguish them at a glance.[5]

Other observers tended to agree there was something distinctive about Mormons, but often cast the differences in more generous terms. Charles Dickens visited an emigrant ship at an English dock about to sail for America "in order to see what eight hundred Latter-day Saints were like, and I found them (to the rout and overthrow of all my expectations) . . . a very fine set of people." In fact, he thought them, "in their degree, the pick and flower of England. . . . It would be difficult," he went on, "to find Eight hundred people together anywhere else, and find so much beauty and so much strength and capacity for work among them."[6] At about the same time, Mark Twain recorded his observations upon touring Salt Lake City, which he called "stronghold of the prophets, [and] capitol city of the only absolute monarchy in America":

> We strolled about everywhere through the broad, straight, level streets and enjoyed the pleasant strangeness of a city of 15,000 inhabitants with no loafers perceptible in it, and no visible drunkard or noisy people. A limpid stream rippling and dancing through every street in place of a filthy gutter; block after block of trim dwellings built of frame and sun-

burned brick—a great thriving orchard and garden behind every one of them, apparently, and a grand general air of neatness, repair, thrift and comfort around and about and over the whole.[7]

At the close of the twentieth century, the old stereotypes—or the cultural continuities—sometimes continued to assert themselves. Harold Bloom, for example, maintains with apparent sobriety that "the visitor to Salt Lake City, after just four days, has learned to tell the difference between certain Mormons and most Gentiles at first sight. There is something organized about the expressions on many Mormon faces as they go by in the street."[8]

As we will see, Mormons cooperate fully in the role history and popular perception have assigned them as a highly distinctive people. A history of exile and persecution, belief in their chosenness and in their church's claim to divine origin, unique health codes and temple rites, a self-sustaining welfare system, and a private cultural vocabulary, all conspire to reinforce their own and everyone else's sense that they are a people apart. Gordon B. Hinckley, current prophet and president of the church, has shown a fondness for the words of Peter, believing they serve as both characterization of and challenge to the Latter-day Saints: "Ye are a chosen generation, a royal priesthood, an holy nation, a peculiar people" (1 Peter 2:9)

Mormonism was once largely confined to white Americans of British or Scandinavian descent centered in Utah; more Mormons worldwide now have Spanish as a native language than English. Even within the United States, it is increasingly inaccurate to refer to Mormonism as a Utah church. True, that state still boasts the highest numbers of Latter-day Saints, but whereas one of every two lived there in 1930,[9] significant numbers are now found scattered broadly across the United States.

With the advantage of sociological analysis, it is now possible to address the question of Mormon distinctiveness in very specific, quantifiable terms. What we discover is that popular perceptions have elements of both truth and error. Mormons as a people do tend to show high levels of religious commitment. They attend church more regularly than Catholics and Protestants, and evangelicals, attending Sunday school twice as often as Baptists and three times as often as Seventh-Day Adventists. They share their faith with others more often than Lutherans and Methodists, and read the Bible as often as members of the most Bible-studious groups—Assemblies of God, Pentecostals, and nondenominational Protestants.[10]

They contribute considerably more money to their church than other church-going Americans.[11] The LDS reputation for a rigorous work and education ethic seem well-founded as well. The Mormon standard of educational attainment is "considerably higher than the national average."[12] Bucking the general rule, the better educated Mormons are, the more likely they are to be religiously committed.[13]

Patterns of family life are even more distinguishing. LDS members in the United States have higher rates of marriage and lower rates of divorce than is true nationally.[14] Compared to members of other religions, Mormons are the most likely to be married to a spouse of their own faith.[15] Large family size in America frequently prompts the assumption that the parents are either Catholic or Mormon and, indeed, Mormon family size is "substantially larger than the national average."[16] But contrary to prevalent notions, this is not a result of either doctrinal or cultural prohibitions against birth control. The practice is not officially discouraged (though it once was), and Mormon mothers use contraception at a rate comparable to the national average.

Mormons are renowned for their wholesome, clean-cut lifestyles—and apparently with good reason. Mormon youth consume tobacco, alcohol, and drugs at rates substantially lower than their peers.[17] And LDS people are considerably less likely to have sexual relations before marriage or outside of marriage; in fact, one study concludes that in the area of sexuality, "findings . . . appear to differentiate LDS people from non-LDS people more than any other set of variables."[18]

The typical role of the woman in Mormon culture is itself a mixture of the expected and the surprising. The church encourages traditional gender roles, teaching that mothers have primary responsibility for child-rearing, while teaching the New Testament principle that it is men's duty to "provide . . . for those of his own house" (1 Tim. 5:8). And indeed, LDS people, in higher numbers than average, favor the man earning the living and disapprove of mothers of small children working and of putting children in daycare. Even so, women work at nearly the same rate as non-Mormons.[19]

Politically, Mormons are generally assumed to be staunch Republicans. And indeed, Utah usually does vote that way. But in 2004, the U.S. Senate majority whip and other prominent members of Congress were LDS Democrats. In addition, studies reveal Mormons to be more open than most Americans to inter-racial association (inter-racial marriage, integrated schooling, and racially mixed neighborhoods), and "among the more 'liberal' of the various denominations in attitudes toward racial justice."[20]

Socioeconomically, Mormons have long had a reputation for industry and thrift. Early stereotypes depicted Mormons as society's castoffs, and Missouri settlers invoked their alleged destitution as one reason for expelling them from their settlements in the 1830s. In actual fact, from their early experiments in communitarian economics to their prodigious feat of carving an empire out of the Utah desert, their industriousness made their territorial name of "Deseret"—a Book of Mormon term meaning honeybee—entirely apt. In contemporary America, their record is respectable but not stupendous. They report slightly higher incomes per household than the average.[21]

In sum, Mormons are a mix of the expected, the surprising, and the ever-evolving. To what extent the distinctness of a Mormon identity is objectively quantifiable, and to what extent it is a product of both self-representation and popular depiction, is a complicated issue. One popular interpretation would have it that Mormonism began as a movement radically at odds with mainstream American culture. The need to assert their uniqueness on a stage crowded with emerging religious sects, to substantiate their claim that Christianity had gone astray and only wholesale restoration would suffice, and to give literal weight, through physical gathering and social peculiarity, to their belief in themselves as a covenant people, all conspired to produce a religious culture that necessitated, enacted, and reified dramatic difference.

But finding protection from mainstream hostility and interference neither in their Missouri enclaves, their city-state of Nauvoo, nor the mountain fastness of Utah, they at last relented and self-consciously began the process of Americanization to achieve acceptance, approval, and statehood. A combination of this strategic campaign and the inescapable forces of modernization and globalization together have produced a religious culture that some would argue not only has reached accommodation with its host culture, but may be its more typical incarnation. "They ain't whites—they're Mormons!" cries a character in a 1914 Jack London novel.[22] By 1989, the hero of Tom Clancy's novel raises no eyebrows in calling the Mormon characters "honest and hardworking, and fiercely loyal," in fact, everything that "America stood for."[23] In the eyes of many observers, it is clear, Mormonism has become "the American religion." But it was a tortuous path that took its adherents there.

Chapter 1 charts the history of the Mormon Church from its organization into the twenty-first century. Because the first three-quarter centuries of that history were characterized by tensions and conflicts with local populations, state militias, the federal government, and orthodox churches—all to a degree unprecedented in American history—chapter 2 examines the several sources of friction characterizing those first generations. Chapter 3 is devoted to expounding Mormon religious doctrine, reviewing what is typically Christian in LDS theology and what is different and innovative. Smith produced not just one extrabiblical book of scripture, the Book of Mormon, but the core of two others as well, in addition to making substantial emendations to the text of the King James Bible. Chapter 4 considers the origin and content of those additions to the Christian scriptural canon. Subsequent chapters examine Latter-day Saint worship in terms of its three principal loci—home, church, and temple (chapter 5); Mormonism's engagement with political and social issues of the modern day (chapter 6); and the role of the arts and education in Mormon culture (chapter 7). Chapter 8 looks at some of the competing varieties in the Latter-day Saint tradition; and considers the challenges and opportunities faced by Mormonism in the new millennium, as it increases its international presence and provokes predictions of attaining world-faith status.

Notes

1. Cited in *The Economist*, 7 February 2002.

2. Richard Burton, *City of the Saints* (1861; reprint, ed. Fawn M. Brodie, New York: Knopf, 1963), 224.

3. Dean May citing Thomas O'Dea, in "Mormons," in Stephan Thernstrom, ed., *Harvard Encyclopedia of American Ethnic Groups* (Cambridge, Mass.: Harvard University Press, 1980), 720.

4. James T. Duke, "Cultural Continuity and Tension: A Test of Stark's Theory of Church Growth," in James T. Duke, ed., *Latter-Day Saint Social Life: Social Research on the LDS Church and its Members* (Provo, Utah: Religious Studies Center, Brigham Young University, 1998), 77–79.

5. The paper by Samuel Cartwright and C. G. Forshey relied upon a report of Roberts Bartholow, assistant surgeon of the U.S. Army. See Surgeon General's Office, *Statistical Report on the Sickness and Mortality in the Army of the United States . . . From January, 1855 to January, 1860* (Washington, D.C.: George W. Bowman, 1860), 301–2.

6. Charles Dickens, *The Uncommercial Traveller* (1861; reprint, New York: Charles Scribner's, 1902), 262–63.

7. Mark Twain, *Roughing It* (New York: Rinehart, 1953), 71–72.

8. Harold Bloom, *The American Religion: The Emergence of a Post-Christian Nation* (New York: Simon and Schuster, 1992), 116.

9. Tim Heaton, "Vital Statistics," in James T. Duke, ed., *Latter-day Saint Social Life: Social Research on the LDS Church and its Members* (Provo, Utah: Religious Studies Center, Brigham Young University, 1998), 109.

10. These comparisons derive from a Barna Research Group poll reported in the *Washington Post*, 9 February 2002.

11. Dean R. Hope and Fenggang Yang, "Determinants of Religious Giving in American Denominations: Data from Two Nationwide Surveys," *Review of Religious Research* 36 (1994): 123–48.

12. Stan L. Albrecht and Tim B. Heaton, "Secularization, Higher Education, and Religiosity," in Duke, *LDS Social Life*, 302.

13. Stan L. Albrecht, "The Consequential Dimension of Mormon Religiosity," in Duke, *LDS Social Life*, 285.

14. Heaton, "Vital Statistics," 124.

15. Twelve percent of Mormons live in a "mixed religion household," according to the *American Religious Identification Survey* (ARIS) conducted in 2001 by the Graduate Center of the City University of New York. Some results of the survey are available on-line at www.religioustolerance.org/chr_prac2.htm.

16. Tim B. Heaton, Kristen L. Goodman, and Thomas B. Holman, "In Search of a Peculiar People: Are Mormon Families Really Different?" in Marie Cornwall, Tim B. Heaton, and Lawrence A. Young, *Contemporary Mormonism: Social Science Perspectives* (Urbana: University of Illinois Press, 2001), 89.

17. Steven Bahr reviews several studies that document, with rare exceptions, lower alcohol and drug use among Mormon youth compared to adolescents from other religions. See his "Religion and Adolescent Drug Use: A Comparison of Mormons and Other Religions," in Cornwall et al., *Contemporary Mormonism*, 122–23.

18. Heaton et al., "In Search," 100.

19. Ibid., 104.

20. Armand Mauss, *All Abraham's Children: Changing Mormon Conceptions of Race and Lineage* (Urbana: University of Illinois Press, 2003), 252–55.

21. Heaton, "Vital Statistics," 130.

22. Jack London, *Star Rover* (1914; reprint, New York: Arcadia House, 1950), 135.

23. Tom Clancy, *Clear and Present Danger* (New York: Putnam, 1989), 480.

Chapter 1

A Homegrown Religion: Mormonism in America and America in Mormonism

> Mormonism [is] history, not philosophy.
> —LDS historian Richard Bushman

> History as theology is perilous.
> —Grant McMurray, president of the Community
> of Christ (formerly the Reorganized Church
> of Jesus Christ of Latter Day Saints)

On 10 September 1846, the bombardment began and continued sporadically for three days. As many as eight hundred (some Mormons said 1,800) militiamen and area citizens with six pieces of cannon had surrounded the virtually deserted city of Nauvoo, Illinois. The two to three hundred remaining Saints converted some steamboat shafts to cannon and threw up barricades. After a stubborn resistance by the besieged and a daring sortie that brought temporary respite but at a cost of three Mormon lives, the combatants signed an agreement of capitulation on 16 September. By October, the Mormon temple in Nauvoo—finished at such tremendous sacrifice even while persecutions raged—was desecrated, the beautiful city that had recently rivaled Chicago in size was a shell of its former self, and the last weary and infirm Saints had joined their fellow believers in forcible exile. They left behind not just the "City of Joseph," but the very borders of the United States of America.

At almost the same time and thousands of miles away, the Mormon Battalion, a group of Mormon volunteers, trudged toward Santa Fe to rendezvous with the federal Army of the West on their way to fight the Mexican War. On 9 October the battalion arrived, and Colonel Alexander

Doniphan of the Missouri Mounted Volunteers ordered a one-hundred gun salute to honor the Mormons for their loyalty to the United States. They had just completed the longest march in American military history, on behalf of a government from whose territory they had just been expelled at cannon-point.

It is one of the great paradoxes of the Mormon experience in the nineteenth century that the American flag suggested to the Latter-day Saints both promise and oppression; it served them as emblem of God's purpose and designs and bitter ensign of a nation that expelled, disenfranchised, and persecuted them. America, Mormons believe, was the seedbed not only of modern democracy, but of the gospel's restoration, a "land choice above all others" (Ether 2:15). As a Mormon apostle wrote, "the Lord prepared America as the site for the restoration of his truth in the latter days."[1] Yet that same country, in the aftermath of extensive mobbings and expulsions, refused to redress the systematic persecution and expulsion of the Mormon people from their homes and lands. From the Mormon perspective, the paradox of this relationship is that, however fractious it may become, it is indispensable to both church and nation achieving their promised destiny. Mormons believe that providential design and purpose informed the founding of both. And while nineteenth-century America felt the faith and practice of the LDS Church to be incompatible with the morality of a Christian nation, and Mormonism's very presence a blight on the body politic, the church considered both itself and America to be players whose roles and destinies were interdependent and divinely scripted.

"An Unusual Excitement on the Subject of Religion": Joseph Smith and the Second Great Awakening

Mormons understand their history in terms of a sweeping drama that spans millennia, involving protagonists who are foreordained (but not predestined) to their roles, predictably hostile adversaries, and conflicts whose broad outlines, if not specific details, are part of a grand, prophesied design. At the same time, and in ways that are not necessarily inconsistent with the Mormon version, secular historians emphasize the social setting behind Mormonism's birth as well as political and constitutional conflicts that surrounded its first generations of growth and processes of accommodation and "Americanization" that mark its recent past and present.

The gospel, according to Latter-day Saints, was known to prophets and patriarchs harking all the way back to father Adam, who they believe was baptized, received the gift of the Holy Ghost, and knew of the atonement of Jesus Christ. In that sense, Mormonism claims to be not an innovation or creation of Joseph Smith, but rather the latest—and final—incarnation of a church that was conceived in heavenly councils before the world was created, and found its first earthly appearance in the days soon after the fall of man. But why this final version of an eternal gospel, the one called Mormonism, should unfold in an American setting is a question that secular historians and Latter-day Saints might answer rather differently. For while historians may assign Mormonism a few lines in the saga of America, the LDS have long held that Mormonism is the real drama, with America blessed to play a special role as important as any character's.

In the interval between Eden and the Industrial Revolution, Mormons believe the descendents of Adam went through recurrent phases of apostasy, or spiritual darkness, and gospel fullness. Noah's generation was the most notorious instance of moral blight, but the Old Testament records numerous occasions when the chosen seed strayed from faithfulness to God, falling prey to the enticements of Mammon, Baal, or any number of golden calves. Patriarchs and prophets such as Enoch, Abraham, Moses, and Jeremiah provoked reform, renewed or reformulated covenant relationships with deity, and restored lost or neglected truths and teachings. Christ's establishment of the gospel and a church organization in "the Meridian of time" (Smith's scriptural expression for the middle epoch in earth's history) is, to the Mormon mind, the most glorious but far from the first occasion that the doctrines of faith, repentance, and salvation were taught in purity and fullness. Not unlike Luther and his myriad brother reformers, Mormons believe that in the generations after Peter and Paul false teachings and wickedness corrupted the fountains of both gospel truth and priesthood authority. But unlike the Protestant reformers, Mormons believe that the contamination occurred earlier than the late middle ages and would have to wait longer than the sixteenth century for an authoritative and efficacious solution to the last and "Great Apostasy."

That America might be the scene of a new Zion, where God could reestablish his gospel and walk among his people, if only figuratively, fired the minds of many who settled there. Early colonizers of America often saw themselves as embarking on an "errand in the wilderness." The Pilgrims who disembarked in Plymouth sought to erect their heavenly city on earth, and with profound assurance that they were enacting sacred history. Mormonism's initial conception of America would be articulated in similar terms—but with a difference. The Mormon experience with America begins over two thousand years before Plymouth. It starts with a prophecy attributed to an Israelite prophet who, speaking shortly after arriving in the New World six centuries before Christ, sees in vision the voyages of an inspired voyager (presumably Columbus) and the colonization of the hemisphere:

> And I looked and beheld a man among the Gentiles, who was separated from the seed of my brethren by the many waters; and I beheld the Spirit of God, that it came down and wrought upon the man; and he went forth upon the many waters, even unto the seed of my brethren, who were in the promised land. And it came to pass that I beheld the Spirit of God, that it wrought upon other Gentiles; and they went forth out of captivity, upon the many waters. (1 Nephi 13:12–13)

Mormons believe that from the time of the Babylonian empire, then, America—or at least the Western Hemisphere—was prophetically seen as a promised land, to which the Lord would one day lead the righteous. After predicting the voyage of Columbus, this same prophet, Nephi, goes on to describe how "the mother Gentiles were gathered together upon the waters, and upon the land also, to battle against them. . . . And I, Nephi, beheld that the Gentiles that had gone out of captivity were delivered by the power of God out of the hands of all other nations" (17–19). In Latter-day Saint thought, these words describe the American independence movement as a divinely inspired and assisted process. Eventually, with a free people established, the tyrant of Great Britain defeated, and the land secure, the main act unfolds:

> For the time speedily cometh, saith the Lamb of God, that I will work a great and a marvelous work among the children of men; a work which shall be everlasting. . . . And it came to pass that I, Nephi, beheld the power of the Lamb of God, that it descended upon the saints of the church of the Lamb, and upon the covenant people of the Lord, who were scattered upon all the face of the earth; and they were armed with righteousness, and with the power of God in great glory. (14:7, 14)

America, in other words, is a land divinely foreordained to be the stage for the concluding acts of the last gospel dispensation of the world's history. After early habitation by various peoples, it is rediscovered by an inspired Christopher Columbus, and settled by those who were directed there by the Spirit of the Lord ("there shall none come into this land save they shall be brought by the hand of the Lord" [2 Nephi 1:6]). Its inhabitants are sustained in their Revolutionary War by "the power of God" (1 Nephi 14:18), and immediately thereafter, another LDS scripture proclaims, the Lord himself "established the Constitution of this land by the hand of wise men whom [he] raised up unto this very purpose" (*Doctrine and Covenants* [DC] 101:80).

By 1796, after doing his part to establish the nation's independence and, as its first president, its stability and political direction, George Washington delivered his farewell address. With America secure in its freedom, and with principles of religious toleration (relatively) established, the field was now ripe for God to plant the seeds of the gospel in "good ground" for the last time.[2] That same year, Joseph Smith Sr., a struggling Vermont farmer, and Lucy Mack, were married in the town of Tunbridge. On 23 December 1805, their fourth child and third son, Joseph Jr., was born in Sharon, Windsor County. By 1820, fourteen-year-old Joseph had become a seeker of true religion.

The immediate context for the founding of the Church of Jesus Christ of Latter-day Saints was a period of intense religious fervor known as the Second Great Awakening. In some ways a reprise of the Great Awakening of the colonial era, this later version was marked by similar religious revivalism, with a more individualistic—and often more radical—edge to it. The movement was given impetus if not birth at a series of camp meetings held at Cane Ridge, Kentucky, in 1801, and soon spread in all directions. Conditions in America generally, and New York State especially, made for a boiling cauldron of religious enthusiasm. Population in the counties to the west of Canandaigua, where the Smiths relocated in 1816, grew from under 17,000 at the turn of the century to over one hundred thousand just twenty years later.[3] The economic promise of the Erie Canal, under construction since 1817, economic depression following the War of 1812, rapid industrialization, agricultural crisis, and other social upheavals constitute one explanation for the large numbers of geographically and emotionally displaced people searching for religious meaning and spiritual security in a shaken world. Whether these pervasive waves of religious fervor were a spiritual response to societal upheaval, radical individualism, a new mechanism for social control (a "quintessentially bourgeois" spirituality that served the interests of a new manufacturing class), or

Joseph Smith Jr. (1805–44)
Prophet and founder of the Church of Jesus Christ of Latter-day Saints. (Courtesy of the Church Archives, The Church of Jesus Christ of Latter-day Saints)

inspired by a sense, as in the case of Joseph Smith's grandfather, Asael, that American independence was a portent of divine favor and a harbinger of an imminent millennium ("the Stone is now cut out of the mountain, without hands, spoken of by Daniel," he wrote[4]), no one could dispute the sea change in religious life sweeping across America.

The tenor of the times can be caught from titles of two works that describe that area of the country at that historical moment: *The Burned-Over District*, a modern study, refers to the fires of religious zeal that swept the western part of the state. A book more contemporary with the era's developments, the 1838 *Humbugs of New York: being a remonstrance against popular delusion; whether in science, philosophy, or religion*, reflects the exasperated response to the myriad -isms of the era that sometimes flashed into existence and then disappeared before they could even be entered in the almanacs. Mormonism is one "Humbug" mentioned, but so are the "kindred enormities of Matthias" and the "multitudes who believe in 'Animal Magnetism,' subscribe to 'Phrenology,' are the willing victims of every form of 'Quackery,' and have adopted the creed and practice of 'ultraism.' "[5] Other newly minted or newly invigorated movements cited—usually disapprovingly—by observers on the sidelines include New Americans, Sabellians, Swedenborgians, Sabbatarians, Necessarians, Hutchinsonians, Sandemonians, Muggletonians, Brownists, Hernhutters, Dunkers, Jumpers, and a host of others.

What distinguished this generation of religious seekers from previous ones was the pervasive intimation that the heavens were opening, Christ was coming, and new prophets were walking the earth. The spiritual egalitarianism so reflective of American individualism, with its emphasis on personal responsibility for salvation and democratic access to gifts of the Spirit, combined with charismatic preachers and contagious enthusiasm to create an unprecedented marketplace of religious options. Still, in Joseph Smith's area as elsewhere, heterodoxy erupted in the context of the more dominant, conventional rivalries. Methodist circuit riders vied with Disciples of Christ preachers, and Presbyterians clashed with Baptists. Fervent, outdoor camp meetings swept the whole countryside and everyone seemed to be competing for converts in a scene vividly described by the young farmboy Joseph Smith:

> There was in the place we lived an unusual excitement on the subject of religion. It commenced with the Methodists but soon became general among all the sects of that region of country. Indeed, the whole district of

country seemed affected by it, and great multitudes united themselves to the different religious parties, which created no small stir and division amongst the people, some crying, "Lo, here!" and others, "Lo, there!" . . . Great zeal . . . was manifested by the clergy, who were active in getting up and promoting this extraordinary scene of religious feeling, in order to have everyone converted.[6]

Joseph was one of thousands who willingly endured a barrage of competing pitches for a new—or renewed—religious engagement. And he was one of dozens who chronicled his personal quest, insisting his prayerful search had been met with miraculous manifestations from on high. His earliest record of his spiritual odyssey captured his sense of both personal and universal fallenness: "I become [sic] convicted of my sins and by searching the scriptures I found that mankind did not come unto the Lord but that they had apostatized from the true and liveing [sic] faith and there was no society or denomination that built upon the gospel of Jesus Christ as recorded in the New Testament."[7]

Desirous of affiliating himself with some religious body, but uncertain where to turn, Smith found direction in a passage from the book of James: "If any of you lack wisdom, let him ask of God that giveth to all men liberally, and upbraideth not, and it shall be given him" (1:5). Retiring to a secluded spot in the woods near the family farmhouse, Smith knelt and prayed, and was rewarded with an epiphany that would soon turn his world—and later the American orthodox establishment—upside down.

In his earliest version of his experience, he emphasized the personal nature of the message he heard from the midst of the resplendent vision: "A pillar of light above the brightness of the sun at noon day come [sic] down from above and rested upon me and . . . I saw the Lord and he spake unto me saying Joseph my son thy sins are forgiven thee." As touching on his desire for denominational guidance, Smith was told "the world lieth in sin at this time and none doeth good no not one they have turned aside [sic] from the gospel and keep not my commandments." In a later revision, he would add important details: "When the light rested upon me I saw two Personages, whose brightness and glory defy all description, standing above me in the air. One of them spake unto me, calling me by name and said, pointing to the other—*This is my beloved Son. Hear Him!*" Also, in this version, he was pointedly instructed that he must join none of the area churches, "for they were all wrong."[8] Skeptics see in these differences inconsistency and progressive elaboration. The faithful see a prophet gradually reassessing the extent to which his private epiphany had more universal implications and giving neglected details new exposure or emphasis accordingly.[9]

From the vantage point of retrospective history, Mormons now refer to this as "the First Vision," implying not just that others would follow, but that the event signaled the commencement of the boy's prophetic career and the heralding of a new dispensation. But Joseph's motives for offering his prayer on this spring day in 1820 were purely personal. Furthermore, his reaction to the epiphany showed that he interpreted it—even long after- ward—as personal in significance. Nothing in his reaction at the time or in later remarks suggests that he understood the event, marvelous as it may have been, as a calling to be a modern Moses—or even as a call to the min- istry. He told few people, engaged in no public sermonizing, and gathered no secret cabal of true believers; he was a teenage farm boy who had just experienced a remarkable vision. That made him unique in his neighbor- hood, but it was certainly not without many precedents in early America. Lorenzo Dow and Charles Finney are just two of the more famous exam- ples of religious seekers who experienced visions of their own.[10]

The response to Joseph's revelation was relatively muted. A Methodist preacher chastened him for his fanciful story. And at some point—though probably later—irritated neighbors ducked the youth in a pond.[11] But reminiscing about this period of his life in 1838, a year when mobs mas- sacred eighteen Mormons and exiled thousands from Missouri, Joseph interpreted his early travails in a more ominous light: "It seems as though the adversary was aware, at a very early period in my life, that I was des- tined to prove a disturber and an annoyer of his kingdom; else why should the powers of darkness combine against me? Why the opposition and per- secution that arose against me, almost in my infancy?"[12]

Joseph said little about his experience to his family ("I have learned for myself that Presbyterianism is not true" was his remark to his mother that day). And surprised by the unsympathetic response of local clergy, Joseph apparently said no more to others except to stubbornly insist, in the face of rumors and ridicule, that he had actually seen a vision. His life fell back into the rhythm of farm labor and nagging poverty. Three years passed, accord- ing to his recollection, before spiritual yearnings and self-doubts again led him to intense supplication of God. On a night in late September 1823, he prayed with "full confidence in obtaining a manifestation, as I previously had one." His room filled with light, and there appeared a white-robed per- son "glorious beyond description," who identified himself as Moroni. As the messenger began to speak, Joseph's preoccupations with personal worthiness and spiritual direction were quickly overshadowed by the announcement that "God had a work for [him] to do," one involving the translation of an ancient record. The angel described a set of gold plates containing an account that chronicled the history of America's ancient inhabitants and contained "the fulness of the everlasting Gospel"—as delivered by the Savior to those same people, he added cryptically.[13] The angel then quoted a number of Old and New Testament prophecies, alluding to a dawning era when young men would see visions, terrible judgments and desolations would precede the Lord's coming, and Daniel's stone cut without hands would roll forth to fill the earth. Moroni warned Joseph to safeguard the plates and associated artifacts when the time came to obtain them, and then departed. The visitation was repeated two more times that night, and again the next morning while Joseph worked the fields. Commanded to rehearse his experience to his father, Joseph did so, then made his way to the depository of the plates, which he had seen in vision during the angel's visits. The place, which is to this day known as Cumorah, was then a nondescript hill "of considerable size" a short walk

Hill Cumorah, New York
It was from this site that Joseph Smith said he retrieved an ancient set of gold plates, which he translated as the Book of Mormon. (Courtesy of the Church Archives, The Church of Jesus Christ of Latter-day Saints)

from the Palmyra farm. Near the top he found the plates secreted in a stone box beneath a large, rounded stone, together with a breastplate, a curious compass-like device called a Liahona, and the "interpreters," an object for translation.

The angel forbade Joseph to retrieve the objects at the time, directing him to return again the next year, which Joseph did. As it turned out, he was made to return at the same time each year for three years, learning more at each "interview," as he called them, about "what the Lord was going to do and in what manner his kingdom was to be conducted in the last days" (JS-H 1:54). At the fourth anniversary, the night of 22 September 1827, a twenty-one-year-old Joseph went to the now familiar hill with Emma (his wife of eight months) and was finally entrusted with the plates and interpreters. When he returned to his parents' home, early in the morning of the 23rd, he had the interpreters bundled in a silk handkerchief, but the plates themselves, he reported, he had hidden in the woods. The next day, he retrieved the plates, wrapped them in a linen frock, and returned home.

Joseph's earlier story of heavenly visitors had elicited no more than mild derision. Now, tales of a new "bible" written on plates of gold quickly spread throughout the area, and soon Joseph was besieged by prying neighbors and would-be thieves who took to violence. Other problems emerged from his earlier experiments with folk magic. Cultural historians now recognize the pervasiveness in that time and place of superstitious beliefs and practices that to a modern audience seem incongruous with Christian religiosity. Divining rods were employed to find water; peep-stones or seerstones were placed in hats and prompted visions of lost objects or buried treasure; and belief in angels, devils, and guardian spirits was rampant. As a historian of the period writes, "many Americans resorted to various forms of folk magic in expressing their religious beliefs . . . and nothing in their occult practices was regarded as contrary to accepted Christian values."[14]

The young Smith had associated with a number of local treasure-seekers and money-diggers, and when word of a buried "gold bible" surfaced, some disgruntled former associates of Joseph apparently felt entitled to a share of any discovered treasure, one even claiming that it was his own seerstone that Joseph was making use of in his new discovery. Rumors of lost silver mines and treasure hordes abounded in the region, and minor finds in Indian mounds farther to the west were common knowledge. Joseph apparently possessed something, opinion seemed to run, and it might be valuable. For a few months, Joseph and his hostile antagonists played cat and mouse, with the young man hiding the plates under hearth stones, beneath floor boards, and in a pile of flax. Smith was anxious to get on with the translation of the record, using the interpreters that accompanied the plates. But in these harried circumstances, translation would be impractical if not impossible. Smith had recently won the trust and friendship of Martin Harris, a middle-aged farmer in the area. So in December 1827, aided by his prosperous friend, Joseph and his pregnant wife slipped away to Harmony (now Oakland), Pennsylvania, with his golden plates tucked away in a barrel of beans.

Harmony was 135 miles distant, and the home of Emma's parents. In relative seclusion but also in taxing poverty, Joseph struggled in fits and starts over the next several months to translate the plates, using at times his seerstone and at times the interpreters. The precise process by which Smith carried out the translation he never described, but he and witnesses did leave a description of the instruments themselves. The interpreters comprised a kind of oversized spectacles, incorporating "two stones set in silver bows" that Joseph came to call the Urim and Thummim, a term used in the Old Testament to refer to a mysterious oracular object associated with the priestly garments of Aaron (Exod. 28:30). Joseph also made use of his seerstone—a common-appearing rock the size of a hen's egg—that he had acquired some years earlier.

In February 1828, his benefactor and friend Harris traveled to New York City with a transcription of some of the characters Joseph copied from the plates, in search of authentication. He sought out Charles Anthon of Columbia College, an expert in classical languages (though not in Egyptology, then in its very infancy). Anthon later insisted that after looking at the transcription, he warned the farmer against fraud. Harris claimed that Anthon pronounced the ancient writings authentic. At any rate, the visit apparently left Harris sufficiently confident in Joseph's role as prophet that the spring found him serving as Joseph's scribe while the translation proceeded apace. By June 1828, the two men had produced over a hundred pages of translated material. Under pressure from his skeptical wife, Harris pleaded with Joseph for permission to show the manuscript to her. Joseph initially resisted but eventually relented and gave Harris the only copy of the manuscript they had produced. Harris soon broke his pledge to reveal the text to close family members only. The manuscript was stolen (suspicion fell on Harris's wife Lucy and has remained there ever since), and Harris reluctantly confessed the loss to Joseph. Not knowing how he could remedy the catastrophe, and fearing he had lost his gift to translate and incurred God's anger, the novice prophet sank into the deepest despair of his life.

In the aftermath of the fiasco, Joseph was required to return the sacred oracles to the angel, was severely rebuked at his hands, and for a time believed he had forever been removed from his calling. With the coming of fall, however, he was reinstated, received back the plates, and returned to the work of translation. Emma now took Harris's place as scribe, but work proceeded slowly as the impoverished couple struggled to eke out a living. Eventually it ceased altogether. The next spring, in April 1829, a young schoolmaster by the name of Oliver Cowdery, who had lodged with the elder Smiths and heard the prophet's story from a local resident, came to Harmony to meet Joseph. Two days later, he was transcribing accounts of ancient American wars between peoples called Nephites and Lamanites, interspersed with sermons, history, and missionary narratives, as fast as they fell from the mouth of an energized Joseph Smith. At a rate of 3,500 words a day, they completed most of the manuscript in the next two months. In June the Smiths and Cowdery moved back across the New York border to Fayette and the home of Joseph's friend David Whitmer, to get away from gathering harassment in Harmony. There Joseph and Cowdery completed the translation, but not before learning from the text they were translating that Joseph would no longer be alone in bearing witness to the world of the reality of gold plates and angelic messengers.

Book of Mormon prophets had spoken of three special witnesses who would assist in establishing the truthfulness of the sacred record (Ether 5:2–4; 2 Nephi 27:12). In the course of approximately two years that the plates were in Joseph's possession, not a single person had ever actually seen them other than Joseph himself. They remained covered, or curtained off by a blanket while he used them, though many family members and friends were allowed to heft them and even leaf the plates while in their covered state. Oliver Cowdery was a logical choice for the role of eyewitness, since he was principal scribe. Martin Harris, though responsible for losing much of the manuscript, had still been a faithful friend and supporter (and would eventually mortgage his farm to cover printing costs). And David Whitmer had provided lodging while Joseph and Oliver completed their work. These three were the obvious candidates, and sometime in June, Joseph reported that he had received a revelation authorizing him to show them the plates. Shortly thereafter, Joseph and his three friends retired to the woods and petitioned God to manifest the sacred record.

When nothing happened, Harris felt he was the cause of their unsuccessful efforts and separated himself from the group. The remaining three continued to pray, and Joseph described what happened next: "we beheld a light above us in the air, of exceeding brightness; and behold, an angel stood before us. In his hands he held the plates which we had been praying to have a view of. He turned over the leaves one by one, so that we could see them, and discern the engravings thereon distinctly." Nearby, the interpreters and other sacred relics were exposed to their view as well. There followed a voice out of the bright light, saying, "These plates have been revealed by the power of God, and they have been translated by the power of God."[15]

Joseph went in search of Harris, joined him in prayer, and the same vision was repeated. A few days later, Joseph gathered about him another group of men, consisting of his father, two brothers, and five members of the Whitmer clan, and retired with them to a favorite family place of prayer. There, in the absence of any angelic messengers or heavenly voices, Joseph matter-of-factly displayed to the group the golden plates. Each man handled and examined the leaves at his leisure. In every edition of the Book of Mormon ever printed, the testimony of the eleven witnesses has been published over their names. The first three witnesses affirmed "with words of soberness that an angel of God came down from heaven, and he brought and laid before our eyes, that we beheld and saw the plates, and the engravings thereon." The eleven others declared that Joseph Smith "has shown unto us the plates of which hath been spoken, which have the appearance of gold; and as many of the leaves as the said Smith has translated we did handle with our hands; and we also saw the engravings thereon, all of which has the appearance of ancient work, and of curious workmanship."[16]

With the translation complete and affidavits of authenticity prepared, Joseph was ready to go to press. E. B. Grandin, a Palmyra bookseller, hesitantly contracted to publish the work (but only after Joseph threatened to move the project to Rochester). Late that summer, publication began. On 26 March 1830, Grandin formally announced the sale of the Book of Mormon in his bookshop. Phase one of the new prophet's work was over.

Organizing Zion: New York Beginnings

Back in September 1827, Moroni had quoted from the eleventh chapter of Isaiah to the seventeen-year-old Joseph: "And [the Lord] shall set up an

The three witnesses
Oliver Cowdery, David Whitmer, and Martin Harris solemnly declared that "an angel
of God came down from heaven" and showed them the gold plates. (Courtesy of the
Church Archives, The Church of Jesus Christ of Latter-day Saints)

ensign to the nations," the Old Testament prophet had written, "and shall assemble the outcasts of Israel, and gather together the dispersed of Judah from the four corners of the earth" (v. 12). Joseph and believers in his message soon came to identify the Book of Mormon as that ensign to the nations, and in both Mormon theology and historical fact, the new scripture served the function of drawing converts together from a multitude of religious and geographical backgrounds. In that context, as Joseph would come to realize, bringing the Book of Mormon to light was a preparatory, not final, prophetic task, as he had believed initially.[17] Only eleven days after the Book of Mormon was offered for sale, Joseph felt directed to organize a church which he called at the time the Church of Christ.

In large part, the timing was the result of publication—the new faith now had something to set it apart, a sign of Joseph's authority as prophet, and evidence that the gathering of Israel so anticipated by thousands of Christians in antebellum America could commence in earnest. But organization had also to wait upon other developments. In the closing weeks of translation, Joseph and Oliver had encountered references to baptism, and sought through prayer a fuller understanding of the principle. Oliver recorded what transpired on 15 May 1829 on the banks of the Susquehanna: "the veil was parted and the angel of God came down clothed with glory and delivered the anxiously looked for message and the keys of the gospel of repentance."[18] These keys constituted what the messenger, who identified himself as John the Baptist, called the "Aaronic priesthood," and consisted essentially of the authority to preach the gospel and perform baptisms. After ordaining the two men to that power, the angelic messenger indicated that in due time, the higher priesthood of Melchizedek would be bestowed, the same authority Christ bestowed upon his twelve apostles. Joseph and Oliver baptized each other, and shortly thereafter about a half dozen friends and family. Sometime in the ensuing weeks, Smith recorded that the apostles Peter, James, and John visited Joseph and Oliver and ordained them as promised.

These were distinctive and significant claims by Joseph. Many Seekers, Primitivists, and Restorationists of the era anticipated a return of Christianity to the supposed purity and power of the New Testament church. The Puritan Roger Williams, for example, founded the Baptist Church in America, but withdrew from his own church months later, declaring its baptism could not be valid "because it was not administered by an apostle." Finding no authorized church on earth, he resigned himself to waiting until "God should stir up himself or some other new Apostles."[19] Smith's claims at least comported with the expectations or hopes of many who yearned for an authorized restoration rather than self-motivated reform of Christianity.

So it was that on 6 April 1830, with priesthood authority, a new book of scripture, and a small but determined cohort of believers, Joseph established the church in Fayette, New York. Conforming to the laws of New York, six men were named as organizers—Joseph; his two brothers Hyrum and Samuel; two of the witnesses, David Whitmer and Oliver Cowdery; and Peter Whitmer Jr., a son in the home where the final translation and now the church's founding took place. In addition, perhaps four dozen other supporters were present—many had joined the cause after reading early portions of the Book of Mormon distributed before final publication. On the occasion of the organization, Joseph produced a revelation in which his own continuing role in the ongoing "restoration" was clarified. He was to be considered "a seer, a translator, a prophet"; the church was directed to "give heed unto all his words and commandments" as he received them from the Lord; and he was recognized as one whom God had "inspired to move the cause of Zion in mighty power" (DC 21:1, 4, 7).

Joseph had established himself as a translator in the course of producing the Book of Mormon. As a seer, according to that text, Joseph could "know of things which are past, and also of things which are to come, and by them shall all things be revealed, or, rather, shall secret things be made manifest, and hidden things shall come to light" (Mosiah 8:17). In the months and years ahead, Joseph would continue to reveal lost gospel truths, temple rituals, and ancient texts, and produce a stream of prophecies foretelling his own martyrdom, the migration of the Saints to the Rocky Mountains, the origin of the Civil War in South Carolina, along with a host of other predictions. But the label of prophet was the most common appellation he bore, used mockingly by the press and affectionately by his own people. Like Abraham and Moses, he was the divinely appointed father of his flock, leading them out of both spiritual blight and physical oppression; he was the enunciator of a new covenant between God and his chosen people; and he was the instrument to whom God revealed himself and through whom he revealed his will and his law in mighty shows of power and by means of his literal voice.

In the weeks that followed, some two dozen more people were baptized into the fledgling flock. Most early converts were relatives and close friends in the immediate vicinity of Fayette and from the prophet's hometown of Palmyra. Another group of strong supporters hailed from Colesville, a town near the Pennsylvania border across from Harmony and home of the Knight family, long-time devoted friends of the Smith family. Three factors soon converged to extend that circle dramatically. First, with the church formally organized and a book of scripture available, public preaching could begin in earnest. Second, Smith understood the Book of Mormon to be not just a history of American Indian origins, but to be directed in large part to their descendents. As one writer of the new scripture prophesied, "there shall be many which shall believe the words which are written; and they shall carry them forth unto the remnant of our seed" (2 Nephi 30:3). Smith therefore saw preaching to the American Indians as both a missionary opportunity and a divine directive. Finally, part of Smith's millennialist worldview was the hope of a literal New Jerusalem, or Zion. Again, the Book of Mormon lent force to this expectation, with its promise—one of the most quoted passages among nineteenth-century Mormons—that though the Jerusalem of old had been destroyed, "it should be built up again, a holy city unto the Lord . . . and that a New Jerusalem should be built up upon this land" (Ether 13:5–6). And in a revelation to Smith in September 1830, the location of that New Jerusalem was identified as somewhere "on the borders by the Lamanites" (DC 28:9). (Lamanites is the Book of Mormon's term for the surviving aboriginal descendants of Moroni's people.) The same revelation commanded Oliver Cowdery to a mission that would take him and three others to the distant frontiers of the United States. The stone cut without hands had begun to roll forth.

The Furnace of Affliction:
Ohio, Missouri, Illinois, and Exile

The four missionaries who embarked for parts west in the fall of 1830—Oliver Cowdery, Parley P. Pratt, Ziba Peterson, and Peter Whitmer—found little success among the tribes they visited en route to Missouri. But between preaching to the Cattaraugus near Buffalo and getting expelled by Indian agents while proselytizing the Delawares across the Kansas River, they passed through northeastern Ohio, where Pratt looked up his former pastor, now successful Reformed Baptist (Campbellite) minister Sidney Rigdon. Before they moved on to Missouri, Pratt and the others had baptized 127 converts, including Rigdon. Almost overnight, the center of church membership had shifted to Ohio.

Back in New York, Smith had determined to move the church west-ward. But the decision was more than a simple relocation under the pressures of persecution. Joseph had produced a revelation a few months earlier in which the Lord told him he was "called to bring to pass the gathering of mine elect; for mine elect hear my voice and harden not their hearts" (DC 29:7). Gathering, or the restoration of Israel, was of course an Old Testament motif. Like the building of Zion, it was generally held to have spiritual rather than literal meaning, at least in the case of Christian believers. But here again, Smith was literally reenacting, rather than rhetorically appropriating, prophetic patterns. As the next words of the revelation continued, "Wherefore the decree hath gone forth from the Father that they shall be gathered in unto one place upon the face of this land, to prepare their hearts and be prepared in all things against the day when tribulation and desolation are sent forth upon the wicked." Ohio, at least for the time being, was to be the literal place for Latter-day Saints to congregate. As Charles Dickens would remark of the Mormons a few years later, "It sounds strange to hear of a church having a 'location.' But a 'location' was the term they applied to their place of settlement."[20]

Just twelve miles from Lake Erie in northeastern Ohio, Kirtland made a convenient point of gathering for Saints arriving from other parts of the United States and from across the lake in Canada. Rigdon had spent a number of years establishing congregations throughout the Ohio region before his conversion to Mormonism. He now turned his contacts to good advantage, and soon the convert population, though centered in Kirtland, spilled over into neighboring communities.

Ohio was fertile soil, and within months of Joseph's arrival in February 1831, the transplanted New Yorkers and area converts brought church membership to a few hundred. Yet even while members poured into Ohio, Joseph traveled west to meet the members of the Indian mission, and in July 1831, in Jackson County, Missouri, he declared that Missouri, too, would be a place of gathering, and "the place for the city of Zion" (DC 57:1).[21] Thenceforward, church gathering would occur around the two locations of Kirtland, Ohio, and Independence, Missouri. Even though Smith himself remained in the east, Mormon settlement was increasingly shifting to Missouri.

The gathering would be a crucial ingredient in the establishment of a peculiar Mormon identity, bringing both strength and opposition to the church. Functioning as a community who lived, farmed, labored, and

worshiped together under one leader, Mormons were inherently committing themselves to a group identity and a collective mentality that Joseph
could shape to powerful ends. By presuming to dictate not just the forms
of worship and ritual, but even the conditions of followers' temporal existence, Joseph was moving beyond the confines of conventional religious
leadership. To the extent that believers acceded to this authoritarianism
that reached beyond the pew, beyond the Sabbath, and beyond the spiritual, building the kingdom of God became an endeavor with more than
metaphorical significance. Soon, temple building would become not just a
distinctive feature of Mormonism, but the crowning emblem and evidence
of a complete restoration of ancient gospel fullness, a sign that the conduit
linking heavenly powers to earthly disciples had been firmly reestablished,
proof that in this House of the Lord, God could once more be fully present to his people. The physical congregating of the Saints made available
sufficient collective resources to construct these holy edifices. As Joseph
Smith would later teach, the object of gathering was precisely this, "to
build unto the Lord an house whereby he could reveal unto his people the
ordinances" of his temple.[22] Accordingly, in the summer of 1833, plans
proceeded for the construction of a temple in Kirtland, and the cornerstones were laid on 23 July. Within three years, largely in response to these
plans, church membership in Kirtland township increased from only 100
to over 1,300.[23]

On the very same day that temple foundations were being established
in Kirtland, anti-Mormon agitation had compelled the Mormons to agree
to abandon their stakes in Jackson County, Missouri. Three days earlier, a
mob of over three hundred had attacked Mormons in the town of Independence. They tarred and feathered two leaders, destroyed the Mormons' printing press, and drove dozens of families from their homes.
Mobs also attacked neighboring townships in the succeeding months and
skirmished with Mormons in a violent encounter known as the "Battle
above the Blue," leaving several casualties. On 7 November 1833, in a
wintry rain, the Saints in Independence were driven across the Missouri
River north into Clay County. Soon, virtually all the Saints in Jackson
County—some 1,200—joined the rest in Clay or scattered elsewhere. The
redemption of Zion would have to wait.

Clay County at this time had some five thousand inhabitants. They at
first welcomed the Mormon refugees, but the sudden influx of a number
amounting to almost a quarter of their own population created tensions.
Soon, the same conflicts that had led to their expulsion from Jackson

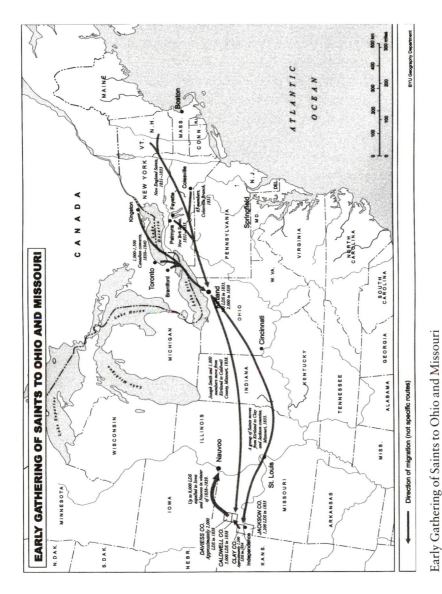

Early Gathering of Saints to Ohio and Missouri

(From *Historical Atlas of Mormonism*, by S. Kent Brown, Donald Q. Cannon, Richard Jackson. Gale Group, © 1994, Gale Group. Reprinted by permission of the Gale Group.)

County appeared here as well. As the temple was completed and dedicated in Kirtland in March 1836, frictions with old settlers in Missouri grew incessantly more heated. Finally, in a mass meeting held in June 1836, the citizens demanded the Saints' ouster from Clay County. Again they moved north, into the new county of Caldwell designated to accommodate them, and into neighboring Daviess County. From Kirtland, Smith urged the Saints to relocate peacefully.

Even in the face of opposition and exile, church growth in the next few years was rapid, and most converts headed to northern Missouri. By 1838, the Mormon population of Caldwell County reached five thousand, with a few thousand more in Daviess and elsewhere. Far West, in Caldwell County, became the church's new commercial and ecclesiastical center, soon boasting 150 permanent homes, seven grocery and dry goods stores, hotels, blacksmith shops, a printing shop, and a schoolhouse.[24] And more converts were pouring in daily. Tensions finally erupted in election-day violence twenty miles to the north in Gallatin, Daviess County, in August, and days later Saints were ordered out of nearby Carroll County to the southeast. In October, hundreds of vigilantes forcibly evicted the Carroll Mormons and Saints in five other counties. Mormons retaliated by attacking Gallatin and another village and expelling non-Mormons from Daviess. A skirmish at Crooked River left four dead, including one Mormon apostle, and exaggerated rumors of Mormon depredations further inflamed tensions. Governor Lilburn Boggs, taking at face value reports that the Mormons were the aggressors in the conflict, responded with his infamous order of extermination on 27 October. Directed to General John B. Clark of the Missouri Militia, it read in part: "The Mormons must be treated as enemies and must be exterminated or driven from the state. . . . Their outrages are beyond all description. If you can increase your force, you are authorized to do so, to any extent you many think necessary. . . . You will proceed immediately to Richmond and there operate against the Mormons.[25]

Three days later, and before the order even reached them, two hundred militia rode into Haun's Mill, a Mormon settlement along Shoal Creek in northeastern Caldwell County. The women fled to the woods with children, while the men retreated into a blacksmith shop. In a matter of minutes, the militia had shot and hacked to death eighteen men and boys. The next day, Clark surrounded Far West with thousands more militia, and demanded the surrender of the Saints.

Meanwhile, the situation in Ohio had not been an idyllic contrast. As early as 1832, mobs had attacked Joseph Smith, beating him almost senseless and then leaving him tarred and feathered, and brutally assaulted Sidney Rigdon. Unlike Missouri opposition, which largely pitted old settlers against new, Ohio tensions were largely fomented by disillusioned and disaffected members who incited both wavering Mormons and skeptical non-Mormons against the personal leadership of Joseph Smith. In early 1834, however, the influx of converts to Kirtland and activity on the Kirtland temple set off alarm bells that evoked a Missouri-type reaction on the part of old citizens. At a public meeting, opponents of the church denounced the Prophet for bringing upon the community "an insupportable weight of pauperism."[26] A committee subsequently announced that they had hired one Philastus Hurlbut to unmask the fraud behind the Book of Mormon. He traveled to the Palmyra area and collected affidavits from boyhood neighbors of Joseph Smith that cast the entire family in an unsavory light. Published in 1834 as *Mormonism Unvailed* [sic] by Eber D. Howe, the attacks were a key ingredient in galvanizing opposition to Mormonism and its founder. (The obvious intention to defame and the canned, repetitive nature of the allegations against Smith have compromised their credibility among modern scholars.)

The early part of 1836, leading up to the April dedication of the Kirtland temple, ushered in a prolonged, Pentecostal season for the Saints. Amid word of the travails in Missouri, and growing dissension and opposition in Ohio, construction of the temple had been the steady focus, both materially and spiritually, of the young church. Smith's successor Brigham Young later recounted how the members were at this time "too few in numbers, too weak in faith, and too poor in purse, to attempt such a mighty enterprise." Still, he recalled "the great Prophet Joseph, in the stone quarry, quarrying rock with his own hands," and "the laborers on the walls, holding the sword in one hand to protect themselves from the mob, while they placed the stone and moved the trowel with the other."[27]

On 21 January of that year, Joseph Smith met in the temple with his counselors and a few dozen leaders. At that time, the prophet's scribe recorded, "the heavens were opened upon us." Joseph saw "the celestial kingdom of God, and . . . the transcendent beauty of the gate through which the heirs of that kingdom will enter, which was like unto circling flames of fire." Seeing a brother who had died unbaptized in the new faith, Smith learned that "all who have died without a knowledge of this gospel who would have received it if they had been permitted to tarry, shall be heirs of the celestial kingdom of God." So also "all children who die before they arrive at the years of accountability, are saved" (DC 137).

Of the other brethren present, some saw what Joseph saw and others beheld "the armies of Heaven protecting the Saints. . . . Some saw the face of the Savior, and others were ministered unto by holy angels, and the spirit of prophecy and revelation was poured out in mighty power."[28] Over the next three and a half months, as reported in countless diaries and letters, individuals and groups as large as a thousand in number reported visions, the voices and visitation of angels, the gift of tongues, and other miraculous manifestations. Even the Mormon children of Kirtland reported throngs of heavenly beings gathered above the temple.

Days after the dedicatory services for the completed edifice in March 1836, the most important events in the ongoing process of gospel restoration occurred since the organization of the church itself six years earlier. Together with Oliver Cowdery, Joseph was praying in the seclusion of the veiled temple pulpit, when they were granted a vision of the Savior. There followed, in turn, visitations from Moses, Elias, and Elijah, each committing to them the respective "keys" of the gathering of Israel, of the Abrahamic covenant, and of the sealing powers spoken of by Malachi—which Joseph would only come to understand fully or elaborate some years later. All in all, the heavenly portents provided strength and comfort to a community soon to be overwhelmed by gathering clouds.

Over the next two years, a third of Joseph's high associates would lose or forsake their good standing in the church, and many of the rank and file rebelled or left the fold. Joseph's involvement in the failed Kirtland Bank (technically an "anti-Banking Society") compounded a widespread sentiment that he had overstepped his authority or misled the church. By the summer of 1837, former supporters even attempted to have Smith replaced by David Whitmer as president of the church. Sufficient support remained for Joseph to maintain his position, but opposition to his leadership intensified. By January, he fled Kirtland for his own safety. In Missouri, he was once again surrounded by his friends and supporters—but he arrived only to find that the Mormons in that state would no longer be tolerated by the old citizens or protected by the civil authorities. So it was that only months later, following the massacre at Haun's Mill and with General Clark demanding the complete surrender of the Saints, Joseph and other leaders agreed to a parley with Missouri militia leaders. The meeting was a ruse, arranged between the militia and Mormon leader Colonel George M. Hinckle. The betrayed Mormon prophet was summarily court-martialed and illegally sentenced to be shot for treason. General Alexander Doniphan refused to carry out the judicial murder, but weeks later, Joseph began a long incarceration in Liberty, Missouri, while his destitute followers again forsook homes and fields to seek a new life to the northeast.

Soon thereafter, finding a scenic location on a bend of the Mississippi, and enticed by the hospitality and sympathy of prominent leaders and citizens of Illinois, Smith encouraged the Saints to buy up lots in the swampy environs of a village named Commerce. The Saints drained the land, began to erect homes, and renamed the city Nauvoo—a Hebrew word meaning "beautiful." The golden age that followed is unique in the annals of American religious history. One historian has listed some of the unprecedented features of Nauvoo's establishment and history:

1. No other city in American history was founded exclusively as a refuge for victims of violent American persecution.
2. No other city of comparable size was ever designed, founded, populated, and administered by a religious body with such exclusive theological control.
3. No other city in recorded history experienced such a phenomenal growth rate without an economic attraction.
4. No other city in modern times trained and supported an army for its protection from hostile fellow nationals.
5. No city since the Middle Ages ever depended so heavily, both economically and culturally, on the construction of a single public edifice (the temple).
6. No other American city in time of peace has ever been besieged by an army of American citizens.
7. From no other American city has such a large percentage of the inhabitants been forced from their homes and driven into exile.
8. No other city in the Western Hemisphere had ever held such significance to a modern religious denomination.[29]

At the time of its transformation into a Mormon Mecca, Commerce could boast no more than a half dozen small houses. Joseph Smith, recently released from Liberty Jail, arrived in May 1839 as settlement by Mormon refugees was already well underway. In the next year's census, Nauvoo was already half the size of Chicago. By early February 1841, an Illinois newspaper reported that the city had "about 3000 inhabitants [and] some 300 buildings." That July, apostle Heber C. Kimball returned from his missionary labors in England and recorded that 1,200 buildings were present, with hundreds of others in progress.[30]

One new feature of the church's growth in this era was the influx of the first foreign converts (besides Canadians). Kimball and a few companions had been the first missionaries to take the Mormon message overseas, having left on their first mission from Kirtland in 1837. By the summer of 1840, the first ships of immigrant converts docked in New York, and their passengers began to wend their way to the banks of the Mississippi. Before the Saints left for the west, almost five thousand British converts would swell the ranks of the Nauvoo community. In March 1843, a convert from Canada wrote enthusiastically about the city's vitality and growth, but perhaps with some exaggeration:

> I think there are more than one hundred handsome brick houses in Nauvoo now. . . . Perhaps there is not any other city on this globe improving as fast as Nauvoo. It is supposed that there are at present ten to twelve thousand inhabitants in the city alone, and the country around it and Montrose is swarming with the Saints. . . . It is supposed that there are at present two thousand from England, Scotland, Wales and the Isle of Man waiting between New Orleans and this place until navigation opens, and two thousand more are expected out next spring and summer from the same places.[31]

The virtual city-state flourished, converts flooded in from regions near and abroad, and new revelations and teachings poured forth from Joseph—to be disseminated by traveling apostles and missionaries and by a vigorous Mormon press. In January 1841, Joseph announced plans for a second temple, and in April the cornerstones were laid. Far more than a house of worship, the towering limestone structure became the symbol of a faith, the religious and social focus of its people, and the virtual raison d'etre for the gathering itself. Toward the end of its construction, "two hundred builders were working on the Temple, requiring six hundred support workers to supply them with lumber and stone."[32] By then, one touring lecturer was calling it the largest building west of Cincinnati and north of St. Louis, and John Greenleaf Whittier predicted that at its completion, it would be "the most splendid and imposing architectural monument in the New World . . . a temple unique and wonderful as the faith of its builders."[33]

The temple in Kirtland had served primarily as a meetinghouse. The temple in Nauvoo would be the site for higher teachings and sacred ceremonies that Smith revealed to the faithful. With the implementation of these temple rituals, some of the most distinctive Latter-day Saint doctrines would be revealed and others more fully expounded. Premortal existence, plurality of gods, the eternal nature of marriage, baptism for the dead—these and other beliefs increasingly distinguished Mormon belief from more orthodox varieties of contemporary Christianity.

Mormonism was now in its short-lived golden age. Converts continued to pour in from England and other states, the city was prosperous, Joseph preached regularly to thousands of faithful saints in his beloved Bowery, and all the while, the beautiful new temple rose majestically against the Illinois skyline. Best of all, the Nauvoo Legion's five thousand drilled and armed men seemed to guarantee that the people would continue unmolested by mobs and hostile militia.

It was not long before the same factors that caused Mormons to rejoice in their newfound autonomy led to the collapse of their brief utopia. Perhaps emboldened by the unprecedented security the city and legion afforded, Joseph began to teach the doctrine of plural marriage more openly. Mormon military might, independent courts, and Joseph's simultaneous titles of prophet, mayor, and lieutenant-general provoked cries of anti-republicanism and theocracy. Newspapers and politicians adopted strident anti-Mormon rhetoric, and a group of dissidents initiated a hostile paper, *The Nauvoo Expositor*, in the very "City of Joseph." The city council declared the paper a public nuisance and ordered the press destroyed.

Legal questionability aside, the move was the worst conceivable public relations misstep, and the immediate outcry was furious. Within days, Joseph had been arrested and jailed in Carthage, a few miles from Nauvoo. With the prophet temporarily beyond the protection of faithful supporters and the powerful Nauvoo Legion, a mob of a hundred men with painted faces stormed the cell where Joseph and three others were held the evening of 27 June 1844. They shot and killed Joseph and his brother Hyrum, and grievously wounded a companion. Fearing reprisal, the mob quickly fled. Conditions seemed ripe for a minor civil war more violent than the Missouri conflicts.

The governor of Illinois, Thomas Ford, had disarmed the Nauvoo Legion just days before. That was no true hindrance to revenge or self-defense, since personal arms quickly replaced state-issued ones. Nonetheless, church leaders urged restraint, and grief rather than vengeance prevailed. Simultaneous with the threat of further violence and displacement came a crisis in the succession of leadership. Joseph had left a trail of mixed signals regarding the inheritance of his authority. Brigham Young, the senior apostle, returned to Nauvoo at the moment of crisis, and contended that Joseph had provided for presiding authority to revert to the

Joseph Mustering the Nauvoo Legion, by C.C.A. Christensen (tempera, ca. 1865)
In Nauvoo, Illinois, the Saints established a powerful presence with a militia several
thousand strong at its height. (Courtesy of Brigham Young University Museum of Art.
All Rights Reserved)

Assassination of Joseph Smith
Joseph, along with his brother Hyrum, was murdered by an armed mob while incarcerated in Carthage Jail, Carthage, Illinois, in 1844. (From *Rocky Mountain Saints,*
1873, by Thomas B. H. Stenhouse)

Brigham Young (1801–77)
Shortly after Joseph Smith's death in 1844, Brigham Young assumed leadership of most of the Saints, as president of the Quorum of the Twelve. From an 1846 daguerreotype attributed to Lucian Foster. (Courtesy of the Church Archives, The Church of Jesus Christ of Latter-day Saints)

Crossing the Mississippi on the Ice, by C.C.A. Christensen (tempera, ca. 1865)
In February 1846, the first waves of Mormon exiles began to flee Nauvoo and regroup
in Winter Quarters, Nebraska, before beginning the long journey west. (Courtesy of
Brigham Young University Museum of Art. All Rights Reserved)

Quorum of Twelve Apostles as a whole. Each of the challengers attracted
some support, but most of the Saints rallied around Young and the Twelve.

If the Saints thought that the murder of their prophet would quench
the anger of their enemies, they quickly learned their mistake. The martyrdom—and lack of response by either authorities or the Nauvoo
Legion—only emboldened the mobs. (A few murder suspects were later
indicted by a jury, but none was ever convicted.) Outlying settlements were
attacked, more than two hundred houses were burned, and the governor
ordered the Saints to leave. Remarkably, the bulk of their energies and
efforts in these months centered not on defense or exodus, but on com-
pleting their sacred temple. For the next year, the Saints worked frantically
to finish the structure, knowing full well it would have to be abandoned
virtually the moment it was completed. By December 1845, the sacred rituals Joseph had introduced were being performed, though completion
would not occur until months later. Such heroic efforts to complete the
temple only to forsake it bear witness to the transcendent significance
Mormons assign to the ordinances they enact there.

It was in the spring that the Saints planned once again to abandon their homes and places of worship and refuge, Young having committed to such an exodus in exchange for a cessation of mob violence against the Saints. And by that point, the Saints had had enough. As one mentioned in his journal, speaking of an October conference where Young's decision was approved, "it was voted unanimously that the Church en masse move from the United States, where we have had nothing but persecution from the beginning, and go to a country far to the west where we can serve God without being molested by mob."[34] But the mobs were unwilling to permit the Mormons even that brief time of preparation and a warm weather departure.

So it was that in early February 1846, under threat of renewed attack by the mobs, and in response to rumors that federal troops would intervene to prevent their departure, the first Saints headed down Parley Street, and crossed the Mississippi on flatboats. Weeks later, the mighty river froze, and waves of refugees crossed on foot and in wagons. About 14,000 other refugees from Nauvoo and surrounding regions would join them in the exodus over the next seven months. Destitute, dispirited, and dispossessed once again, hampered by dreadful weather and muddy prairies, the Saints took four arduous months to struggle a mere 300 miles across the state. They formed a number of temporary settlements along the way, but concentrated along the Missouri River, creating a town called Kanesville (present-day Council Bluffs) on the eastern shore, and a larger town, Winter Quarters (North Omaha) on the bluff above the west bank. Winter Quarters would serve as the major point of departure for west-bound Mormon emigrants for several years to come. Four hundred men, women, and children would die the first winter there, from exposure and cholera.

While the first Saints were struggling across the Iowa prairie, a representative of Brigham Young traveled in the opposite direction, seeking aid from President James K. Polk for the hard-pressed Saints. The federal government had just declared war against Mexico, and Polk agreed to permit the raising of a battalion of five hundred Mormon volunteers. Mormons were understandably reluctant when, weeks later, Captain James Allen arrived in Iowa to enlist soldiers for the U.S. Army. But as Young recognized, the effort served the self-interest of both parties. The homeless Mormons sorely needed the $42 clothing allowance given each volunteer, and Polk could use a hardy corps ready to march nearly 2,000 miles to join the Army of the West in California. Over five hundred men were mustered into the service on 16 July, and six months later they crossed the Colorado River into California, having completed one of the longest infantry marches in

Mormon Battalion reunion, 1896
Even as the Saints began their exile in 1846, over five hundred Mormons volunteered
for service in the Mexican War, bringing in desperately needed cash for the migration.
(Courtesy of the Church Archives, The Church of Jesus Christ of Latter-day Saints)

military history. A volunteer corps thus participated in the very war that
guaranteed that their land of intended exile and refuge, envisioned as
beyond the reach of American arms and oppression, would fly the stars
and stripes almost upon their arrival.

Meanwhile, Young continued to direct preparations for the westward
trek of his people. Thrown into a leadership role under the most tragic and
trying of circumstances, Brigham Young quickly showed his genius for
organization and administration. He arranged the thousands of Saints
into the Camp of Israel, comprised of companies of tens, fifties, and hundreds, with captains over each unit. Specialized talent was distributed
evenly among the groups, and regulations governing the order in the
camps and for supplying the trains were approved. Permanent settlements
at Garden Grove and Mt. Pisgah, in Iowa, provided respite and a source
of crops for succeeding pioneers. Young organized a mail service between
the scattered camps, sent apostles to England to supervise both missionary
work and emigration, and organized a relief expedition for the last of the
beleaguered Saints in Nauvoo.

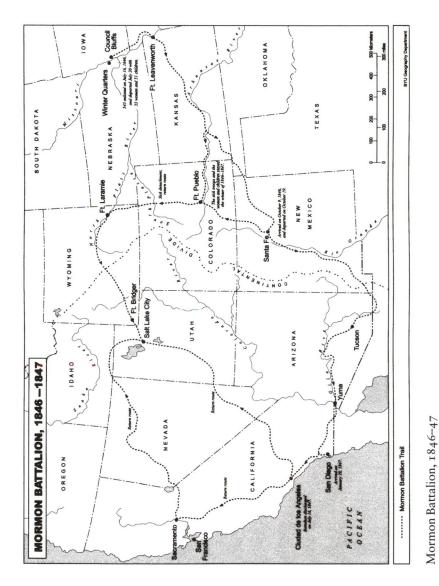

Mormon Battalion, 1846–47

(From *Historical Atlas of Mormonism*, by S. Kent Brown, Donald Q. Cannon, Richard Jackson. Gale Group, © 1994, Gale Group. Reprinted by permission of the Gale Group.)

Making the Desert Blossom: Brigham Young and the Mormon Empire of the West

By the spring of 1847, Young was ready to strike out with the advance company of 150 pioneers, intent on blazing the trail to the Salt Lake Valley and laying the foundations for a permanent settlement there. Young and others decided that rather than follow an established route to the west, they would create their own for most of the way, in part to avoid potential conflict with non-Mormon emigrant trains. So it was that they followed the northern bank of the Platte River across modern-day Nebraska (the Oregon trail followed the south bank). At Ft. Laramie, just inside present-day Wyoming, they picked up the Oregon trail and followed it to the southwest corner of the state, the site of Ft. Bridger. From there, Young followed a trail to Salt Lake pioneered by the Donner party the year before. From Winter Quarters to the Salt Lake Valley was just over 1,000 miles, and Young's party made the trip in a little over three months—an indication of the hellish conditions under which the body of Saints had spent four months crossing Iowa the previous year.

The exact tally is hard to determine, but as many as six thousand Saints are thought to have perished along the trail in the waves that followed. The high toll notwithstanding, Young's feat in orchestrating the migration that ensued for the next generation and more were without precedent in American history. The organization of the exodus as well as the provisions made for planting crops and building shelters and establishing ferries along the way, all gave order and discipline to the largest displacement and resettlement of American citizens ever. Only the Cherokee exodus along the Trail of Tears in the winter of 1838–39 compares with it in volume and in human suffering. Sixty-two thousand Mormons would follow in their wake over the next two decades (the railroad transformed westward travel when completed in 1869).

Young, delayed at the end of his trek by mountain fever, entered the valley on 24 July, a few days after the advance scouts. Ever after celebrated as Pioneer Day, the 24th was generally commemorated by Utah Saints with a good deal more fervor than the Fourth of July. (Even today, the date is a major holiday in Utah and receives some kind of commemoration throughout the worldwide church.) Days after their arrival in the Salt Lake Valley, Orson Pratt began a survey of the valley, and others began to erect a fort. Soon irrigation ditches were dug and seeds planted, while back in

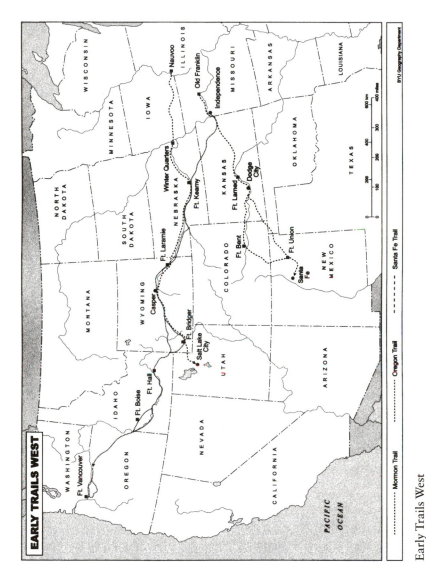

Early Trails West

(From *Historical Atlas of Mormonism*, by S. Kent Brown, Donald Q. Cannon, Richard Jackson. Gale Group, © 1994, Gale Group. Reprinted by permission of the Gale Group.)

Winter Quarters, the first of three hundred wagon trains to use the Mormon trail was setting out.

Settlement proceeded quickly, and like the trek itself, the community's growth was planned, organized, and astutely anticipated, with city planning, public works projects, and land surveys and distribution. The first autumn harvest was hopelessly meager, and starvation shadowed the Saints through the first winter. But their resilience once again prevailed, and in spite of feeble resources, arid, alkaline soil, and swarms of crickets, a modest 1848 harvest saved the Saints from their diet of roots, crows, and tree bark. Months later, flocks of gold-seeking forty-niners streamed through the settlement, happy to unload burdensome goods for a pittance. The transients brought temporary respite from the Saints' destitution, and foreshadowed the role the city would play as the crossroads of the west. Salt Lake City was soon firmly established as a thriving community that within five years of settlement boasted twenty thousand inhabitants, more than Nauvoo at its height. It was bursting at the seams, and with hundreds of thousands of square miles of sparsely inhabited land, Young directed colonizing efforts to settle the regions in every direction. Almost a hundred towns were established in the Saints' first decade in the valley. An astounding five hundred Mormon-settled communities would eventually dot the intermountain west.

Rumors had circulated at the time of the exodus from Nauvoo that Missouri was planning an expedition to pursue and destroy the Mormons as a people, even as they fled the country.[35] With half the continental United States now separating the Saints from their oppressors, they must have felt secure in their mountain fastness. Both the experiences of the past and the reality of their geographical isolation now led Young to emphasize economic self-sufficiency for the Saints. Emboldened by their isolation and self-sufficiency, and by his appointment as governor over the new Utah Territory in 1850, Young would wait only two more years to drop the most potent bombshell in the history of the Mormon Church's fractious relationship with America. On 29 August 1852, Orson Pratt, an apostle acting at the behest of Brigham Young, stood in the tabernacle and publicly announced for the first time that the Saints were practicing the principle of plural marriage: "I have not been in the habit of publicly speaking upon this subject," he began, and then with an understatement few could yet appreciate, added, "and it is rather new ground to the inhabitants of the United States."[36]

For the next generation and more, Mormonism would come to be synonymous, in the eyes of the American public, with a marriage practice until then associated with the patriarchs of the Old Testament, the followers of Muhammad, or the harems of oriental despots. Then and now, the myths and the realities of plural marriage seldom coincided, but it was public perception, largely shaped by inflammatory depictions and condemnations from pulpits, politicians, and novelists, that fueled immediate and drastic repercussions. Novelists of the era depicted the practice as white slavery, and portrayed Mormon missionaries as little more than abductors in search of fresh stock. In a "Buffalo Bill" nickel weekly, Brigham Young dispatches (or countenances) raiding expeditions on wagon trains for the purpose of bringing back young virgins, and Arthur Conan Doyle's Sherlock Holmes begins his famous detective career when he tracks his first murder case to Mormon kidnappers of gentile women.[37] Other fictional representations emphasized the bondage, torture, and forced marriages of reluctant women.

In actual fact, plural marriage was practiced solely as a consequence of a felt conviction among Latter-day Saints that God had commanded the practice, as part of the "restoration" or "restitution of all things" prophesied by Peter (Acts 3:21) and inaugurated by Joseph.[38] Contrary to sensationalized accounts and glib assumptions, plural marriage was not practiced by whim or personal initiative. Those whom Joseph taught the doctrine and enjoined to live it generally did so, if at all, only after overcoming a fiercely ingrained monogamous morality. Brigham Young's famous remark may have been greeted with skepticism by outsiders, but countless diaries and letters of those engaged in "the practice" testify to the genuine anguish and discomfort they experienced. Young wrote, "Some of these my brethren know what my feelings were at the time Joseph revealed the doctrine; I was not desirous of shrinking from any duty, nor of failing in the least to do as I was commanded—but it was the first time in my life that I had desired the grave, and I could hardly get over it for a long time. And when I saw a funeral, I felt to envy the corpse its situation."[39] His colleague and fellow apostle John Taylor echoed the feelings of countless others when he initially considered the practice "an appalling thing" which "nothing but . . . the revelations of God . . . could have induced me to embrace."[40] The financial and emotional burdens, not to mention the exposure to contempt and persecution entailed in plural marriage, could have all been avoided by engaging in the informal liaisons of casual promiscuity rather than entering into the formal, binding, and increasingly public relationships of polygamy if sexual satisfaction were the motive. Most practitioners of the principle, male and female, seem to have found little pleasure amid the pressures of maintaining harmony and good will in the context of multiple relationships.

Asked by Horace Greeley if the majority of women found the system acceptable, Young responded, "they could not be more averse to it than I was when it was first revealed."[41] Although women privately recorded their struggles and difficulties with this trial of faith, they rallied publicly in overwhelming support for the principle when politicians and would-be liberators meddled. In practice, Mormon women showed a surprising tendency to marry into a plural relationship, even when younger, single males were available, and Brigham Young granted divorces readily to any women who petitioned him. Estimates are notoriously diverse and contested, but probably less than 10 percent of the male population was involved in the practice. Most men who did practice the principle took only one additional wife, and almost always housed her in a separate domicile, usually in a different community. Small comfort that, to a public blitzed with images of bearded patriarchs accompanied by legions of young wives.

Within a year of Pratt's public announcement, the first wave of anti-Mormon novels focusing on the theme of plural marriage came off the press. A moral crusade against Mormonism by preachers, politicians, and prominent figures quickly gained steam, and the public was alternately enthralled and enraged, revealing an uneasy mix of prurient interest and righteous indignation. In 1856, the new Republican Party organized their platform by tying the issue of slavery to polygamy and promising eradication of those "twin relics of barbarism." The next year three federally appointed judges, feeling insulted and rebuffed in their efforts to exercise authority in Utah, returned to Washington and complained that the territory was in a state of virtual rebellion, instigated by the despotic Brigham Young. Coming soon after reports of intransigence and disloyalty made in Washington by a thwarted surveyor general and suspicious Indian agents, these depictions convinced President Buchanan that federal intervention was called for. So it was that in July 1857, President Buchanan ordered a federal army of 2,500 to invade the Territory, seat a new governor (Alfred Cummings), and restore order.

Mormon raiders harassed the troops along their western march, torching grazing land, scattering their cattle, blocking routes, burning baggage trains, and otherwise impeding their progress. Colonel E. B. Alexander, commanding the expedition's vanguard, wrote indignantly to Brigham Young that Mormon tactics were "far beneath the usages of civilized warfare, and only resorted to by those who are conscious of inability to resist by more honorable means."[42] But the strategy worked, and the army, now under the command of Colonel Albert Sidney Johnston, was forced to winter well short of Salt Lake Valley, at the charred site of Ft. Bridger, burned by the Mormons.

The Mormons succeeded in bringing the troops to the verge of starvation, but had managed to avoid bloodshed. The troops settled into winter quarters as the crisis simmered on. The next spring, Johnston was still intent on occupying Salt Lake City to humble the Mormons, avenge his army's own humiliation, and establish uncontestable federal control. Knowing the futility of continued resistance to American troops, Young still had one drastic option he was willing to consider. "President Young preached yesterday at the Tabernacle," a contemporary who had weathered the eastern persecutions recorded, "that he thought it best to move southward and if the United States were determined to send their army into the Valley without some treaty, or agreement, we would burn our houses, cut down our orchards and make the country as desolate as it was when we came here. He then called for a vote of the congregation. They all voted aye."[43]

Thousands of refugees were soon moving southward, but further conflict was narrowly avoided in part by the timely intervention of skilled negotiator and friend-to-the-Mormons Colonel Thomas Kane. Governor Cumming entered the city, assumed his post, and discovered—probably to his surprise—not a mutinous horde of barbarians but a respectful and decent people justly in fear for their peace and safety. With Cumming's report in hand, President Buchanan declared an amnesty. The army made a token pass through the mostly deserted city, then retired to a discreet distance, where they established Camp Floyd. The whole affair eventually wound down—but the tension and paranoia had precipitated the darkest chapter in the Mormon saga.

At the height of the "Utah War," in early September, the Baker–Fancher wagon train, a group of Arkansas and Missouri emigrants headed for California, provoked local Indians and Mormon settlers while passing through southern Utah. Word circulated that they had boasted of complicity in the atrocities against Missouri Mormons, and Indians accused them of poisoning wells. It has never been possible to sort out all the facts and to separate real causes from after-the-fact rationalization. But the complex mix of wartime tensions, wounds of the past, and bad judgment all around led to a massacre of the emigrant train by native Americans and

Federal soldiers from Camp Floyd
As part of the compromise ending the Utah War of 1857, the federal government set-
tled into Camp Floyd as a token army of occupation, 36 miles south of Salt Lake.
(Courtesy of the Church Archives, The Church of Jesus Christ of Latter-day Saints)

Salt Lake City, ca. 1861–64
The pole and sagebrush Bowery, earliest site used for public worship, and the first tab-
ernacle, completed in 1852. (Courtesy of the Church Archives, The Church of Jesus
Christ of Latter-day Saints)

The telegraph office and Main Street businesses
(Courtesy of the Church Archives, The Church of Jesus Christ of Latter-day Saints)

Down and back trains, 1867
By 1860, the Utah leadership was organizing wagon trains that traveled eastward to pick up emigrating Saints, returning to the Salt Lake Valley the same season. (Courtesy of the Church Archives, The Church of Jesus Christ of Latter-day Saints)

local Mormons. Eighteen young children were spared, but none of the hundred adults survived. Only one of the Mormon leaders, John D. Lee, was eventually tried and executed for the crime. Suspicion has long lingered on the question of Brigham Young's complicity, but it is more likely that local Mormon authorities orchestrated the atrocity.

The Mormons had escaped the Utah War without suffering casualties. But their sovereignty, self-government, and isolation were at an end. Reports of the Mountain Meadows Massacre, the coming of the railroad, and the explosive conflict over plural marriage guaranteed that Mormonism, though lodged in the remote Wasatch Mountains, would occupy center stage in the American consciousness and in American politics for the next fifty years.

Impervious as Mormons appeared to be to assimilation into the American mainstream, and resistant as they had proven to extermination, the American government was determined to at least eliminate their most egregious affront to conventional morality—the practice of plural marriage. The first legislative effort to do so was the Morrill Anti-Bigamy Act. Even as the Civil War raged in the east, Congress mustered the resources to pass this 1862 legislation, which made marriage to more than one wife a crime and disincorporated the Mormon Church. Lincoln, however, believed the Mormons were best left alone and refused to enforce the legislation. As for the Civil War itself, the Mormons—understandably—stood aloof during the conflict. "We have frequently been mobbed, pillaged and plundered, without redress," said apostle John Taylor. "Our men have been whipped, banished, imprisoned, and put to death without a reason. . . . Shall we join the north to fight against the south? No! Shall we join the south to fight against the north? As emphatically, No! Why? They have both . . . brought it upon themselves, and we have had no hand in the matter."[44] At Lincoln's request, however, Young did supply guards to protect mail routes in Utah.

With the war over and with slavery eliminated, the country turned renewed attention to slavery's "twin relic." In 1870 the House passed the Cullom Bill, imposing harsh measures against polygamists and authorizing another federal army to invade Utah and eradicate polygamy. With ironic timing, in the very same month, the Utah legislature bestowed upon women the right to vote, and they soon became the first females in the country to exercise the franchise. Hearing of the Cullom Bill's provisions, between three and six thousand of them massed in the tabernacle to protest government intrusion and to affirm their right to "believ[e] and practic[e] the counsels of God, as contained in the gospel of heaven."[45]

An incredulous public could only witness the protest in amazement, accustomed as they were to hearing that polygamy was essentially a form of white slavery in which uncooperative women were punished or killed. The Cullom Bill failed in the Senate, but Congress successfully increased the severity and scope of antipolygamy legislation in the next decade. In 1882, President Chester Arthur signed into law the Edmunds Act, which mandated fines, disenfranchisement, and imprisonment for the practice of plural marriage. Over the next ten years or so, over a thousand Mormons would be convicted of unlawful cohabitation (easier to prove than polygamy), and hundreds of men, along with a handful of women, spent time in prison.[46] Thousands of others, including many church leaders, went underground to avoid the federal authorities.

The final blow fell in 1887. The Edmunds–Tucker Act aimed to effectively destroy the Mormon Church as a political, economic, and religious entity, since it could not curb its practices. The bill dissolved the church, its Perpetual Emigrating Fund, and its militia, the reconstituted Nauvoo

Joseph F. Smith family portrait
Taken with his five wives and children on occasion of his sixtieth birthday, 1898.
(Courtesy of the Church Archives, The Church of Jesus Christ of Latter-day Saints)

Unidentified Latter-day Saint and his two wives

Contrary to popular impressions, most Mormons did not practice plural marriage, and for those who did, two wives was the usual number. (Courtesy of the Church Archives, The Church of Jesus Christ of Latter-day Saints)

Thompson Dunbar elopes with Mrs. Ballygag's entire boarding school
Comic writers from Mark Twain to Artemus Ward and others added humor to an arsenal of weapons directed against Mormon polygamy. (From *The Tragedy of Thompson Dunbar*, by Max Adeler [pseudo.], 1879)

Legion. Church property was confiscated, and an obedience and loyalty test oath stripped virtually all Mormons of their political rights. Since it was clear that the women of the territory were too independent-minded to comply with the government's vision of their own best interests, Congress repealed their right to vote as well, whether or not they were polygamists or even Mormon. A few months later, church president John Taylor died in hiding, and for the next three years, the Mormons endured more imprisonments, bankruptcy, dismembered families, and virtual criminal status for membership in their church.

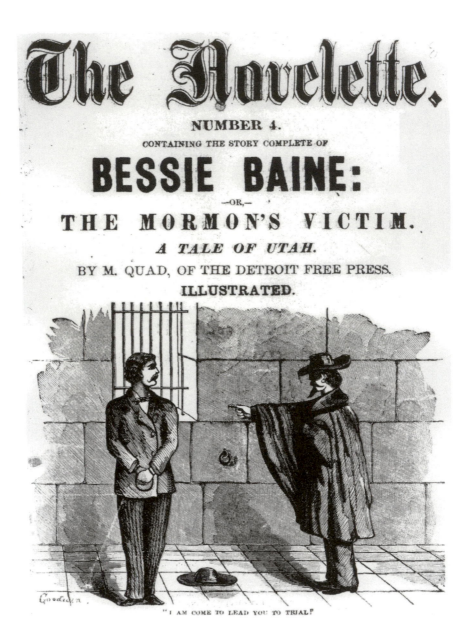

Bessie Baine; or, The Mormon's Victim
Exploiting nativist sentiment, authors and illustrators of anti-Mormon works frequently portrayed Mormons as exotic or foreign in appearance and manner. (By M. Quad [pseud.], 1898)

Utah penitentiary orchestra, ca. 1888

A wave of federal antipolygamy statutes empowered judges to subject dozens of Mormon men—and some women—to prison terms ranging from months to years. (Courtesy of the Church Archives, The Church of Jesus Christ of Latter-day Saints)

At last, in September 1890, new church president Wilford Woodruff revealed to a shocked congregation that he intended to submit to the federal legislation and urged his followers "to refrain from contracting any marriage forbidden by the law of the land."[47] Some members thought they discerned in his words a strategy of ostensible compliance but tacit resistance. And indeed, some plural marriages were performed by church leaders for a few years thereafter. But eventually it became clear that the era of plural marriage was, for faithful members of the church, finally at an end. Cessation of the practice was certainly as traumatic a transition as instituting the practice had been half a century earlier. Members were by now profoundly attached to a practice that had required such extreme sacrifices and that had come to be viewed by many as a visible sign of their costly devotion and status as a "peculiar people." Households were now forcibly broken up, sister wives separated, and thousands of women abruptly cut off from loving and established, however unconventional, relationships

Salt Lake temple capstone ceremony
The largest group ever assembled in Utah witnessed the laying of the capstone on 6
April 1892, forty years after construction began. (Courtesy of the Church Archives,
The Church of Jesus Christ of Latter-day Saints)

with their husbands. Children too suffered, as in so many cases their contact with their fathers was circumscribed and redefined. And many of the women who had become plural wives were, in fact, older unmarrieds, aged widows, or indigent immigrants, with whom the husband had a benevolent rather than sexual relationship. Therefore, writes one scholar, "whatever polygamy's faults were, in destroying it the federal government also destroyed what had been an effective social welfare system."[48]

Some Mormons fled to Canada or Mexico to continue the practice and preserve their families, but most acceded to the new regimen as faithfully—though reluctantly—as they had initially embraced the old. Today, significant numbers of polygamists persist in the practice, scattered primarily throughout the four corners area of the Southwest. No such group, however, has any official connection with the Church of Jesus Christ of Latter-day Saints. The Mormons today are no more tolerant of plural marriage than the Episcopalians or Lutherans. But the historical origins of the practice in the days of Joseph and Brigham, and the persistence of media stereotypes and misinformation, continue to wed Mormonism and polygamy in the popular imagination.

With the abandonment of polygamy, Mormonism turned a corner in the history of its place in American society. Signs of a new age of respectability were quick to replace the old indicators of isolation and difference. Months after Woodruff's Manifesto, he directed the disbanding of the People's Party, the political party dominated by Mormon citizens and church interests. Henceforth, Mormons would affiliate with the same parties as other American citizens. In October 1891, the president of the church and his counselors (the First Presidency) felt safe enough from arrest to appear together in public for the first time in seven and a half years. In 1893, the federal government restored voting rights in Utah (at least to the men). In April of that year, the Salt Lake temple was dedicated, just in time to furnish a striking and durable symbol of a reemergent church. Months later, the Mormon Tabernacle Choir took second place in competition at the Chicago World Fair. From this moment on, Mormonism would begin to gain world attention for its beauties as well as for its idiosyncrasies. And the increasing scope of this attention was foreshadowed two years later when the first stake—or ecclesiastical unit comprising several congregations—was organized outside the United Sates in Alberta, Canada. Mormonism's process of Americanization was by no means complete. But as the church abandoned polygamy, moved toward a genuine two-party political system in Utah, and began to shed its insularity, its distance from the mainstream narrowed perceptibly. Enough barriers to harmony had been eliminated for Congress to finally grant Utah's petition for statehood. The request had been rebuffed in 1848, 1856, 1861, 1872, and 1887. Finally, on 4 January 1896, Utah became the forty-fifth state of the Union.

Out of Isolation

The polygamy controversy did not end with statehood; the drama had at least two acts left to unfold. In 1898, Utah elected polygamist B. H. Roberts to the House of Representatives. A House committee, reinforced by nationwide petitions and public clamor, denied him his seat, though his plural marriages had been contracted before the manifesto. Then in 1903, Reed Smoot was elected to the Senate. He was not the first Latter-day Saint elected—Frank Cannon had been in 1896. But Cannon's position in the church had been ambiguous at best, and he soon became a virulent anti-Mormon. Smoot, on the other hand, was one of the church's Twelve Apostles, and the election to public office of such a high-ranking Mormon rekindled all the suspicions and rancor that had delayed statehood for half a century to begin with. For the next few years, Senate committees weighed the rumors of continuing polygamous unions in Utah, of Mormon disloyalty, and of church authoritarianism. Finally, in 1907, Smoot was granted his seat in the Senate, where he would serve for three decades.

American involvement in World War I came two generations after the Civil War, and Latter-day Saint response to the conflict revealed their new place in American society. In contrast with their studied indifference to the claims of regionalism or patriotism in the Civil War, Mormons now supported the war effort with resources and enthusiasm equal to or exceeding the national mean. Volunteer enlistments were far above quota; Red Cross contributions and the purchase of Liberty Bonds in Utah both exceeded federal requests by around 50 percent.[49]

The most dramatic change in the LDS Church in the years following World War I was the transition from a Utah-based church to a population dispersed throughout the United States. Arriving in the desolate valley in 1847, Young had expressed his dream of Mormon autonomy: "We do not intend to have any trade or commerce with the gentile world, for so long as we buy of them we are in a degree dependent upon them. The Kingdom of God cannot rise independent of the gentile nations until we produce, manufacture, and make every article of use, convenience, or necessity among our people. . . . I am determined to cut every thread of this kind and live free and independent, untrammeled by any of their detestable customs and practices."[50]

In the process of their Americanization, Latter-day Saints had to abandon that dream of economic and cultural autonomy. At almost the same moment statehood was granted, effectively ending the political isolation of Utah, church leaders declared an end to the practice of the gathering, marking the beginning of the end to the physical isolation of Mormonism. The new direction was first suggested in 1898; by 1907 the First Presidency was formally declaring that "the policy of the Church is not to entice or encourage people to leave their native lands; but to remain faithful and true in their allegiance to their governments, and to be good citizens."[51] Missionaries continued to fan out throughout the world, but converts were encouraged to stay in their own areas and "build Zion."

In an ironic reversal of the Mormon image, Latter-day Saints gradually went from being perceived and portrayed as un-American, immoral, and peculiar, to quintessentially American, respectable, and even admirable. For even as they shed their countercultural polygamy and clannishness, they came to reemphasize those principles that situated them in the mainstream of popular values. Beginning in 1899, they had begun to give new emphasis to the neglected principle of tithing. Commitment to financial sacrifice and generosity expanded, during the Great Depression, into a highly efficient and comprehensive welfare system. The church thereby launched a program that replaced what President Heber J. Grant called "the curse of idleness" and the indignity of the dole with principles of self-reliance and industry. Renewed emphasis on the Word of Wisdom soon led to an association of Mormonism with a clean, healthy lifestyle.

Other influences were at work to consolidate Mormonism's recognition as a church that had entered the mainstream. Beginning around the turn of the century, Temple Square and the Tabernacle Choir and its 12,000-pipe organ were promoted as tourist attractions. Visitors who once flocked to Salt Lake to write about the American Moses and his harem, now came away impressed by the wholesome, middle-class values in evidence. By 1905, two hundred thousand visitors were visiting the famed Square annually[52] (the current figure is in the millions). With the polygamy issue at last laid to rest, national media showed a willingness to grant more favorable coverage. In 1930, *Time Magazine* actually featured President Heber J. Grant on its cover, commemorating the centennial of the church's founding.

Missionaries had also been effective in enlarging the church's membership and enhancing its public image. In 1901, missions were opened in Japan and reopened in Mexico. Over the next five decades, numerous others throughout South America, Asia, and Europe were opened or reorganized, and church membership tripled. Church organization responded to the rapid growth by requiring full-time service from General Authorities, and, beginning in 1941, by calling several Assistants to the Twelve to full-time service as well. As the church membership diffused beyond the Utah borders, governance was decentralized as well, with local leaders given more authority.

By the end of World War II, the Latter-day Saints were approaching one million members. With the cessation of hostilities, the church enjoyed the same resurgence of an available male labor pool as the rest of the nation—and they quickly took advantage of the opportunity for a vastly

Downtown Salt Lake City
Once the dominant feature on the skyline, the Mormon Temple is now dwarfed by the
hi-rise Church Office Building to its east. The tabernacle, home of the famous choir, is
adjacent to the west, and the sprawling Conference Center is on the north. (Courtesy
of the Church Archives, The Church of Jesus Christ of Latter-day Saints)

increased missionary force. With those greater numbers came new efforts
to increase the efficiency, the professionalism, and the standardization of
missionary work. In 1952, Salt Lake introduced the first uniform method
for teaching the gospel systematically in a series of six discussions. In 1961,
the first worldwide training seminars for mission presidents began, and
President David O. McKay's popular slogan, "Every member a missionary," helped propel the church into a new era of missionary-mindedness.
That same year, the church first began providing preparatory language
training to missionaries called to serve in Mexico and Argentina. By 1978,
a $15 million complex near Brigham Young University had been dedicated
for the exclusive purpose of training all missionaries in the areas of language, culture, and gospel teaching methods.

The consequences of Mormonism's new and improved (and enlarged)
missionary force were dramatic. From 1950 to 1980, church membership

grew more than 50 percent per decade, with strongest growth in Latin America and along the western coast of the United States.[53] Clearly, one of the major challenges of the new half-century would be dealing with an explosive growth rate, and with a membership that would be increasingly drawn from foreign cultures.

Many of the pressures of a worldwide church were addressed by a program initiated in 1961 by apostle Harold B. Lee. He headed an effort to eliminate redundancy in, improve cooperation and consistency between, and generally streamline all church programs, curricula, and activities. The resulting "Priesthood Correlation" continues to be a guiding principle of church governance today, allowing a highly efficient centralization of church organizations. It is one of the legacies of correlation, and one of the hallmarks of Mormon efficiency and organization, that a member can travel to any ward in the world and find a Sunday School or Primary or Relief Society class organized in the same way, doing the same lesson, and using the same manuals, as in the member's home ward. Not only does the Priesthood Correlation program instill efficiency and (what some consider an excessive) conformity, but it works to forestall the doctrinal innovations and schisms that could easily follow in the wake of globalization.

Challenges Facing the Contemporary Church

The LDS Church faced other significant challenges in the late twentieth century that ensued from the political and cultural upheavals of the 1960s. In this era, the church still maintained a policy dating to the Brigham Young years of barring from the priesthood (and thus from significant leadership positions) anyone of African ancestry. (This subject will be addressed in chapter 6.) Public opposition to this LDS racial policy grew in the 1960s and 1970s especially. In addition, the sexual revolution, feminism, abortion, and the perceived breakdown of family values presented the church both with challenges and with opportunities to assert their own defining values.

In 1978, President Spencer W. Kimball announced an epochal revelation that opened the priesthood to all worthy males in the church, without regard to race, thus paving the way for dramatic progress in missionary work among African and Brazilian populations. A barrier that was coming to assume the cultural magnitude of nineteenth-century polygamy was effectively removed with one official pronouncement.

The Washington D.C. temple
Dedicated in 1974, a temple on the outskirts of the nation's capital—and the first east of the Rockies—betokened a church that was moving to the respected mainstream of a country that had once exiled its members. (author photograph)

Two other emphases of the later twentieth century would be families and temple building. Family Home Evening, a program whereby families gather informally on a weekly basis for both instruction and meaningful time together, received renewed emphasis starting in the 1960s, and came to epitomize the church's devotion to strengthening the family. The program inspired favorable recognition, frequent endorsements by media and local governments, and occasional imitations around the country. In a rare gesture, the church formally issued a "Proclamation to the World on the Family" in 1995, reaffirming cardinal Mormon doctrines on the eternal nature of the family unit. Related to this emphasis on the family was a major commitment to building those temples where Mormons believe families are eternally welded together. Primarily under the administration of the peripatetic Gordon B. Hinckley, temple building received unprecedented emphasis, with the number of Mormon temples in operation going from under twenty in 1980 to over a hundred by the new millennium. The Mormon doctrine of the family, rooted in fairly conventional gender roles and reliant upon patriarchal models of home and church governance, proved fairly resilient in the face of the feminist revolution. The women's movement provoked no major crisis in the church, although there were a few scattered—and publicized—excommunications over the issue. At the same time, the public discussion of women's issues did prompt healthy debate and fresh attention to the place of women in the church.

The real development of significance, however, was the changing face of church demographics as the century ended. In 1950, only half of the church's congregations were in Utah, and over 90 percent of members lived in the United States or Canada. By 1990, the percentage of congregations in Utah had shrunk to one-fourth, and over one-third lived abroad. That same period saw Mormonism's organized presence abroad expand from fifty nations to 128. In September 2000, church membership reached 11 million, and over half of those did not speak English as their first language. Mormonism was no longer a Utah church, nor even primarily an American church. The era of the international church had begun.

Notes

1. Mark E. Petersen, *The Great Prologue* (Salt Lake City: Deseret, 1975), 7.

2. In the allegory of the olive trees, recounted at great length in Jacob 5, LDS readers generally see the "good spot of ground" where transplantation occurs as referring to America.

3. Horatio Gates Spafford, *A Gazeteer of the State of New York* (Albany: B. D. Packard, 1824), 80; cited in Bushman, *Joseph Smith and the Beginnings of Mormonism* (Urbana: University of Illinois Press, 1984), 45.

4. Asael Smith to Jacob Perkins Town, 14 January 1796, in Mary Audentia Smith Anderson, *Ancestry and Posterity of Joseph Smith and Emma Hale* ... (Independence, Mo.: Herald Publishing House, 1929), 60–62; cited in Donna Hill, *Joseph Smith: The First Mormon* (Salt Lake City: Signature, 1977), 21–22.

5. David Meredith Reese, *Humbugs of New York: being a remonstrance against popular delusion; whether in science, philosophy, or religion* (New York: Taylor, 1838), 265.

6. Joseph Smith-History 1:16–17, *Pearl of Great Price.* Recent scholarship has cast some doubt on the exact chronology of Smith's account, since in his fourteenth year the records indicate little revivalist activity in his immediate vicinity. Milton V. Backman defends the 1820 dating in *Joseph Smith's First Vision* (Salt Lake City: Bookcraft, 1971). No one doubts, however, that such an ambience characterizes some period or periods of his youth, since his area saw enough missionary activity to be named the "burned-over district." See Whitney R. Cross's classic study of that name (Ithaca, N.Y.: Harper and Row, 1950).

7. Dean Jessee, ed., *Papers of Joseph Smith*, 2 vols. (Salt Lake City: Deseret, 1989–92), 1:5.

8. The earliest account, of 1832, is from ibid., 1:1–14. The standard, canonized account from 1838 is in *The Pearl of Great Price*, Joseph Smith-History 1:16–17.

9. For a study of the different accounts of the First Vision, see Milton V. Backman Jr., *Joseph Smith's First Vision* (Salt Lake City: Bookcraft, 1980).

10. Richard Bushman has found over thirty-two pamphlets relating personal visions in the period 1783 to 1815—and those are just the published ones. Bushman's tally does not include visionary experience embedded in longer narratives. "The Visionary World of Joseph Smith," *BYU Studies* 37, no. 1 (1997–98): 183–204.

11. The ducking was remembered by neighbor Thomas H. Taylor, reported in *Deseret Evening News*, 20 January 1894, 167.

12. Joseph Smith-History 1:20.

13. Joseph Smith-History 1:29–34.

14. Robert Remini, *Joseph Smith* (New York: Viking, 2002), 6.

15. Joseph Smith Jr., *History of the Church of Jesus Christ of Latter-day Saints*, 7 vols., ed. James Mulholland et al. (Salt Lake City: Deseret, 1951), 1:54–55.

16. Originally published at the end of the volume, the testimonies are now printed in the front of every edition, and have been since 1841.

17. David Whitmer even recorded that soon after the book was published, Joseph handed his seerstone to Oliver Cowdery and said "he was through with it, and he did not use the stone any more. He said that he was through the work that God had given him the gift to perform, except to preach the gospel." *Address to All Believers in Christ* (Richmond, Mo.: author, 1887), 32.

18. *Messenger and Advocate* 1, no. 1 (October 1834): 16.

19. William Cathcart, ed., *The Baptist Encyclopedia* (Philadelphia: Everts, 1881), 1253; Williams' awaiting of new apostles was characterized as such by his contemporary John Cotton, in James Ernst, *Roger Williams: New England Firebrand* (New York: Macmillan, 1932), 479.

20. Charles Dickens, "In the Name of the Prophet—Smith!" *Household Words* 8 (19 July 1851): 340.

21. Just before his Kirtland departure, on 7 June, Smith had pointed more generally to Missouri as the place for the faithful to assemble (DC 52:42).

22. Andrew F. Ehat and Lyndon W. Cook, eds., *The Words of Joseph Smith: The Contemporary Accounts of the Nauvoo Discourses of the Prophet Joseph* (Provo, Utah: Religious Studies Center, Brigham Young University, 1980), 212.

23. Milton V. Backman Jr., *The Heavens Resound: A History of the Latter-day Saints in Ohio, 1830–1838* (Salt Lake City: Deseret, 1983), 140, 147–49.

24. Clark V. Johnson, "Northern Missouri," in S. Kent Brown, Donald Q. Cannon, and Richard H. Jackson, eds., *Historical Atlas of Mormonism* (New York: Simon and Schuster, 1994), 42.

25. Smith, *History of the Church*, 3:175.

26. Backman, *The Heavens Resound*, 201.

27. *Journal of Discourses*, 26 vols., reported by G. D. Watt et al. (Liverpool: F. D. and S. W. Richards et al., 1851–86; reprint, Salt Lake City: n.p., 1974), 2:31.

28. Smith, *History of the Church*, 2:379–82.

29. George W. Givens, *In Old Nauvoo: Everyday Life in the City of Joseph* (Salt Lake City: Deseret, 1990), x–xi.

30. Ibid., 4–5.

31. E. Cecil McGavin, *Nauvoo the Beautiful* (Salt Lake City: Stevens and Wallis, 1946), 72.

32. Ibid., 43.

33. Glen M. Leonard and Edgar T. Lyon, "The Nauvoo Years," *Ensign* 9 (September 1979): 11; Mulder, "Among the Mormons," 159.

34. Warren Foote, *Autobiography of Warren Foote*, 3 vols. (privately printed typescript n.p., n.d.), 1:82. Originals in the Historical Department of the Church of Jesus Christ of Latter-day Saints, Salt Lake City, Utah.

35. Sen. Thomas H. Benton of Missouri was the alleged instigator, and Young even suspected President Polk of complicity. See Leonard J. Arrington and Davis Bitton, *The Mormon Experience: A History of the Latter-day Saints* (New York: Vintage, 1980), 98–99.

36. *Journal of Discourses*, 1:53–54.

37. [Ingraham, Prentiss] "Author of *Buffalo Bill*," "Buffalo Bill and the Danite Kidnappers; or, The Green River Massacre," *The Buffalo Bill Stories: A Weekly Devoted to Border History* (1 February 1902); Arthur Conan Doyle, *A Study in Scarlet* (London: Ward Lock, 1887).

38. In the Book of Mormon, the prophet Jacob teaches that plural marriage is an exceptional, not normative practice. When specially commanded to "raise up seed" through this practice, it is countenanced. Otherwise, "there shall not any man among you have save it be one wife" (Jacob 2:27–30).

39. *Contributor* 5, no. 2 (November 1883): 58.

40. B. H. Roberts, *The life of John Taylor, third president of the Church of Jesus Christ of Latter-Day Saints* (Salt Lake City: G. Q. Cannon, 1892), 100.

41. Arrington, *Mormon Experience*, 185.

42. Nels Anderson, *Desert Saints: The Mormon Frontier in Utah* (Chicago: University of Chicago Press, 1966), 176.

43. Foote, *Autobiography*, 150.

44. B. H. Roberts, *The Comprehensive History of the Church of Jesus Christ of Latter-day Saints*, 6 vols. (Provo, Utah: Church of Jesus Christ of Latter-day Saints, 1957), 5:11.

45. Sarah M. Kimball, quoted in Edward W. Tullidge, *The Women of Mormondom* (New York: Tullidge & Crandall, 1877), 380–81.

46. For a half dozen examples of incarcerated women, see George W. Givens, *Five Hundred Little Known Facts in Mormon History* (Springville, Utah: Bonneville, 2002), 233.

47. Official Declaration-1, DC.

48. Edwin B. Firmage, "The Judicial Campaign Against Polygamy and the Enduring Legal Questions," *BYU Studies* 27, no. 3 (summer 1987): 116.

49. "A total of 24,382 enlisted. . . . The Red Cross asked for $350,000; they received $520,000. When the government began to sell Liberty bonds, Utahns were requested to raise $6,500,000; they purchased $9,400,000 worth." Richard O. Cowan, *The Church in the Twentieth Century* (Salt Lake City: Bookcraft, 1985), 61.

50. "Norton Jacobs Record," 28 July 187, in Eugene England, *Brother Brigham* (Salt Lake City: Bookcraft, 1980), 161.

51. James R. Clark, comp., *Messages of the First Presidency of The Church of Jesus Christ of Latter-day Saints*, 6 vols. (Salt Lake City: Bookcraft, 1965–75), 4:165.

52. Daniel H. Ludlow, ed., *Encyclopedia of Mormonism: The History, Scripture, Doctrine, and Procedures of the Church of Jesus Christ of Latter-day Saints*, 4 vols. (New York: Macmillan, 1992), 2:633.

53. Richard O. Cowan, *The Church in the Twentieth Century* (Salt Lake City: Bookcraft, 1985), 263.

Chapter 2

"These War-like Fanatics": Anti-Mormonism in American History

Our institutions, which guarantee the freedom of religious opinion to the Jew, the Mahometan, the Pagan, and even to the *Atheist*, afforded no protection to the Mormon.
—John Russell, *The Mormoness, 1853*

We should be patient and rational in dealing with these . . . self-professed defender[s] of truth.
—Jay Newman, *Foundations of Religious Tolerance, 1982*

Early Mormonism's relationship to America, as we have seen, was a fractious one at best. But persecution can carry with it an aura of self-righteousness, and historians are rightly skeptical of any group making too much of its victimized status. Because persecution also provokes powerful group loyalty and cohesion, and can be a sign to believers that the forces of Satan are alarmed ("we expect the rage of all hell to be aimed at us to overthrow us," said Brigham Young[1]), emphasizing opposition to Mormonism throughout American history serves both social and ideological purposes as well. Nevertheless, no historian would deny that among religious groups in nineteenth-century America, none experienced such persistent, vehement, and widespread opposition, or incurred such extensive hostility from the federal government. In the twentieth century and beyond, the record is more debatable.

Religious Roots of Anti-Mormonism

Reasons for conflict between the Latter-day Saints and American society varied with time and place, and generally involved a range of factors and agendas. Although some constants persist through the historical record, the tensions and hostilities were largely shaped by radically different contexts in which political, social, cultural, and theological practices and perspectives collided. But the popular hostility that Mormonism engendered was, from first to last, rooted in—if not confined to—religious challenges to Christian orthodoxy, and its American Protestant variety in particular. As we saw earlier, the initial antagonisms that Joseph Smith recorded were provoked by his claim to have experienced personal manifestations from on high. Prophets, seers, and mystics in all ages have courted derision and opposition by presuming special spiritual gifts and privileged access to God and his mysteries. In this regard, Joseph Smith was no different from the beleaguered Portuguese children of Fatima who claimed to be visited by the Virgin Mary, or Jemima Wilkinson, the "Publick Universal Friend," whose reception in Rhode Island and Pennsylvania was neither universal nor friendly. On at least one occasion she had to flee a stone-throwing mob. "Mother" Ann Lee, founder of the Shakers, discovered her gender was no protection against hostility that erupted at times into violent abuse, and even the eighteenth-century visionary Emanuel Swedenborg, esteemed among European nobility and intelligentsia, was likewise not immune to contempt and ridicule. Aggravating the hostility in Smith's case were at least two factors. First, he claimed not just dreams of Jesus or visitations by angels, but actual contact with God himself. And this at the unlikely age of fourteen. Second, rather than retreat behind linguistic ambiguity by fudging the nature of the epiphany (vision? dream? out-of-body experience?), he insisted stubbornly on the literal reality of his encounter: "I had actually seen a light," he would write of his First Vision, "and in the midst of that light I saw two Personages, and they did in reality speak to me" (JS-H 1:25).

The Book of Mormon

By 1830, Smith had published his translation of the Book of Mormon and was offering it for sale, both from the Palmyra publisher E. B. Grandin and from a fledgling corps of missionaries who spread out in ever-increasing orbits from their New York base. If Joseph Smith's claim to divine favor was a misdemeanor of rash youthfulness, disseminating a work that challenged the canonical uniqueness of the Bible was a religious felony. The first could be dismissed as so much impudence. The second was an affront to Christianity's very rootedness in the Bible as the canonically complete word of God. Immediately upon the Book of Mormon's publication, newspapers trumpeted its "Blasphemy!"[2] The earliest clerical response known, a letter of the Dutch Reformed minister Diedrich Willers, complained that Smith, "now established as a prophet through the transmission of his nonexistent plates, wants to elevate his book to the status of a canonical work through which the Spirit of God is revealed to men. Even with this he is not satisfied, but introduces a second Bible, and thereby expects it to be acknowledged that the Word of God is not complete."[3]

Willers himself admitted that he had "read only a little of it" (he "would wish to be excused from this effort"[4]). He was one of several critics who exemplified the reality behind Thomas O'Dea's humorous jibe that "the Book of Mormon has not been universally considered by its critics as one of those books that must be read in order to have an opinion of it."[5] The critics, like the believers, understood that what was at stake in the *claim* to a new revelation was of greater theological significance than the particular *content* of any such revelation. In 1841, the first book-length apologia for the Book of Mormon listed the six objections "commonly urged against it." It was criticized, noted Mormon author Charles Thompson, because (1) it was an "imposition" to claim to be a revelation from God, (2) God would "never give any more revelations to man after the [Bible]," (3) "the Bible is full and complete," (4) "God has imperatively forbidden any addition," (5) the Book of Mormon is seen as an attempt "to do away" with the New Testament, and (6) it was actually written by Solomon Spaulding and Sidney Rigdon.[6] None of these criticisms, then or now, challenged the theological value or content of the record. Christians by and large have taken the Lord's words to Moses, like John's similar injunction in reference to his revelation on Patmos, as a comment on biblical sufficiency itself (in spite of the fact that they could only have been referring to the immediate context of their own writings): "Ye shall not add unto the word which I command you, neither shall ye diminish ought from it" (Deut. 4:2; see also Rev. 22:18).

New Definitions of the Sacred

Other critics have seen Smith's additions to the canon as part of a larger process that undermined the way religious faith itself has come to be predicated on a kind of sacred distance. In *The Idea of the Holy*, religious scholar Rudolf Otto writes that within this category of experience (the sacred or holy), mystery, the *mysterium tremendum*, is not merely an attribute of divinity, but "the deepest and most fundamental element in all . . . religious devotion." It is something "beyond conception or understanding, extraordinary and unfamiliar, . . . before which we therefore recoil in a wonder that strikes us chill and numb." In sum, the mysterious is "that which lies altogether outside what can be thought, and is, alike in form, quality, and essence, the utterly and 'wholly other.'"[7] Elizabeth Johnson agrees, insisting that

> the history of theology is replete with this truth: recall Augustine's insight that if we have understood, then what we have understood is not God; Anselm's argument that God is that than which nothing greater can be conceived; Hildegard's vision of God's glory as Living Light that blinded her sight; Aquinas's working rule that we can know *that* God is and what God is *not*, but not *what* God is; Luther's stress on the hiddenness of God's glory in the shame of the cross; Simone Weil's conviction that there is nothing that resembles what she can conceive of when she says the word God; Sallie McFague's insistence on imaginative leaps into metaphor since no language about God is adequate and all of it is improper.[8]

Against this backdrop, Joseph Smith's religion-making was brazenly lacking in transcendence, mystery, or ineffability. The god he preached was accessible, communicative, as bodily and vocally real as the God of Moses; scripture was not a timeless revelation whose origins were shrouded in the mists of history, but an ongoing reality in whose enunciation, transcription, canonization, and publication Joseph and his colleagues had hands-on participation. Priesthood was not a nebulous potential residing in all believers or derived from faith in the Bible, but an actual authorization committed to men through resurrected apostles who visited Joseph Smith and placed physical hands upon his head to effect a tangible connection between his authority to minister and the ministry of Jesus Christ in Palestine. Physical plates with real heft confirmed by a dozen witnesses, seerstones and oracular spectacles, temples of stone rather than flesh, a Zion that could be located on a map, and a gathering that entailed wagons and later handcarts rather than a figurative unity of belief—in these and other ways Mormonism collapsed the historical, psychological, and ontological distance that became integral to so much of the Christian tradition. As such, Mormonism invited accusations of both banality and blasphemy.

Historians have in recent years turned increasingly to nonreligious factors to explain the Mormon conflict with American society. But hostility to Mormonism emerged long before—and would persist long after—Mormonism's practices of centralized gathering, economic communalism, or polygamy. From the start, opponents were contemptuous of Mormonism's ill-suitedness to embody the sacred or the sublime, as those concepts developed in Christianity. From the prophet's pedestrian background and name ("'Smith!' said Miss Priscilla, with a snort. 'That's a fine name for a prophet, isn't it?'"[9]) to his church's relentless pragmatism ("no association with the sacred phrases of Scripture could keep the inspirations of this man from getting down upon the hard pan of practical affairs," observed Josiah Quincy[10]), to the specificity and proximity of the Book of Mormon's origin and story ("It is far superior to some modern productions on western antiquities, because it furnishes us with the names and biography of the principal men who were concerned in these enterprises. . . . But seriously, . . ."[11]), Mormonism resisted those ruptures with historical reality that have served to ground the idea of the holy and sense of the sacred. And rather than obscure or apologize for this brashness, Mormonism explicitly celebrates the immediacy and particularism of God's manifestations in modern history:

And again, what do we hear? Glad tidings from Cumorah! Moroni, an angel from heaven, declaring the fulfilment of the prophets—the book to be revealed. A voice of the Lord in the wilderness of Fayette, Seneca County, declaring the three witnesses to bear record of the book! The voice of Michael on the banks of the Susquehanna, detecting the devil when he appeared as an angel of light! The voice of Peter, James, and John in the wilderness between Harmony, Susquehanna County, and Colesville, Broome County, on the Susquehanna river, declaring themselves as possessing the keys of the kingdom, and of the dispensation of the fulness of times! And again, the voice of God in the chamber of old Father Whitmer, in Fayette, Seneca County, and at sundry times, and in divers places through all the travels and tribulations of this Church of Jesus Christ of Latter-day Saints! And the voice of Michael, the archangel; the voice of Gabriel, and of Raphael, and of divers angels, from Michael or Adam down to the present time, all declaring their dispensation, their rights, their keys, their honors, their majesty and glory, and the power of their priesthood; . . . Let the mountains shout for joy, and all ye valleys cry aloud; and all ye seas and dry lands tell the wonders of your Eternal

King! . . . And again I say, how glorious is the voice we hear from heaven, proclaiming in our ears, glory, and salvation, and honor, and immortality, and eternal life; kingdoms, principalities, and powers! (DC 128:21–23)

Mormon Elitism and Theocracy

The triumphalism and audacity of Mormon religious claims were to skeptics prima facie evidence of an outrageous imposition. Citizens in Missouri, even as they denied engaging in religious persecution, revealed hearty contempt for the miraculous and the supernaturalism that so pervaded Mormon preaching. In an 1833 document Jackson County residents composed to justify their expulsion of the Mormons, they vented their exasperation that, among other concerns, the Mormons "do not blush to declare, and would not upon occasion hesitate to swear, that they have wrought miracles . . . and supernatural cures, have converse with God and His angels, and possess and exercise the gifts of divination and of unknown tongues."[12] Scattered throughout an extensive body of redress petitions signed by Mormons exiled from Missouri are references to religious beliefs as the reason the citizens gave for expelling the Saints.[13] But Mormon claims to special spiritual status and powers would soon be accompanied by social and institutional dimensions of the faith, more threatening because more durably and materially grounded.

American culture has long been rooted in the rhetoric if not the reality of religious pluralism. Consequently, it is no surprise to find the religious dimensions of anti-Mormonism sometimes obscured by appeals to patriotism, moral rectitude, generic "Christian" values, and the American way of life. During the "nativist" period in American history, overzealous patriots embarked upon a campaign that pitted American loyalties against a perceived threat of inundation by waves of immigrants. Catholics suffered extremely during this period for two reasons. As a foreign, authoritarian religious institution commanding worldwide devotion, the papacy seemed sharply inimical to the ideals and institutions of American democracy. And most of the flood of Irish immigrants who poured into the country in the post–Civil War era, competing for scarce American jobs, were of course Catholic.

The leadership of Mormonism was perceived as a similarly despotic regime, and in the popular imagination, the Vatican and Salt Lake City were interchangeable as seedbeds of antirepublicanism. The difference, of course, was that Mormonism was not as readily associated with an ethnic group that reinforced this perception of an entity that was foreign, threatening, and un-American. For even if the case could be made that Mormons were largely a foreign import, they could not, like the Catholics, be easily identified by association with a particular ethnicity. That fact itself may have exacerbated tensions; at times, popular fiction reflected a resulting, peculiar anxiety that Mormonism provoked. The popular image of Mormonism as a "viper on the hearth" suggests a public dread of a creeping menace that insinuated itself into the domestic sphere with none of the visible characteristics usually associated with foreign menaces. Lacking ethnic markers, foreign origins, and distinctive language or dress or features, Mormons were doubly dangerous precisely *because* their apparent family resemblance belied an inner core of contagious heresy.

Two responses emerged as a consequence. First, was the guilt-by-association strategy. Novels of the era could refer to Mormons in the same breath as "Mahometans," "Indians," "Turks," and Chinese ["rat-eaters"].[14] The specific groups linked to Mormons in period magazines, report Gary Bunker and Davis Bitton, were the "Irish, Catholics, blacks, Chinese, [and] native Americans"[15]—all groups outside the American mainstream of the era. Political cartoons depicted "the Mormon Question" as of a piece with "the China Question" and "the Indian Question," thus insinuating that Mormonism was another in a line of problems that were foreign and political by nature, not religious or domestic.

A more creative response to the Mormon paradox was a pattern of representation that served to create difference where none existed, to endow Mormonism with those very characteristics and features that would erect clear, discernible parameters to a nebulous and fluid community. At times, this was accomplished by describing Mormonism as a foreign ethnicity in very vague, generic terms, with frequent allusions to the foreign makeup of Mormon numbers. And those making the allegations could do so in very public, incendiary ways. During his campaign for the presidency, for instance, Stephen A. Douglas alleged that "nine-tenths of the inhabitants [of Utah] are aliens by birth who have refused to become naturalized, or to take the oath of allegiance, or do any other act recognizing the government of the United States as the paramount authority in that territory."[16] Statistically speaking, the fears were unwarranted: the 1880 Utah census, for instance, revealed that of 144,000 people in Utah, fewer than 31 percent were foreign-born. (And this in a year when

Idaho, Wisconsin, California, Dakota, Arizona, Nevada, Minnesota, all had higher percentages of foreign-born citizens.[17])

Still, the lack of conspicuous markers of genuine ethnicity did not stop writers from creating their own. Orientalism, as Edward Said has shown, has always been more about Western fantasy than Asian reality, serving as a convenient category that authors can employ to denote the exotic, the erotic, the mysterious, or the threatening. And in the case of Mormonism, writers borrowed liberally from that construct to impute to LDS characters menace, lasciviousness, and physical strangeness. *Mormonism: The Islam of America*, reads one typical title.[18] "Orientalism in the extreme Occident," was what Charles Heber Clark called the religion, referring in part to the polygamous connection. But he insisted that the city even looked like Damascus, and the Utah sky itself was "of more than Oriental appearance."[19] Dane Coolidge wrote in the early twentieth century, but his leading Mormon character still "stood out . . . like a man of a different race," and all of them have "in their eyes, or so it seemed, . . . a strange, foreign look."[20] Jack London's character cuts through the complicated details of ethnic differentiation to conclude simply, "They ain't whites . . . They're Mormons."[21]

Of course, the frequent allusions to Joseph Smith and Brigham Young as American Mohammeds revealed very particular objections to Mormonism as well. Arthur Conan Doyle's allusions to the "harems of the elders" in a Sherlock Holmes mystery and James Oliver Curwood's reference to the "harem of the king" in his anti-Mormon novel were blatant attacks on the system of Mormon polygamy.[22] But other criticism was implicit as well. When Doyle also compared Mormonism to "the inquisition of Seville [and] the German Vehmgericht," it becomes clear that spiritual tyranny, not lasciviousness, is the common denominator of his allusions. Whether Joseph Smith was represented as, in novelist Sydney Bell's words, "an oriental despot," or as Robert Richards insisted, a Romish conspirator,[23] the perceived authoritarianism would become an increasing target of hostility. In spite of Mormonism's emphasis on "personal revelation," church authority was unquestionably hierarchical, with the prophet as supreme spiritual head on earth, and members were enjoined to heed "all his words and commandments . . . as if from [God's] own mouth" (DC 21:4–5). It was not only outsiders and nativists who reacted against this Mormon authoritarianism. In staking out his role as prophet of a new dispensation, Joseph Smith, as we have seen, went far beyond mere sermonizing or even scriptural authorship. The Kingdom of

God that he envisioned had social, economic, and political dimensions, and he believed his stewardship encompassed all of them. To the extent that dissidents and enemies resisted Joseph's claim to such sweeping prerogatives, the stage was set for conflict, charges of tyranny and priestcraft, and anxieties about cult behavior and religious imperialism. Conflict in this regard first surfaced in Kirtland. Much of the disaffection of this era was exacerbated by economic conditions and activities in and around Kirtland. The Mormon presence in Kirtland had grown from a mere one hundred in 1833 to 1,300 in 1836, at which point it was showing no signs of abating. Even as the gathering focused increasingly in Missouri, Joseph Smith apparently foresaw continuing growth in the Kirtland area, even drafting a master plan for city improvements in 1836.

Economic Tensions

A complex mix of factors led to challenging economic vicissitudes and disparities in the Kirtland area. First, as a gathering place, it was naturally receiving a daily influx of uprooted converts, generally without funds or immediate prospects of employment. The resulting "insupportable weight of pauperism" of which neighboring citizens complained was no exaggeration.[24] Church leaders admitted the problem (the Kirtland Saints, they acknowledged, were "poor from the beginning"), and even addressed the problem by counseling leaders of outlying branches not to send their emigrants to Kirtland without making financial provision for them.[25]

At the same time, Kirtland was becoming a booming town, and huge profits were there to be made by the ambitious. Many Saints dutifully shared their abundance with the destitute. But many members translated their optimism about the future into a rising debt load and speculative land purchases. Then in early 1837, with their economy stymied by lack of money and credit, Smith and other church leaders made plans to establish a bank. Denied authority to do so by the state legislature, they instead organized the Kirtland Safety Society Anti-Banking Company. Such circumvention was not unprecedented, and the issuing of banknotes without a charter was not clearly prohibited by law. Nevertheless, weeks after its opening, the institution began to unravel. Undercapitalization, the spread to Ohio of a national banking panic, wild land speculation, and an alleged run on the company's limited specie by opponents of the church have all been cited as contributing factors. By November the anti-banking company was out of business, and investors—many of whom were backers of modest means—were left with $400,000 in losses.[26] Joseph suffered greater personal loss in the failed venture than any other, but that fact did little to dampen resentment or console those who were ruined by the collapse—or who watched the failure and wondered how a genuine prophet could suffer financial disaster. Joseph and many of his colleagues were charged with banking violations and fined. For members already inclined to murmur about the prophet's intrusion into secular affairs, the whole episode spurred disaffection.

In early 1838, the man who had transcribed almost the entirety of the Book of Mormon, Oliver Cowdery, left the church over just this issue. Cowdery had sold some of his land holdings in Missouri, in defiance of a revelation by Smith. Charged by a church council in Far West, Missouri, with "virtually denying the faith by declaring that he would not be governed by any ecclesiastical authority or revelations whatever in his temporal affairs," Cowdery readily admitted the offense: "I will not be influenced, governed, or controlled, in my temporal interests by any ecclesiastical authority or pretended revelation whatever, contrary to my own judgment."[27] That the high council subsequently rejected the charge against Cowdery suggests the extent to which Smith's authority to dictate in temporal matters was still a matter of controversy, uncertainty, and discontent.[28]

Once in Utah, the problem was rendered an issue of national concern, since personal subordination to perceived spiritual tyranny was one thing—the institutionalization of theocracy was another all together. "The essential principle of Mormonism is not polygamy at all but the ambition of an ecclesiastical hierarchy to wield sovereignty" warned an eastern newspaper in 1885.[29] And indeed, the institutions of church and state were virtually indistinguishable in the kingdom administered by Brigham Young, where temporal and spiritual realms converged. In this connection, critics and historians have made much of Mormonism's Council of Fifty, a shadow government Smith set up with alleged designs for eventual political domination, an instrument for an audacious subversion of American democracy and the bald imposition of theocracy. In reality, as one scholar has written, "the primary role of the Council of Fifty was to symbolize the otherworldly world order that would be established during the millennial reign of Christ on earth. Aside from its symbolic value, the singular importance of the Council of Fifty is that it reveals Joseph Smith, Jr., as Mormonism's greatest Constitutionalist."[30]

Plural Marriage

Constitutionalist Smith might have been, but in Kirtland the prerogatives he claimed led many besides Oliver Cowdery into discontent and rebellion. For it was during this same period of economic crisis that rumors circulated in Kirtland about another disturbing aspect of the prophet's life—his involvement in plural marriages. It is not clear at what point in his life Joseph Smith first contemplated the practice, or felt he received heavenly direction on the subject. In the popular imagination, Mormonism—especially early Mormonism—continues to be associated with polygamy (technically "polygyny"), or plural marriage. Like the question of ecclesiastical authority, the doctrine of plural marriage fractured the church from within before it invited wrath from without. As Joseph himself predicted, "should he teach and practice the principles that the Lord had revealed to him and now required of him that those then nearest him . . . would become his enemies & the first to seek his life."[31] Though it is unclear exactly when Smith first practiced or preached the principle, evidence suggests he first considered the idea during his work revising the Old Testament in 1831. Most revelations that came to Joseph occurred in response to particular questions he asked of God, often as he read or revised the scriptures. It would have been consistent with this practice to inquire of the Lord when he encountered the plural marriage of the patriarchs and sought understanding or a connection between that abandoned practice and the "restoration of all things" he had been called to effect. That much is indicated by the opening words of the revelation on plural marriage that Joseph at last recorded in 1843: "inasmuch as you have inquired of my hand to know and understand wherein I, the Lord, justified my servants Abraham, Isaac, and Jacob, as also Moses, David and Solomon, . . . as touching the principle and doctrine of their having many wives and concubines" (DC 132:1).

At any rate, Smith apparently took as his first plural wife Fanny Alger, probably in 1835 in Kirtland. It was during this same period that Joseph came under increased criticism from his brethren, and undoubtedly the rumors of Joseph's unconventional marriage system was a factor. Initial practice of the principle provoked his followers and associates to become estranged from the church in one of two ways. Some members were simply aghast at the rumors, and could not reconcile themselves to a practice so at odds with inherited Christian norms, no matter its alleged sanction by a modern-day prophet. Even his erstwhile scribe and right-hand-man Oliver

Cowdery would later vehemently denounce Smith's relationship with Fanny Alger as adultery, and though he later reconciled with the church, Cowdery never reconciled himself to the principle of plural marriage.

Some members, on the other hand, not only accepted the radical new doctrine, but began to practice their own version of polygamy, either in the mistaken view that the practice was open to all or using the prophet's purported example as a justification for their own unsanctioned liaisons. Ironically, it was this same Oliver Cowdery along with other leading elders, loyalists later alleged, who initiated extramarital relationships in spite of Smith's insistence that they were unauthorized to do so. He alone held the keys to legitimize the practice, he taught; nonetheless, once word of the practice spread, self-prescribed polygamy became a magnet for sexual opportunists like John Bennett, who invoked "spiritual wifery" as a cloak for what amounted to seduction pure and simple. He was exposed and excommunicated, and others who entered the practice without authorization found themselves rebuked and corrected. In fact, many of those who alleged sexual misconduct on Smith's part over the next decade were, in turn, accused and excommunicated for using the principle of plural marriage as a pretext for their own immoral behavior. Charges and counter-charges of gross immorality flourished in this increasingly secretive, contentious climate.

The combination of hostile nonmembers and the more vociferous disgruntled members, in a milieu of financial failures, swirling innuendo, and authoritarian leadership, proved too much for the survival of the church in Kirtland. Dissident leaders staged an effective coup a month after the bank failure. Brigham Young, the prophet's staunchest defender, fled for his life from mob fury at the end of December 1837. Joseph and Sidney Rigdon, believing their lives were in danger, followed three weeks later.

Politics, the Gathering, and Church Growth

With the removal of most Kirtland Saints to Missouri, the gathering gained momentum and church growth itself became a factor in hostility. Willers had complained in his 1830 letter that within months of its organization, the Mormon Church was "winning over many members of the Baptist Church," as well as "members of the Lutheran, Reformed, [and] Presbyterian" persuasions.[32] In Missouri just three or four years later, the press reported a Mormon's claim that there were already gathered

"20,000 converts to the doctrines he professes."[33] The claim was wildly exaggerated, but perceptions, not fact, fueled frontier anxieties. And the principle of Mormon gathering compounded those anxieties. Even 20,000 members, dispersed throughout a state or two, might have passed unnoticed. Only 2,000, settling compactly in the midst of the sparsely settled counties of Missouri, were impossible to ignore. And settle compactly they did. By 1833, there were 1,200 Mormons in Jackson County, who relocated in Clay County the next year. By 1838, when church membership totaled near 18,000, 5,000 of those were living in Caldwell County and another 2,000 in the adjacent Daviess County.[34]

However innocently conceived or spiritually grounded, the Mormon doctrine of gathering was inescapably charged with menace to a frontier society especially where so many factions maintained a fragile balance—whether the issue was presidential politics, slavery, or clashing cultures of east and west. The remarks a naïve but probably representative woman made to Warren Foote, leader of a Mormon wagon train on his exodus from Nauvoo to the west, provide a window on the estrangement and apprehension that accompanied popular impressions of Mormon solidarity:

> She asked, "How many do you suppose there are of the Mormons." I answered, I cannot tell, some thousands I suppose. She said with surprise, "Do you not know them all?" O no madam, but a few of them I replied. "You don't," said she. "I thought they all knowed one another." I said that they were like other folks about that.
>
> She went on to add, tellingly, "If the Mormons would scatter around amongst the white folks, they could live in peace."[35]

Foote found her advice amusing. But the tragedy behind the humor was that such gathering, in the view of militia General John B. Clark, was the direct cause of the destruction, beatings, and violence that preceded the Saints' expulsion from Missouri in 1838. In his speech to the exiles, he admonished them "to scatter abroad, and never again organize yourselves with Bishops, Presidents, etc., lest you excite the jealousies of the people, and subject yourselves to the same calamities that have now come upon you."[36]

As the unsympathetic journalist J. H. Beadle editorialized about the persecutions: "the same results would soon overtake the Methodist or any other church, if it should concentrate its forces in one state, every man voting . . . at the command of the bishop."[37] And as for the political threat the Mormons posed, the statistics reveal that old settlers were not unduly alarmist in believing they had suddenly and perhaps irrevocably lost their franchise in a veritable flood of Mormon immigrants. The citizens' 1833 document had referred to invading "swarms" of Mormons, and indeed, as many as eight thousand Saints settled there in the next five years. In Daviess County, where old settlers used violence to prevent Mormons from voting in August 1838, their actions can be understood as a desperate reaction to a recent influx of Mormons that had suddenly given the newcomers a two to one advantage at the polls. Because the Mormon Question was a hot political issue, the Saints tended to vote en bloc for whatever candidate promised to be the most sympathetic to their cause. In Caldwell County that year, for example, the Mormon-favored Democratic candidate for Congress received 337 votes to his Whig opponent's 2.[38] The town of DeWitt, home to 40 or 50 Missourians, was transformed virtually overnight into a Mormon enclave of perhaps 200 Saints, with a corresponding shift of political power.[39] This pattern was repeated throughout northern Missouri.

During the Saints' Illinois period, another element introduced into the volatile mix of anti-Mormon hysteria was Smith's decision to run for president in the 1844 election. Having unsuccessfully sought redress in Washington for the Missouri depredations, and finding politicians in general and the presidential candidates for the 1844 election in particular unwilling to pledge support or guarantee justice for the Mormon people, the prophet decided to position himself as a candidate. His decision was probably a calculated move to gain greater visibility for his cause, to leverage the considerable Mormon electorate in Illinois into a bargaining chip that would give him influence and a role in the national campaign, and have a platform for the dissemination of both personal and doctrinal views relevant to the election. Most important, he hoped to parley his visibility into protection from the church's persecutors. "We will whip the mob by getting up a president," he said.[40] In April, 340 special electioneer missionaries were called to spread the gospel and the platform, heading out for all twenty-six states in the Union and the Wisconsin territory.

Smith's campaign received a good amount of press coverage, and while he was never a serious contender, the remote possibility must have been alarming to his enemies, and in the suspicious climate of the day, his decision could only be read by outsiders as an exercise in either megalomania or insatiable ambition. One Dr. Southwick reported to Mormon leaders that he had been at a June meeting in Illinois attended by men from twenty-three states, convened to consider "the best way to stop Joseph Smith's career, as his views on government were widely circulated and took like wildfire. They said if he did not get the Presidential chair this election, he would be sure to the next time."[41]

When the national Republican Party officially aimed to eradicate polygamy as a "relic of barbarism" in 1856, they guaranteed that political solidarity for Mormons would continue to be a matter of life and death struggle for the church. A few years later, non-Mormons and dissenters in Utah made opposition local, when they formed the Liberal Party to counter the hegemony of the church. In response, the Mormons formed the People's Party in 1870 to represent their interests, solidifying the political polarization. For the next two decades, politics and religion were inescapably intertwined in the Territory. As Utah Mormons campaigned for statehood, it became necessary to gain the support of the historically unsympathetic national Republican Party, and to emulate the national two-party system as a sign of their Americanness. Stories still circulate about church leaders assigning half of each congregation to register as Republicans. So prevalent were such tales at the time that in March 1892, the First Presidency published a statement "declaring that the rumors of their directing members of the Church which political party they should support were false and without foundation in fact. The Presidency had no disposition to direct in such matters, but desired the people to choose for themselves."[42]

From the beginning, Mormons had been warned about the dangers of too much cliquish solidarity. In the Jacksonian period, guidebooks even advised new settlers to the frontier "to mingle freely and familiarly with neighbors, and above all to pretend to no superiority."[43] An inescapable feature of life on the frontier was a social leveling born of necessity, the virtual irrelevance of class and rank once the entertainments and amenities of eastern culture were left behind. "The leveling spirit of Western democracy," writes Ray Allen Billington, "sought not only to elevate the lowly but also to dethrone the elite. Any attempt at 'putting on airs,' was certain to be met with rude reminders of the equality of all men."[44]

Not only did the Saints not mingle freely, they emphasized by word and deed their radical distinctness from their neighbors. Their principle of gathering, their self-identification with the House of Israel, and their relegation of all others to the status of gentiles did little to help. And their gathering was no placid conventicle of Shakers. Theirs was at times a rhetoric of defiance, elitism, and confrontation. It had begun before the first Saints even arrived in Jackson County. Writing in Kirtland, Ohio, Smith had proclaimed the word of the Lord with neither tact nor diplomacy: "Ye shall assemble yourselves together to rejoice upon the land of Missouri, which is the land of your inheritance, which is now the land of your enemies" (DC 52:42). Such doctrine did not go over well with the old settlers, all too aware of Mormon intentions: "We are daily told," they protested in their 1833 document, "and not by the ignorant alone, but by all classes of them, that we, (the Gentiles,) of this country are to be cut off, and our lands appropriated by them for inheritances. Whether this is to be accomplished by the hand of the destroying angel, the judgments of God, or the arm of power, they are not fully agreed among themselves."[45]

Actually, the Saints hoped to accomplish the conquest of Zion through fairly pedestrian means—by the dollar. "Wherefore, it is wisdom that the land should be purchased by the saints," counseled an 1831 revelation, "and also every tract lying westward, ... and also every tract bordering by the prairies, inasmuch as my disciples are enabled to buy lands" (DC 57:4–5). Still, the swelling numbers, the rhetoric about rights of inheritance, language that cast Mormons as "saints" and old settlers as "gentiles" and "the wicked," would soon incite tensions that principles of the marketplace could do little to abate.

And in the later stages of the Missouri conflicts, Mormon rhetoric went far beyond spiritual polarities. Rejected by former supporters and associates, Smith had fled his Kirtland enemies and arrived in Missouri in March 1838. In his personal experience, the dangers from the dissenters had weighed more heavily than the threats from without. Perhaps it was out of this background that he immediately proceeded to cleanse the inner vessel, determined to eradicate apostasy in Missouri. On 19 June, his most vociferous orator, Sidney Rigdon, delivered his rousing "salt sermon." Based on Matthew 5, wherein Jesus admonished that salt without savor was "to be cast out and trodden under the feet of men," Rigdon's fiery speech prompted the creation of a secret, militant organization, the "Danites," or "Destroying Angels," determined to enforce orthodoxy and purge the ranks of the disloyal. Joseph's role in their formation and subsequent activities has been alleged but never established. They appear to have directed at least some of their fury in the coming months against some of their Missouri persecutors, further inflaming a virtual civil war by responding to illicit violence with illicit violence.

A few weeks after Rigdon's "salt sermon," he delivered a Fourth of July speech that marked a decisive shift in Mormonism's response to persecution. Formerly the Mormons had, for the most part, passively acquiesced to their trials. They had been driven out of Jackson County in 1833, shattering their dreams of establishing a Zion there, and they were forcibly evicted from Clay County three years later. Twice dispossessed without compensation, they were in no mood to be burned or driven out of their homes again. While expressing indignation and seeking redress through legal channels, they had nevertheless offered virtually no armed resistance to their oppressors. But on Independence Day, 1838, Rigdon gave the American public fair notice that Mormons would no longer submit to oppression, and the church's publication and dissemination of his remarks left no room for doubt that the line had been drawn in the sand. If mob action against the Saints were to persist, Rigdon promised, "it shall be between us and them a war of extermination, for we will follow them, till the last drop of their blood is spilled, or else they will have to exterminate us; for we will carry the seat of war to their own houses, and their own families, and one party or the other shall be utterly destroyed."[46] When Governor Boggs issued his infamous order less than four months later, his insistence that the Mormons must be "exterminated or driven from the state," so shocking to Americans now, was actually a rejoinder to Rigdon's challenge, framed in the terms Rigdon had himself employed.

Slavery and the American Indians

In the state of Missouri in the 1830s, slavery was the most contentious of all political issues, and in this regard, the Mormon influx was especially alarming. Missouri had been admitted to the Union as a slave state only a decade before the church was founded. It was populated mostly by southerners with little use for northerners or anyone inclining toward abolition. Most of the incoming Mormons were clearly northerners, and the Missouri citizens' 1833 document of protest had accused the newcomers of extending "an indirect invitation to the free brethren of color in Illinois, to come up . . . to the land of Zion."[47] The touring Englishman Edward Abdy confirmed the presence, if not the validity, of that rumor.[48] In actual fact, Mormons were sensitive enough to the political winds to tread cautiously in regard to slavery. Shortly before the Jackson County citizens convened to express their grievances, the church's newspaper, the *Evening and Morning Star*, had reprinted the Missouri law against the immigration of "free people of color," and warned members to "shun every appearance of evil" in this regard.[49] And following a skeptical response by Missourians to that advisory, Mormons followed up with another article that went so far as to insist that "our intention was not only to stop free people of color from emigrating to this state, but to prevent them from being admitted as members of the church" (far from actually disallowing blacks, the church did baptize several).[50] But Mormon efforts to assuage the fears of Missourians could hardly have been more inept. For the editor of the hastily composed and posted broadside, W. W. Phelps, apparently could not resist an approving aside about "the wonderful events of this age" that were tending "towards abolishing slavery." And a few months later, in December 1833, Smith would declare by revelation that "it is not right that any man should be in bondage one to another" (DC 101:79).

Still walking a fine line, in August 1835, the church published a document—immediately canonized—that again attempted to set out its position in clear terms: "we do not believe it right to interfere with bondservants, neither preach the gospel to, nor baptize them contrary to the will and wish of their masters, nor to meddle with or influence them in the least . . . ; such interference we believe to be unlawful and unjust, and dangerous to the peace of every government allowing human beings to be held in servitude" (DC 134:12). Even so, Mormons could not deny that the Book of Mormon itself condemned slavery unambiguously. "It is against the law of our brethren," the Nephite Ammon had said, "that there should be any slaves among them" (Alma 27:9). And by the time Smith ran for president in 1844, he proposed an ambitious scheme for freeing all the slaves and subsidizing their emancipation through the sale of public lands. The Missourians did not mistake the true leanings of the Mormons, their efforts to diffuse concern notwithstanding. So pervasive was the perception of Mormonism as hostile to slavery that more than sixty years after the prophet's death, writers on Mormonism would still claim that Joseph "was shot and killed for his anti-slavery sympathies."[51]

African Americans were not the only ethnic group to complicate the Mormon problem. On the frontier, unconventional policies and attitudes toward the American Indians could engender misunderstanding and ignite conflict. In this regard, the Book of Mormon was not exactly an asset. That Mormon missionaries marketed the volume as a history of the American Indians was not itself a problem; the idea that America had been settled by offshoots of the house of Israel (whether from the lost ten tribes, as popularly depicted, or the tribe of Joseph, as the Book of Mormon held) had a long history in American and colonial writing. But the Book of Mormon insisted that the descendents of those settlers, whom Joseph Smith associated with modern native Americans, were in fact heirs of the covenant with

Israel, a people of promise, and future participants in the building of a New Jerusalem. "One of the most important points in the faith of the Church of the Latter-day Saints, through the fullness of the everlasting Gospel," declared Smith plainly, "is the gathering of Israel (of whom the Lamanites constitute a part)."[52]

Even the foreign visitor Abdy, touring a Missouri that bordered Indian territory, could see this was an inflammable doctrine: "As the promulgators of this extraordinary legend maintain the natural equality of mankind, without excepting the native Indians or the African race, there is little reason to be surprised at the cruel persecution by which they have suffered. . . . The preachers and believers of the[se] . . . doctrines were not likely to remain, unmolested, in the state of Missouri."[53] Indeed, a mass meeting of citizens that convened in Liberty, Missouri, specified as one reason for their expulsion of the Mormons from Clay County the fact that they were "keeping up a constant communication with our Indian tribes on our frontiers, [and declare], even from the pulpit, that the Indians are a part of God's chosen people, and are destined by heaven to inherit this land."[54]

During the Mormons' Nauvoo period, these accounts had been supported by credible and influential persons. Brigadier General Henry King, who had been present as interpreter during a meeting of Smith with three Potawatomi chiefs, wrote to the Iowa governor, John Chambers, that "it seems evident, from all that I can learn, . . . that a grand conspiracy is about to be entered into between the Mormons and Indians to destroy all white settlements on the frontier."[55] Either King's language skills or his motives must be questioned, but as the Saints began their exodus from Illinois to present-day Omaha in 1846, the rumors of Mormon meddling with Indians had taken their toll on public perceptions. One refugee recounted in his journal the atmosphere of alarm:

> The inhabitants are very much scared. They are afraid that the "Mormons" will soon be upon them and slay men, women, and children. I called into a house to see if I could sell any thing. The man was not at home. As I turned to go out the woman said "You are a Mormon I suppose it is a fair question." Yes Madam I replied. She said "There are a great many Indians up there where you are camped." I replied that I had not seen any. Said she, "You have not seen any! Why we hear that you are building forts and your women are marrying in with the Indians, and that you are combining togather [sic] and are coming down here to kill us all off." . . . She then said, "There are a great many women here that are

almost scared to death, they are just ready to run." Well, Said I, if they are not killed until the "Mormons" kill them they will live a long time.[56]

After the Saints resettled in Utah, politicians joined the chorus of critics alleging the Mormons were again plotting with the native inhabitants. Stephen Douglas would claim in 1857 that "the Mormon government, with Brigham Young at its head, is now forming alliances with Indian tribes in Utah and adjoining territories—stimulating the Indians to acts of hostility."[57] While that was mostly fanciful invention, Indians *were* involved with the Mormons in the massacre of emigrants a few months later at Mountain Meadows in a unique instance of collaboration that seemed to fulfill Douglas's most dire predictions.

Communitarianism

Only a few years into its history, Mormonism acquired institutional dimensions and a numerous following that presented more overt threats to social stability. Once established in Ohio and Missouri, Joseph implemented, in addition to the gathering itself, another in a line of unconventional practices that would be perceived as a threat to the established social order. Called the Law of Consecration and revealed in 1831, this principle required heads of household to deed their property over to the church and receive in return "as much as is sufficient for himself and family" (DC 42:32). The residue was to be "kept in [a] storehouse, to administer to the poor and needy, as shall be appointed by the high council of the church, and the bishop" (DC 42:34). External pressure and conflicts made the utopian ideal difficult to implement, but internal weaknesses presented obstacles as well. In June 1834 the Lord rebuked the Saints because they did not "impart their substance, as becometh saints, to the poor and afflicted among them." Accordingly, he warned, they "must needs be chastened until they learn obedience, ... by the things which they suffer" (DC 105:3, 6).

Although the Saints did not succeed in replicating a society that shared "all things [in] common" as alluded to in the book of Acts (4:32), they did practice an unprecedented degree of communal, economic self-sufficiency. To what extent their clannish business practices and experiments in economic communalism disturbed the old settlers is not clear. It has been said that such a practice ran counter to the ruggedly individualistic frontier ethos that dominated near the boundaries of civilization. Other historians, however, have emphasized the extent to which survival on the frontier was always a cooperative enterprise, and hold that the myth of individualistic self-sufficiency is overblown.[58] In addition, the Missourians claimed the indigence of church members was a factor in their being expelled from Jackson County, and indeed, the continual displacement and disruption of Mormon life was more conducive to destitution than affluence. But even given the imperfect implementation of the church's communitarian principles, it is likely Mormon economic insularity and cohesiveness were themselves to some degree threatening. In any case, it is probable that the clannishness of which the Law of Consecration was an emblem was really the irritant.

Cultural Conflicts

Finally, there was the simple problem of cultural conflict. The same Missouri document that specified motives for the expulsion of the Mormons twice mentioned the fact of their being, largely, "eastern men, whose manners, habits, customs, and even dialect, are essentially different from our own."[59] And it was true that most of the first generation of church members were drawn from New York, Pennsylvania, and Ohio. Though few were exactly eastern aristocrats, it is clear that early Mormons aspired to a level of cultural and intellectual attainment that was not exactly consistent with the level of civilization one found on the frontier. (They established schools and adult education programs, and would even plan a university in the midst of recently drained swampland just three years after their forcible eviction from Missouri.)

The Missourians, on the other hand, were not renowned at that point in time for their decorum or level of cultural achievement. Missouri in 1831, the year of the Saints' arrival, was still very much a frontier state, with all that that implied. The English traveler J. S. Buckingham remarked in 1842 that "no one can approach the frontier settlements . . . without being struck with the lawless spirit . . . everywhere manifested by the inhabitants."[60] Another historian of the Old Northwest writes that the perception of inhabitants of that era as "coarse, ignorant, lawless, and violent" was true at all times for some and at some time for most.[61] Joseph Smith himself first arrived in Missouri in the summer of 1831, and in spite of his hopes of establishing Zion there, was filled with foreboding by what he saw:

our reflections were many, coming as we had from a highly cultivated state of society in the east, and standing now upon the confines or western limits of the United States, and looking into the vast wilderness of those who sat in darkness; how natural it was to observe the degradation, leanness of intellect, ferocity, and jealousy of a people that were nearly a century behind the times, and to feel for those who roamed about without the benefit of civilization, refinement, or religion.[62]

These perceptions were not limited to European visitors and Yankee prophets. William Walker, at one time the provisional governor of the Nebraska Territory, visited Independence, nerve center of the Mormon gathering in Missouri, a few years after the Saints' expulsion. He found the citizens "the most selfish, exacting, grinding, mercenary people I ever saw in any country, barbarian or Christian. Hospitality is an utter stranger and foreigner to them."[63]

Autonomy and Militarism in Nauvoo

Once the Mormons were established in their haven of Nauvoo, Illinois, two additional factors entered the picture to foment antagonisms. First was the nature of the Nauvoo charter itself. Much of the unique character of Nauvoo resulted from the unusual powers and privileges given the Saints by its charter, under which the city operated from February 1841. Granted by the state legislature, the charter provided for the establishment of a university and an independent militia that would be called the Nauvoo Legion. From the point of view of the Mormons, the charter's best feature was that the mayor and city councilmen were also designated as municipal court judges. As one writer points out, "this feature allowed the Saints to place trusted church leaders in key positions, and provided an avenue of escape from illegal and trumped-up arrest by the issuing of writs of habeas corpus. Of course, enemies of the Church chafed against this power as much as the Saints rejoiced in it."[64] Perceptions grew that Mormon courts would protect not only Smith, but any Mormon in the commission of any crime. Fiction writers, journalists, and hostile editors like Thomas Sharpe added to the rumors that Nauvoo had become a robbers' roost and safe haven for counterfeiters, thieves, and evildoers of every stripe.

Second was the size and prominence of the Nauvoo Legion. America in this period had a standing army of fewer than ten thousand men. Most states, including Illinois, required service in the militia, but given their oppression at the hands of the Missouri militia, Mormons petitioned the Illinois legislature for the right to fulfill their military obligation to the state by serving in a militia under local control. The Nauvoo Legion, authorized by the Nauvoo Charter, was the result. Nominally under the control of the governor, the Legion was actually declared "totally independent" by state authorities in 1843, probably to avoid state responsibility for financial support.[65] Numbering six hundred men under arms at its inception, the Legion would boast five thousand at the time of the prophet's death—making it the second largest group of trained soldiers in the country and over half the size of the federal army.

That Joseph Smith took the title of lieutenant general (echoes of George Washington!) probably didn't help dispel fears about Mormon militarism and motives. The Legion engaged in drills, parades, and sham battles, providing a source of both spectacle and conspicuous pride to the inhabitants of Nauvoo. But the highly public displays involving thousands of armed troops under the command of the Mormon prophet were probably ill-considered, in light of the church's history in Missouri. Thomas Sharp, who would become a virulent anti-Mormon as editor of the Warsaw, Illinois Signal, was a guest in April 1841 when a splendidly bedecked Lieutenant General Smith drilled and paraded fourteen companies of the Legion. Months later, Smith continued to note with satisfaction the attention the Legion was attracting: "Such was the curious and interesting excitement which prevailed at the time in the surrounding country, about the Legion," he wrote in January 1842, that "Judge [Stephen A.] Douglas adjourned the circuit court . . . and came with some of the principal lawyers, to see the splendid military parade of the Legion."[66] Soon, however, it became apparent that outsiders were paying attention more out of alarm than amusement. A few months later, the New York Herald printed the observations of a U.S. artillery officer, who wrote alarmingly (and inaccurately) of the area's "30,000 warlike fanatics," warned of the Mormon "tendency . . . to annihilate all other sects," and prophesied that "the time will come when this gathering host of religious fanatics will make this country shake to its centre."[67] The same year, doubtless with images of Smith and his thousands of armed minions still fresh in his mind, Sharp alleged in his increasingly hostile Signal that "everything [the Mormons] say or do seems to breathe the spirit of military tactics. . . . Truly fighting must be the creed of these Saints [emphasis original]."[68]

Fictional Representations

"This is the age of reading." So proclaimed Joseph Story in a Phi Beta Kappa address at Cambridge, Massachusetts, in 1826.[69] So it was that in this very period the paranoia about organized Mormon violence found another powerful mode of expression in the work of a popular British naval hero and novelist, Frederick Marryat. His *Monsieur Violet: His Travels and Adventures among the Snake Indians* (London, 1843) was the first full-length work to treat Mormons fictively (if one discounts the pseudo-documentary accounts), and its depictions were alarming. His fanciful descriptions of the bloodthirsty Danites, report of Rigdon's "salt sermon," and exaggerated portrait of a heavily militarized fortress Nauvoo were sprinkled with enough factual elements—including contemporary newspaper accounts like the one above from the *Herald*—to successfully feed the flames of paranoia. And renegades in Joseph's inner circle, whether sincerely affronted by polygamy or simply thwarted in their personal prurient agendas, were in a perfect position to fuel the fires of outrage. When the inflammatory *Nauvoo Expositor* was published, allegations that plural marriage was just Smith's ploy to mask his licentiousness and adultery, made by Smith's excommunicated, former confidants featured prominently in its tirades.

Most notable in this regard was the case of John C. Bennett. He had served in Nauvoo as Smith's counselor, city mayor, chancellor of Nauvoo University, second-in-command of the Nauvoo Legion, and in other responsible positions. Embarrassed by revelations of his sordid past, sexual predation, and subsequent excommunication, he retaliated in print. First he published a series of scurrilous letters impugning the prophet's character, and then expanded his accusations into a book published in 1842 as *The History of the Saints, or, An Exposé of Joe Smith and Mormonism*. Given the unparalleled prominence of such a defector and a catalog of accusations ranging from arson to rape to treason, Bennett's widely disseminated accusations found a vast, receptive audience. Starting in the 1850s, scores of novels would combine with countless periodicals, nickel weeklies, short stories, and other forms of popular fiction, to promulgate stereotypes of Mormons as evil, lustful, deceitful, and generally dangerous to Christian values and American women. Novelized accounts of Mormon perfidy were even cited on the floor of the U.S. Senate during debate on the Mormon question. The media war would continue for generations as a powerful factor in shaping and exacerbating public animosity toward the Latter-day Saints.[70]

The Utah Period

Once ensconced in the Wasatch Mountains of Utah, the Mormons must have felt themselves well free of mobs, militia, and dissidents. In their first five years in Utah, they were preoccupied with laying out a city, irrigating the desert, contending with swarms of crickets, and fending off starvation. With the 1852 announcement of polygamy, a new era in anti-Mormonism was initiated that this time incorporated federal legislation, a federal army, and a national crusade by politicians, journalists, and novelists. With public acknowledgment of the practice, visitors and reporters could chronicle the details of an institution displayed with brazen openness.

Good evidence exists that in many cases the antipolygamy crusade could be motivated by something more than disinterested concern for the sanctity of conventional marriage. Scholars have noted, for example, that the federal invasion of Utah occurred on the eve of the Civil War, and was largely orchestrated by the ardent secessionist John B. Floyd, secretary of war in the Buchanan Cabinet. It is possible that he urged the expedition in order to displace a substantial proportion of the standing army and leave federal forts and arsenals in the South vulnerable to southern attack. Alternately, it has been suggested that the show of force against a territory portrayed as rebellious and semi-autonomous was meant as an object lesson to other states contemplating secession.

In launching the expedition, President Buchanan articulated exactly what it was that most distressed other Americans: "The great mass of these [Mormons are] acting under the influence of leaders to whom they seem to have surrendered their judgment."[71] That thousands of professed Christians would embrace en masse a practice so clearly antithetical to established morality and natural inclination seemed disturbing evidence that some malevolent tyranny over the minds of Mormons was at work. What Mormons practiced in response to that supposed surrender to ecclesiastical tyranny—polygamy or political conformity or anything else—might be considered secondary to the primary complaint that theocracy prevailed in Utah. One scholar of the era cites the testimony of anti-Mormon Frederick Dubois as representative of a subterfuge that invoked the practice of plural marriage issue as a weapon in a crusade against something many considered even more insidious:

> Those of us who understood the situation were not nearly as much
> opposed to polygamy as we were to the political domination of the

> Church. We realized, however, that we could not make those who did not
> come actually in contact with it, understand what this political domina-
> tion meant. We made use of polygamy in consequence as our great
> weapon of offense and to gain recruits to our standard. There was a uni-
> versal detestation of polygamy, and inasmuch as the Mormons openly
> defended it we were given a very effective weapon with which to attack.[72]

Furthermore, the editorialist J. H. Beadle, writing at the height of the
antipolygamy crusade in 1877, discounted polygamy as the real cause of
Mormon persecution. The record, he insisted, clearly shows that "the
Mormons had more trouble with the world before they adopted polygamy
than since. . . . Polygamy will do for a scape-goat, but the trouble is far
more radical than that."[73]

As the practice of polygamy faded into history, so too did the church's
physical concentration, its geographical isolation, and, to a lesser extent,
its political homogeneity. As a consequence, the church ceased to operate
as a hegemonic institution exerting influence over every aspect of Mormon
life. The process of assimilation into the American mainstream solved the
problem of plural marriage even as it softened perceptions of an overly
intrusive Utah theocracy.

Modern Mormonism and American Society

In the modern era, Mormonism's place in American society and the American religious community continues to be paradoxical. Once considered
pariahs and persistently characterized as foreign, un-American, and exotic,
Mormons are now viewed by some in precisely the opposite terms. American literary critic Harold Bloom has endorsed the reputed comment of a
famous Russian novelist that "if there is already in place any authentic version of the American Religion then, as Tolstoy surmised, it must be Mormonism."[74] In part this view reflects the degree to which Mormons have
become equated, in popular perception, with American values considered
mainstream at mid-century and into the "culture wars" of the late twentieth century. Their disproportionately high representation in Congress, the
CIA, and the FBI reflects the degree to which they are accepted as patriotic,
clean-cut, family-centered, and civic-minded. Among intellectuals and the
cultural elite, these attributes may be more cause for satire and ridicule than
esteem, as the case with the LDS characters in British novelist John Le
Carré's *Russia House*. Their "Mormon cleanliness," the narrator finds, is

"slightly revolting."[75] Similarly, in the award-winning gay fantasia, *Angels in America* (1993–94), the emblem of American sanctimonious hypocrisy is Joe Pitts, Utah Mormon and closet homosexual. But in these and kindred instances, Mormonism is not so much an object of derision for its own religious or cultural particularities, as it is for its embodiment of American values at their most conservative and traditional.

Outright hostility to Mormonism per se is for the most part confined to conservative religious groups who object to the Latter-day Saint claim to membership in the Christian faith group—for reasons to be explored subsequently—and to political operatives who still find it effective to use the Mormon label as code for fanatic, extremist, or otherwise socially or religiously undesirable. In the 1994 elections, for example, both Massachusetts Senator Ted Kennedy, in his contest against Mitt Romney, and Virginia Representative L. F. Payne, in his race against challenger George Landrith, publicly exploited the Mormon affiliation of their opponent. Payne's polling firm went so far as to circulate campaign literature that said, "George Landrith is a Mormon" and then proceeded to ask voters if his background raised "serious doubts, minor doubts, or no doubts."[76]

Joseph Smith's run for the presidency in 1844 may not ever be duplicated by a standing Mormon prophet. But the fact that an LDS Michigan governor (George Romney) could run for the Republican presidential nomination in the 1960s and an LDS senator (Orrin Hatch) could repeat the attempt in 2000 suggests that Mormons are finding a comfortable place in American society and political life. The question of Mormonism's place in the American religious community, as we will now see, is slightly more complicated.

Notes

1. *Journal of Discourses*, 26 vols., reported by G. D. Watt et al. (Liverpool: F. D. and S. W. Richards et al., 1851–86; reprint, Salt Lake City: n.p., 1974), 1:348.

2. *Rochester Daily Advertiser*, 2 April 1830.

3. D. Michael Quinn, trans. and ed., "The First Months of Mormonism: A Contemporary View by Rev. Diedrich Willers," *New York History* 54 (July 1973): 330.

4. Ibid., 327.

5. Thomas O'Dea, *The Mormons* (Chicago: University of Chicago Press, 1957), 26.

6. Charles Thompson, *Evidences in Proof of the Book of Mormon* (Batavia, N.Y.: D. D. Waite, 1841), 149–67.

7. Rudolf Otto, *The Idea of the Holy*, trans. J. W. Harvey, 2nd ed. (London: Oxford University Press, 1950), 12, 13–28, 146.

8. Elizabeth A. Johnson, *She Who Is: The Mystery of God in Feminist Theological Discourse* (New York: Crossroad, 1992), 7. Her citations are: Augustine, *Sermo* 52, c. 6, n. 16 (PL 38.360); Anselm, *Proslogium* chaps. 2–3, *Saint Anselm: Basic Writings*, trans. S. N. Deane (LaSalle, Ill.: Open Court, 1974); Hildegaard of Bingen, *Scivias*, trans. Mother Columba Hart and Jane Bishop (New York: Paulist, 1990), bk. 1, vision 1.*ST* I, q. 3, preface; Luther, theses 19 and 20, "The Heidelberg Disputation," *Luther: Early Theological Works*, trans. and ed. James Atkinson (Philadelphia: Westminster, 1962); Simone Weil, *Waiting for God*, trans. Emma Craufurd (New York: Harper and Row, 1973), 32; and Sallie McFague, *Models of God: Theology for an Ecological, Nuclear Age* (Philadelphia: Fortress, 1987), 35 and passim.

9. Charles Pidgin, *House of Shame* (New York: Cosmopolitan, 1912), 90.

10. Josiah Quincy, *Figures of the Past* (Boston: Little, Brown, 1926), 326.

11. J. M. Peck, *A Gazeteer of Illinois* (Jacksonville: Goudy, 1834), 53–54.

12. Joseph Smith Jr., *History of the Church of Jesus Christ of Latter-day Saints*, 7 vols., ed. James Mulholland et al. (Salt Lake City: Deseret, 1951), 1:397.

13. Clark V. Johnson, *Mormon Redress Petitions: Documents of the 1833–1838 Missouri Conflict* (Provo, Utah: Religious Studies Center, Brigham Young University, 1992).

14. Pidgin, *House of Shame*, 89.

15. See the chapter, "Troublesome Bedfellows: Mormons and other Minorities," in Gary L. Bunker and Davis Bitton, *The Mormon Graphic Image, 1834–1914: Cartoons, Caricatures, and Illustrations* (Salt Lake City: University of Utah Press, 1983).

16. Speech delivered 12 June 1857 in the state house in Springfield, Illinois. Cited in Joseph Fielding Smith, *Church History and Modern Revelation,* 4 vols. (Salt Lake City: The Church of Jesus Christ of Latter-day Saints, 1946–49), 4:146.

17. Utah Legislature's Memorial to Congress, *Congressional Record,* 13 January 1887, house proceedings, cited in B. H. Roberts, *A Comprehensive History of The Church of Jesus Christ of Latter-day Saints,* 6 vols. (Salt Lake City: Deseret, 1930), 6:136.

18. Bruce Kinney, *Mormonism: The Islam of America* (New York: Revell, 1912).

19. Charles Heber Clark [Max Adeler, pseud.] *The Tragedy of Thompson Dunbar: A Tale of Salt Lake City* (Philadelphia: Stoddart, 1879), 10.

20. Dane Coolidge, *The Fighting Danites* (New York: Dutton, 1934), 37–38.

21. Jack London, *Star Rover* (1914; reprint, New York: Arcadia House, 1950), 135.

22. Arthur Conan Doyle, *A Study in Scarlet* (London: Ward Lock, 1887; New York: Burt, n.d.), 129; James Oliver Curwood, *The Courage of Captain Plum* (Indianapolis: Bobbs-Merrill, 1908), 261. In his allusion to the king, Curwood has in mind James Strang, who broke with the main body of Mormons and founded his own religious mini-empire on Beaver Island, Michigan.

23. Sydney Bell, *Wives of the Prophet* (New York: Macaulay, 1935), iv; Robert Richards [pseud.], *The California Crusoe, or The Lost Treasure Found; a Tale of Mormonism* (London: Parker, 1854).

24. *Painesville Telegraph,* 31 January 1834, 3. In Milton V. Backman Jr., *The Heavens Resound: A History of the Latter-day Saints in Ohio, 1830–1838* (Salt Lake City: Desert, 1983), 340.

25. *Messenger and Advocate* 3 (January 1837): 443. See also Smith, *History of the Church,* 2:468–69.

26. Backman, *Heavens Resound,* 320.

27. The nine formal charges against Cowdery and his letter of response are in Roberts, *Comprehensive History*, 1:431–34.

28. Cowdery's reply to the nine charges was largely confined to the one issue of the limits of ecclesiastical authority. As a result, he was excommunicated for those charges to which he had not deigned to respond, including legal harassment of church leaders and dishonesty. See ibid., 1:432.

29. Gustive O. Larson, "Federal Government Efforts to 'Americanize' Utah Before Admission to Statehood," *BYU Studies* 10, no. 2 (winter 1969–70): 218.

30. D. Michael Quinn, "The Council of Fifty and Its Members, 1844 to 1945," *BYU Studies* 20, no. 2 (winter 1979–80): 163.

31. Benjamin Franklin Johnson to George S. Gibbs, Salt Lake City, 1903. In E. Dale Lebaron, "Benjamin Franklin Johnson in Nauvoo: Friend, Confidant, and Defender of the Prophet," *BYU Studies* 32, nos. 1–2 (winter–spring 1992): 184.

32. Willers, "First Months," 331.

33. Edward Strutt Abdy, *Journal of a residence and tour in the United States of North America, from April 1833 to October, 1834*, 3 vols. (London: Murray, 1835), 3:54.

34. Total membership numbers from *Deseret News 2001–2002 Church Almanac* (Salt Lake City: Deseret, 2000), 582; other figures from Richard H. Jackson, "First Gathering to Zion," in S. Kent Brown, Donald Q. Cannon, and Richard H. Jackson, eds., *Historical Atlas of Mormonism* (New York: Simon and Schuster, 1994), 35.

35. Warren Foote, *Autobiography of Warren Foote*, 3 vols. (privately printed typescript n.p., n.d.), 1:96.

36. The speech is recorded in *History of Caldwell and Livingston Counties, Missouri* (St. Louis: St. Louis National Historical Company, 1886); cited in Smith, *History*, 3:203–4.

37. J. H. Beadle, "The Mormon Theocracy," *Scribner's Monthly* 14, no. 3 (July 1877): 392. Seven years later, when Beadle was a much harsher critic of Mormonism, he repeated the diagnosis. In an 1877 volume on "the Mysteries and Crimes of Mormonism," he stated that "the great cause of popular hostility, which finally led to the worst result, was the Mormon system of voting solidly, at the dictation of a few men." See his *Life in Utah* (Philadelphia: National Publishing, 1870), 67.

38. Marvin Hill, *Quest for Refuge: The Mormon Flight from American Pluralism* (Salt Lake City: Signature, 1989), 228.

39. Alma R. Blair, "Conflict in Missouri," in S. Kent Brown, Donald Q. Cannon, and Richard H. Jackson, eds., *Historical Atlas of Mormonism* (New York: Simon and Schuster, 1994), 46. In DeWitt, the 40 to 50 Missourians were rapidly overwhelmed by 150 to 200 Saints.

40. Smith, *History*, 6:243.

41. Ibid., 6:605–6.

42. Andrew Jenson, *Church Chronology: A Record of Important Events Pertaining to the History of The Church of Jesus Christ of Latter-day Saints* (Salt Lake City: Deseret, 1914), 17 March 1892 entry.

43. Ray Allen Billington, "Frontier Democracy: Social Aspects," in *The Turner Thesis: Concerning the Role of the Frontier in American History*, ed. George Rogers Taylor, 3rd ed. (Lexington, Mass.: D. C. Heath, 1972), 178.

44. Ibid.

45. Smith, *History*, 1:396.

46. "Oration delivered by Mr. S. Rigdon, 4th Day of July, 1838, at Far West, Caldwell County, Missouri" (Far West: Elders' Journal Press, 1838). Reprinted in *BYU Studies* 14 (summer 1974): 523.

47. Smith, *History*, 1:397.

48. Abdy, *Journal*, 3:41.

49. *Evening and Morning Star* 2, no. 14 (July 1833): 109.

50. *Evening and Morning Star* "extra" (18 July 1833); Smith, *History* 1:379. Blacks were among the audience of Smith's preaching as early as 1831, and at least two converts are known from those first years in Ohio—Elijah Abel and "Black Pete." Donna Hill, *Joseph Smith: The First Mormon* (Salt Lake City: Signature, 1999), 379.

51. R. C. Evans, interview in the Toronto, Canada *Daily Star*, 28 January 1905; cited in Joseph F. Smith and Richard C. Evans, *Blood Atonement and the Origin of Plural Marriage: A Discussion* (Salt Lake City: Deseret, 1905), 9.

52. Smith, *History*, 2:357.

53. Abdy, *Journal*, 3:59.

54. The entire report of the citizens' committee is in Smith, *History*, 2:448–52.

55. Lawrence G. Coates, "A History of Indian Education by the Mormons, 1830–1900" (Ed.D. diss., Ball State, 1969), 55–56.

56. Foote, *Autobiography*, 96.

57. Speech delivered on 12 June 1857 in Springfield, Illinois State House. Smith, *Church History*, 4:148.

58. The historian of religious bigotry, Gustavus Myers, for example, felt that "animus was directed at Mormons partly because their ideas and ways differed so greatly from the customary, and in part because of their phenomenally industrious co-operative system which, while essentially individualistic, was planned harmoniously for the common benefit." Gustavus Myers, *History of Bigotry in the United States* (New York: Random House, 1943), 173.

59. Smith, *History*, 2:450.

60. James Silk Buckingham, *The Eastern and Western States of America* (London: Fisher, Sons, 1842), 194.

61. R. Carlyle Buley, *The Old Northwest: Pioneer Period 1815–1840*, 2 vols. (Indianapolis: Indiana Historical Society, 1950), 1:394.

62. Smith, *History of the Church*, 1:189.

63. William Walker, journal, 7 April 1851. Cited in Herman C. Smith, "Missouri Troubles," *Journal of History* 4 (October 1909): 440–41.

64. Susan Evans McCloud, *Brigham Young: An Inspiring Personal Biography* (American Fork, Utah: Covenant Communications, 1996), 105.

65. Givens, *In Old Nauvoo*, 132.

66. Smith, *History of the Church*, 5:3.

67. *New York Herald*, 17 June 1842.

68. Robert Bruce Flanders, *Nauvoo: Kingdom on the Mississippi* (Urbana: University of Illinois Press, 1965), 113.

69. William J. Gilmore, *Reading Becomes a Necessity of Life: Material and Cultural Life in Rural New England, 1780–1835* (Knoxville: University of Tennessee Press, 1989), 19.

70. For a thorough treatment of anti-Mormonism in fiction, see Terryl L. Givens, "They Ain't Whites . . . They're Mormons: Fictive Responses to the Anxiety of Seduction," in *The Viper on the Hearth: Mormons, Myths, and the Construction of Heresy* (New York: Oxford University Press, 1997).

71. Roberts, *Comprehensive History*, 4:425.

72. Klaus J. Hansen, *Quest for Empire: The Political Kingdom of God and the Council of Fifty in Mormon History* (Lincoln: University of Nebraska Press, 1974), frontispiece.

73. Beadle, "Mormon," 392.

74. Harold Bloom, *The American Religion: The Emergence of the Post-Christian Nation* (New York: Simon and Schuster, 1992), 97.

75. John Le Carré, *The Russia House* (New York: Bantam, 1990), 211.

76. "Payne Survey Angers Landrith," *Lynchburg News and Daily Advance,* 28 September 1994.

Chapter 3

Christians with a Difference:
Orthodoxy and Heresy
in LDS Thought

> The fundamental principles of our religion are the testimony of
> the Apostles and Prophets, concerning Jesus Christ, that He
> died, was buried, and rose again the third day, and ascended into
> heaven and all other things which pertain to our religion are
> only appendages to it.
> —Joseph Smith, *Elders Journal*

> O God, tell me I beg, . . . whether my infancy followed upon
> some earlier stage of my life that had passed away before it. . . .
> And is God bounded by a bodily shape and has he hair and
> nails? And are those [patriarchs] to be esteemed righteous who
> had many wives at the same time?
> —St. Augustine, *Confessions*

> What the Mormons do, seems to be excellent; what they say is
> mostly nonsense.
> —Charles Dickens, *Household Words*

Mormons espouse belief in and salvation through Jesus Christ, the
divine Son of God. In that sense, they are unambiguously Christian.
However, they do not descend, as Catholics and Protestants do, from a faith
tradition defined principally in terms of allegiance to creedal statements
going back to Nicaea and Chalcedon (formative church councils held in the
fourth and fifth centuries). Mormons, for example, reject the conventional
Trinity. Their unorthodox conception of deity is a central factor in the
refusal of some Christians to consider Mormons kindred believers. In addi-

tion, Mormons have peculiar beliefs about the scriptural canon, the origin of man, and his eventual destiny—all at variance with contemporary mainstream Christians, though not inconsistent, they believe, with the Bible or what they refer to as "the primitive Church" (Christianity in the first hundred years or so, before the "apostasy" or corruption of Christ's organization and teachings). On the other hand, Mormons are unarguably Christian if measured by their embrace of New Testament ethics and their unqualified acceptance of Jesus as the divine son of God, the Savior and Redeemer of the world. Even here, their conception of Christ's role in human redemption has generally been imperfectly understood and represented by outsiders.

In examining LDS doctrines, a few caveats are necessary. Mormonism has no systematic theology as such. In fact, there is in some Mormon thought a hostility to the very notion of such an enterprise. Mormon scholar and apologist Hugh Nibley explains the case as a matter of what he calls a choice between "Sophic" and "Mantic" modes of apprehending and organizing knowledge. The first, he writes, is the path of conventional Christianity. This Sophic approach represents the application of reason and intellect to religious questions, or the turn to theology. This turn, continues Nibley, was originally an effort "'to overcome the objections of reason to revelation'—that is St. Augustine's famous reconciliation of Classical and Christian learning. But how can you call it reconciliation when it is always the church that gives way? It is always reason that has to be satisfied and revelation that must be manipulated in order to give that satisfaction; this is no compromise but complete surrender, by which Theology 'becomes the train-bearer of the Old Queen Philosophy.'"[1]

On the other hand, the Mantic, according to Nibley, believes the grand scheme of things "is incomprehensible to people of as little knowledge and experience as ours, and insists for that reason that if we are to know anything at all about it, our knowledge must come from a higher source, by revelation. . . . Whenever revelation is resumed, the holy order of things revives, while that holy order cannot survive after revelation has ceased, no matter how hard men try to preserve and imitate its institutions. The sacral order is thus completely dependent on revelation."[2]

Continuing Revelation and the Development of Theology

To put it more simply, Mormonism is founded on the principle of modern, continuing revelation from God. By revelation, Mormons mean something fairly different from what many theologians intend by the term. Catholic scholar Avery Dulles, in his classic study of revelation, indicates that most Christians understand the term to refer to either the Bible "viewed as a collection of inspired and inerrant teachings" or the process by which "God reveals himself . . . in his great deeds."[3] Alternately, revelation can mean for some theologians an inner experience of the divine. In most all cases, the common feature of revelation from a theological point of view is the lack of particular, communicated content. As religious scholar William Abraham summarizes, "revelation in the fully personal sense characteristic of personal agents has been abandoned."[4]

Mormonism, on the other hand, embraces the position of sociologist Rodney Stark, who has insisted that by definition, "a revelation is not an insight or an inspiration. A revelation is a communication. . . . A revelation presupposes a divine being capable of wishes and intentions."[5] Accordingly, Mormonism is rooted both historically and theologically in a concept of revelation that is striking in its literalness. When Joseph Smith returned from his first epiphany in the Sacred Grove, his summative comment was not a statement about the visitation he experienced, the nature of the God he beheld, or the apostate condition of Christianity that God described. It was, rather, a simple affirmation of the apostle James' promise that when an individual asks God a question in childlike faith and guilelessness, God may choose to answer with articulate, discernible, unmistakably human words: "I asked the Personages who stood above me in the light, which of all the sects was right . . . and which I should join. I was answered that I must join none of them."[6]

The Book of Mormon that Joseph Smith would translate a few years later is suffused with this same principle, carrying it much further even than its Old Testament incarnation. In Genesis, it is true, God often engages in literal dialogue with human beings, querying Adam in the garden or Cain outside it, bargaining with Abraham over the fate of Sodom, or in Exodus, expounding the Decalogue to Moses. But in these and kindred biblical examples, as scholars have noted, revelation is generally the province of patriarchs and Israel's leaders. "Prophecy was preeminently the privilege of the prophets," writes one authority.[7] Mormonism resurrects this conception of literal communication with deity, making it the basis for a modern church's organization and teaching. As pertaining to the latter, Joseph recorded in 1830 the Lord's directive that

> no one shall be appointed to receive commandments and revelations in this church excepting my servant Joseph Smith, Jun., for he receiveth

them even as Moses. And thou shalt be obedient unto the things which I shall give unto him . . . to declare faithfully the commandments and the revelations, with power and authority unto the church. . . . For I have given him the keys of the mysteries, and the revelations which are sealed, until I shall appoint unto them another in his stead. (DC 28:2–7)

Consistent with the principle of prophetic succession, Mormons continue to believe that the right to declare God's will—as commandment, policy, doctrine, or theology—is vested in the current president of the church, but extend revelation to lay individuals. So believing as they do that God makes his will known both personally to seeking individuals, and institutionally and collectively to the prophet of the church, Mormons are resistant to the notion that scholars or theologians are necessary to determine church doctrines. Theology, simply stated from the Mormon perspective, is what happens when revelation is absent. As such, theology is an activity largely associated, in the Mormon historical consciousness, with a foundering Christian tradition. John Taylor, Brigham Young's successor, expressed this view with typical nineteenth-century Mormon bluntness: "We had had Methodism, Presbyterianism, Dunkerism, Shakerism, Catholicism, Quakerism, and every other ism that you could think of; but there was none that had the ancient Gospel,—no, not one. I was, however, well acquainted with theology. I consider that if ever I lost any time in my life, it was while studying the Christian theology. Sectarian theology is the greatest tomfoolery in the world."[8]

Such rhetorical excess does not characterize mainstream Mormon attitudes today, but it is certainly true that Taylor, like Young, was more concerned with "building the kingdom" than mastering or erecting theological systems. Taylor's successor, Wilfred Woodruff, similarly embodied something closer to Brigham Young's pragmatism than Joseph Smith's doctrinal insatiability:

How much longer I shall talk to this people I do not know; but I want to say this to all Israel: Cease troubling yourselves about who God is; who Adam is, who Christ is, who Jehovah is. For heaven's sake, let these things alone. Why trouble yourselves about these things? . . . God is God. Christ is Christ. The Holy Ghost is the Holy Ghost. That should be enough for you and me to know. If we want to know any more, wait till we get where God is in person. I say this because we are troubled every little while with inquiries from elders anxious to know who God is, who Christ is, and who Adam is. I say to the elders of Israel, stop this. Humble yourselves before the Lord; seek for light, for truth, and for a knowledge of the common things of the kingdom of God.[9]

Resisting as it does an officially sanctioned theology, then, Mormonism has produced few texts by way of official, systematic doctrinal exposition. The four "standard works" of the church are indisputable guides to Mormon belief, but as we have seen, the Bible used is not a distinctive Mormon version (it is the King James), and the Book of Mormon has only recently become a prominent source of church teaching. Many principles pertaining to church governance, sacraments, and doctrines are expounded in the *Doctrine and Covenants*, and the *Pearl of Great Price* makes some important contributions on the subject of the purpose of life, premortal existence, and the spirit world. From time to time, the First Presidency issues proclamations, declarations, and manifestoes that have the force and authority of scripture, but such "official" doctrinal declarations and proclamations have been few. A public disavowal of polygamy was issued in 1890; a statement on "The Origin of Man" (1909) insisted that Moses' account that "God created man in his own image" comprised "the truth concerning the origin of the human family"; a 1925 statement on "The Mormon View of Evolution" excerpted portions of the prior document, again affirming that man is "the direct and lineal offspring of Deity"; a 1916 "Doctrinal Exposition" on "The Father and the Son" explained four senses in which Jesus Christ, though separate and distinct from the Father, is appropriately referred to by that title on certain scriptural occasions; the 1978 proclamation extended the priesthood to "all worthy males"; and most recently, the 1995 "Proclamation on the Family" confirmed LDS teachings and values regarding marriage and family.

For two generations, many Latter-day Saints have relied for matters of doctrinal clarification upon an encyclopedic tome called *Mormon Doctrine* (first printing 1958) as the definitive statement on the subject, because of its authoritative title, tone, and authorship by a prominent apostle, Bruce R. McConkie. But it never received official sanction, and it expresses what an increasing number of Mormons see as an overly rigid fundamentalism. Less encyclopedic in scope (even such key theological concepts as "grace" and "sanctification" are not represented in its index), but bearing the imprint of the church itself, is James Talmage's *Articles of Faith*, an 1890 examination of thirteen core tenets first articulated by Joseph Smith. The *Encyclopedia of Mormonism* lacks official church sanction, but is a reliable guide to a broad array of church beliefs and teachings.

The general lack of official theologizing and reticence to publish or endorse doctrinal positions seems to suggest a church devoid of an extensive or detailed belief system. Judged by the standard of formal theologizing, Mormonism may appear undeveloped, a relative newcomer lacking an august tradition of *Summa Theologica*s, catechisms, creeds, and treatises. But this is to miss the distinctive nature of Mormonism as, in Harold Bloom's words, an instance of audacious religion-making in the broadest sense.[10] The sheer volume of Joseph's visionary pronouncements and the magnitude of the overall conception he pieced together—a history of the human soul that recedes into an infinite human past and stretches forward into deification and world-making, a multidispensational gospel that extends from Adam to the present day, and a conglomeration of gospel keys and ministries participated in by prophetic figures from Abraham and Moses to John the Baptist and Peter, James, and John, all dispensations and keys and practices converging in one great Dispensation of the Fullness of Times—this brash assertion of a final and definitive script that encompasses all religious precedents as mere preparation for the final act called the Restoration is what Mormonism presumes to offer. In this sense, Mormonism is better understood as enacting its central doctrines rather than systematically articulating them. Prophets are called, visions are received, new scripture is produced, the elect are gathered, temples are built, angels visit the earth, priesthood authority is bestowed by resurrected beings, and prophetic succession follows upon martyrdom and exile. That is the sense in which Mormonism is history rather than a collection of beliefs. Which is not to say that Mormonism has not had its share of earnest apologists and expounders. The Pratt brothers, Orson and Parley P., added shape and detail to Joseph Smith's teachings. In a later generation, B. H. Roberts and John A. Widtsoe, as well as the above-mentioned James Talmage provided thoughtful and informed explorations of Mormon theology.

As for LDS leaders themselves, although all prophets following Joseph Smith inherited his mantle and full title, none would ever pursue revelatory production with the same vigor and bravado. Although neither Joseph nor any other LDS leader ever declared the "restoration" of the gospel a fait accompli, in the Mormon mind Joseph's death signaled the end of a distinct phase of this "last dispensation." Joseph was the innovator. Brigham Young was the organizer and colonizer. Subsequent prophets have been more like Brigham than like Joseph, emphasizing the pragmatic concerns of gathering, consolidation, and expansion, rather than doctrinal innovation or elaboration. Having successfully negotiated the process of Americanization, Mormonism is increasingly seen as a respectable, mainstream institution, even a plausible contender, in some circles, for the designation of "the American religion."[11]

What this means is that Mormonism is now characterized by a tension between two imperatives: on the one hand, Mormonism is consumed by a sense of divine commission to take the gospel—the "restored" gospel—to all the world. The good news, for Mormons as for Christians generally, is that Christ died for the sins of the world. What makes their version of the news a little different is their insistence that Joseph Smith is the first in a contemporary line of prophets authorized to preach that gospel in its purest and fullest form, and that he restored the essential authority to administer the saving ordinances of that gospel. Joseph Smith and his story of heavenly manifestations, angels, and gold plates is therefore inseparable from the gospel that he restored and that Mormon missionaries teach. And it is a gospel that encompasses teachings, practices, and dimensions unfamiliar to mainstream Christians (like baptism for the dead, premortal existence, and eternal families), though, Mormons are adamant, central to ancient dispensations of Christianity.

On the other hand, Mormonism continues to strive for the kind of legitimacy and reputation that will provide those missionaries with the broadest access to an audience of receptive listeners. Consequently, Mormonism increasingly emphasizes its core Christian doctrines and the fruits of its religion more than its theological innovations. Family values and happy homes are more celebrated than the plurality of gods (see below). The church welfare program is more touted than a mother in Heaven (also see below), and healthy lifestyles and Mormon longevity are more advertised than the original location of the Garden of Eden (Missouri, according to a Smith revelation). This practice has been construed by some as a misleading sales pitch, one that entices converts with its more attractive features while concealing its more unorthodox and unusual teachings.

In actual fact, Mormonism, like the Christianity of the New Testament, *is* a religion more interested in ethical behavior than correct belief. (Members may be excommunicated for immoral acts, for instance, but not for privately held heresies.) Whether gathering the Saints in Ohio, making the Utah desert "blossom as a rose," or building Zion worldwide, Mormon leaders have perennially emphasized the practical over the abstract. At the same time, many of the most heterodox teachings imputed to Mormonism are *not* official church dogma, appearing in their standard works or in teaching manuals or in other LDS publications. Several of Joseph

Smith's revelations and original teachings—like occasional teachings of his successors—were never presented to the body of the church for acceptance and canonization, because of either their speculative nature, inessential role in personal salvation, or dubious accuracy. Only doctrines expounded in LDS scriptures or promulgated through official church manuals, publications, or official pronouncements of the prophet or First Presidency, in addition to teachings presented in the LDS temples, are binding on LDS members. Even within that category, however, Mormon doctrine can at times pose a vibrant challenge to conventional theological concepts, and some unofficial pronouncements, like the "King Follett" discourse Smith delivered shortly before his death, have been so incorporated into Mormon discussions about God and salvation as to achieve virtual canonical status.

None of this is meant to suggest that Mormon leaders do not have a powerful interest in delineating and maintaining religious orthodoxy of belief. Affirmation of cardinal concepts—Christ as savior, Joseph's status as a prophet, the current church president's authority as God's mouthpiece—is a requirement for admittance to the temple, the official litmus test of true Mormon faithfulness. And even sympathy with practitioners or expounders of teachings hostile to Mormon tenets (like modern-day polygamists), is grounds for refusing a temple pass (called a recommend). And since 1963, a Priesthood Correlation Program has served to centralize and coordinate all church organizational structures, planning, programs, and teaching curricula and manuals. This has been an extremely efficient factor in maintaining strict control over how the Latter-day Saint version of the gospel is taught and administered.

Lacking a professional clergy, the onus for knowing and understanding LDS doctrines is on individual rank-and-file members. Leaders constantly enjoin individuals to be students of the scriptures, and daily study of the canon is common with many members, especially the numerous former missionaries for whom scripture study was long part of the daily routine.

By and large, however, church leaders show little inclination to foster or engage in theologizing about the more abstruse points of Mormon doctrine. When President Gordon B. Hinckley was asked by a *Time* magazine interviewer about Joseph Smith's teaching that God the Father was once a man, he replied that the church doesn't really teach, emphasize, or discuss that doctrine.[12] His answer was taken by some listeners to be either evasive or disingenuous. It may be more accurate to interpret his response as reflecting a very real historical trend (since Smith, at least) away from the speculative and theoretical and toward the practical. For it is the Latter-day Saint practical religion of clean living, hard work, and family-centeredness, with which Mormons are increasingly—and more positively—associated.

Beyond Reformation: "They Shall Know That There is a Prophet in Israel"

"I speak boldly and faithfully and with authority," said Joseph Smith. "How is it with the kingdom of God? Where did the kingdom of God begin? Where there is no kingdom of God there is no salvation. What constitutes the kingdom of God? Where there is a prophet, a priest, or a righteous man unto whom God gives his oracles, there is the kingdom of God; and where the oracles of God are not, there the kingdom of God is not."[13] In the nineteenth-century lexicon, oracles could refer both to divine messages and to the ancient, sacred artifacts known as the Urim and Thummim, emblem of privileged priestly status and revelatory power.[14] The first meaning was presumably primary with Joseph Smith, according to a revelation proclaimed on the day of the church's establishment. "Thou shalt be called a seer, a translator, a prophet," it declared, uniquely authorized among men "to receive commandments and revelations," and alone possessing "the keys of the mysteries and the revelations which are sealed" (DC 21:1; 28:2, 7). But Smith's literal possession of the Nephite interpreters, or Urim and Thummim as he came to call them, aptly doubled the sense in which the oracles of God were committed to him.

Clearly, this literal conception of prophetic revelation and vocation means that Mormonism is not a smorgasbord religion. From its inception, the Church of Jesus Christ of Latter-day Saints has been based on an authoritarian model for which even the prophetic figures of the Old Testament are inadequate patterns or precedents—save perhaps Moses or Abraham. As we have seen, Mormonism entails a vision of the gospel rooted in a particular variety of dispensationalism. In this view, God reveals anew to mankind in various ages the plan of salvation through his messengers the prophets, who have the priesthood authority necessary to officiate in saving ordinances and to dispense the fullness of gospel truth. Different prophets are associated with particular commissions or keys. In the Mormon version, Moses, for instance, holds the keys of the gathering of Israel. Elijah, as suggested by Malachi's words, holds the keys of sealing families within and across generations (Mal. 4:5–6). In what Latter-day

Saints call the Dispensation of the Meridian of Time, Christ came and taught the gospel once again, as he had with Adam and Enoch and Moses and others, establishing his church for the next to the last time. Like the Catholics and some Protestants, Latter-day Saints believe that this church was a formal entity, organized with various offices and callings, authorized to perform necessary ordinances, given the keys to preach the gospel, and administered by a quorum of twelve apostles and presided over by Peter. Catholics take Christ's utterance to Peter in Mathew 16:18 ("thou are Peter, and upon this rock I will build my church") as effective institution (or foreshadowing) of an authoritative line that would become the papacy. Latter-day Saints believe the key to that passage is in the preceding verse: "flesh and blood hath not revealed it [that Jesus is the Christ] unto thee, but my Father which is in heaven." And upon that rock, that is, the rock of both institutional and personal revelation, Mormons believe Christ designed to institute his church. And unlike Catholics but like many Protestants, Latter-day Saints believe that the demise of that church was both prophetically described and historically accomplished.

This demise, which Mormons call "the Great Apostasy," is of course an implicit feature of Protestant belief. Where Mormonism's conception of this apostasy takes a unique form is in the immediacy, extensiveness, and irreparability of the decay that Mormonism alleges. By its very definition, writes Mormon scholar Hugh Nibley, the very idea of Christian history "requires unquestioning acceptance of the basic proposition that the church did survive." But in the Mormon view, the lights went out almost as soon as they were lit. Nibley insists that this came as no surprise, since two "convictions of the early church [were] that the end was near and that it was to be disastrous. . . . No one suggests that only a distant and partial disruption was expected."[15]

What, exactly, was lost? A church organization headed by a prophet and twelve apostles, and the priesthood itself—or authority to preside over the church, teach the gospel, and administer the ordinances of salvation—to start with. And the primitive gospel and its teachings. What, do Mormons believe, was introduced in place of the gospel's "plain and precious truths" (1 Nephi 13)? A triune God, creation ex nihilo, original sin, infant baptism, a closed canon, the end of prophets and prophecy, suppression of vernacular scriptures, and a professional clergy all followed in turn. The Reformation, in spite of the movement's well-intentioned leaders, was in the Latter-day Saint view too little too late to restore lost truths and authority. But it was precisely the step necessary to prepare the seedbed of a fuller restoration. As LDS President Joseph F. Smith wrote in 1907, "Calvin, Luther, Melanchthon, and all the reformers, were inspired in thoughts, words, and actions, to accomplish what they did for the amelioration, liberty, and advancement of the human race. They paved the way for the more perfect gospel of truth to come. Their inspiration, as with that of the ancients, came from the Father, his Son Jesus Christ, and the Holy Ghost, the one true living God."[16]

But minor course corrections, believe Mormons, could not reestablish the authority to act in God's name, open the conduits of heavenly communication, and thus provide a vehicle for restoring the plenitude of gospel truth. It was not a reforming Joel that was needed, but an Abraham, reestablishing the terms of a covenant relationship with God and founding an utterly new era in human history. No zealous Jeremiah decrying the sins of the contemporary age would suffice, but a veritable Moses was required, one who communed with God, dictated the terms of a renewed covenant, and both figuratively and literally would gather his people out of bondage and reestablish them as a peculiar people guided by living oracles of God.

Joseph Smith and his followers claim he was a prophet in *that* mold. And that he had the authority, the inspiration, and the visionary power to effect a restoration in which two ingredients were paramount: (1) the fullness of gospel truth, including not only the ethical teachings of Christ, but a corpus of knowledge that redefines the origins and potential of the human soul (literal children of deity with an interminable premortal existence and a destiny as gods), and (2) the priesthood keys necessary not just to establish the Church of Jesus Christ, to baptize and preach the gospel, but to perform sealing ordinances that bind wedded couples and their posterity together for eternity and confer upon them a literal version of the blessings promised Abraham, thereby endowing them with the full blessings of salvation.

Bodies, Parts, and Passions: Mormon Doctrine of Deity

God Himself who sits enthroned in yonder heavens is a Man like unto one of yourselves—that is the great secret! If the veil were rent today and the great God that holds this world in its sphere and the planets in their orbit and who upholds all things by His power—if you were to see Him today, you would see Him in all

the person, image, fashion, and very form of a man, like yourselves. . . . The first principle of truth and of the Gospel is to
know for a certainty the character of God, and that we may converse with Him the same as one man with another, and that He
once was a man like one of us and that God Himself, the Father
of us all, once dwelled on an earth the same as Jesus Christ himself did in the flesh and like us.
—Joseph Smith[17]

It would be hard to say which LDS belief is most distinctive when
measured against orthodox Christian theology—but the Mormon conception of God is certainly a contender. Perhaps surprisingly, in light of
what Joseph Smith taught in his discourse on the occasion of King Follett's
death, Mormons pray to and worship God in ways that are virtually indistinguishable from the manner in which many other Christians do. Latter-
day Saints believe that God is the Eternal Father, the Supreme Being, the
deity they reverence and worship. As to his prior incarnation or habitation, Joseph Smith said little, and the LDS scriptures are silent. As to how
such a conception of an evolved God can be reconciled with belief in his
omnipotence, omniscience, and eternal nature, the sources are likewise
silent; the way in which God was once "as man now is" has received no
elaboration through official church channels.

In a further challenge to orthodoxy, Joseph Smith declared by revelation in 1843 that "the Father has a body of flesh and bones as tangible as
man's; the Son also; but the Holy Ghost has not a body of flesh and bones,
but is a personage of Spirit. Were it not so, the Holy Ghost could not dwell
in us" (DC 130:22). Clearly, this is well outside the traditional doctrine of
the Trinity. Since the Council of Nicaea (A.D. 325), it has been a central
tenet of Christian belief that God and Christ, along with the Holy Spirit,
are all "of one substance." In fact, many theologians would agree that the
doctrine of the Trinity is "*the* central dogma of Christian theology, that the
one God exists in three Persons and one substance."[18] Reaffirmed recur-
rently in early Christian councils, this doctrine is still general throughout
Catholic and Protestant branches of the church.

Mormon belief in an anthropomorphic god is not a mere peculiarity of
the faith, nor is it, from an LDS perspective, a doctrinal innovation. It is
integrally bound up with a Mormon cosmology that denies conventional
dualism (immaterial spirit versus physical matter), with a view of revelation

that takes divine speaking literally, and with a belief in human perfectibility that gives new meanings to eternal life. And Mormons believe that their doctrine of deity is consistent with both biblical texts and historical Christianity. It is a virtual commonplace among scholars of early Christianity that Trinitarian conceptions of deity do not receive full articulation or command Christian assent until the fourth century, with the advent of the famous church councils.[19]

What many theologians would view as a progressive movement away from the naive and figurative representations of an Old Testament deity, with bodily form and usable vocal chords, Mormons see as an apostate rejection of simple, unchangeable truths. Though clearly outside the mainstream, some scholars find Mormon conceptions of deity not entirely unsupported by precedent or sound reason. Edmond LaB. Cherbonnier has written at length in the *Harvard Theological Review* on "The Logic of Biblical Anthropomorphism."[20] More recently, he has written that "neither Jews, nor Mormons, nor other Christians need be embarrassed by the idea that God is a Person. They need not apologize for literal interpretation, for that does most justice to what the Bible authors meant."[21] And Walter Eichrodt writes that "an unprejudiced evaluation of the Old Testament" leads to the clear recognition that "the foundation of Old Testament faith . . . is [God's] personhood."[22] Though such secular pronouncements cannot establish the theological legitimacy of Mormon conceptions of deity, they suggest why Mormons can plausibly claim, albeit never prove, that Joseph was restoring, rather than inventing, gospel doctrines.

It is in light of such an anthropomorphic God that the Mormon concept of revelation, explained above, is best understood. To attribute literal speech acts to God is to defy modern Christianity's persistent hostility to the anthropomorphism that speech implies. That is why, in the Western religious tradition, genuine dialogic exchange between God and human beings generally becomes metaphorized into the more nebulous concepts of "revelation" we have seen. As William Abraham reasons, "when the theist speaks of divine revelation, the activity of human revealing serves as the model for conceiving that revelation." But here "we sense immediately a certain awkwardness."[23] This awkwardness, of course, is the possibility that conceptions of God will be contaminated by human analogies.

As Nicholas Wolterstorff argues:

> The traditional assumption that divine speech is reducible to divine revelation was not just fortuitous error; an interesting reason was sometimes

offered. Since God has no vocal cords with which to utter words, and no hands with which to write them down, God cannot literally speak, cannot literally be a participant in a linguistic communication. Accordingly, attributions of speech to God, if not judged bizarrely false, must be taken as metaphorical.[24]

Sandra M. Schneider agrees that outside of an anthropomorphic model, divine discourse cannot be taken literally for the obvious reason that language "is a human phenomenon rooted in our corporeality as well as in our discursive mode of intellection and as such cannot be literally predicated of pure spirit."[25]

It should be clear from the above that if God the Father is a physically embodied person, then Christ is not a dimension of God, God's earthly embodiment, or the godhead manifest as a particular function or mode. Jesus Christ is a separate and distinct member of the godhead. Mormons believe, as the book of John states, that Christ was God (the Son) from before the foundations of the world. In the Book of Mormon, the prophet known as the brother of Jared sees a divine personage, who identifies himself as Jesus Christ in his premortal form, and explains his appearance as a manifestation of "the body of my spirit" (Ether 2:16). In his premortal state, Mormons believe, Christ was known to the ancients as Jehovah. (At just what point Joseph came to make this identification is not clear.) Latter-day Saints believe that Christ was born into the world as the literal son of God and the son of Mary, inheriting the power of immortality from his father and the seeds of mortality from his mother. As James Talmage wrote in a work deemed semi-scriptural by Latter-day Saints, "in [Christ's] nature would be combined the powers of Godhood with the capacity and possibilities of mortality; and this through the ordinary operation of the fundamental law of heredity. . . . The Child Jesus was to inherit the physical, mental, and spiritual traits, tendencies, and powers that characterized His parents—one immortal and glorified—God, the other human—woman."[26]

A Three-Act Play: Premortality, Probation, and Plural Worlds

In 1833, Joseph Smith revealed the first hints of a doctrine that has since become one of the distinctive hallmarks of LDS theology. "I was in the beginning with the Father, and am the Firstborn," Joseph Smith records

Jesus as saying. And then Christ adds the portentous words: "Ye were also in the beginning with the Father" (DC 93:21, 23). This primordial beginning turns out to be in fact an infinite past: "Man was also in the beginning with God. Intelligence, or the light of truth, was not created or made, neither indeed can be" (DC 93:29). The connection between this primordial "intelligence" and the human spirit has not been officially explicated. Some Mormon writers have held that God fashioned intelligence, or this self-existent material, into spirits; others that the expression is itself another term for human spirits. In any case, this assertion that man existed in the beginning with God would gradually be elaborated into a doctrine of preexistence or, more properly, premortal existence. The fullest doctrinal exposition would come two years later, in 1835, with Joseph's production of the Book of Abraham. There a vision of the premortal realms is presented in which the premortal Christ and foreordained prophets, heavenly councils, and Satan's rebellion all begin to assume their places in an increasingly comprehensive panorama.

"Now the Lord had shown unto me, Abraham," the account begins,

> the intelligences that were organized before the world was; and among all these there were many of the noble and great ones; . . . And there stood one among them that was like unto God, and he said unto those that were with him: We will go down . . . and make an earth whereon these may dwell; And we will prove them herewith, to see if they will do all things whatsoever the Lord their God shall command them; And they who keep their first estate shall be added upon . . . and they who keep their second estate shall have glory added upon their heads for ever and ever. And the Lord said: Whom shall I send? And one answered like unto the Son of Man: Here am I, send me. And another answered and said: Here am I, send me. And the Lord said: I will send the first. And the second was angry, and kept not his first estate; and, at that day, many followed after him.[27]

Mormons refer to this setting as the Council in Heaven (a common theme in ancient Middle Eastern literature[28]). It was on this occasion, they believe, that mortal probation and bodily incarnation were proposed as necessary stages leading to spiritual progression toward godliness. (It was also in this setting, Smith taught, that servants of God received their assignments: "I suppose that I was ordained to this very office in that Grand Council."[29])

In exuberant response to the presentation of these plans, Latter-day Saints hold, "the morning stars sang together and all the sons of God shouted for joy," as recorded in the Old Testament book of Job (38:7). Lucifer, Son of the Morning, contended for the role of savior, and conspired "to destroy the agency of man" on which the plan of upward progression depended (Moses 4:3). As a result, for attempting to usurp Christ's role and for opposing free will, he was cast out, "and his tail drew the third part of the stars of heaven" (Rev. 12:4). One of every three premortal spirits, according to an LDS reading of John's revelation, rebelled with Lucifer and lost the opportunity for mortal life, growth, and physical incarnation.

But Christ and mankind, as it turns out, are not unique in regard to their eternal existence. For "the elements are eternal," Smith's 1833 revelation continued, in an early version of the Law of Conservation of matter. Smith would later elaborate:

> Doesn't the Bible say he *created* the world? And they infer, from the word create, that it must have been made out of nothing. Now, the word create came from the word *baurau*, which does not mean to create out of nothing; it means to organize; the same as a man would organize materials and build a ship. Hence we infer that God had materials to organize the world out of chaos—chaotic matter, which is element, and in which dwells all the glory. Element had an existence from the time he had. The pure principles of element are principles which can never be destroyed; they may be organized and re-organized, but not destroyed. They had no beginning, and can have no end.[30]

Mormon belief that all mankind came from a premortal existence informs the LDS worldview in subtle but pervasive ways. To the riddle of human nature, generally seen as a contest between the two simple ingredients of nature and nurture, the burden of genetic inheritance on the one hand and the shaping forces of environment on the other, Mormons add a third factor: the choices, experiences, and schooling of shadowy aeons that precede our mortal incarnation. Character was presumably shaped, friendships forged, family relationships assigned, promises made, and myriad transactions occurred, whose influence permeates a veil of forgetfulness. What the poet William Wordsworth called "intimations" of heavenly realms and "shadowy recollections" inform and infuse Mormon sensibility about an ineluctable relationship between a forgotten Act I and the present Act II that we call mortality. In obliviousness to the play's full scope, most mortals, Mormons believe, are trying to understand a three-act play, having forgotten the exposition or not even knowing that the play did not begin after the intermission.

Few Latter-day Saints would presume to connect the dots between present afflictions or blessedness and prior merit or deficiency in any particular causal chain. But the general sense that there is a connection between what we suffer here, and what we did or contracted for there, softens the impression upon Mormons of an earthly existence that can appear random, capricious, and senseless. The lament "I didn't ask to be born" rings hollow in a faith tradition that literally believes, in church President Lorenzo Snow's words, "we were willing to come" and "very likely we put ourselves under certain obligations that we would discharge certain duties devolving upon us when we came here."[31] Indeed, both membership in the church and accompanying stewardships are often associated with premortal faithfulness. In a cryptic Book of Mormon passage, Alma teaches that holders of the priesthood were "called and prepared from the foundation of the world" (Alma 13:3),[32] and Joseph Smith himself taught that "every man who has a calling to minister to the inhabitants of the world was ordained to that very purpose in the Grand Council of Heaven before this world was."[33]

Joseph also suggested that personal relationships on this side of birth may mirror—albeit imperfectly—ones formed on the other side. In commenting on the impact of this doctrine on the LDS character, an official publication suggests that "the belief that we knew each other there increases our appreciation of each other here."[34] Patriarchal blessings (special, personalized blessings given to each Mormon by a "Patriarch," usually in adolescence) commonly include prophetic promises as well as references to past conduct in the preexistence. Mormonism's cultural language allows for references to premortal friendships, family bonds, and even romances rooted in sketchy notions of past affections and commitments. A popular Mormon musical of the 1970s, *Saturday's Warrior,* adapted the classical conventions of comedy (scrambled relationships and misdirected romance that all gets happily sorted out in the end) to a setting that reached from premortal friendships, sibling loyalties, and romance to the friendship, family stresses, and thwarted loves of mortality.

The decision to make the jump into mortality was provoked by the promise of spiritual advance (hence the rejoicing recorded by Job) but colored by the recognition of the odyssey's spiritual peril (and so the defection of one-third of the heavenly hosts). Earth life, the so-called second estate, offered at least two opportunities lacking in premortality—the acquisition of physical bodies of flesh and the faith-building and faith-testing circumstance of absence from God. The Book of Mormon twice refers to mortality as a "probationary" state, a time of testing and preparation to meet

God (Alma 12 and 42). Character, Mormons believe, is both revealed and shaped on the far side of certainty; hence the veil of forgetfulness that spiritually isolates man in this mortal sphere. But earth life is emphatically more than a test for two reasons.

First, according to the Mormon doctrine of eternal progression, the human soul is not inherently evil, is not consigned by God's foreknowledge to either salvation or damnation, and is never a finished product simply given an eternal room assignment once its true nature is manifested or ascertained. Believing themselves to be literal progeny of God, Mormons emphasize the open-ended potential for endless growth and development. "All the minds and spirits that God ever sent into the world are susceptible of enlargement and improvement. The relationship we have with God places us in a situation to advance in knowledge," taught Joseph Smith.[35] To the timeless query about human nature, Mormonism responds that man is neither inherently good nor inherently evil; he is inherently free. "All truth is independent in that sphere in which God has placed it, to act for itself, as all intelligence also; otherwise there is no existence" (DC 93:30). Earth provides an ample forum for human agency to operate without the dampening effects of divine guardianship, while providing the abundance of options that make choice meaningful and conducive to growth.

Second, Mormons consider the opportunity for human incarnation itself to be a doctrinal principle as important as the miracle of *the* incarnation. "We came to this earth that we might have a body and present it pure before God in the celestial kingdom. The great principle of happiness consists in having a body. The devil has no body, and herein is his punishment. . . . All beings who have bodies have power over those who have not."[36] Because Mormons reject conventional dualism, it is not clear what advantages a physical body offers over a spiritual body. Joseph Smith taught as revealed truth that "there is no such thing as immaterial matter. All spirit is matter, but it is more fine or pure, and can only be discerned by purer eyes" (DC 131:7). Still, it is an article of their faith that only when these two dimensions are united, when "spirit and element [are] inseparably connected, [does man] receive a fulness of joy" (DC 93:33). Part of this joy is consequent upon the introduction of opposites into the realm of human experience. "They taste the bitter," says the Lord in the *Pearl of Great Price*, "that they may know to prize the good" (Moses 6:55).

Man's entrance upon the stage of mortality, then, is part of a preconceived plan, in whose ratification and participation man himself played a willful part. Why transgression appears to be the necessary precondition for human birth as well as human death is not entirely clear in Mormonism. Still, Mormon scriptures emphasize that man's fall was not to be lamented as the loss of paradise, but celebrated as the gateway to mortality for the countless souls of men and women who inhabited the premortal realms. In their Edenic state, Adam and Eve (whom Mormons take to be literal progenitors) were apparently incapable of procreation. As the Book of Mormon states, had not Adam and Eve fallen, they "would have had no children; wherefore they would have remained in a state of innocence" (2 Nephi 2:23). That is why the father of the human race is heralded as a kind of Christ figure, enabling the eternal progression of humankind: "Adam fell that men might be," says Lehi in the Book of Mormon, "and men are that they might have joy" (2 Nephi 2:25).

According to Genesis, of course, the woman was first to partake of the Tree of Knowledge of Good and Evil. Timothy writes in the New Testament that being deceived and first to eat, Eve was in transgression, but not Adam (1 Tim. 2:14). Indeed, Adam could not fulfill the command to multiply and replenish the earth in her absence, so it is possible to read his action as the decision to break the lesser of two commandments. But LDS scripture insists that since both had to assume a mortal condition to bring about God's purposes, Eve was simply leading the way, and was the first to recognize the need to transgress one command in order to fulfill another. As she later confirms, "were it not for our transgression we never should have had seed, and never should have known good and evil, and the joy of our redemption, and the eternal life which God giveth unto all the obedient" (Moses 5:11). The penalty attached, of expulsion from the garden and its Tree of Life (associated, apparently, with the gift of immortality), not only initiated the conditions that made possible the human race, but was itself an act of mercy rather than punishment in Mormon thought. For once having violated God's injunction against eating the forbidden fruit, Adam and Eve incurred guilt—or spiritual death—along with mortality— physical death. At this point, their expulsion from the garden prevented them from making a temporary and reparable degradation into a permanent condition. "If it were possible that our first parents could have gone forth and partaken of the tree of life," explains Alma in the Book of Mormon, "they would have been forever miserable, having no preparatory state," that is, no interval for repentance and sanctification to operate in their lives, between first fatal choice and final reward (Alma 12:26).

The fall is indeed a fortunate fall in Mormon thought; Adam's sin, like Eve's, is a selfless gesture, and any doctrine of original sin or original guilt is without any basis whatsoever. "Every spirit of man was innocent in the beginning; and God having redeemed man from the fall, men became again, in their infant state, innocent before God" (DC 93:38). Accordingly, Smith would later write, "men will be punished for their own sins, and not for Adam's transgression."[37] As for the difficult question of why God would impose two incompatible commandments, some Mormons have speculated that the conditions of mortality are so physically harrowing and spiritually perilous, that it was necessary for mankind to demonstrate his embrace of such a plan through a willful act, one that contravened divine command. It has also been pointed out that the choice foreshadowed the recurrent earthly dilemma of choosing between orders of good, a more taxing and anguishing test than the mere choice of good over evil.

Adam and Eve's expulsion from the garden was a literal, as well as symbolic, alienation from God. And consequent upon man's inheritance of a mortal condition, with its attendant appetites, weaknesses, and temptations, individuals create their own alienation from God. Mormons are under no delusions about the moral makeup of what the Book of Mormon calls the "natural man"—indeed, scripture's King Benjamin calls the natural man "an enemy to God" (Mosiah 3:19), and other prophets of that record lament his wickedness and frailty and quickness to sin. But in the context of man's eternal existence and nature, his mortal incarnation represents, absent Christ's empowering grace, a stage in which the vulnerabilities of the spirit are painfully apparent, but are not an inherent or abiding condition. "Natural man," in other words, suggests more a condition or state that man acquires through willful disobedience or through succumbing to the corrupting influences of mortality, than the original nature of his soul.

The literalism of the Mormon conception of heavenly parentage leads inescapably to heavenly *parents*. Nineteenth-century Mormon poetess Eliza R. Snow provided the most famous formulation of the belief: "In the heavens, are parents single, no the thought makes reason stare / Truth is wisdom, truth eternal, tells me I've a mother there." The doctrine has been officially endorsed by the First Presidency of the church, as when Joseph F. Smith and his counselors affirmed that as "the infant son of an earthly father and mother is capable in due time of becoming a man, so the undeveloped offspring of celestial parentage is capable, by experience through ages and aeons, of evolving into a God."[38] Nevertheless, church leaders have tended to avoid elaborating upon the belief or even general mention of it, probably for two reasons. First, they consider such a topic too sacred and delicate a matter to expose to public speculation or sensationalizing. Second, dissident feminists have latched onto the principle as a way of furthering a feminist theology in the church, and leaders have censured as heretical certain feminist initiatives aimed at encouraging prayer to a female deity. So outside of singing the hymn "Oh My Father," with its words by Eliza R. Snow, members are not likely to hear many references to a Heavenly Mother in the modern church.

Closely related to Mormon belief that God was once a mortal like us, is the belief that his present condition is one attainable by man. As fifth Mormon President Lorenzo Snow (Eliza's brother) famously put it, "As man now is, God once was; as God now is, man may become."[39] The first half of that couplet, we have seen, has been little elaborated through official church channels. The second half has been a subject of great attention and development. The First Presidency in 1909, and again in 1925, affirmed that "man is the child of God, formed in the divine image and endowed with divine attributes, and . . . is capable, by experience through ages and aeons, of evolving into a God."[40] For Brigham Young, this was the whole point of our mortal probation: "Man is destined to be a God and has to act as an independent being—and is left without aid to see what he will do, whether he will be for God and to practice him to depend on his own resources [*sic*], and try his independency—to be righteous in the dark—to be the friend of God and do the best I can when left to myself— act on my agency as the independent Gods."[41]

Called deification (or theopoiesis or theosis in the language of theology), exaltation has an extensive prehistory in Christianity, though its parallels with the Mormon version are subject to dispute. The clearest biblical precedent for this concept ("the only explicit biblical support," opines one authority)[42] is Peter's wish that his auditors "might be partakers of the divine nature" (2 Peter 1:4). Mormon scholars also cite in this regard both Psalm 82:6 ("I said, ye are gods") and Jesus' quotation of that verse in John 10.

Some question the translation of these passages, but it is certain that many early Christians believed at least something akin to the Mormon conception.[43] "Let the interpretation of the Psalm [82] be just as you wish," wrote Justin Martyr, "yet thereby it is demonstrated that all men are deemed worthy of becoming 'gods', and of having power to become sons of the Highest." According to LDS scholar Daniel Peterson, the idea was common even in the Jewish community at Qumran. Among the Dead Sea Scrolls, he writes, "several texts . . . indicate that a human being could hope to be enthroned among the gods."[44] And Mormon Stephen Robinson enumerates a host of Christian precedents:

> Saint Clement of Alexandria wrote, "Yea, I say, the Word of God became a man so that you might learn from a man how to become a god." . . . In the early fourth century Saint Athanasius [stated] . . . "The Word was made flesh in order that we might be enabled to be made gods." . . . On another occasion Athanasius stated, "He became man that we might be made divine." Finally, Saint Augustine himself, the greatest of the Christian Fathers, said: "But he himself that justifies also deifies, for by justifying he makes sons of God. 'For he has given them power to become the sons of God' [John 1:12]. If then we have been made sons of God, we have also been made gods."[45]

Mormons also cite popular Christian apologist C. S. Lewis's belief in the process by which "finite beings (with free wills) [may progress] into—well, Gods."[46]

So Mormon aspirations to divinity are seen as heretically reminiscent of Lucifer's yearning to "be like the most high" (Isa. 14:14) by some Christians, and as logical fulfillment of Paul's promise that we can be "heirs of God, and joint-heirs with Christ" (Rom. 8:17) by Latter-day Saints. In any case, this three-stage epic that is conceived before the earth's foundations are laid and culminates in the epiphany of a glorified, resurrected divinity, is a distinctive and powerful vision of human origins and human potential. The result is a distinctive conception of salvation that is predicated on the continuation of family relationships into the eternal sphere.

Calvary as Anticlimax: Gethsemane and Mormon Atonement

For most Christians, Christ's role in human salvation is the defining ingredient in their faith. Any assessment of Mormonism as a Christian faith, therefore, must begin with a look at the LDS doctrine of Christ. Latter-day Saints continue to be frustrated by what they see as persistent misunderstandings and misrepresentations of the Mormon doctrine of Christ's atonement by critics, the media, and even otherwise astute observers of the religion. News magazines perennially report that Mormons are "unlike orthodox Christians [in believing] that men . . . earn their way to godhood by the proper exercise of free will, rather than through the grace of Jesus

Christ."[47] Equally misguided are the authors of a popular account of Mormonism who write that since Latter-day Saints deny the doctrine of original sin, they believe "men and women are saved because [Christ's] example moves their hearts to respond; this grace . . . guides their lives and moral choices" in a manner similar to atonement as understood in "liberal Protestant theology."[48] Both views are simply wrong. As a canonized revelation to Joseph Smith unambiguously states, "For behold, I, God, suffered these things for all, that they might not suffer if they would repent; But if they would not repent, they must suffer even as I; Which suffering caused myself, even God, the greatest of all, to tremble because of pain, and to bleed at every pore, and to suffer both body and spirit" (DC 19:16–17).

From this we learn that the atonement was a vicarious expiation, an actual displacement of suffering from mankind onto Christ. James Talmage, the LDS apostle and author most revered for his writings on Christ and the atonement, summarizes how, "in some manner, actual and terribly real though to man incomprehensible, the Savior took upon Himself the burden of the sins of mankind from Adam to the end of the world."[49] According to the Book of Mormon, there can be nothing which is short of an infinite atonement which will suffice for the sins of the world" (Alma 34:12). Therefore, "this is the whole meaning of the law, every whit pointing to that great and last sacrifice; and that great and last sacrifice will be the Son of God, yea, infinite and eternal" (Alma 34:14).

The current president of the LDS Church, Gordon B. Hinckley, said in 1997:

> no one believes more literally in the redemption wrought by the Lord Jesus Christ. No one believes more fundamentally that He was the Son of God, that He died for the sins of mankind, that He rose from the grave, and that He is the living resurrected Son of the living Father. All of our doctrine, all of our religious practice stems from that one basic doctrinal position: "We believe in God, the Eternal Father, and in His Son, Jesus Christ, and in the Holy Ghost." This is the first article of our faith, and all else flows therefrom.[50]

At the same time, it is true that Mormon theology defines salvation existentially, that is to say, as a condition of being that man attains to developmentally. Therefore, while Christ's atonement may remit the punishment of sin, it cannot impute to man a condition of holiness he has not attained. To do so would violate the principle of moral agency, or what the Book of Mormon calls the principle of restoration (Alma 11:40–42), according to which all people find the fate they most desire (as manifest through their choices). For this reason, Latter-day Saints make a distinction between the unconditional gift of immortality, which Christ's atonement conveys to the entire human family without exception, and salvation, a condition that depends upon an individual's righteous desires as manifest through his choices (but a condition that is still utterly contingent upon God's enabling grace). So it is both fair and fitting that man is "raised to happiness according to his desires of happiness, or good according to his desires of good; and the other to evil according to his desires of evil" (Alma 41:5). The atonement allows man to escape the punishment of a sinful choice for which he has repented, meaning, he is free to choose afresh, to redirect his life in accordance with principles of virtue and truth. And that process of atonement, choice, forgiveness, and redirection allows man to move progressively closer and closer to a condition of godliness.

In this regard, the exemplary life of Christ, and the empathy he earned through both personal and vicarious suffering, are powerful catalysts to human faith and striving. The Book of Mormon records that "he will take upon him death, that he may loose the bands of death which bind his people; and he will take upon him their infirmities, that his bowels may be filled with mercy, according to the flesh, that he may know according to the flesh how to succor his people according to their infirmities" (Alma 7:12). But those functions are clearly secondary in Mormon theology to the redemptive power of Christ's vicarious suffering itself.

Man is saved by grace in this conception, because he cannot escape the consequences of his own sinfulness and partake of what Peter calls the divine nature without some kind of intervention that remits the punishment of his wrongful choices, works upon him to purify his desires, and empowers him to overcome the allure and bondage of sin. And that act of intervention, of Christ's expiation on mankind's behalf, is unmerited, freely given, and indispensable to human salvation. That is why Mormons accept the doctrine of grace as taught in the New Testament, but believe the Book of Mormon prophet Nephi articulates the most accurate synthesis of Pauline and Jamesian emphases: "For we know that it is by grace that we are saved, after all we can do" (2 Nephi 25:23). Human insufficiency to attain salvation is powerfully argued by King Benjamin in his address on the atonement in the Book of Mormon. "Are we not all beggars," he asks, "do we not all depend on the same Being?" Even the bases of physical sustenance, life and breath "that ye may live and move and do according to your own will" are not yours to command, he insists; our fragile existence "from one moment to another" is sustained only by Christ's gift, how infinitely more so redemption and eternal life. And if man should labor all his days to earn such gifts, "yet ye would be unprofitable servants" (Mosiah 4:19; 2:21–22).

The role of works in this view is not that of "earning" salvation, for the most righteous individual cannot, by his own efforts, attain to godliness. Good works do not represent some minimum standard of righteous proficiency—because if God could determine that some arbitrary standard is sufficiently "good" for his reward, an infinitely kind and compassionate God would simply do away with the standard altogether and dispense salvation indiscriminately to all his children. And *that* version of grace is untenable for two reasons. First, because works represent choice, not merit, and are thus the guarantor of human agency, not of human worthiness. The role of works in human salvation is that they embody the enacted will of the freely choosing individual. Reward is not a function of what is earned, but of what one chooses to accept as a consequence of God's grace, as Joseph Smith recorded in a revelation to that effect: "they shall return again to their own place, to enjoy that which they are willing to receive, because they were not willing to enjoy that which they might have received" (DC 88:32). Works are simply the evidence, in this regard, of a choice to accept that gift. Salvation in the absence of works that reflect human choice would not be grace but coercion.

In the second place, works in Mormon theology mean adherence to eternal principles which of themselves—and indispensably—conduce to virtue, purity, and holiness. These principles must be embraced under conditions of choice that are offered and then continually offered afresh in the eternally present aftermath of the atonement, leading us to be *what* God is rather than simply *where* God is. In this context, as one Mormon leader writes, "mercy and repentance are rehabilitative, not retributive. The Savior asks us to repent not just to repay him for paying our debt to justice, but also to induce us to undergo the personal development that will purify our very nature. The 'natural man' will remain an enemy to God forever— even after paying for his own sins—unless he also 'becometh a saint through the atonement of Christ the Lord (Mosiah 3:19).'"[51]

In this model, commandments and divine directives are not mere tests of obedience or arbitrary decrees, but a template for godliness and a pattern for the divine nature. As another revelation to Joseph Smith states, the faithful are "crowned," not burdened, "with commandments not a few"

(DC 59:4). So when the Book of Mormon records that "wickedness never was happiness," and that to go "contrary to the nature of God" is to exist "in a state contrary to the nature of happiness," Mormons learn that freely rendered obedience to law, godliness, and eternal happiness are all part of the same fabric of divinity. Eternal happiness is the natural consequence of abiding by those laws prescribed for us, but an act of unwarranted and unfathomable kindness on God's part makes our embrace of those laws both possible and efficacious.

Families are Forever: Temples, Genealogy, and Eternal Marriage

On the great day of judgment, according to Jewish legend,

> the children of the wicked who had to die in infancy . . . will be found among the just, while their fathers will be ranged on the other side. The babes will implore their fathers to come to them, but God will not permit it. Then Elijah will go to the little ones, and teach them how to plead in behalf of their fathers. . . . God will give assent to their pleadings, and Elijah will have fulfilled the word of the prophet Malachi; he will have brought back the fathers to the children.[52]

The legend is one attempt to make sense of the cryptic words of Malachi that conclude the Old Testament, wherein that prophet promises in the name of the Lord, "Behold, I will send you Elijah the prophet before the coming of the great and dreadful day of the Lord: And he shall turn the heart of the fathers to the children, and the heart of the children to the fathers, lest I come and smite the earth with a curse" (Mal. 4:5–6). When John the Baptist preached in the wilderness, Jewish priests thought perhaps the desert prophet was the predicted Elijah and asked him for confirmation. "I am not," he said plainly (John 1:21). Whether John was being overly literal and evasive or frank and truthful is in dispute. Many Christians opt for the former reading, insisting that John did indeed fulfill the prophecy, coming "in the spirit and power" if not in the actual person of Elijah. "This is meant alone of John the Baptist," writes respected commentator Adam Clarke of the Malachi passage, typifying a common Christian reading of the prophecy.[53] Some have seen in Elijah's appearance on the Mount of Transfiguration (Mark 9:4) a more literal fulfillment.

Devout Jews, on the other hand, anticipate the prophecy's future fulfillment. Some of them still set an empty place at the Passover table, a perpetual reminder of their hope in the prophet's eventual return.

One such Passover transpired on April 2, 1836. The next day, Mormons found their own meaning behind Malachi's promise. On that occasion, Joseph Smith was in the Kirtland, Ohio temple, which had been dedicated a few days earlier. With Oliver Cowdery, he retired behind a pulpit veil to pray. In an ensuing vision, he beheld the Christ, as well as Moses, Elias (whom Mormons believe to be an individual distinct from Elijah), and, finally, Elijah himself. As the latter, he "who was taken to heaven without tasting death," stood before them, he announced "the time has fully come, which was spoken of by the mouth of Malachi—testifying that he [Elijah] should be sent before the great and dreadful day of the Lord come— To turn the hearts of the fathers to the children, and the children to the fathers, lest the whole earth be smitten with a curse—Therefore, the keys of this dispensation are committed into your hands" (DC 110:14–16).

It would be some time before the meaning of these words was clear. The temple at Kirtland, the first one erected by the Latter-day Saints, was a beautiful structure three years in the building. Its appearance and actual purpose was that of a large meetinghouse; its interior was used for teaching and public worship, but not the more sacred rituals and ordinances of Mormon practice. (Smith performed in the Kirtland temple some washings of feet patterned on New Testament descriptions, but not the ceremonies that have since become the staple of Mormon temple worship. The relationship between temples, children and their fathers, and the "keys" restored by Elijah, was yet to be developed.) Five years after the Kirtland temple was dedicated, the Saints had moved from Ohio and fled Missouri persecutions for the swampy village of Commerce, which soon became the flourishing city of Nauvoo, Illinois. By the time the Saints had been driven to Nauvoo, Mormon doctrine was much further along in development. Here, in January 1841, revelation directed them to build another temple, in which newly revealed ceremonies would be performed.

The point of Elijah's visitation, Joseph explained, was to deliver those priesthood keys that linked husband to wife and children to parents in a continuous "chain that binds the hearts of the fathers to the children, and the children to the fathers," spanning generations and annulling the effects of deathly separation.[54] This eternal family unit actually becomes both the acme of Latter-day Saint aspiration, and the essence of what they mean by salvation in the world to come. Mormons interpret this destiny as the true focus of the Abrahamic covenant, a compact they believe was made with the ancient patriarch but persists through all earthly eras, and whose promises even the Christian dispensation preserves rather than supplants. "Thou shalt be the father of many nations," Jehovah tells Abraham in one of many versions of the covenant. "I will make nations of thee, and kings shall come out of thee" (Gen. 17:4, 6). "I will multiply thy seed as the stars of heaven, and as the sand upon the shore," he adds on Mount Moriah. "And in thy seed shall all the nations of the earth be blessed" (Gen. 22:17–18).

Mormons interpret the covenant's promise of vast inheritance, a progeny of kings, and a seed as numerous as the dust of the earth, as all pertaining not to time but to eternity. Exaltation, or eternal life, the life that God leads, includes not only immortality and a fullness of joy, but a "continuation of the seeds forever and ever," the power to sire and "bear the souls of men" (DC 132:19, 63). As LDS philosopher Truman Madsen writes, "divine families encircled by [Christ's] fire and light are the very essence of life and eternal life and . . . without them this earth—indeed this cosmos—will have missed the measure of its creation."[55]

If this is true, then the sealing rites of the temple need to be administered to the living as well as those who have departed life without benefit of those sealing powers. Since entrance into the gospel covenant itself is heralded by baptism, baptism for the dead is a necessary precursor to other vicarious ordinances. The subject of the salvation of the unbaptized had first been broached by Joseph in an 1836 vision, wherein he saw his deceased brother Alvin in the celestial kingdom of God. Wondering how that could be, since his brother died without seeing the gospel restored or receiving the ordinance of baptism, Joseph heard a voice saying, "all who have died without a knowledge of this gospel, who would have received it if they had been permitted to tarry, shall be heirs of the celestial kingdom of God" (DC 137:7).

As a fuller doctrine of salvation of the dead took shape, two conditions of such salvation emerged. First, it became apparent that in the realm of the departed, the gospel would have to be taught to those who died "in ignorance." Explicating 1 Peter 4:6, which refers to the gospel being "preached also to them that are dead," Joseph said that "all those who have not had an opportunity of hearing the Gospel, and being administered unto by an inspired man in the flesh, must have it hereafter, before they can be finally judged."[56] The fullest LDS description of this process came in a 1918 vision to President Joseph F. Smith, the sixth Mormon prophet. While contemplating those same passages in Peter, Smith wrote, he saw "the hosts of the dead, both small and great," and the appearance in that realm of the Son of God, "declaring liberty to the captives who had been faithful." Then Smith watched as, "from among the righteous, he organized his forces and appointed messengers, clothed with power and authority, and commissioned them to go forth and carry the light of the gospel to them that were in darkness, even to all the spirits of men; and thus was the gospel preached to the dead" (DC 138:11, 18, 30).

Second, taking baptism (like the soon-to-be-revealed temple ordinances) to be essential to salvation, Joseph declared that proxies could stand in for those who died without baptism—or more particularly, without baptism performed by an authorized (LDS) priesthood holder. Joseph's understanding of this principle, he said, was based on knowledge "independent of the Bible."[57] Still, he, like generations of Mormons ever since, quoted Paul's first epistle to the Corinthians as evidence of ancient precedent. "Else what shall they do which are baptized for the dead," the apostle queried, "if the dead rise not at all? why are they then baptized for the dead?" (15:29). Latter-day Saints perform vicarious ordinance work, then, with the understanding that the divinely mandated ordinance is required of all who will enter the kingdom of God. But it is performed with the belief that the departed must hear—and accept—the gospel message as taught in the spirit world, for the baptism performed on their behalf to have any value.

It was in 1840 that Joseph first taught the principle that the deceased could be baptized vicariously in order to satisfy the requirement for baptism and the first proxy baptisms were performed in the Mississippi River. As work on the temple progressed, river baptisms were halted until they could be done in the proper setting of a completed temple. In May 1842, Joseph administered what came to be known as "the endowment" to select members, using the upper room of his brick store, while waiting for the temple to be completed. In these ceremonies, members were instructed in a series of covenants, or obligations, and blessings, that accompany the representation of a journey from the preexistence, into earth life, through telestial and terrestrial states, and culminating in the celestial kingdom, which represents exaltation in the presence of God. It was not until after the prophet's death that the first group of Saints participated in endowment ceremonies in the temple, on 11 December 1845.

About this same time, the first sealings were performed in the temple. In this ordinance, a man and his wife, or the parents and their children, are bonded together by the power of the priesthood. Like Catholics, Mormons believe that Christ gave Peter important power and authority when he bestowed upon him "the keys of the kingdom." But in his promise that whatsoever the apostle "bound on earth" would be "bound in heaven" (Matt. 16:19), the Latter-day Saints see a reference to the "sealing powers" that Elijah restored to Joseph Smith and that forge the eternal chain of family ties Smith referred to. This is certainly an unusual Christian doctrine, but is an essential ingredient in the Mormon concept of family. Latter-day Saint couples who enter the temple for a marriage ceremony stand in the midst of opposing mirrors, which reflect infinitely receding images of themselves at the marriage altar. The vivid symbolism emphasizes the eternal nature of the relationship they believe themselves to be entering upon.

Since none can discern who will or will not accept the gospel, proxy ordinances (including baptisms, endowments, sealings, and others) are performed for all names submitted to the temple by living members. The goal of documenting all names and relationships in the history of the human family seems patently impossible. Nonetheless, the effort to link the myriad branches of the race into one stupendous family tree has resulted in a program of genealogical research that is mind-boggling. Hub of the massive effort is the Family History Library in Salt Lake City. An army of over four hundred professionals and volunteers assist some two thousand daily visitors to trace their "kindred dead," relying upon 3 million rolls and fiche of microfilm and over three hundred thousand published sources. Literally thousands of rolls of additional microfilm pour in monthly, from hundreds of cameras capturing records in over forty countries at any one time.

With the advent of the Internet, genealogical research was catapulted into the digital age. The church launched a Family Search Web site in 1999, and by early 2003, almost one billion names were in searchable databases. Public response to the Web site has been remarkable. The first three and a half years witnessed over 10 billion hits to the site by 143 million different users.[58] Obviously, the church's unparalleled resources in this area have made it possible for millions of families—in and outside the church—to reconnect with their ancestors through genealogical research, and have fostered a Mormon mindset that enlarges and enriches the concept of "family" in unprecedented ways.

The faith tradition's emphasis on family and marriage is further reflected in the fact that Mormons are more likely to marry, and marry at an earlier age, than non-Mormons.[59] Not surprisingly, perhaps, Mormon divorce rates are related to the level of religious commitment of the partners. However, when Latter-day Saints marry within their faith, they are

The LDS genealogy program
Well over 2 billion microfilmed names of deceased persons from more than 150 countries are stored at the church's Granite Mountain Records Vault, east of Salt Lake Valley. (Courtesy of the Church Archives, The Church of Jesus Christ of Latter-day Saints)

the least likely of all Americans to divorce.[60] Furthermore, when measuring the rate of divorce among Mormons married in the temple (the rite observed by most active, committed Mormons), the rate falls tremendously. One study indicates that for men with temple marriages, 5.4 percent have been divorced compared to 27.8 percent of nontemple men. For women, the numbers are 6.5 percent for temple marriages and 32.7 percent for the others.[61]

In the 1970s, an American survey posed the question, "Do you anticipate reunion with your loved ones in an afterlife?" Of the Lutherans, Baptists, and Roman Catholics polled, about 53 percent responded in the affirmative. Ninety percent of Mormons did.[62] Clearly, Mormon teachings

The church's main family history library
The library is in Salt Lake City, and is open to the public. Patrons may do research in branch libraries scattered throughout the world. (Courtesy of the Church Archives, The Church of Jesus Christ of Latter-day Saints)

on the eternal nature of family relationships correspond to more durable earthly unions and an expectation of durable eternal bonds as well.

A Peculiar People: Tithing, Health Laws, and Missionary Work

Faith and Finance

"Let us here observe, Joseph Smith wrote, "that a religion that does not require the sacrifice of all things never has power sufficient to produce the faith necessary unto life and salvation."[63] For a time, the Latter-day Saints experimented with the Law of Consecration, a principle of communalism such as the early church is described as living in the book of Acts ("they had all things in common," 4:32). After the Saints had failed to successfully live such a challenging principle, the law of tithing was first given as the standing law of the church in July 1838, to the members in Missouri. The principle, as the etymology of the term suggests, enjoined members to "pay one-tenth of all their interest annually," with interest interpreted to mean income.

The law of tithing is a remarkably efficient system of church finance, as well as a continuing principle by which individual commitment to the gospel is both measured and fostered. Originally, tithing was frequently paid in kind, with members contributing 10 percent of their produce or new livestock. Goods were gathered in the bishop's storehouse, from where they were dispensed to the poor and needy under the authority of the bishop. Today, members generally make cash payments through their local bishop. Local contributions are gathered and deposited weekly and immediately transferred to Salt Lake City. From church headquarters, all decisions pertaining to the disposition of tithing funds are made.

No collection plate is passed, and donations are not solicited. Nevertheless, the principle is taught frequently in church sermons, and members must pay a full tithe to be eligible for temple worship. The consequence of such an emphasis is that Mormons donate funds to their church at a substantially higher rate than is true in other faiths. In one study, those donating a full 10 percent of their income to the church ranged from 40 to 80 percent of the sample, depending on educational level.[64] The church does not release financial figures, so the total income from tithing (and from other sources as well) is not known, though it is a subject of widespread speculation. Estimates range from a few billion dollars a year to $6 billion or more.

The Body as Temple

Like devout Jews, Hindus, Muslims, and members of some Christian denominations, Mormons abide by a dietary law that forbids the ingestion of certain substances. While the revelation known as the Word of Wisdom also enjoins the eating of fresh fruits and grains ("in the season thereof"), it is the prohibitions that dominate Mormon consciousness regarding this law. Tradition holds that Joseph Smith was prompted to inquire of the Lord regarding tobacco use in response to his wife's complaints about the unsavory aspects of the practice, as evidenced in the stained floor of her Kirtland, Ohio home above the Whitney store, used by Joseph's School of the Prophets (a forum of both gospel and secular instruction). The ensuing revelation singled out the use of tobacco, alcohol ("wine and strong drink"), and "hot drinks," which the prophet's brother Hyrum (and subsequent leaders) interpreted to mean tea and coffee, as "not good . . . for the body neither for the belly" (DC 89:7–8).

Received in 1833, the principle was framed as coming neither by way of "commandment [n]or constraint, but by revelation and the word of wisdom" (DC 89:2). And apparently, few members or even leaders of the church did feel constrained by the revelation, since the prohibited substances continued to find fairly general use among them all. Brigham Young gave new emphasis to the revelation in 1851, but more than ten years later, he was more concerned about the economic than religious implications of noncompliance. Noting the vast sums going outside the Territory to import tobacco, he insisted that the crop could be produced in southern Utah so as to avoid "paying outsiders from sixty to eighty thousand dollars annually."[65] With the advent of America's prohibition movement, church attention focused more sharply on alcohol consumption, and the Word of Wisdom received powerful new attention. In the 1920s, adherence to the Word of Wisdom became a requirement for temple admission—the ultimate measure of good standing in the church.

The same revelation also encouraged the sparing use of meat, advising it be limited to "times of winter, or of cold, or famine" (DC 89:13). If the past is any predictor, perhaps at some future time leaders will move Latter-day Saints to embrace more fully the quasi-vegetarianism the law mandates as they did in the case of the other prohibitions—but at present Mormons probably consume Big Macs and steaks at the national average. Even so, current Mormon practices governing the body may have a dramatic effect on the longevity of those bodies. One researcher concludes that "the healthiest active Mormons have a life expectancy that is 8 to 11 years longer than U.S. whites as a whole."[66]

It is important to realize that in Mormon thought, the Word of Wisdom forms part of a theology of the body that has roots in Paul's admonition to treat our physical selves as a "temple of God," with reverence and care (1 Cor. 3:16). Accordingly, in the spirit of the Word of Wisdom, any substance—or quantity of substance—that is detrimental to health or the independence of the spirit, is to be shunned. Clearly, that proscription applies to illegal drugs. For the most orthodox of Mormons, it even applies to any caffeinated beverage, since they too can be addictive.[67]

In the realm of human sexuality, Mormon conceptions of the body as a holy tabernacle find powerful expression as well. Like John Milton and C. S. Lewis, Mormons believe that sexuality is neither a sign nor consequence of fallenness, but a characteristic of godliness having a role in the eternal worlds. "Gender is an essential characteristic of individual premortal, mortal, and eternal identity and purpose," the church recently pronounced.[68] But the embrace of sexuality—along with gender—as an eternal constant, as God-given and -sanctioned, leads in the case of Mormon sexual morality not to less inhibitions on sexual expression, but more. This is because Mormons associate the procreative power not just with God's power to engender life, but with human potential to be parents in the eternal realms. Correct exercise of this creative prerogative now, they believe, will result in the power to create life eternally. Mormons are thus required to practice sexual abstinence before marriage and fidelity after marriage. In fact, Mormon scripture characterizes sexual immorality as "most abominable above all sins save it be the shedding of innocent blood or denying the Holy Ghost" (Alma 39:5).

Mormon emphasis on premarital chastity and marital fidelity appears to bear measurable fruit. Studies reveal LDS youth to have a significantly lower incidence of premarital sex than non-LDS teenagers.[69] In fact, Latter-day Saints register rates consistently lower than national averages for premarital sex, teen pregnancy, and extramarital relations.[70]

Missionary Service

On 14 September 1839, Brigham Young left his home in Montrose, Illinois, and headed for England. He was so enfeebled by sickness that he had to be assisted the short distance from his house to the ferry. His impoverished family had recently been driven out of Missouri and were all sick, including a ten-day-old baby. Across the river at Heber C. Kimball's house, Young collapsed and needed several days to recover. Kimball and his family were likewise sick with ague, and when the two commenced their journey together, Heber could not climb into the wagon unaided. He later described feeling "as though my very inmost parts would melt within me, at the thought of leaving my family in such a condition, as it were, almost in the arms of death. I felt as though I could scarcely endure it." At this point, he ordered the teamster, who had just started the horses on their way, to hold up. "Brother Brigham," he reportedly said, "this is pretty tough, but let us rise and give them a cheer." At that point, Young rose to his feet, and the two swung their hats and shouted, "Hurrah, hurrah, hurrah for Israel!" The wives, hearing the cheer, came to the door and returned the farewell, then Young and Kimball resumed their journey to England. It would be almost two years before the two apostles returned.[71]

Mormon missionary work is rooted in a legacy of personal sacrifice, and in those early years of persecution and vulnerability especially, manifested a risky dispersal of both human and monetary resources. Ambitious proselytizing efforts continue to be a core element of both church growth and institutional strength. The first exposure that most people have to the Church of Jesus Christ of Latter-day Saints is most likely to be in the form of two clean-cut young men in suits and ties knocking on their door. Most Christian missionaries trace their charge to Matthew 28:19, when the Lord commissioned the eleven disciples just before his ascension, saying, "Go ye, therefore, and teach all nations, baptizing them in the name of the Father, and of the Son, and of the Holy Ghost." For Mormons, this injunction was renewed by revelation through the prophet Joseph Smith, with numerous references to a field "white and ready to harvest" and admonitions to "thrust in the sickle" and to "establish and bring forth Zion." Even before the first Book of Mormon was off the press, Mormon faithful were taking portions of the printed text with them on missions to preach and convert, traveling south to Pennsylvania and north into Canada. But it was not until the church was established and priesthood authority restored, that Joseph formally authorized missionaries to begin the harvest of souls.

On 11 April 1830, the first Sunday after the organization of the church, Oliver Cowdery preached the first public discourse of the new dispensation. Then in June, Samuel Harrison Smith, brother of the prophet, filled a knapsack with copies of the new scripture and headed out on a series of journeys that would take him 4,000 miles, covering ground from Maine to Missouri. Response to the Book of Mormon, Samuel learned, was generally tepid, though his efforts resulted in the important conversions of Brigham Young and Heber C. Kimball.

Other missionaries soon followed, and small branches of the church were established in the eastern states, principally New York and Pennsylvania, and Canada. (West Virginia would see branches in 1832 and Tennessee and Kentucky in 1834.) In the fall of 1830, Oliver Cowdery and three companions were directed to take the gospel to the American Indians on the western borders of Missouri. They found little success there, but converted many along the way in Ohio, laying the foundations for the church's first westward migration to Kirtland. In the early history of the church, missionaries could be called to a variety of tasks in addition to preaching the gospel. Early missionary assignments, as one historian notes, included the call "to mine gold in California, smelt iron in Parowan, process lead ore near Las Vegas, transport mail for the Brigham Young Express and Carrying Company, study at eastern universities, colonize various settlements in the West, or build chapels, schools, and temples."[72] Today, while proselytizing missions are the norm, young men and women, and older couples, may be called to serve in the areas of education, health, or welfare.

Most missionaries are trained today at the Missionary Training Center (MTC) in Provo, Utah. An 1833 revelation of Joseph Smith foretold a day when "every man [should] hear the fulness of the gospel in his own tongue, and in his own language, through those who are ordained unto this power" (DC 90:11). Helping make that audacious prediction a reality is this multimillion-dollar sprawling complex with dormitories, classrooms, auditoriums, and gyms. Together with more than a dozen satellite MTCs around the world, the institute trains some thirty thousand missionaries a year. The Provo Center receives almost five hundred recruits every week, and spends several weeks immersing them in the study of any one of some forty-eight languages, then sends them off to a combined total of more than 120 foreign nations. For the most part, they leave with a

LDS missionary work
Sister missionaries study sign language at the Missionary Training Center, Provo, Utah.
(Courtesy of the Church Archives, The Church of Jesus Christ of Latter-day Saints)

The church's 60,000 strong full-time missionary force
Missionaries include growing numbers of older couples who serve alongside young
men and women. (Courtesy of the Church Archives, The Church of Jesus Christ of
Latter-day Saints

remarkably functional (if not fluent) knowledge of the language and an
understanding of basic cultural practices and expectations.

Missionary service in the Church of Jesus Christ of Latter-day Saints
serves a number of purposes. Clearly, the expectation that every young
man will serve a two-year mission, culturally and doctrinally emphasized,
produces a large cadre of full-time missionaries—by far the largest, pro-
portionally, of any Christian denomination. Almost as many, in fact, as all
American Protestant groups combined. According to the church, about
one-third of eligible U.S. Mormon males answer the call.[73] Such a large
group of missionaries in the field—around sixty thousand at the beginning
of the twenty-first century—is a vital ingredient in sustaining vibrant
church growth. (A sizeable portion of that number are female missionaries. They are welcome to join the ranks if they feel the call, and many do;
but missionary work is considered, in the case of males, an obligation that
pertains to the priesthood, not a mere option.)

Second, missionary service provides a two-year period of leadership
training. Most elders have the opportunity at some point to serve as district or zone leaders, supervising the work of other missionaries in their
regions. In addition, in many areas of the church, the missionaries are
the only members with sufficient church experience to preside over local

congregations of relatively new members. The LDS practice of requiring, as a rule, that missionaries pay their own way deters those simply looking for world travel or an interlude from work and schooling, and ensures that those who do go are more self-selecting, committed, and serious about their work. These factors tend to prepare a generation of future leaders, and work to foster and cement loyalty to the church.

Third, Mormonism has no theological seminaries of any kind. But two years spent proselytizing, added to the four years of early-morning scripture and church history study most missionaries complete, produce a corps of returned missionaries who are unusually biblically literate if not theologically sophisticated.

Mormons and the Christian Community

With the abandonment of polygamy and Mormonism's nineteenth-century geographical and cultural isolation, the most dramatic objects of social tension and criticism largely vanished. Still, it is clear that in spite of Mormonism's respectability in the modern world, many other Christians recognize that Latter-day Saints are Christians with a difference. In May 2000, the United Methodist Church passed a resolution insisting that the Church of Jesus Christ of Latter-day Saints "does not fit within the bounds of the historic, apostolic tradition of Christian faith," citing "radically differing doctrine on such matters of belief as the nature and being of God; the nature, origin, and purpose of Jesus Christ; and the nature and way of salvation." The Presbyterian Church (U.S.A.) and the Southern Baptist Convention passed similar resolutions.[74] The Vatican declared Mormon baptisms invalid in 2001.[75]

From one perspective, these prohibitions seem poorly reasoned. Rodney Stark and Charles Glock, in their study of *American Piety* (after acknowledging the virtual impossibility of finding any "universally acceptable standards" of orthodoxy), selected four "belief items" from which they constructed an "Orthodoxy Index."[76] The beliefs were "existence of a personal God, the divinity of Jesus Christ, the authenticity of biblical miracles, and the existence of the Devil." For good measure, they included as "other central Christian tenets: life beyond death, the virgin birth, and Christ's walking on water." In all seven cases, Mormon belief is in unambiguous accord with these core beliefs. This is why Mormons are often hurt and confused by the tendency of some in the Christian community to exclude Latter-day Saints from full membership.

From another perspective, however, these decisions are not at all unfair. Mormonism *does* insist that its doctrines are a restoration, not a reformation, of original Christian teachings; the LDS believe that priesthood authority to perform church sacraments has been absent in the historic Christian tradition; and Mormons teach that the Church of Jesus Christ of Latter-day Saints is "the only true and living Church upon the face of the earth." Their vigorous and successful missionary force derives converts largely from established Christian denominations, so the LDS Church is not exactly poised to persuade leaders of those Christian denominations to embrace Mormons as fellow laborers in the vineyard. So Mormonism's place in the Christian community is necessarily defined by unbridgeable difference and irresolvable tension at some levels. But sharing a belief in God, in Christ as Savior, and in core Christian values, Latter-day Saints and fellow Christians have found entirely sufficient grounds for friendly fellowship and shared respect. In recent years, Latter-day Saints have vigorously supported multifaith humanitarian efforts, participated in interdenominational organizations, and engaged in interfaith dialogue at many levels.

Some critics both within and outside the church have suggested that a steadfast devotion to literally believing Joseph Smith's story of heavenly visitations and gold plates is, ultimately, a barrier to full participation in a larger Christian community. But the Book of Mormon is not negotiable for Latter-day Saints. For the church cannot repudiate the story of its composition by ancient American prophets, its delivery to Joseph by a resurrected being, and its translation by means of the miraculous Urim and Thummim, without eviscerating the very foundations of the church itself. From its inception, the Church of Jesus Christ of Latter-day Saints has made the Book of Mormon the litmus test for Joseph Smith's credibility as a prophet and for the legitimacy of the church he founded. "It is the keystone of our religion," Joseph declared, and leaders ever since have reaffirmed this fact. Elder Bruce R. McConkie's declaration is typical: "The Book of Mormon . . . stands as a witness to all the world that Joseph Smith was the Lord's anointed through whom the foundation was laid for the great latter-day work of restoration."[77] It is a good bet that Mormonism could indeed be rendered more acceptable to those who inhabit a world of space shuttles and PDAs, if the church would relinquish its insistence on angels and seerstones. But given the role the new scripture and Joseph Smith's narrative have had in the construction of a Mormon religious identity, the resulting church would not be recognizably Latter-day Saint.

That the Book of Mormon is only becoming devotionally and doctrinally more central in the LDS Church cannot be disputed. In 1977, 19 million copies of the Book of Mormon had been printed in twenty-seven languages.[78] By 2000, the number printed had more than quintupled to 100 million copies in one hundred languages. So while Mormonism may be placing less public emphasis on those doctrines inimical to orthodox, historical Christianity—theosis and God's anthropomorphic nature—the church stands irrevocably poised increasingly to emphasize truth-claims inimical to secular modernism—a God who continues to intrude miraculously and conspicuously into human history and who dispenses heavenly epiphanies and revelations to both modern prophets and seeking individuals.

Clearly, the pressures to move closer to the Christian mainstream seem to register little or not at all to "the Brethren," those General Authorities who dictate in all matters of church doctrine. *Sunday Times Magazine* journalist Keith Wheatley captures the logic of that resistance in his 1987 observation: "The phenomenal growth of the Latter-day Saints in recent times shows that they have no need to dilute their doctrines. . . . They seem to be a church whose hour has come."[79]

Notes

1. Hugh Nibley, "Three Shrines: Mantic, Sophic, and Sophistic," in *The Ancient State: The Rulers and the Ruled*, in *The Collected Works of Hugh Nibley*, 15 vols. (Provo, Utah: Deseret and FARMS, 1986–), 10:370, 372, 367.

2. Ibid., 372.

3. Avery Dulles, S.J., *Models of Revelation* (New York: Doubleday, 1983), 27–28.

4. William J. Abraham, *Divine Revelation and the Limits of Historical Criticism* (New York: Oxford University Press, 1982), 24.

5. Rodney Stark, "A Theory of Revelations," *Journal for the Scientific Study of Religion* 38, no. 2 (1999): 289.

6. Joseph Smith-History 1:18–19, *Pearl of Great Price*.

7. "Prophecy," in F. L. Cross and E. A. Livingstone, eds., *Oxford Dictionary of the Christian Church* (Oxford: Oxford University Press, 1997), 1336.

8. *Journal of Discourses*, 26 vols., reported by G. D. Watt et al. (Liverpool: F. D. and S. W. Richards et al., 1851–86; reprint, Salt Lake City: n.p., 1974), 5:240.

9. G. Homer Durham, ed., *The Discourses of Wilford Woodruff* (Salt Lake City: Bookcraft, 1946), 235–36.

10. See *The American Religion: The Emergence of the Post-Christian Nation* (New York: Simon & Schuster, 1992).

11. Most famously, Leo Tolstoy used this term, according to U.S. Ambassador Andrew White. See *Autobiography of Andrew Dickson White,* 2 vols. (New York, 1907), 2:87. More recently, Harold Bloom uses this term to designate a composite group, but Mormonism features prominently in that construct. "There is something of Joseph Smith's spirit in every manifestation of American religion," he writes, claiming that "what matters most about Joseph Smith is how American both the man and his religion have proved to be." *American Religion,* 127.

12. Richard N. Ostling and Joan K. Ostling, *Mormon America: The Power and the Promise* (San Francisco: HarperSanFrancisco, 1999), 422.

13. Joseph Smith, *Discourses of the Prophet Joseph Smith,* ed. Alma P. Burton (Salt Lake City: Deseret, 1977), 167.

14. The *Oxford English Dictionary* (1980 ed.) indicates both "divine revelation" and "breastplate of the Jewish High Priest, the Urim and Thummim" as nineteenth-century meanings of the term.

15. Hugh Nibley, *Mormonism and Early Christianity,* in *The Collected Works of Hugh Nibley* (Provo and Salt Lake City: FARMS and Deseret, 1987), 169, 193.

16. Joseph F. Smith, "Editor's Table: Fountain of Truth," *Improvement Era* 10 (June 1907): 629.

17. The sermon from which this excerpt comes is known as the "King Follett Discourse." Joseph Smith, *Teachings of the Prophet Joseph Smith,* ed. Joseph Fielding Smith (Salt Lake City: Deseret, 1976), 345.

18. "Trinity," in F. L. Cross and E. A. Livingstone, eds., *Oxford Dictionary of the Christian Church* (Oxford: Oxford University Press, 1997), 1641.

19. Bernhard Lohse writes, for example, that "one does not find in [the New Testament] an actual doctrine of the Trinity"; it was "well into the fourth century before the doctrine of the Trinity was dogmatically clarified." R. L. Richard writes that "the formulation of 'one God in three Persons' was not solidly established, certainly not fully assimilated into Christian life and its profession of faith, prior to the end of the 4th century. . . . among Apostolic Fathers, there had been nothing even remotely approaching such a mentality or perspective," and *Harper's Bible Dictionary* acknowledges that "the formal doctrine of the trinity as it was defined by the great church councils of the fourth and fifth centuries is not to be found in the New Testament." Bernhard Lohse, *A Short History of Christian Doctrine* (Philadelphia: Fortress, 1966), 37–38, 53; R. L. Richard, "Trinity, Holy," in *New Catholic Encyclopedia* (New York: McGraw-Hill, 1967), 14:299; P. Achtemeier, ed., *Harper's Bible Dictionary* (San Francisco: Harper and Row, 1985), 1099.

20. Edmond LaB. Cherbonnier, "The Logic of Biblical Anthropomorphism," *Harvard Theological Review* 55 (1962): 187–206.

21. Edmond LaB. Cherbonnier, "In Defense of Anthropomorphism," in Truman G. Madsen, ed., *Reflections on Mormonism: Judeo-Christian Parallels* (Provo, Utah: Brigham Young University, Religious Studies Center, 1978), 171.

22. Cherbonnier, "In Defense of Anthropomorphism," 161.

23. Abraham, *Divine Revelation,* 11.

24. Nicholas Wolterstorff, *Divine Discourse: Philosophical Reflections on the Claim that God Speaks* (Cambridge: Cambridge University Press, 1995), 10.

25. Sandra M. Schneider, *The Revelatory Text* (San Francisco: Harper, 1991), 27–29, cited in ibid., 10.

26. James E. Talmage, *Jesus the Christ* (Salt Lake City: Deseret ["Published by the Church"], 1915 [reprint, 1973]), 81.

27. Abraham 3:22, 24–28, *Pearl of Great Price.*

28. See, for example, Daniel C. Peterson, "'Ye are Gods': Psalm 82 and John 10 as Witnesses to the Divine Nature of Humankind," in Stephen D. Ricks, Donald W. Parry, and Andrew H. Hedges, eds., *The Disciple as Scholar: Essays on Scripture and the Ancient World in Honor of Richard Lloyd Anderson,* 2 vols. (Provo, Utah: FARMS, 2000), 2:484–87.

29. Smith, *Teachings,* 365.

30. Smith, *Discourses,* 345.

31. Lorenzo Snow, *Conference Report* (April 1901): 2; *Conference Report* (April 1898): 12.

32. Mormons generally—and probably inaccurately—read the words following ("on account of their faith and good works") to refer to conduct in the preexistence, ignoring the crucial fact that the conduct referred to is according to God's *"foreknowledge"* of the righteousness of some "while others *would* reject the Spirit of God" (Alma 13:3–4).

33. Smith, *Teachings,* 365.

34. "Mutual Messages," *Improvement Era* 34, no. 12 (October 1931).

35. Smith, *Teachings,* 348.

36. Ibid., 181.

37. This denial of original sin is now canonized as the second of the Thirteen Articles of Faith, *Pearl of Great Price.*

38. James R. Clark, comp., *Messages of the First Presidency,* 6 vols. (Salt Lake City: Bookcraft, 1965–75), 4:199–206.

39. Eliza R. Snow Smith, *Biography and Family Record of Lorenzo Snow* (Salt Lake City: Deseret, 1884), 46, 47.

40. The two official declarations are reproduced in Daniel Ludlow, ed., *Encyclopedia of Mormonism,* 4 vols. (New York: Macmillan, 1992), 4:1665–70.

41. President's Office Journal, 28 January 1857, Brigham Young Papers, LDS Church Archives.

42. "Deification," in Cross and Livingstone, *Dictionary of the Christian Church,* 465.

43. Daniel C. Peterson, in his study of the debate, quotes Julien Morgenstern to the effect that except for "one modern scholar, Kittel," seeing in these verses a reference to human judges rather than 'gods' "has been definitively rejected by all others on ample grounds." "'Ye are Gods',," 480.

44. Justin Martyr, *Dialogue with Trypho,* in *Ante-Nicene Fathers,* 10 vols., ed. Alexander Roberts and James Donaldson (Grand Rapids: Eerdmans, 1977), 1:262, cited in ibid., 517; Peterson, "Ye are Gods," 511.

45. All citations are given in Stephen Robinson, *Are Mormons Christian?* (Salt Lake City: Bookcraft, 1991), 61.

46. C. S. Lewis, letter to Mrs. Edward A. Allen (1 November 1954), in *Letters of C. S. Lewis,* rev. Walter Hooper (New York: Harcourt, Brace, 1993), 440.

47. *Newsweek* (1 September 1980): 68.

48. Ostling, *Mormon America,* 328.

49. Talmage, *Jesus the Christ,* 613.

50. Gordon B. Hinckley, "Excerpts from Recent Addresses of President Gordon B. Hinckley," *Ensign* 28, no. 2 (February 1998): 73.

51. Bruce C. Hafen, "Beauty for Ashes," *Ensign* 20, no. 4 (April 1990): 9.

52. Louis Ginzberg, *Legends of the Bible* (New York: Simon and Schuster, 1956), 601.

53. Adam Clarke, *The Holy Bible Containing the Old and New Testaments with a Commentary and Critical Notes*, 3 vols. (Nashville: Abingdon, n.d. [reprint]), 2:806.

54. Smith, *Discourses*, 145–46.

55. Truman G. Madsen, "Are Christians Mormon?" *BYU Studies* 15, no. 1 (1974–75): 89.

56. Smith, *Discourses*, 271.

57. "Joseph Smith to the Traveling High Council and Elders of the Church of Jesus Christ of Latter-day Saints in Great Britain," 19 October 1840, in Clark, *Messages*, 1:124.

58. "Facts and Statistics," FamilySearch Web site.

59. Tim B. Heaton, K. L. Goodman, and T. B. Holman, "Are Mormon Families Really Different?" in Marie Cornwall, Tim B. Heaton, and Lawrence A. Young, eds., *Contemporary Mormonism: Social Science Perspectives* (Urbana: University of Illinois Press, 2001), 94.

60. After five years of marriage, only 13 percent of LDS couples have divorced, compared to 20 percent for same-faith marriages of other Christians and 27 percent among Jews. See Evelyn Lehrer and Carmel Chiswick, "Religion as a Determinant of Marital Stability," *Demography* 30 (August 1993): 393.

61. Darwin L. Thomas, "Family Life," in Daniel H. Ludlow, ed., *Encyclopedia of Mormonism: The History, Scripture, Doctrine, and Procedures of the Church of Jesus Christ of Latter-day Saints*, 4 vols. (New York: Macmillan, 1992), 2:489.

62. Glen M. Vernon, "Comparative Mormon Attitudes Toward Death," in Glenn M. Vernon, ed., *Research on Mormonism* (Salt Lake City: Association for the Study of Religion, 1974), 642–47.

63. Joseph Smith, *Lectures on Faith*, comp. N. B. Lundwall (Salt Lake City: Bookcraft, n.d.), 58.

64. Perhaps surprisingly, but consistent with Mormonism's exception to the secularization hypothesis, a higher educational level correlated with more faithful observance of the principle of tithing. Sam L. Albrecht and Tim B. Heaton, "Secularization, Higher Education, and Religiosity," in James T. Duke, ed., *Latter-day Saint Social Life: Social Research on the LDS Church and its Members* (Provo, Utah: Religious Studies Center, Brigham Young University, 1998), 305.

65. Leonard Arrington, *Great Basin Kingdom: An Economic History of the Latter-day Saints 1830–1900* (Lincoln: University of Nebraska Press, 1958), 216.

66. James E. Enstrom, "Health Practices and Mortality among Active California Mormons, 1980–93," in Duke, *Latter-day Saint Social Life*, 461.

67. Under the heading of "Cola Drinks," an official LDS publication stated: "The leaders of the Church have advised, and we do now specifically advise, against use of any drink containing harmful habit-forming drugs." Conference Report, April 1975, 102.

68. A Proclamation "To the Church and to the World," *LDS Church News* 30 September 1995.

69. Brent C. Miller and T. D. Olson, "Sexual Attitudes and Behavior of High School Students in Relation to Background and Contextual Factors," *Journal of Sex Research* 24(1988):194–200; another study indicated that the lowest levels of premarital sexual activity occur among three groups: Latter-day Saints, Pentecostals, and

Jehovah's Witnesses. See S. H. Beck, B. S. Cole, and J. A. Hammond, "Religious Heritage and Premarital Sex: Evidence from a National Sample of Young Adults," *Journal for the Scientific Study of Religion* 30(1991):173–80.

70. Tim B. Heaton, "Four C's of the Mormon Family: Chastity, Conjugality, Children, and Chauvinism," in D. Thomas, ed., *The Religion and Family Connection: Social Science Perspectives* (Provo, Utah: Religious Studies Center, Brigham Young University, 1988), 107–24.

71. Roberts, *Comprehensive History*, 2:23–24.

72. A. Glen Humphreys, "Missionaries to the Saints," *BYU Studies*, 17, no. 1 (Autumn 1976): 75.

73. *Ensign* 14, no. 12 (December 1984): 66.

74. "United Methodists claim LDS not really Christian," *Idaho Statesman*, 11 May 2000, A2.

75. "Striving for Acceptance," *Washington Post*, 9 February 2002, B9.

76. Rodney Stark and Charles Y. Glock, *American Piety: The Nature of Religious Commitment* (Berkeley: University of California Press, 1968).

77. Bruce R. McConkie, *Mormon Doctrine* (Salt Lake City: Deseret, 1989), 99.

78. *Ensign* 7, no. 9 (September 1977): 37.

79. Keith Wheatley, *Sunday Times Magazine,* 15 November 1987.

Chapter 4

Making Scripture:
The Mormon Canon

> Take away the Book of Mormon and the revelations, and where
> is our religion? We have none.
> —Joseph Smith, *History of the Church*

> [Mani] seem[s] to suggest that already in the third or fourth cen-
> tury the idea had got around, at least to perceptive minds, that
> religious movements have each a book, that a new religious
> movement must have a new written book.
> —William Cantwell Smith, *Rethinking Scripture*

In a revelation to Joseph Smith in 1831, the Lord declared that his servants "shall speak when moved upon by the Holy Ghost. And whatsoever they shall speak when moved upon by the Holy Ghost shall be
scripture, shall be the will of the Lord, shall be the word of the Lord, and
the power of God unto salvation" (DC 68:3–4).

It was in such a context that Brigham Young in the 1830s made a dramatic statement comparing the claims upon Latter-day Saints of scripture
and modern prophetic utterance:

> Brother Brigham took the stand, and he took the Bible, and laid it down;
> he took the Book of Mormon, and laid it down; and he took the Book of
> Doctrine and Covenants, and laid it down before him, and he said:
> "There is the written word of God to us, concerning the work of God
> from the beginning of the world, almost, to our day. And now," said he,
> "when compared to the living oracles those books are nothing to me;
> those books do not convey the word of God direct to us now, as do the
> words of a Prophet."[1]

In the final result, even as Mormon doctrine subordinates its own canon to the principle of living revelation, these distinctions may count for little. Given the very fluidity of the canon we have seen, any relationship between living oracles and printed scripture is always subject to renegotiation. As Mormon canonical history shows, today's inspired utterances may become part of tomorrow's Standard Works.

Mormonism stands virtually alone among Christian denominations in embracing extracanonical scriptures. In other words, in addition to accepting the Bible "as the word of God, as far as it is translated correctly," Latter-day Saints accept as equal in status to the Bible three other collections: the Book of Mormon, the *Pearl of Great Price*, and the *Doctrine and Covenants*. And while endorsing the King James translation as their official English version of the Bible, Latter-day Saints have incorporated into their published edition of the KJV changes made to the text by Joseph Smith when he was working on what he called his "translation" of the Old and New Testaments.

Joseph's Golden Bible: The Book of Mormon

Joseph Smith's rapid rise in notoriety was commensurate with his quick ascent as a spiritual leader. The event that launched him into the public glare, to the permanent glory and detriment alike of his reputation, was his publication of the Book of Mormon. Those who reviled him as a charlatan, like those who revered him as a prophet of God, based their judgment largely on his alleged translation of a set of gold plates he claimed to have retrieved from a hillside in Upstate New York in the fall of 1827. Joseph himself would later date his role as a prophet from that September day when Moroni, an angel who in his mortal life commanded vast armies in pre-Columbian America, allowed Joseph to extract the ancient record from the depository where it had lain for 1,400 years.[2] Moroni had first appeared to Joseph in 1823, telling the seventeen-year-old boy about a great civilization that originated with an Israelite migration to the Western Hemisphere in the days of Jeremiah and King Nebuchadrezzar. Moroni, their last surviving spiritual and military leader, buried an abridgment of his people's history that had been faithfully maintained since the migration from Jerusalem. It was this same Moroni who now appeared to Joseph Smith, alluded to an undefined "work" that God had for him to do, and prophesied his name would be "had for good and evil among all nations, kindreds, and tongues."[3]

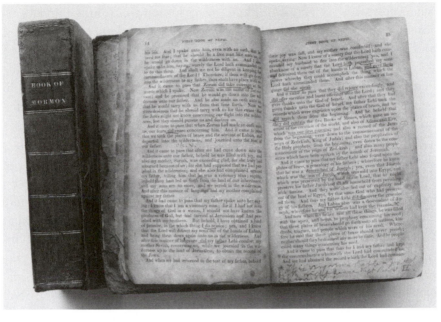

First editions of the Book of Mormon
From 1830 to 2000, over 100 million copies of this "keystone of Mormonism" were printed in several dozen languages. (Photograph by Bradley Sheppard. George Givens collection)

The content of the new scripture contained little revolutionary doctrine. Its most startling information, besides asserting the Israelite origins of at least two ancient American peoples, was a description of a visit by the resurrected Christ to the inhabitants of the Western Hemisphere not long after his ascension from Jerusalem. To Joseph and the first missionaries who peddled volumes of the Book of Mormon door to door, the record's content was of interest primarily because of the Israel-Indian connection. "Do you wish to purchase a history of the origin of the Indians?" was the sales pitch used by the prophet's brother Samuel. The Book of Mormon does present history of a sort—but it is more in the nature of personal and then clan history, than a hemispheric history. The account opens just prior to the expedition of Nebuchadrezzar against Jerusalem, when "many prophets" descend upon the area, forecasting the doom of the city if the people persist in their wickedness. Nephi, the first chronicler of the plates, refers to his father Lehi as one such figure, crying repentance. Predictably, his father is rejected and then persecuted. But he is not made captive like Daniel or exiled in Egypt like Jeremiah. Rather, he is warned to flee into the wilderness with his family. Nephi narrates his family's journey, and a harrowing dash back to the city to retrieve sacred records kept on brass plates, and then again to persuade another family with marriageable sons and daughters to join their exodus. They spend years in the Arabian peninsula before reaching the coast in present-day Yemen or Oman. There, Nephi constructs a ship under divine guidance, and the family embarks for a distant "land of promise."

Making landfall in the Western Hemisphere (most Mormon scholars think it was the west coast of Central America), the immigrants soon divide into two warring factions: a righteous, God-fearing people who await the coming of Christ, and a rebellious group who become a warlike and cursed race. Over time the respective designations of Nephite and Lamanite become indices of discipleship and apostasy, rather than of lineal descent from the original clans, but the animosities and bloodshed persist for hundreds of years. Finally, in the late fourth century, a cataclysmic war of extermination finishes off the Nephites. Mormon, the last Nephite commander, delivers the sacred history of his people to his son Moroni, who narrates his civilization's extinction and seals up the record.

The narrative itself is complex. Parts purport to be intact records lifted from other ancient sources (Isaiah passages from the brass plates of Laban, for instance), while the framing narrative of those passages is itself supposedly transmitted intact for a thousand years, and preserved without redaction until received by Joseph Smith. The bulk of the record, however, purports to be an abridgment of the last five hundred years of Nephite history, as engraved by Mormon (whose editing gives the record its name), father of the prophet/angel Moroni. Within his abridgment we find accounts of wars, missionary journeys, sermons, epistles, a description of coinage, the history of a pre–Common Era Christian church, editorial commentary, apostrophes to future generations, prophecies, visions, and more. At times, the story line fragments and details simultaneous stories, and at times we find ourselves following narratives within narratives within narratives, like children's nesting blocks. In addition to Lehi's exodus from the Old World, two other migrations are recounted in the Book of Mormon, one contemporary with Lehi and one thousands of years earlier, and the briefer accounts of those two peoples intersect and are assimilated into Mormon's abridgment.

The King James English, together with long stretches of Isaiah's writings, can make for difficult going ("chloroform in print," jibed Mark Twain). But there are also passages of real poignancy, beauty, and rhetorical power, like Nephi's psalm of lamentation, Alma's conversion account, and Mormon's valediction to his slain people. Early in his narrative, Nephi digresses to express frustration at his own human frailties:

> when I desire to rejoice, my heart groaneth because of my sins; nevertheless, I know in whom I have trusted.
>
> My God hath been my support; he hath led me through mine afflictions in the wilderness; and he hath preserved me upon the waters of the great deep.
>
> He hath filled me with his love, even unto the consuming of my flesh.
>
> He hath confounded mine enemies, unto the causing of them to quake before me.
>
> Behold, he hath heard my cry by day, and he hath given me knowledge by visions in the nighttime.
>
> And by day have I waxed bold in mighty prayer before him; yea, my voice have I sent up on high; and angels came down and ministered unto me.
>
> And upon the wings of his Spirit hath my body been carried away upon exceedingly high mountains. And mine eyes have beheld great things, yea, even too great for man; therefore I was bidden that I should not write them.
>
> O then, if I have seen so great things, if the Lord in his condescension unto the children of men hath visited men in so much mercy, why should my heart weep and my soul linger in the valley of sorrow, and my flesh waste away, and my strength slacken, because of mine afflictions?
>
> And why should I yield to sin, because of my flesh? Yea, why should I give way to temptations, that the evil one have place in my heart to destroy my peace and afflict my soul? Why am I angry because of mine enemy?
>
> Awake, my soul! No longer droop in sin. Rejoice, O my heart, and give place no more for the enemy of my soul.
>
> Do not anger again because of mine enemies. Do not slacken my strength because of mine afflictions.
>
> Rejoice, O my heart, and cry unto the Lord, and say: O Lord, I will praise thee forever; yea, my soul will rejoice in thee, my God, and the rock of my salvation. (2 Nephi 4:19–30)

Several hundred years later, the prophet Alma recounts to his rebellious son the story of his own dramatic conversion to Christ.

> And it came to pass that as I was thus racked with torment, while I was harrowed up by the memory of my many sins, behold, I remembered also

to have heard my father prophesy unto the people concerning the coming of one Jesus Christ, a Son of God, to atone for the sins of the world.

Now, as my mind caught hold upon this thought, I cried within my heart: O Jesus, thou Son of God, have mercy on me, who am in the gall of bitterness, and am encircled about by the everlasting chains of death.

And now, behold, when I thought this, I could remember my pains no more; yea, I was harrowed up by the memory of my sins no more.

And oh, what joy, and what marvelous light I did behold; yea, my soul was filled with joy as exceeding as was my pain!

Yea, I say unto you, my son, that there could be nothing so exquisite and so bitter as were my pains. Yea, and again I say unto you, my son, that on the other hand, there can be nothing so exquisite and sweet as was my joy. (Alma 36:17–21)

And few passages can match the pathos of Mormon's farewell as he surveys a quarter million of his slain countrymen, after the annihilation of the Nephite armies.

And it came to pass that my people, with their wives and their children, did now behold the armies of the Lamanites marching towards them; and with that awful fear of death which fills the breasts of all the wicked, did they await to receive them. And . . . they came to battle against us, and every soul was filled with terror because of the greatness of their numbers. And . . . they did fall upon my people with the sword, and with the bow, and with the arrow, and with the ax, and with all manner of weapons of war.

And it came to pass that my men were hewn down, yea, even my ten thousand who were with me, and I fell wounded in the midst; and they passed by me that they did not put an end to my life. And when they had gone through and hewn down all my people save it were twenty and four of us, (among whom was my son Moroni) and we having survived the dead of our people, did behold on the morrow, when the Lamanites had returned unto their camps, from the top of the hill Cumorah, the ten thousand of my people who were hewn down, being led in the front by me.

And my soul was rent with anguish, because of the slain of my people, and I cried: O ye fair ones, how could ye have departed from the ways of the Lord! O ye fair ones, how could ye have rejected that Jesus, who stood with open arms to receive you! . . . O ye fair sons and daughters, ye fathers and mothers, ye husbands and wives, ye fair ones, how is it that ye could have fallen! But behold, ye are gone, and my sorrows cannot bring your return. (Morm. 6:7–11, 16–20)

The climax of the sweeping historical saga is a visit the resurrected Christ makes to the Nephites soon after his Old World ascension. In this New World context, he tells the Nephites they are the "other sheep" he mentioned in his Jerusalem ministry (John 10), thereby providing one of many threads that connect the Book of Mormon to the Bible, reinforcing its claim to be a companion volume rather than a substitution for the Christian scriptures.

Compared to the Bible, the Book of Mormon is lacking in conspicuously novel doctrines. One contribution of the Book of Mormon that has been insufficiently noted—because it is implicit rather than explicit—concerns the way the scripture reconceptualizes the principle of divine revelation. We have seen that the primary role of the Book of Mormon in LDS history has been to serve as evidence that Joseph Smith was a prophet of God. And as a proselytizing tool, missionaries in Smith's era and in recent years have appealed, though less so today, to the historical curiosity of readers, if only to get a hearing. (Until the 1980s, editions of the Book of Mormon included photographs of Mayan ruins, a glossy counterpart to the Frederick Catherwood illustrations of Mesoamerican temples that piqued Joseph Smith's interest.) Doctrinally, the Book of Mormon presents a radically positive interpretation of the fall as fortunate, and a discussion of atonement that reconciles grace with human agency and accountability, though doctrinal content has been little explored until recent years. But one of the record's most appealing and innovative contributions comes in both depicting and exemplifying a notion of revelation that combines the literalism of the Old Testament with the egalitarianism of a democratic age. Like the books of Moses and the books of the Prophets, the Book of Mormon abounds with patriarchs and prophets who converse with God. In Abraham dickering with God over Sodom's fate, or Moses receiving the Decalogue, we see a conception of revelation, or divine communication, that is rooted in an anthropomorphic conception of deity and that is directed at prophet-leaders.

In the Book of Mormon, the opening scene is of a Jerusalem to which there came in the days of Jeremiah "many prophets prophesying unto the people" (1 Nephi 1:4). When God speaks to these prophets, it is likewise in human language, using discernible words and directives, and it rises frequently to the level of genuine, interpersonal exchange (as when Enos bargains with God over the fate of his people [Enos 5–17] or Nephi argues with the Holy Ghost over the dispatch of Laban [1 Nephi 4:10–18]). Where the Book of Mormon diverges dramatically from the Old Testament pattern is in extending both the recipient range and the subject range of these revelations. In the Bible, as one authority has written "Prophecy was preeminently the privilege of the prophets."[4] And as for subject matter, the concern of these prophets is generally with the fate of kings and nations and tribes, with the workings and purposes of God in history, with the spiritual destinies of covenant peoples and fledgling churches. Even more grandly, as Abraham Heschel writes, "Prophecy . . . may be described as exegesis of existence from a divine perspective."[5] Not so in the Book of Mormon.

Following a magnificent, panoramic vision given to the patriarch Lehi, his son Nephi finds himself "desirous also that I might see, and hear, and know of these things, by the power of the Holy Ghost, which is the gift of God unto all those who diligently seek him" (1 Nephi 10:17). That expression of hunger for—and hopeful expectation of—personal, confirmatory revelation, is perhaps the most persistent thematic thread in the Book of Mormon, an indispensable key in understanding Mormonism's (and the Book of Mormon's) historical and ongoing appeal, and the basis of that experiential element behind conversion, commitment, and membership in the Mormon faith community.

Nephi's request finds powerful validation when the Spirit of the Lord reveals to him a vision even surpassing the epic scope of his father's. The significance of his experience is heightened by the text's clear insistence that it is Lehi who embodies clan leadership, patriarchal authority, and visionary aptitude. Nephi's request would thus seem either presumptuous or redundant—and that possibility is suggested by the Spirit of the Lord himself, who asks Nephi if he does not believe the account of his father. "Thou knowest that I believe all his words," Nephi replies. To which the Spirit replies with a loud voice, "Hosanna to the Lord, the most high God," and reveals to Nephi a vision whose description surpasses in detail and splendor even his father's.

The clear moral, repeated time and again throughout the narrative, is that "he that diligently seeketh shall find; and the mysteries of God shall be unfolded unto [him]" (1 Nephi 10:19). That invitation emphatically extends beyond prophets to seeking sons and concerned fathers, followers as well as leaders. Such characters seek and receive revelations in the Book of Mormon in response to queries on everything from the location of game to the disposition of enemy troops, on subjects of doctrinal import and in regard to personal fears and insecurities. Those who, lacking high office and priestly qualifications, share the opinion of Nephi's faithless brothers that "the Lord maketh no such thing known unto us" are chastised for the hardness of their hearts and for denying the "spirit of revelation" (1 Nephi 15:9–10; Hel. 4:23).

At the conclusion of the Book of Mormon record, Moroni addresses future readers in the most cited passages from the scripture, reasserting and universalizing the principle of personal revelation:

> And when ye shall receive these things, I would exhort you that ye would ask God, the Eternal Father, in the name of Christ, if these things are not true; and if ye shall ask with a sincere heart, with real intent, having faith in Christ, he will manifest the truth of it unto you by the power of the Holy Ghost. And by the power of the Holy Ghost ye may know the truth of all things. (Moro. 10:4–5)

This promise resonated with a nineteenth-century public steeped in a Protestant culture that was increasingly democratized. Mormonism was not the only frontier religion of the era that answered the yearning of religious seekers for personal spiritual manifestations. But it did offer a concrete object that served as a provocation to such spiritual encounters, and it carried the principle of personal, dialogic revelation further than most. So much so that it prompted Alexander Campbell, the founder of the Disciples of Christ, a kindred restorationist sect, to fume that Joseph Smith had gone too far in this regard.

> I would ask [Book of Mormon witnesses Oliver Cowdery, David Whitmer, and Martin Harris] how they knew that it was God's voice which they heard—but they would tell me to ask God in faith. *That is, I must believe it first, and then ask God if it be true!* . . . If there was anything plausible about Smith, I would say to those who believe him to be a prophet, hear the question which Moses put into the mouth of the Jews, and his answer to it—"And if thou say in thine heart, *How shall we know the word which the Lord hath not spoken?*"—Does he answer, "*Ask the Lord and he will tell you?*" . . . Nay, indeed [emphases his].[6]

Similarly, Gilbert Wardlaw, an Edinburgh minister, admonished his American audience in 1830 in words uncannily pertinent to the Mormon example:

> I am aware that prayer for the outpouring of the Holy Spirit has been, and may be recommended in terms which Scripture sobriety does not justify. Some have spoken of this divine gift as if they expected something actually miraculous, something altogether new to the church in the present

day, conferred independently of the word, and in a manner almost perceptible to the senses.[7]

The Book of Mormon's most important role in Mormonism would seem to be its embodiment of the very principle that Campbell and Wardlaw denounced: its promise of access to a personal spiritual manifestation that confirms to the individual the truthfulness of that Book of Mormon, and by extension, the divine role and mission of Joseph Smith as the restorer of the gospel of Jesus Christ. The remarkable growth and success of Mormonism cannot be separated from the hunger this record satisfied. As the poet John Greenleaf Whittier recognized, Mormonism spoke "a language of hope and promise to weak, weary hearts, tossed and troubled, who have wandered from sect to sect, seeking in vain for the primal manifestations of the divine power."[8] And the Book of Mormon was the vehicle through which those manifestations were channeled.

Recognizing the Book of Mormon's essential role in sustaining the history and doctrine of Mormonism as a whole, apologists within the church and critics without have expended vigorous efforts to sustain or impugn the book's claims to historical validity. It never occurred to Joseph Smith or early Saints that the Book of Mormon represented anything other than a literal history that unfolded somewhere in the Western Hemisphere. In fact, next to serving as prima facie evidence of Joseph Smith's divine calling, elucidating the origins of the American Indians was the most prominent role the Book of Mormon played in the nineteenth century. In that era, speculation linking the native Americans to the lost tribes of Israel was a popular topic, and the Mormon variation—linking those peoples to a Jewish migration—was close enough to exploit public interest in the general theme.[9] "The idea . . . that the Indians are descendents of the Jews . . . is generally entertained among the learned," was how a Mormon writer put the case.[10] So the sales pitch of Joseph's brother Samuel Smith and fellow missionaries—"[do you] wish to purchase a history of the origin of the Indians?"—was an appeal to the familiar, not the novel.

Indian mounds throughout the Mississippi and Ohio valleys and other remnants of aboriginal cultures were mysteries to which, early Mormons believed, the Book of Mormon held the key. When the first descriptions of Central American ruins reported by Alexander Humboldt and Juan Galindo filtered through to the Saints in the 1830s, and with the publication in 1841 of John Lloyd Stephens' book especially (*Travel in Central America, Chiapas, and Yucatan*), LDS interest shifted to Mesoamerica as the center of Book of Mormon history. "Their ruins speak of their great-ness; the Book of Mormon unfolds their history,"[11] wrote Smith confi-dently. Such confidence continued unabated into the twentieth century. With more enthusiasm than textual justification, the 1879 edition of the Book of Mormon even keyed Book of Mormon place names to their mod-ern counterparts: arrival in the promised land occurs "on the coast of Chili"; "the land southward" becomes "South America"; the River Sidon empties into "the Caribbean Sea," and so on.

Gradually, insuperable problems with such hemispheric assumptions about Book of Mormon geography and peopling became evident. The multiplicity of Indian languages does not suggest a common source a few millennia removed; migrations across the Bering Straits are more scientif-ically plausible than transatlantic voyages; native American population figures upon Columbus's arrival seem impossibly large if traced entirely to a clan of a few dozen just two thousand years earlier. By the late twentieth century, Mormon apologists were pointing out that a more careful analy-sis of the Book of Mormon revealed a theater of action of only a few thou-sand square miles. Not only the landfall, but the entire history of the Nephites and Lamanites, they argue, took place within an area 500 miles long and 200 miles wide. Accordingly, the Book of Mormon was more accurately viewed as the clan history of a few local groups—not a history of semi-global empires.

This interpretive framework obviates many of the most immediate objections to Book of Mormon historicity, but not all. Most anthropolo-gists and archaeologists cite a list of anachronisms and improbabilities that, they are sure, condemn the record to the realms of fiction. Herds of horses, steel bows, other weapons of iron and metal coins, the chariot and barley, cement and silk—these stand out as blatant textual missteps, they claim. Defenders respond with carefully documented—though highly debatable—instances of horse remains, iron artifacts, and arguments about the translator's prerogative to find near equivalents for unfamiliar terms. Archaeology has not proven a friend to Book of Mormon believers, though a remarkable discovery in Yemen has been touted by Mormons as "dramatic new evidence" of Book of Mormon historicity. In the late 1990s, a number of altars were excavated at a temple complex in the vicin-ity of Sana'a. Scholars found the inscriptions on three of the altars referred to a tribe of NHM. Except for one reference on an eighteenth-century map discovered in 1978, that name had never been associated with any site in that region in modern times. In the Book of Mormon, however, the name appears as an apparently established locality, where a member of Lehi's party is buried. Given Nephi's description of his family's journey from Jerusalem to the Arabian coast, the burial would have occurred while they were somewhere in the vicinity of present-day Yemen. In other words, as one Mormon scholar writes, "Nephi implied that a place in southern Arabia named Nahom already existed in his day, and now three chiseled blocks of stone from a pagan temple in Yemen provide incontrovertible evidence that, in fact, it did."[12]

In general, however, believers and defenders recognize that archaeology may not be the most useful tool to establish the book's historicity. What kind of an archaeological discovery *would* establish its credibility? they ask. A Mayan inscription post that says, "Nephi slept here"? The altars in Yemen corroborated a place name unique, in 1830, to the Book of Mormon. Yet no one outside Mormon circles took note, let alone deemed the find conclusive.

Accordingly, the textual approach of LDS scholars has focused in recent years on assessing the record's internal evidences and compatibility with Middle Eastern culture and languages. Following the lead of Hugh Nibley, the most influential church intellectual since World War II, scholars working at the Foundation for Ancient Research and Mormon Studies have embraced the kind of interrogation he pioneered:

> Does it correctly reflect "the cultural horizon and religious and social ideas and practices of the time"? Does it have authentic historical and geographical background? Is the mise-en-scène mythical, highly imaginative, or extravagantly improbable? Is its local color correct, and are its proper names convincing? Until recent years men were asking the same questions of the book of Exodus, and scholars were stolidly turning thumbs down until evidence accumulating in its favor began to turn the scales. As one student described it, the problem "is rather to prove, by innumerable small coincidences, that which Ebers has so well called the 'Egypticity' of the Pentateuch, than to establish any particular historical point by external and monumental evidence." Just so the problem of 1 Nephi is to establish both its "Egypticity" and its "Arabicity" by like innumerable coincidences.[13]

Scholars working mostly in association with the Foundation for Ancient Research and Mormon Studies, affiliated with Brigham Young University, currently produce a journal, books, reviews, and a newsletter

with updates on new discoveries that buttress Book of Mormon apologetics. Mormon scholars have shown that the unlikely claim of Smith that the
record was written on gold plates in a language called reformed Egyptian
finds circumstantial plausibility. Many examples of record keeping on precious metal plates have been found, and at the time the Book of Mormon
opens, sixth century B.C., Israel's cultural and economic ties to Egypt were
leading to "a process of fusion for which a great deal of evidence now
exists."[14] William Foxwell Albright, doyen of American Ancient Near
Eastern studies, calls it "surprising that there are two Egyptian names,
Paanch[i] and Pahor[an] which appear together in the Book of Mormon
in close connection with a reference to the original language as being
'Reformed Egyptian.'"[15]

Many studies have found evidence of Hebraic grammatical construc-
tions in Smith's translation of the Book of Mormon. Forms like the cog-
nate accusative ("dreamed a dream," "curse with a cursing," or "yoke
with a yoke") are compatible with Hebrew syntax, but unusual in English—yet they appear in the Book of Mormon. So, too, the construct state
("plates of brass," "altars of stone," "words of plainness," rather than
brass plates, stone altars, and plain words) is frequently employed in the
Book of Mormon.

Some supposed gaffes in the Book of Mormon have been subsequently
revealed as historically substantiated. Two examples are the reference to
Christ's nativity in "the *land* of Jerusalem" and the proper name Alma.
The first case turns out to be consistent with Middle Eastern practice of
naming areas for their principal cities. (The Amarna letters—ca. 1400
B.C.—for example, refer to "a town of the land of Jerusalem, Bit-
Lahmi.")[16] In the second, the Book of Mormon name for a male character, once derided as a Latin feminine, was discovered in 1961 by Israeli
scholar Yigael Yadin on a land deed near the western shore of the Dead Sea
dating from the early second century. One of the names on the document
was "Alma, son of Yehudah."[17]

One of the most persuasive claims to an ancient origin to the Book of
Mormon regards a poetic device common in ancient literatures called chi-
asmus, or inverted parallelism. A sequence of terms or ideas is sequentially
embedded, then those same elements reappear in reverse order. These literary patterns can range in length from a simple phrase or sentence to
examples of remarkable complexity and length. One example of average
size is found in Mosiah 5:

(a) And now ... whosoever shall not take upon them *the name* of Christ

  (b) must be *called* by some other name;

   (c) therefore, he *findeth himself on the left hand of God.*

    (d) And I would that ye should *remember* also, that this is *the name* ...

     (e) that never should be *blotted out,*

      (f) except it be through *transgression*; therefore,

      (f′) take heed that ye do not *transgress,*

     (e′) that the name be not *blotted out* of your hearts. ...

    (d′) I would that ye should *remember* to retain *the name* ...

   (c′) that ye are not *found on the left hand of God,*

  (b′) but that ye hear and know the voice by which ye shall be *called,*

(a′) and also, *the name* by which he shall call you.[18] (Emphasis added)

Such examples as these and others may buttress the confidence of the faithful, but do not yet appear to constitute a critical mass of evidence sufficient to interest more than a handful of scholars in ancient studies. In a famous address given in 1997, two evangelical scholars agreed that Book of Mormon apologists have, since the 1970s especially, shown commendable "sophistication and erudition" in their work, "producing serious research which desperately needs to be critically examined."[19] Still, to most scholars, the stigma of supernaturalism surrounding the Book of Mormon is too daunting even though, as one determined skeptic admits, it is hard to ignore the "striking coincidences between elements in the Book of Mormon and the ancient world and some notable matters of Book of Mormon style."[20]

Meanwhile, skeptics interested in the Book of Mormon as a cultural product have worked to find cultural consistencies with nineteenth-century American religion, culture, and folk traditions: the book's frequent references to "secret combinations" strike some historians as suspiciously reminiscent of anti-Masonic rhetoric of the era; commonplace assumptions about a link between native Americans and the lost tribes of Israel provide a plausible context for Smith's invention of a story about Israelite migrations to the New World; Book of Mormon injunctions against infant baptism and universal salvation were both relevant to nineteenth-century theological controversies; and Joseph's own family history includes dreams and visions with some similarities to one detailed in the first book of Nephi. Additionally, Joseph Smith's own personal engagement in digging for buried treasure, and his youthful use of a seerstone, may be interpreted as precedents for his own story of how he retrieved and translated the sacred record.

In the nineteenth century, it was possible to point to the enigmatic vestiges of erstwhile empires and maintain that the Book of Mormon made a plausible claim to be the Rosetta stone of ancient American civilization. But archaeology has proved to be a two-edged sword and historians of American culture have provided critics with alternative explanations of Book of Mormon origins. All that is certain is that as Mormon membership continues to climb, and as the Book of Mormon becomes even more central to Mormon religious life (a trend underway since the 1970s), the stakes surrounding its claim to be a true account of happenings in an ancient American setting will only get higher. And even if the historicity of the Book of Mormon turns out to be a question that never engages the interest of secular scholars, its keystone role in the development of a new world religion will itself make the record an inescapable focus of growing interest and scrutiny.

Recent years have seen an effort by evangelicals and dissident Mormons to pressure the church into shedding its absolutist claims about the historicity of the Book of Mormon. It is not really necessary, they claim, to impugn Joseph Smith's character or sincerity. All Mormons need to do is to admit that consciously *or* unconsciously, Joseph Smith inserted cultural influences, prevalent ideas, and contemporary material into his narrative. The story of Moroni and the gold plates must be jettisoned, or explained away as hallucination or delusion. Since "truth" is a notoriously pliable concept, and since the Bible has successfully weathered the assaults of higher criticism, geological science, and Darwin to remain a powerful locus of religious experience and spiritual "truth," the diplomats of spiritual détente reason, believers in the Book of Mormon can safely relinquish their fundamentalism as well. This is the explicit strategy, for example, of one critic who writes that people need to "challenge . . . simplistic assumptions about the nature of revelation" in order to arrive at a "more refined . . . definition of revelation and scripture."[21]

In a similar vein, a disaffected Latter-day Saint asserts that there are "overwhelming scientific proofs of [the Book of Mormon's] fictional character," and pleads for an abandonment of Mormon preoccupation with the scripture's historicity, to be replaced by a focus on its spiritual message.[22] He quotes approvingly another Mormon, who fashions an argument based on William James' famous distinction: "some might think . . .

the conclusion that Joseph Smith is the author of the work requires reject-
ing the work as religiously relevant and significant. . . . [But] such a rejection does not follow from this critical judgment. Historical conclusions
about a scriptural text, such as who authored it, are *existential* judgments,
. . . and can and should be separated from judgments about *spiritual* values."[23] Indeed, it sounds no more than generous to accommodate Joseph's
perceived prophetic fallibility by redefining scripture "as both record and
metaphor of human striving for the divine, rather than as religious icon or
documentary history"[24] and arguing that the Book of Mormon, like the
Bible, can be read as pseudo-history without compromising its spiritual
value. Yet another dissident Mormon tries to promote this same analogy:
"It is unclear to me," he earnestly writes, "how the Old Testament's great
expression of human fear and hope in God or its message of ethical
monotheism and social concern or of human liberation are compromised
in the least when we recognize that many of its narratives do not tell accurate history or that its view of the natural world is contrary to the facts."[25]

As tempting and conducive to greater Mormon respectability as these
strategies might be, the story of the prophet and the plates simply doesn't
cooperate in such a reconstruction. Because Smith's persistent references to
the plates as physical artifacts, dug from a hillside, hidden in bean barrels,
under hearthstones, and in smocks, and his displaying of them to eleven cor-
roborating witnesses, not to mention his transcription of them into hieroglyphics and translation of them into English—these continual, extensive,
and prolonged references to a tangible, visible, record are not compatible
with a theory that makes Smith an inspired "writer" reworking the stuff of
his own dreams into a product worthy of the name of scripture. Even if the
analogy were otherwise apt, affirming the Bible's status as scripture in spite
of historical inaccuracies or transmission errors is not comparable to
embracing the Book of Mormon's "spiritual values" while simultaneously
asserting the fraudulence of its entire conception and execution.

Besides giving its name to the new religious movement, the Book of
Mormon has served first and foremost as the primary evidence by which
Joseph Smith's claim to prophetic stature is established. To the casual
reader, the Book of Mormon is conspicuously lacking in theological novelty. One searches it in vain for clues to the origin of Mormonism's most
distinctive teachings. It does not expound on man's premortal origins or
postmortal exaltation; it makes no explicit assertions about the nature of
God, the purpose of temples, the necessity for health codes, or the eternal
durability of families. Joseph Smith himself seldom if ever relied upon the

Book of Mormon as a source of doctrine or sermonizing, and few prophets have since—until very recently. What early Saints and present-day missionaries *do* say about the Book of Mormon is that by reading it, and coming to believe it is true, one can know that Joseph Smith was a prophet of God. It is for this reason that Smith called it the keystone, rather than the foundation, of Mormonism. The church did not grow out of Book of Mormon doctrine, but rather, the Book of Mormon is so inextricably tied to Joseph's authority as prophet, founder, and revelator, that it cannot fall without precipitating a collapse of the entire structure he instituted. Given his claims about the book's origin, it is hard to label him another in a line of religious figures writing inspirational literature.

This is why, from the church's earliest days to the present, the Book of Mormon has been the key to proselytizing and conversion. The story of its coming forth as an ancient record, burial by ancient American prophets, announcement by an angel, and translation by means of a seerstone— this account does not permit much flexibility in the way readers assess Joseph's role.

Modern Revelation: *The Doctrine and Covenants*

The Book of Mormon may be the keystone of Mormonism—the sign of Joseph Smith's prophetic authority and the sign to the faithful of Latter-day gathering and Christ's imminent return. But that prophetic authority itself found utterance in numerous revelations and visitations received by Joseph over a quarter century. The meaning of "revelation" as used by Latter-day Saints is itself best understood as a spectrum that ranges from virtual transcript of heavenly communication to utterance that is authoritative by virtue of the speaker's status alone. Joseph recorded as revelation some words that he claimed to hear from the mouths of angels or even Deity himself. At other times, he saw and heard things in a kind of trance, while others present in the room felt and saw nothing.[26] The majority of his revelations were apparently pronouncements that he uttered while feeling himself under the influence of spiritual guidance, but in the absence of supernatural manifestations of any kind.

In most instances, the words that he recorded took the form of divine address, with Joseph included as part of the audience. "Thus sayeth the Lord" typically prefaces an admonition, directive, or commandment. But some of his revelations took the form of epistles (DC 127, 128), "items of instruction" (DC 130), and even a "declaration of belief regarding Governments and Laws" (DC 134). Initially, Joseph circulated texts of some revelations at church conferences, beginning with the organizational meeting of April 1830. Within three months of the church's founding, Joseph Smith and John Whitmer began to collect and arrange the revelations Joseph had received. At a conference in Hiram, Ohio, in November 1831, a decision was made to compile and publish the "many revelations . . . received from the Lord prior to this time" in an edition of ten thousand (later revised downward to three thousand).[27] Months later, Joseph began publicly promulgating revelations in the church's official periodical, *The Evening and the Morning Star*, beginning with the first issue of June 1832. The next year, a selection of revelations went to press in Independence, Missouri. Before they could be published, a mob destroyed the press and scattered the printed sheets. A few hundred salvaged copies containing some sixty-five revelations to the prophet were bound as *The Book of Commandments*. More revelations were added to an edition newly titled the *Doctrine and Covenants* in 1835, and more yet again to an 1844 edition.

Not all of Joseph's revelations were incorporated into LDS scriptures. At least forty known revelations given to him have never been included.[28] Additional revelations were again incorporated into a new edition of the *Doctrine and Covenants* in 1876, and a "Manifesto" of Wilford Woodruff included from 1908 on; in 1921, Joseph's "Lectures on Faith" that had been included since 1835 were removed.[29] In 1976, two revelations received in 1836 and 1918 were added to another collection of scripture, the *Pearl of Great Price*. In 1981, they were transferred to the *Doctrine and Covenants*, along with an "Official Declaration" on the priesthood. Joseph obviously meant it when he wrote that "we believe all that God has revealed, all that He does now reveal, and we believe that He will yet reveal many great and important things pertaining to the Kingdom of God" ("Articles of Faith," *Pearl of Great Price*).

Though not as well known outside Mormon circles (and not as well studied within them) as the Book of Mormon, the *Doctrine and Covenants* has been more influential in grounding LDS doctrines. Section 89, known to Mormons as the revelation on the Word of Wisdom, provides members with their famous code of health, "showing forth the order and will of God in the temporal salvation of all saints," and section 119 establishes tithing as the economic law of the church. The magnificent epiphany of the three degrees of glory recorded in section 76 was so celebrated in Joseph's day, it was known simply as "The Vision," a title that most Mormons would today associate with the original visitation of the Father and Son to the boy prophet. Joseph had felt impressed in his work on the Bible that "if God rewarded every one according to the deeds done in the body, the term 'Heaven,' as intended for the Saints' eternal home, must include more kingdoms than one."[30] Pondering the apostle John's reference to resurrection in John 5:29, Joseph and his companion Sidney Rigdon both experienced a detailed vision of three distinct spheres of heaven, named by them as the celestial, terrestrial, and telestial kingdoms. Mormon understanding of a graded salvation, and one that is nearly universal, derives from this section.

Section 20 lays out the principles of church organization and government, and along with section 107, discusses the priesthood and defines the duties pertaining to its several offices. Section 130 canonizes the Mormon doctrine of a corporeal God, and section 132 comprises the prophet's official pronouncement on both plural and eternal marriage.

Other notable sections include Joseph's 1832 prophecy that a Civil War would erupt, beginning in South Carolina (87); his "Olive Leaf" revelation that defines the Light of Christ as both the power that enlightens the human mind and "the light which is in all things, which giveth life to all things" (88); Joseph's plaintive plea to the Lord for succor while incarcerated in Liberty Jail, Missouri: "O God, where art thou? And where is the pavilion of thy hiding place?" (121); and the Lord's gentle rebuke: "The Son of man hath descended below them all. Art thou greater than he? . . . Thy days are known, and thy years shall not be numbered less; therefore, fear not what man can do, for God is with thee forever and ever" (122).

Restoring Plain and Precious Things: The "Inspired King James Version"

Joseph would refer in his ministry to three signs that the work of the last days had commenced. All pertained to his role as revelator and creator of new scripture. The first, he said, was the publication of the Book of Mormon. "The covenants given to the Latter-day Saints"—certainly including the directives published in the *Doctrine and Covenants*— was the second. Third, and so important that he referred to it as "a branch of [his] calling,"[31] was what he called "the translation of the Bible."[32] Translation is a bit of a misnomer here—since Joseph did not actually use original manuscripts in his work of revision. It was actually a recension, involving some wholesale insertions, but mostly minor changes.

In June 1830, a few short months after the Book of Mormon had gone on sale to the public, Joseph presented to the church a "precious morsel" that he had received by revelation. But this June revelation was unlike all others that he had received up to this time, consisting as they had of inspired words that directed him in the work of translation and church organization, or provided general admonition or personal direction. The revelation was also unlike the writings comprising the Book of Mormon, since that work had purported to be a distinct body of scripture, and while Book of Mormon prophets had quoted Isaiah liberally, the completed translation stood alone as representing a kind of New World Bible. Now, it looked as if Joseph were returning to the Old Testament itself, augmenting or tampering with the words of its venerated prophets. For this new revelation purported to be "the words of God, which he spake unto Moses at a time when Moses was caught up into an exceedingly high mountain" (Moses 1:1). In the vision, Moses describes his encounter with both Satan and Deity. He learns that God created "worlds without number," that each one "was called earth, and [that] there were inhabitants on the face thereof" (Moses 1:33, 29). But like Raphael disappointing the curious Adam in *Paradise Lost*, God responds to Moses' query about "why these things are so" saying he will give "only an account of this earth" (30, 35). The vision ends with God promising Moses that in a day of disbelief in Moses' own writings, God will "raise up another like unto thee" (41). (As with the similar prophecy of Deut. 18:15, Latter-day Saints take the reference to be Christological.)

This "precious morsel" from the lost writings of Moses grew over the next several months to include a number of revisions and additions to the first five chapters of Genesis. Then, in December 1830, Joseph announced another substantial revelation, comprising "the Prophecy of Enoch," which gave a much fuller account of the life and ministry of that patriarch than is found in the Old Testament. By this time, Joseph was referring to his work as "a translation" of the scriptures. Joseph did not at any point in this process work with original manuscripts. He clearly was using the term in the sense, common in the nineteenth century and still sanctioned by the *Oxford English Dictionary* today, of translate as "to render or express in other words." Joseph apparently saw his translation as an inspired reworking of the text that included both clarification and inspired interpolation.

By the following March, Joseph had extended his work into the New Testament. Almost a year later, at Kirtland, Ohio, the prophet wrote that he had "completed the translation and review of the New Testament, on the 2nd of February, 1833, and sealed it up, no more to be opened till it arrived in Zion."[33] At this point, Joseph turned back to further revisions of the Old Testament, and on the second of July his associate Sidney Rigdon recorded that work was that day completed on the entire Bible.[34] There are several indications, however, that Joseph did not consider the work complete. Both statements by his wife Emma and Brigham Young, as well as textual evidence (such as partial changes and unevenness of apparent attention to different biblical books and sections), suggest that the revision had come to a provisional or tentative conclusion at best. Emma wrote to her son Joseph in 1867, "My heart is made glad by your report of your progress in the translation as you know something of my fears with regard to its publication, on account of what your father said about the unfinished condition of the work."[35] And Brigham Young was reported to have said that Joseph spoke of "going through the translation of the Scriptures again and perfecting it upon points of doctrine which the Lord had restrained him from giving in plainness and fulness at the time."[36]

It is clear that as early as 1833, Joseph anticipated publishing his translation "in a volume by itself; [with] the New Testament and the Book of Mormon . . . printed together."[37] However, other than portions of Genesis that he printed in the church newspaper *Evening and Morning Star* (August 1832), and the substantially revised Matthew 24 printed as a single sheet in Kirtland a few years later, little of his work saw print before the prophet's death in 1844. In 1851, in England, extensive portions of Genesis, together with Matthew 24, were published (with additional writings) in a separate volume, the *Pearl of Great Price*. For the greater part of the church's history, then, the work that occupied Joseph Smith intermittently for years received little exposure among members and never came, in its entirety, to assume the status of scripture. That situation may be said to have changed in 1979. In that year, the LDS Church published a new edition of the Bible. Though still using the text of the King James Version as its official translation, the new edition incorporates into its footnotes many (but far from all) of the changes Joseph Smith made. His translation thus is assimilated into, rather than replaces, the King James Version of the Bible.

The reasons for keeping the King James Version as the official translation are probably several. First, since Smith's translation was a redaction of that version, the two are effectively—and permanently—interconnected.[38] Equally important are proselytizing considerations. Until 1884 (when the American Standard Version was published), there was no competing version in America. Using a version that was widely accepted as authoritative by mainstream Christianity gave Latter-day Saints an important common scriptural ground with other believers, and provided their missionaries with a source for teaching biblical prophecies about and doctrines of the Restoration that nonmembers could regard as authoritative. That justification will continue to lose weight as other translations continue to supplant the King James in the American religious establishment. On the other hand, the language of the other LDS scriptures is King Jamesian. So although that language sounds increasingly archaic to modern readers, it is indelibly associated in the Mormon mind with a scriptural voice, reinforced across a wide spectrum of Mormon sacred texts. For these reasons, it is not likely that the King James Version, supplemented by Joseph's emendations, will ever cease to be the official version of their Bible for English speakers.

Out of thousands of changes the prophet made, the following examples suggest some of the more doctrinally significant. (Additions to and changes from the KJV are in italics.)

Genesis 15:9–12 "*And Abram said, Lord God, how wilt thou give me this land for an everlasting inheritance? And the Lord said, Though thou wast dead, yet am I not able to give it thee? And if thou shalt die, yet thou shalt possess it, for the day cometh, that the Son of Man shall live; but how can he live if he be not dead? he must first be quickened. And it came to pass, that Abram looked forth and saw the days of the Son of Man, and was glad, and his soul found rest,* and he believed in the Lord; and *the Lord* counted it unto him for righteousness." [In these changes, the Book of Mormon theme of pre-Christian knowledge of Christ is extended to the Old Testament patriarch Abraham.]

Genesis 17:11 "And I will establish *a covenant of circumcision with thee, and it shall be* my covenant between me and thee, and thy seed after thee, in their generations; *that thou mayest know for ever that children are not accountable before me until they are eight years old.*" [As indicated in the Book of Mormon and later confirmed by revelation in the *Doctrine and Covenants* (29:46–47), Mormons believe "that little children are redeemed from the foundation of the world through mine Only Begotten; Wherefore, they cannot sin" and baptism is unnecessary.]

Genesis 17:23 Then Abraham fell on his face and *rejoiced*, and said in his heart, *There* shall a child be born unto him that is an hundred years old, and Sarah that is ninety years old shall bear. [Abraham's laughing skepticism is transformed in Smith's revision into a celebratory affirmation.]

Exodus 34:1–2 "And the Lord said unto Moses, Hew thee two *other* tables of stone, like unto the first, and I will write upon *them* also, the words *of the law, according as they were written at the first on the* tables which thou brakest; *but it shall not be according to the first, for I will take away the priesthood out of their midst; therefore my holy order, and the ordinances thereof, shall not go before them; for my presence shall not go up in their midst, lest I destroy them. But I will give unto them the law as at the first, but it shall be after the law of a carnal commandment; for I have sworn in my wrath, that they shall not enter into my presence, into my rest, in the days of their pilgrimage.*" [The story of Israel's worship of the golden calf while Moses communes with God becomes in Smith's revision an account of how the fullness of the gospel and the blessings of the higher (Melchizedek) priesthood, entailed in the original stone tablets, were *replaced* by a lesser gospel known as the Mosaic law in consequence of their faithlessness.]

Matthew 17:10–14 "And Jesus answered and said unto them, Elias truly shall first come, and restore all things, *as the prophets have written.* . . . Then the disciples understood that he spake unto them of John the Baptist, *and also of another who should come and restore all things, as it is written by the prophets.* [Although Mormons understand Elias to be a prophet as well as a role (that of forerunner), most of them understand in these words an allusion to Joseph Smith specifically, and a confirmation of the extensive foreknowledge among the prophets of the latter-day Restoration.]

John 4:26 (KJV 4:24) "*For unto such hath* God *promised his* Spirit. And they *who* worship him must worship in spirit and in truth." [Recasting the phrase "God is Spirit" into this new language, Smith avoided that verse most directly at odds with LDS conceptions of an embodied Deity.]

1 Corinthians 7:1, 29 "Now concerning the things whereof ye wrote unto me, *saying,* It is good for a man not to touch a woman. . . . *But I speak unto you who are called unto the ministry. For* this I say, brethren, the time that remaineth is but short, *that ye shall be sent forth unto the ministry.* [The first change puts the endorsement of celibacy in the mouth of the Corinthians rather than Paul, and the subsequent interpolations suggest that Paul's counsel to avoid marriage pertains to imminently departing missionaries.]

Mummies and Manuscripts: The *Pearl of Great Price*

The year 1835 found Joseph and his circle of Saints gathered in two locations. The original scene of gathering, Kirtland, Ohio, was still presided over by Joseph Smith, but he was under increasing criticism from fellow leaders and many in the rank and file for his growing tendency to blur the lines of spiritual and secular counsel to his flock. In Missouri, mobs had already displaced the Mormon settlers from Jackson County and now tensions in Clay County were growing as well. In the midst of these circumstances, an entrepreneur from Pennsylvania, one Michael H. Chandler, passed through Kirtland with four Egyptian mummies and various scrolls of papyri. These mummies, along with seven others, had originated near the ancient city of Thebes, and been excavated under the direction of an Italian, Antonio Lebolo. Lebolo died in 1830, and his mummies found a new owner in Chandler a few years later. Having sold most of the group in the eastern United States, Chandler settled with Joseph Smith on the then hefty sum of $2,400 for the remaining four in early July.

Joseph immediately began working to translate the texts, though by what means he never made clear. Upon commencing, he announced that at least some of the papyri included the writings of the patriarch Abraham. What emerged next was a remarkable first-person account of Abraham fleeing an attempt on his life in Chaldea by Egyptian priests practicing human sacrifice. Rescued by an angel, he emigrates to Haran, then moves on to Canaan where God establishes his covenant with him. When famine comes to Canaan, Abraham departs for Egypt. Later Abraham recounts being taught celestial cosmology, and describes a vision in which he sees the premortal souls of many "noble and great ones" and a council where the plan of salvation is outlined and a Redeemer of the world chosen (Abraham 3). (This is the principal foundation for Mormon belief in the premortal existence of the human family.) Finally, the record narrates the creation story essentially as it reads in Genesis, but emphasizing the process as one of shaping and ordering by the Gods (a challenge to trinitarianism that Smith would elaborate later), rather than a creation ex nihilo (out of nothing) as in conventional Christian understanding. Smith also transcribed from the papyri three elaborate Egyptian illustrations.

Financial obstacles and a stormy history of forced migrations and persecution delayed publication of the translation until 1842, which occurred in serial form in the church newspaper, *Times and Seasons*. The next year, Smith promised more was forthcoming, but his death forestalled those plans. In 1851 the *Pearl of Great Price* was published, incorporating both the Book of Abraham and eight chapters constituting the Book of Moses. These latter portions include the vision of Moses revealed to Joseph in 1830 and mentioned above, along with Smith's retranslation of Genesis up to 6:13 (at which point God reveals to Noah his intended destruction of the earth). The Genesis material also incorporates the Enoch passages

Smith had revealed in 1830. The entire collection was canonized as church scripture in 1880. Later, Joseph's revision of Matthew 24 and an excerpt from his personal history were added to the volume.

As for the Egyptian manuscripts, after the death of the prophet's mother in 1856, the Smith family sold the mummies and papyri to one Abel Combs. Soon thereafter, they disappear from the record, and were supposed to have been destroyed in the Chicago Fire of 1871. In 1962 eleven fragments of the papyri were found to be in the possession of the New York Metropolitan Museum, and in 1967 the church acquired them. The church promptly published them, and translations followed quickly.

During Joseph Smith's lifetime, Egyptology was in its infancy. By 1967, the discipline was well established. Translated by modern Egyptologists, the fragments were judged by most to have no connection to the Abraham of the Bible, but to be fragments of an Egyptian text known as the Book of Breathings. What was a potentially damaging blow to Joseph Smith's credibility as a translator has elicited a number of responses from Mormon apologists. First, Mormons have pointed out that the few surviving fragments by no means represent the entire collection possessed and worked on by Joseph Smith. Evidence in fact suggests that from three-quarters to about seven-eighths or more of the original manuscript is still missing.[39] (One contemporary remembered one of the unrolled scrolls two rooms in length;[40] the surviving fragments are no more than a few square feet.) And both Joseph and contemporaries described the Book of Abraham originals as having extensive rubrics—that is, passages written in red ink. None of the Metropolitan remnants contain such writings.

Second, it has been pointed out that Joseph's translation may in reality have been something closer to a prompted revelation. "Though the connection between the papyri and the 'Book of Abraham' is unclear," writes Kent Jackson, "it appears that Joseph Smith's possession of the Egyptian texts influenced his attraction to things Egyptian and led to his bringing forth of the document concerning Abraham."[41] As with both the Book of Mormon and his revision of the Bible, Joseph Smith used the word *translation* to cover a range of inspired activity that did not always involve reworking of original texts.

Finally, what is beyond dispute are a number of striking parallels between Smith's version of the Moses and Abraham "translations," and numerous ancient texts discovered in the last century and more that were unavailable to Joseph Smith. The attempted sacrifice of Abraham is recounted in the Pseudo-Philo 6; his struggles against idolatry are described in Jubilees 12; and his vision of premortal spirits, God's dwelling place, and events in the Garden of Eden find striking parallels in the Apocalypse of Abraham.

While many secular scholars are scornful of anything connected with Joseph Smith and seerstones, others find his scriptural production harder to dismiss. The great Egyptologist Klaus Baer, for instance, wrote that the "Egyptian alphabet and grammar" Joseph derived from his study of the papyri "is not the kind of thing a man does who is perpetrating a fraud," and chided fellow Egyptologists for behaving like "pompous asses with a claim to infallibility" who indulged in "ill-considered snap judgments in dealing with Mormons."[42] Literary critic Harold Bloom has also referred to the astonishing parallels between these writings of Smith and ancient Jewish mystical texts (kabbalistic writings), saying "I can only attribute to his genius or daemon his uncanny recovery of elements in ancient Jewish theurgy."[43]

Mormon luminary Hugh Nibley has been indefatigable in finding intertextual corroboration for the antiquity and historical plausibility of the Abraham material, but also of the Book of Moses Smith produced, especially the sections on Enoch. One of the more moving—and striking—parts of this section, depicts God mourning over his creation prior to the great flood:

> And it came to pass that the God of Heaven looked upon the residue of the people, and he wept; and Enoch bore record of it . . . . And Enoch said unto the Lord: How is it that thou canst weep, seeing thou art holy, and from all eternity to all eternity? And were it possible that man could number the particles of the earth, yea, millions of earths like this, it would not be a beginning to the number of they creations; . . . how is it thou canst weep?

God responds by explaining that this human race is "the workmanship of mine own hand," that he gave them both knowledge and agency, and the commandment "that they should love one another and that they should choose me, their Father." Then the Lord

> told Enoch all the doings of the children of men; wherefore Enoch knew, and looked upon their wickedness, and their misery, and wept and stretched forth his arms, and his heart swelled wide as eternity; and his bowels yearned; and all eternity shook. (Moses 7:28–41)

This weeping God motif, Nibley points out, is found in apocryphal Enoch texts, as are a number of other elements in Smith's version. One of these is the "Son of Man" title, which appears nowhere in the Book of Mormon or *Pearl of Great Price*, except for the Enoch passages; the title is common in the Enoch texts found since Smith's day. And more dramatically, Smith's Enoch travels through the "land Mahujah." In the Aramaic fragments from Qumran, the place name appears repeatedly.[44] Even a non-Mormon scholar of the subject has been reported to have called the author of this Book of Moses "saturated in pseudepigraphal Enoch literature."[45]

Once little heralded or studied even by the LDS faithful, the publicity of the last few decades that the *Pearl of Great Price* has garnered has thrown it into greater prominence. Like the Book of Mormon, the *Pearl of Great Price* is now as enthusiastically embraced and touted as a sign of Joseph Smith's calling by Mormons, as it is considered prima facie cause for disdain by critics. Nibley captures a kind of quirky logic behind the opposite responses the book elicits. Addressing the apparent failure of Joseph to accurately translate the book of Abraham from the Egyptian papyri, he insists: "Of course Joseph Smith didn't know Egyptian. That is why we can safely say that the Book of Abraham is inspired."[46]

Notes

1. Wilford Woodruff, *Conference Reports of the General Conference of the Church of Jesus Christ of Latter-day Saints* (October 1897): 22–23.

2. "I have been laboring in this cause for eight years," he wrote in a letter published in *Messenger and Advocate* 1, no. 12 (September 1835): 179.

3. Joseph Smith Jr., *History of the Church of Jesus Christ of Latter-day Saints*, 7 vols., ed. James Mulholland et al. (Salt Lake City: Deseret, 1951), 1:32.

4. "Prophecy," in F. L. Cross and E. A. Livingstone, eds., *Oxford Dictionary of the Christian Church* (Oxford: Oxford University Press, 1997), 1336.

5. Abraham Heschel, *The Prophets* (New York: Harper and Row, 1962), xviii.

6. Alexander Campbell, "Delusions: An Analysis of the Book of Mormon," *Millennial Harbinger* 2 (7 February 1831): 85–96. Reprinted in part in Francis W. Kirkham, *A New Witness for Christ in America*, 2 vols. (Independence, Mo.: Zion's Printing and Publishing, 1951), 2:101–9.

7. Gilbert Wardlaw, *The Testimony of Scripture to the Obligations and Efficacy of Prayer* (Boston: Peirce and Williams, 1830), 8, 59, 97n.

8. J.F.C. Harrison, *The Second Coming: Popular Millenarianism, 1780–1850* (New Brunswick, N.J.: Rutgers University Press, 1979), 191. Cited in Gordon S. Wood, "Evangelical America and Early Mormonism," *New York History* 61 (October 1980): 380.

9. Strictly speaking, Lehi was of the tribe of Manasseh (Alma 10:3)—but he and his clan identified themselves as part of the kingdom of Judah, which incorporated remnants of many other tribes.

10. The remark represents one consensus between the debaters in a fictitious dialogue on the Book of Mormon, published in the *Times and Seasons*, 2, no. 18 (15 July 1841): 473.

11. "American Antiquities," *Times and Seasons* 3, no. 18 (15 July 1842): 860. As of 15 March 1842, Joseph Smith had assumed editorial responsibility for the paper, with John Taylor acting as managing editor.

12. Warren P. Aston, "Newly Found Altars from Nahom," *Journal of Book of Mormon Studies* 10, no. 2 (2001): 61.

13. Hugh W. Nibley, *Lehi in the Desert*, in *The Collected Works of Hugh Nibley*, 14– vols. (Provo, Utah: Deseret and FARMS, 1988), 5:4.

14. Nibley, *Lehi in the Desert*, 14.

15. William F. Albright to Grant S. Heward (25 July 1966). Cited in John A. Tvedtnes, John Gee, and Matthew Roper, "Book of Mormon Names Attested in Ancient Hebrew Inscriptions," *Journal of Book of Mormon Studies* 9, no. 1 (2000): 45.

16. Daniel C. Peterson, "Is the Book of Mormon True? Notes on the Debate," in Noel B. Reynolds, ed., *Book of Mormon Authorship Revisited: The Evidence for Ancient Origins* (Provo, Utah: FARMS, 1997), 156.

17. Peterson, "Is the Book of Mormon True?" 145–46. Terence L. Szink provides evidence of an even earlier provenance, third millennium B.C., in "Further Evidence of a Semitic Alma," *Journal of Book of Mormon Studies* 8, no. 1 (1999). Of course, Hebrew script at the time did not include vowels, so "Alma" is a reconstruction from 'lm'. It is, however, the reconstruction favored by Yigael Yadin himself, as well as Paul Hoskisson, "Alma as a Hebrew Name," *Journal of Book of Mormon Studies* 7, no. 1 (1998): 72–73.

18. Welch describes the discovery in an interview by James P. Bell, "Taking the Stand," *This People* (February–March 1987): 49–63.

19. Carl Mosser and Paul Owen, "Mormon Apologetic, Scholarship and Evangelical Neglect: Losing the Battle and Not Knowing It?" *Trinity Journal* (1998): 181, 185, 189. James White is an evangelical who does not share Owen's and Mosser's respect for the work at FARMS. An author himself of anti-Mormon works, White provides some anecdotal evidence to support his claim that FARMS scholarship is at times smug, ad hominem, and misapplied. See his "The Impossible Task of Mormon Apologetics," *Christian Research Journal* 19, no. 1 (summer 1996): 28–35. Of this article, Mosser and Owen say it is "nothing more than straw man argumentation" (202). The only other example of an attempt to refute Mormon scholarship they can identify is *Behind the Mask of Mormonism: From its Early Schemes to its Modern Deceptions* by John Ankerberg and John Weldon (Eugene, Oreg.: Harvest House, 1992). They dismiss it as "ugly, unchristian, and misleading" (203).

20. David P. Wright, "'In Plain Terms that We May Understand': Joseph Smith's Transformation of Hebrews in Alma 12–13," in Brent Lee Metcalfe, ed., *New Approaches to the Book of Mormon* (Salt Lake City: Signature, 1993), 165n.

21. Dan Vogel, *The Word of God: Essays on Mormon Scripture* (Salt Lake City: Signature, 1990), viii–ix.

22. It is hard to take seriously this writer's suggestion that Mormons should "emphasize the religious and spiritual values in the Book of Mormon" when he simultaneously declares the book fraudulent and Joseph Smith's contributions "as a religious teacher . . . not only useless, but mischievous beyond human comprehending." Brigham D. Madsen, "Reflections on LDS Disbelief in the Book of Mormon as History," *Dialogue* 30, no. 3 (fall 1997): 95–97.

23. Wright, "'In Plain Terms That We May Understand.'" Cited in ibid., 94. Wright was excommunicated from the Mormon Church some time after his article was published.

24. Ian G. Barber, "Beyond the Literalist Constraint: Personal Reflections on Mormon Scripture and Religious Interpretation," *Sunstone* 20, no. 3 (October 1997): 21.

25. Anthony A. Hutchinson, "The Word of God is Enough: The Book of Mormon as Nineteenth-Century Scripture," in Dan Vogel, ed., *The Word of God: Essays on Mormon Scripture* (Salt Lake City: Signature, 1990), 5.

26. In reference to the extensive revelation known as "the Vision" (DC 76), Philo Dibble recorded that "during the time that Joseph and Sidney were in the spirit and saw the heavens open, there were other men in the room, perhaps twelve, among whom I was one during a part of the time—probably two-thirds of the time,—I saw the glory and felt the power, but did not see the vision." *Juvenile Instructor* 27(1892):303–4.

27. Smith, *History*, 1:222; Peter Crawley, "A Bibliography of the Church of Jesus Christ of Latter-day Saints in New York, Ohio, and Missouri," *BYU Studies* 12, no. 4 (summer 1972): 480–82.

28. John W. Welch and David Whittaker, "Mormonism's Open Canon: Some Historical Reflections on its Religious Limits and Potentials" (Provo, Utah: FARMS, 1986), 10.

29. These lectures, presented at the School of the Prophets in Kirtland, Ohio, were probably not authored by Joseph Smith, though he doubtless approved of their published form.

30. Heading to DC 76 (Smith, *History*, 1:245).

31. Smith, *History*, 1:238.

32. "To the Elders of the Church," *Messenger and Advocate* 2, no. 3 (December 1835): 229. The third sign was "the covenants given to the Latter-day Saints."

33. Smith, *History*, 1:324.

34. *Times and Seasons* 6:803.

35. Emma Smith Bidamon to Joseph Smith III, 10 February 1867, archives of RLDS, cited in *Joseph Smith's New Translation of the Bible*, intr. F. Henry Edwards (Independence, Mo.: Herald, 1970), 11.

36. George Q. Cannon, *The Life of Joseph Smith, the Prophet* (Salt Lake City: Juvenile Instructor Office, 1888), 142.

37. Smith, *History*, 1:341.

38. J. Reuben Clark, in *Why the King James Version* (Salt Lake City: Deseret, 1956), gives this reason on page 28.

39. Estimates of non-Mormon scholar Klaus Baer and Mormon Egyptologist John Gee are in Boyd Peterson, *Hugh Nibley* (Salt Lake City: Greg Kofford, 2002), 320.

40. Hugh Nibley et al., "The Joseph Smith Egyptian Papyri: Translations and Interpretations," *Dialogue* 3, no. 2 (1968): 101.

41. Kent P. Jackson, "The Sacred Literature of the Latter-day Saints," in Ernest S. Frerichs, ed., *The Bible and Bibles in America* (Atlanta: Scholars, 1988), 183.

42. Cited in Peterson, *Hugh Nibley*, 320–22.

43. Harold Bloom, *The American Religion: The Emergence of the Post-Christian Nation* (New York: Simon & Schuster, 1992), 101.

44. Nibley, *Enoch the Prophet*, in *The Collected Works of Hugh Nibley* (Provo, Utah: Deseret and FARMS, 1986), 69, 277–78.

45. Nibley quotes Matthew Black, Enoch scholar and professor of divinity and biblical studies at the University of St. Andrews in Scotland. Letter to Robert F. Smith, 11 January 1976, cited in Peterson, *Hugh Nibley,* 328. Apocryphal refers to texts produced by early Christians, but never canonized as part of the Bible. Pseudepigraphal refers to Jewish or Christian texts produced from 200 B.C. to A.D. 200 that claim to be inspired texts authored by famous Old Testament figures.

46. Hugh Nibley, Letter to "Brother Baker," 30 October 1986, in Peterson, *Hugh Nibley,* 328.

Chapter 5

Temple, Church, and Family: LDS Worship and Organization

It was my endeavor to so organize the Church, that the brethren might eventually be independent of every encumbrance beneath the celestial kingdom, by bonds and covenants of mutual friendship, and mutual love.
—Joseph Smith, *History of the Church*

The organization of the Mormons is the most nearly perfect piece of social mechanism with which I have ever, in any way, come in contact, excepting alone the German army.
—Richard Ely in *Harper's,* 1903

Sunday Worship

On the first Sunday of every month, Mormons typically attend a special worship service called Fast and Testimony Meeting. They will have fasted the two previous meals, and contributed the value of those meals—or several times their value—to the church's "fast offering fund," to be administered by the local leader (bishop or branch president) for the care of the poor and needy in the congregation or for nonmembers within local boundaries. After the usual greetings, hymn, and invocation, the leader conducting the meeting turns the remainder of the time over to the congregation for "the bearing of testimonies." What unfolds next illustrates continuity at the deepest level of the Mormon experience from Joseph Smith to the present day. When young Smith returned from his first epiphany in the Sacred Grove, he said that his words to his mother were, "*I have learned for myself* that Presbyterianism is not true," and summed up the experience for posterity with the observation that "I have found the testimony of James to be true—that a man who lacked wisdom might ask of God, and obtain" (emphasis added).[1]

In a testimony meeting members rise, as the urge strikes them, to proclaim the assurance they believe the Spirit has granted them of core LDS truths: that Joseph Smith was a prophet of God, that President Gordon B. Hinckley is one today, that the Book of Mormon is true, and that Jesus Christ is their personal Savior. In addition to mini-conversion narratives, testimonies take other personal and at times idiosyncratic directions as well, often including evidences of God's hand recently encountered or moral precepts newly learned or relearned. They not uncommonly contain as much of testimonial as testimony, expressing love for family and friends.

The effect of these services in welding a close-knit community and forging a distinctive Mormon identity would be hard to exaggerate. The public sharing of sacred experience, the emotional openness and vulnerability produced by such collective participation, the uninhibited expressions of love and affection, the affirmation of uniquely held and uniquely received heavenly truth, and the socialization of the young and newly converted into a particular vocabulary of religious language and religious experience may do more than anything else to create the remarkable sense of spiritual kinship and unity that characterizes the Latter-day Saint people.

An essential component of this "testimony" is an emphasis on the church's exclusivist claims. In the opening section of the *Doctrine and Covenants*, the Lord declares through Joseph Smith that the Church of Jesus Christ of Latter-day Saints is "the only true and living church upon the face of the whole earth with which I, the Lord, am well pleased" (1:30). Such absolutist claims are not conducive to ecumenicalism, but are inseparably wedded to the church's history and origin. "I was answered that I must join none of them," Joseph had been told when asking God which church he should join, "for they were all wrong; and . . . all their creeds were an abomination in his sight" (JS-H 1:19).

The sense that they are possessed of a unique stewardship for pristine Christianity, and that the LDS faith is therefore the only "true and living church," accounts for the urgency Mormons feel to spread the gospel even among peoples already heavily Christianized, but it also accounts in large measure for the feeling of spiritual solidarity among members. While nonmembers can interpret these claims as elitist and chauvinistic, Latter-day Saints believe they are merely echoing the Lord's own endorsement, and to suggest otherwise would be to deny the very necessity for the church's restoration under Joseph Smith.

Interdependency and interaction are fostered at a number of other levels as well. Wards are organized along strict geographical lines, rather like Catholic parishes but with some crucial differences. First, Mormon membership records are scrupulously maintained, and individual member records often arrive at a new ward house before a relocating member does. Those records alert ward leaders to new members in the area, and indicate the availability of active Mormons for local service. Having no professional clergy at the local level, almost all Mormons have some official position ("calling") they fill in the local ward. Mormons attending outside of their assigned geographical unit, therefore, would have no membership record, receive no calling, and therefore could hardly worship or attend services as fully participating members of the congregation. It is therefore rare, and simply foreign to Mormon culture, to resist attending the assigned ward and shop for one with a more congenial leader or membership.

This geographical organization facilitates ward organization, stabilizes ward population, and expedites the process by which relocating members are assimilated into a new congregation. To move to a new ward is automatically to acquire at the same time an identity as member of a new community. Wards (and the smaller units called branches) are organized into stakes (like Catholic dioceses). Generally five to twelve wards and branches comprising a total of two to seven thousand members constitute a stake, which is presided over by a president and two counselors, assisted by an advisory group of twelve high councilmen. While Mormons congregate occasionally by stakes for leadership training or special sessions, their public religious lives are almost entirely organized around activity and worship at the ward or branch level.

The focus of LDS Sunday worship is the ordinance of the Lord's Supper, which Mormons call simply "the sacrament." Two priests, usually youths of sixteen or seventeen, read the only rote prayers used in Mormon worship services, the first a blessing on the broken bread, and the second a blessing on the water, which is dispensed in small cups. (Water was substituted for wine by commandment four months after the church's organization.)[2] First the bread, and then the water, are passed to every member of the congregation, usually by twelve- and thirteen-year-old boys who are "deacons."

Latter-day Saints believe that by participating in the sacrament, they are fulfilling the Lord's injunction to partake of those emblems in remembrance of his body and blood, as enjoined at the Last Supper. Specifically, they consider the occasion to be a renewal of covenants (or rehearsal for covenants, in the case of young children) they made individually at the time of baptism. Members frequently cite a Book of Mormon passage as expressing those covenants that implicitly accompany that decision to be baptized: "as ye are desirous to come into the fold of God, and to be called his people, and are willing to bear one another's burdens, . . . to stand as witnesses of God at all times and in all things, and in all places . . . if this be the desire of your hearts, what have you against being baptized in the name of the Lord as a witness before him that ye have entered into a covenant with him that ye will serve him and keep his commandments?" (Mosiah 18:8–10). The words of the sacrament prayers that consecrate the bread and water include injunctions to remember the atoning sacrifice of Christ, manifest in his broken body and spilled blood. The principal act of weekly worship for Latter-day Saints is therefore the silent gesture of gratitude, reverent contemplation, and recommitment that accompanies the administration of those emblems. Speaking of the centrality of this ritual in LDS religion, one apostle has written that "every ordinance of the gospel focuses in one way or another on the atonement of the Lord Jesus Christ, . . . [but] this particular ordinance with all its symbolism and imagery comes to us more readily and more repeatedly than any other in our life. It comes in what has been called "the most sacred, the most holy, of all the meetings of the Church."[3]

On Sundays other than the first, the worship service (Sacrament Meeting) features "talks" rather than the Fast Sunday testimonies or the sermons typical of other denominations. Speakers are chosen from the adults and young people of the ward. Obviously, such a system means quality varies widely, but virtually everyone takes a turn in the rotation. Usually, one youth speaker will be followed by two adult speakers. Prayer and congregational singing both introduce and conclude the meeting.

LDS worship services are therefore strikingly plain. No formal liturgy or recitations take place, the messages are of uneven polish delivered by youth and laypersons, and the Lord's Supper is administered quietly by twelve- to eighteen-year old boys. Because of larger than normal family size in the Mormon faith, and a family-centered worship, services in Mormon chapels tend to be characterized by a level of background noise from cooing infants and fussy children that can be alienating to visitors. Mormon churches are entirely lacking in crosses, candles, and most religious iconography, and chapels are almost sterile in their simplicity. A basketball gym (called a "cultural hall") is typically adjacent to the chapel, set off by a folding curtain. This ambience, combined with the fact that Mormons reserve their most sacred rites for the precincts of special buildings called temples, can create the perception that Mormon worship lacks the reverence and somberness that characterize certain varieties of Christianity.

In the Sunday School classes that follow immediately after Sacrament Meeting, as in all other ward organizations, teaching, music directing, and all other positions are staffed by members "called" to their positions by the bishop (or the branch president in smaller congregations). Latter-day Saints believe that the process represents a literal calling from God, issued through an inspired bishop. (The bishop is always a male, since Mormons believe in a male-only priesthood.) As President Spencer W. Kimball explained, "when [bishops] have prayed and fasted and thought and pondered and weighed and measured [individuals] for a long time, there come impressions to them, and finally the bishopric calls in a brother [or sister] and asks him [or her] to [serve], called of God through the bishopric, through the proper channels."[4] Subsequent to the issuing of a call, members are sustained in their callings in Sacrament Meetings. More than a formality, this procedure represents a public commitment on the part of all members to support the individual in his or her calling, manifest by their raising their right hands in token of agreement. Then the individual is "set apart" to his or her calling in the bishop's office, receiving a special blessing and the necessary spiritual gifts and powers and access to revelation appropriate to the new position.

Members serving in the LDS Church are thus possessed of the confidence that their calling originates with God and is transmitted through an inspired leader; they receive public show of support in their new undertaking; and they receive a blessing that fortifies them and inspires them with the confidence that they have been made spiritually adequate to the task.

Bishops are themselves called through a similar process, with the stake presidency making the recommendation to the church's First Presidency and the Quorum of the Twelve, who approve every candidate. Like all other ward and even stake leaders, the bishop himself is uncompensated for his service, which averages around twenty hours per week in a typical ward. He is the presiding authority over his congregation, conducts Sacrament Meetings and other services (though he usually rotates that task with his two counselors), performs marriages (though not of the temple variety), conducts funerals, oversees the staffing of all ward organizations (as many as a hundred positions or more, typically), does pastoral counseling, visits ward members, attends training meetings and conducts ward leadership meetings, supervises welfare assistance to the needy, interviews temple-goers, and spends what time he can participating in the activities of the young people in his ward. He serves up to five or six years or more. The bishop's calling is probably the most time-consuming in the ward, and the most spiritually and emotionally taxing as well. But almost every adult and many youth besides have some calling that requires a commitment of time, often in addition to Sunday service. Closest to the calling of bishop in scope of influence and time invested is probably the Relief Society president. As the head of the church's women's organization (founded in 1842 under Joseph Smith's direction), the Relief Society president is on the front lines of assessing welfare needs in the ward. She may be more likely than the bishop to be connected to lines of communication that alert her to sick members, financial crises, or domestic problems. In her role as supervisor of the visiting teaching program (the assigning of female couples to visit every adult woman in the ward), she, as much as anyone, has her finger on the pulse of the congregation.

Following the seventy-minute Sacrament Meeting and fifty-minute Sunday School, women attend an hour-long meeting of the Relief Society, and the men and boys over twelve retire to Priesthood Meeting. Going to church for Mormons, then, means attending a three-hour block of meetings in which most members are, to varying degrees, active participants as well as passive worshipers. (Prior to 1980, those meetings were interspersed through the Sabbath day and during the week. The decision to consolidate was initially a response to the energy crisis of that era, but became permanent policy.)

Ward Organization and Leadership

For those in local leadership positions, the day is even longer. In a typical ward with a 9:00 A.M. Sacrament Meeting, the bishop might meet with his two counselors, an executive secretary, and a ward clerk, at 6:30 A.M. After discussing ward needs, considering new callings, and reviewing the agenda for the worship service, they would wrap up the meeting at 7:30. At that time, they would open the doors to the waiting members of the Ward Council. This expanded leadership group includes the elders quorum president, the high priest group, the ward mission leader, the young men's president, the young women's president, the primary president, the Relief Society president, the Sunday School president, the ward activities chairman, and perhaps the missionary pair or two serving in the ward as well as the ward's high councilman.

The elders quorum president presides over those men in the ward who are elders or prospective elders—usually most men in the ward between the ages of eighteen and fifty or sixty. He supervises home teaching in the quorum (the male counterpart to visiting teaching), organizes service and teaching in the group, and is in general responsible for the temporal and spiritual welfare of his members and their families. The presidents of the young men's and young women's organizations (a man and a woman, respectively) supervise the youth between the ages of twelve and eighteen, who meet during the third block of Sunday meetings, and one weeknight a week. The primary president is the woman who is in charge of the children's auxiliary, whose members range from nursery age through eleven. They meet during the second and third hours of Sunday services. Also under her direction are weekly activity nights for the children, yearly sacrament programs, and special activity days throughout the year. The Sunday School president and ward activities chair function in ways their titles suggest, and the ward mission leader coordinates missionary work between the full-time missionaries and ward members, and organizes and conducts baptism services. Wards have a member of the stake high council assigned to them as an advisor and liaison with the stake, who attends leadership meetings and worship services once or twice a month with the assigned ward.

The ward council serves as the principal mechanism through which important communications from Salt Lake or within the ward are transmitted, the work of ministry is correlated, ward goals and progress are assessed, individual needs are discussed, and particular assignments and responsibilities are assigned to the local leaders. As the name suggests, the council also exists to advise and counsel the bishop, though votes are not taken and the authority to decide virtually all matters of ward policy is his alone as the presiding officer. Meeting at least once a month, the ward council deliberates until the time for Sacrament Meeting approaches. On other Sundays, stripped-down versions of the council, operating as the priesthood executive committee, or the ward welfare council, meet to discuss a more limited agenda.

Beyond the Sunday Routine

In addition to Sunday meetings that tax almost anyone's post-Puritan capacity for endurance, early morning "seminary" classes challenge the commitment of LDS teenagers. In areas of the church with sufficient membership to justify the program, high-school age Mormons spend an hour before school classes each weekday attending seminary in either the meetinghouse or a private home (or in western states, often in a class building adjoining the high school during regular class hours). There, instructed by a volunteer (or a paid full-time instructor in Mormon-saturated areas), students complete a four-year course of study in church history and doctrine, the Book of Mormon, the Old Testament, and the New Testament.

Adults too have church commitments that extend into the week. If testimony meetings are one crucial factor in explaining the emotional and spiritual cohesiveness of Mormon culture, the home teaching and visiting teaching program would be another. Every adult male, and every boy fourteen and older, is assigned a number of ward families—usually two to six—to whom he is expected to minister on a monthly basis. Serving in a companionship, these home teachers bring an uplifting message or informal greeting to their families, ascertain family or individual needs, serve as liaisons to the ward leaders, and generally provide friendship and support to those they visit. Many Mormons facing crises, major or minor emergencies, or a simple doctrinal question are apt to call their home teacher before anyone else. Mormon culture is rife with instances of home teachers called to home or hospital to administer to the sick, assist members stranded with car problems, or help repair a member's roof.

On average, most active Mormons are likely to visit at least half their assigned families in any given month. Overlapping this program, and generally executed with even greater consistency, is the visiting teaching program, coordinated by the Relief Society and involving adult women visiting other adult women of the ward. Although socials and service projects and worship services provide the same opportunities for social contact found in other religious traditions, home and visiting teaching are the most reliable, comprehensive, and perhaps more significantly, horizontally structured mechanism in Mormonism for fostering personal interaction and reciprocal service among members.

Like other Christians, Latter-day Saints do not confine religious practice to Sunday worship. On Monday evenings, Mormons throughout the world observe Family Home Evening. The practice has roots in a 1915 declaration of President Joseph F. Smith, that parents should convene a weekly meeting with their families to teach the gospel and share time together. He declared that "if the Saints obey this counsel, we promise that great blessings will result. Love at home and obedience to parents will increase. Faith will be developed in the hearts of the youth of Israel, and they will gain power to combat the evil influences and temptations which beset them."[5] But it was not until 1964 that the church renewed the initiative, providing formal lesson manuals; then in 1971 church leaders standardized the program by designating Monday evenings for its observance. Parents typically gather their children, begin with a song and prayer, teach—or encourage children to teach—a short gospel lesson, then follow with games and refreshments.

In addition to the semi-formal Family Home Evening, daily family prayer and scripture study are strongly urged by church leaders. It is hard to measure the extent to which members follow such counsel, but the admonition is a constant theme in General Conferences (the semi-annual two-day marathon of sermons by General Authorities broadcast from Salt Lake City), in church publications, and in Sacrament Meeting talks. Under the presidency of Ezra Taft Benson, the Book of Mormon in particular received unprecedented emphasis in the religion and lives of the Latter-day Saints. He encouraged members to hold a daily devotional, in which the Book of Mormon would be read throughout the year. Insisting that its study should supersede reading of other scripture, he urged that members "need to read daily from the pages of the book that will get a man 'nearer to God by abiding by its precepts, than by any other book.'"[6]

The Temple

Personal or family scripture study, home teaching activity, and service in ward or stake callings—all these forms of religious activity serve to gauge levels of religious commitment on the part of Latter-day Saints. But the most important bellwether of a member's discipleship is generally held by Mormons to be temple worship. In the Mormon view, as church apostle Boyd K. Packer has said, "all roads lead to the temple."[7] As is the case with most religions and denominations, one can distinguish between practicing and nonpracticing members. Mormons prefer the designations "active" and "less active." But in addition to that fairly mundane distinction, Mormons may be further divided into two classes, with no clear counterpart in other faith groups: temple attendees and non-temple attendees (or "endowed" and "unendowed" members).

As we have seen, Joseph made the temple and its ordinances an increasing focus of his work of restoration in the final years of his life. As Joseph drew together the threads of Latter-day Saint theology, uniting premortal existence, mortal probation, and exaltation into a grand scheme of human progress, the temple became the sacred space where these realms converge in dynamic interaction. In the fully evolved temple ceremony, participants are reminded of their history as spirit children in a premortal world. They witness the reenactment of man's fall and redemption, and enter into ordinances, covenants, and obligations that extend to them an opportunity for eternal progress and progeny in the eternal worlds.

Like many of their fellow Christians, Mormons believe that faith in Christ, repentance, baptism, and the gift of the Holy Ghost are essential principles and ordinances of salvation. Unlike them, they believe that additional ordinances performed only in the temple prepare mankind for the fullest blessings and most glorious destiny that God makes available to the human family. Only after being "endowed" in the temple and "sealed" to a husband or wife through the priesthood power restored by Elijah, do Mormons believe they have complied with the full range of ordinances necessary for salvation. It still remains for them to live a life of devotion and faithfulness to their temple covenants—which is one reason why Mormons return frequently to renew them in the temple.

Temple worship for Mormons, then, has varied meanings. It refers to the act of faithful compliance with ordinances they believe to be every bit as imperative as Christ's command to be baptized for the remission of sins. Going to the temple also represents, for Mormons, one of the purest forms of service they may render in this life. This is because after their first temple ceremonies, subsequent participation is generally the vicarious performance of ordinances for those who have died. In this way, Latter-day Saints serve as "saviors on Mount Zion," rendering essential service for those who cannot perform the ordinances for themselves. As Joseph Smith described this principle of responsibility for temple work,

> The greatest responsibility in this world that God has laid upon us is to seek after our dead. The apostle says, "They without us cannot be made perfect"; for it is necessary that the sealing power should be in our hands to seal our children and our dead for the fulness of the dispensation of times—a dispensation to meet the promises made by Jesus Christ before the foundation of the world for the salvation of man.[8]

In earlier LDS history, the scarcity of temples made it difficult for most Saints outside Utah to attend them. Travel to a temple was often a once in a lifetime experience, the journey made with the devotion and sacrifice of a Muslim making an arduous and costly pilgrimage to Mecca. With the proliferation of temple-building presided over by Gordon B. Hinckley, the vast majority of Latter-day Saints now live within a 200-mile radius of a temple. Endowed members are likely to do "temple work," as it is called, anywhere from once a week to once or twice a year.

The exclusivity of LDS temple rituals has been a source of frequent tensions and misunderstandings between LDS members and the larger community. In 1870, a U.S. senator stood in the Senate to report hysterical rumors "that an altar of sacrifice was actually built . . . in the temple block, upon which human sacrifices were to be made."[9] The Mormon practice of holding public tours of temples before they are dedicated has defused some of the silliest of such allegations, and defectors from the faith have long since revealed the details of Mormon temple worship, tempering much of the sensationalism but not all the resentment that restrictions on temple access can invite. Even to nonmembers willing to recognize the difference between sacred privacy and exclusionary secrecy, the barriers can be painful. This is especially the case in Mormon temple weddings. In most cultures, a wedding is a time for extravagant celebration and communal participation. Mormon temple weddings generally have very few celebrants—twenty to fifty—and are limited to those with valid temple recommends permitting them entry into the sacred precincts. This means that even nearest family members may be unable to attend the wedding of an LDS son, daughter, sibling, or grandchild. The ceremony itself entails a few remarks by a temple "sealer" or officiator, and a brief exchange of vows across an altar. The entire affair lasts only a few minutes. Brevity and simplicity, however, are in this case seen by Mormons as accentuating, rather than diminishing, the sanctity of the occasion. And while it is true that almost all Christians consider marriage a sacrament, Mormons may have good reason to consider the event with even more than usual solemnity. Not only is the rite considered the last step necessary for candidacy to exaltation, but the eternal rather than earthly duration of the relationship must give even the youngest, most starry-eyed couple pause. Believing that the human soul has an eternal past as well as future, and that marriage does indeed make one flesh out of two, marriage can aptly be considered by the Latter-day Saint as the event that divides his or her eternal existence in twain, and marks the first day of a new identity that will never end.

Church Organization Beyond the Ward

With Sunday meetings, weekly youth meetings, early morning seminary, temple worship, home teaching, and other service and commitments, it may be no coincidence that faithful Latter-day Saints are referred to as "active" Mormons. As we have seen, most members also fulfill a church calling that may require substantial time commitments as well. From the nursery leader to the bishop and stake president, these callings are unremunerated and undertaken in addition to private careers. This level of commitment is also evident at the next unit of church organization after the stake, which is the area, presided over by an area presidency (a president and his two counselors). These presidencies are also members of the church's Quorums of Seventy, and are called to serve in particular geographic areas for terms ranging from three to five years.

Higher in the church hierarchy than the Area Authorities, or Area Seventies, is the Second Quorum of Seventy. Members of this group are typically called for five years, but they have churchwide jurisdiction, hence the term *General Authority*. They serve in area presidencies, travel widely, train and supervise stake presidents, and administer other church business. The First Quorum of Seventy consists of a presidency (over all Seventies) of seven men, and several dozen other General Authorities. They abandon their professions or businesses to serve full-time until age seventy, which in practice generally means terms ranging from five to twenty-five years. While it is true that Mormons have no paid clergy at the congregational level, members of the First and Second Quorums of Seventy (like three-year mission presidents, who preside over full-time missionaries) do receive a living allowance, the amount of which is not made public, but is generally believed to be modest.

Finally, there is the Quorum of the Twelve Apostles (or, "The Twelve"). These men are called to be "special witnesses of Christ" in all the world. Like the prophet, they are formally sustained twice a year by the general membership as "prophets, seers, and revelators." Their number includes former lawyers, educators, and businessmen, and they serve for life. The only church leaders with greater authority are the members of the First Presidency of the church, which consists of the prophet or president of the church, and his counselors. (Usually the president has two counselors, but he has at times had three or more.) These men also receive a living allowance for their service.

When Joseph Smith was martyred in 1844, the principle of prophetic succession had by no means been fully developed. In one sense, Joseph's status as prophet was without modern precedent and has found no full and subsequent reiteration, though church members do regard his successors as prophets who lead the church by divine guidance. But when Mormons refer to "the prophet" in any past sense, they are referring to Joseph as certainly as Muslims mean Muhammad. Joseph's status is formally as well as culturally established. "Joseph Smith, *the* Prophet and Seer of the Lord," as an official statement calls him even after his death, "has done more, save Jesus only, for the salvation of men in this world, than any other man that ever lived in it" (DC 135:3). His role in opening a new dispensation through a cascade of revelations, receiving priesthood authority and keys, founding the church, and translating the Book of Mormon is without parallel among subsequent Mormon leaders. Nevertheless, with the church firmly established as an institution in 1830, the role of prophet was transformed from an informal designation of special spiritual authority to a formal ecclesiastical office. "Behold," decreed a revelation on the day the church was organized, "there shall be a record kept among you; and in it thou shalt be called a seer, a translator, a prophet, an apostle of Jesus Christ" (DC 21:1). Eventually, Joseph would subscribe himself more simply, "prophet and seer of the Church of Jesus Christ of Latter-day Saints" (DC 127:12), and was considering the question of his successor in a church he clearly considered a durable institution under God's direction.

Young assumed leadership of the church in his capacity as president of the Quorum of the Twelve Apostles, but only after leading the greatest migration in American history and serving as de facto leader of his people for more than three years was he designated president of the church (on 5 December 1847). John Taylor would again wait three years, and Wilford Woodruff two, before assuming the title of their predecessor. Only with the death of Woodruff would the principle of succession be both clearly assumed and promptly acted upon. From Lorenzo Snow's ordination to the present, the senior member of the Quorum of the Twelve is understood to be the divinely intended successor to the presidency, and he is duly ordained to the position within days of his predecessor's death and henceforth regarded by members as God's living prophet.

Two facts result from this pattern of succession to the leadership of the Mormon Church. First, ever since the death of Brigham Young, the transition from one tenure to the next has been seamless and devoid of politicking and uncertainty. Barring unexpected deaths, church leaders transition predictably and consistently through positions of increasing seniority in the Quorum, receiving final training and experience as president of that group before moving on to direct the entire church. Second, the presiding official of the Mormon Church, like the apostles in general, tends to be aged, and the church leadership has often been characterized as a gerontocracy. It is true that church presidents typically serve into their 90s. David O. McKay died at 96. Joseph Fielding Smith served from age 93 to 95. Harold B. Lee was a relatively young and healthy 73, but died after a year and a half in the post. Spencer W. Kimball assumed the role at 78, but was renowned for a level of energy that kept younger colleagues panting to keep pace, until the final few years before his death at age 90. Ezra Taft Benson served until 94, though he was incapacitated at the end of his tenure as well. After the 9-month presidency of 86-year-old Howard W. Hunter, Gordon B. Hinckley became president at the age of 84. Even so, he is easily one of the last century's most dynamic, vigorous Mormon presidents, maintaining a hectic pace well into his 90s.

A few voices in the church have clamored for an abandonment of a system that works to perpetuate an increasingly aged leadership. Beginning in 1978, the church began the practice of granting emeritus status to some aging General Authorities, but that practice has not been extended to members of the Quorum of the Twelve. Nor is it likely to ever be, given their unique position as potential heirs of the presidency. Mormons would prefer to allow God the prerogative of winnowing out the top leadership through natural causes, than to meddle in the process. Given the stupendous growth of the church in the twentieth century, one would be hard pressed to argue that the church has been crippled by a system that values experience over youthfulness.

The LDS Welfare System

The foremost economic historian of Mormonism has pointed out that many distinguished observers (Weber and Schmoller in Germany, Bousquet in France, Katherine Coman and Frederick Jackson Turner in the United States) have found the "most startling aspect of Mormonism" to be disappointingly unsensationalisitic. It is "not the practice of plural marriage, not the belief in a highly personal God, not even the restoration of biblical Christianity or the Book of Mormon or the belief that Joseph Smith received visitations from Heavenly Beings, but the exaltation of economics and economic welfare into an important, if not indispensable, element of religious salvation."[10] That is why the LDS welfare system is integral to the very structure of the church, and inseparable from church practice.

The sixth prophet of the church, Joseph F. Smith, taught that "a religion which has not the power to save people temporally and make them prosperous and happy here on earth, cannot be depended upon to save them spiritually and exalt them in the life to come."[11] One researcher found that of 112 revelations announced by Joseph Smith, "eighty-eight dealt partly or entirely with matters that were economic in nature," and concluded that "Mormonism, though a religion, is largely, if not primarily, an economic movement, at least insofar as it offers to the world anything that is new."[12]

Mormonism has long been renowned for taking care of its needy. In 1976, the Teton Dam in Idaho collapsed, releasing a 50-foot-high wall of water upon the communities below. The flood did a billion dollars' worth of damage, but the speed and efficiency of the Mormon response to the disaster became a subject of national press coverage. In localities throughout the area, stake presidents called bishops, bishops called elders quorum presidents and high priest group leaders, who in turn called home teaching companionships. Such clear, economical, and regularly employed lines of organizational communication made it possible to turn out between thirty and forty-five thousand volunteers almost at once.

When Hurricane Andrew devastated Florida during the summer of 2002, the response was equally amazing. As one newspaper reported,

> The Mormon Church mobilized like a mighty army, fixing 3,700 homes, a synagogue and a Pentecostal church and dumping 2,100 truckloads of debris. The Mormons sent a "spearhead unit," a tractor-trailer with food, water, tools and bedding from its Atlanta base before the storm hit South Florida, setting up even as Andrew left. . . . [They] set up distribution centers in Kendall and Homestead. Living out of tents, the Mormons worked in crews of seven. They filled immediate needs from the Bishops' Storehouse, a warehouse in Davie stocked by South Florida's 18,000 church members. To coordinate efforts, the Homestead Stake Center asked for 10 Spanish translators, says church welfare official Albert Benzion of Miramar. He found 100.[13]

Of course, Mormonism's experience with disaster relief has a long history. A stake president evoked the precedent of the great migration west of thousands of Mormon refugees when he matter-of-factly described LDS relief efforts after Hurricane Andrew: "we organized ourselves, in accordance with the scriptures, with 'captains of hundreds, captains of fifties, captains of tens.' We deployed our members in various parts of the neighborhoods."[14] In 1831, when Joseph Smith directed the New York Saints to gather to Ohio, he was imposing some two hundred transient, frequently destitute members on about three hundred converts who were already settled and established in the Kirtland area. Borrowing loosely from a New Testament model of early saints who had "all things in common" (Acts 4:32), Joseph instituted the Law of Consecration, according to which members covenanted to "remember the poor, and consecrate of [their] properties for their support" (DC 42:30). "Few complied," writes one historian, "but enough did to make the temporary gathering viable."[15] In its ideal form, the Law of Consecration required members to deed over their assets to the church. Each would receive in return "an inheritance," which meant a stewardship over assets sufficient to engage in his chosen trade or profession. On a regular basis, members would continue to return excess profits back into the system, where they would be used to support new start-ups or sustain the financially failing and destitute.

A full-fledged effort was begun in Thompson, Ohio, in May, and other attempts took place in Kirtland and in Missouri intermittently over the next seven years. None was entirely successful, owing to both the perpetual impoverishment exacerbated by persecutions and relocations, and to the human frailties and selfishness of those participants who did prosper but chose to withhold their profits or withdraw from the system. In 1838, the Law of Tithing effectively replaced the Law of Consecration and stewardship. Mormons often interpret their failure in the same way they read the Old Testament episode of the golden calf. Failing to prove themselves worthy of the higher gospel law dispensed to Moses on Sinai (in Joseph Smith's redaction of the story), the Israelites received instead the lower law of Moses, a "schoolmaster to bring us unto Christ," in Paul's words (Gal. 3:24). Just as the higher law was eventually restored to a chastened Israel through the ministry of Christ, so do Mormons anticipate the day when once again, the Law of Consecration will replace the lesser Law of Tithing as the economic law of Zion. As LDS apostle Marion G. Romney explained, "From the very beginning I have felt that the [welfare] program would eventually move into the law of consecration and that this is the trial pattern. Until I can pay my tithing and make liberal contributions of my money and labor . . . I will not be prepared to go into the United Order, which will require me to consecrate everything I have and thereafter give all my surplus for the benefit of the kingdom. I think the United Order will be the last principle of the gospel we will learn to live and that doing so will bring in the millennium."[16]

Some Mormons believe that having covenanted to live the Law of Consecration in the temple ceremonies, they are obligated to follow the spirit of the law at present, in their own spheres of influence. LDS scholar and gadfly Hugh Nibley, for instance, has asked, "what is there to stop me from observing and keeping the law of consecration at this very day as I have already covenanted and promised to do without reservation? . . . I have promised to keep a law, and to keep it now."[17] The church welfare program is therefore seen by Latter-day Saints not just as a temporary expedient for dealing with poverty, but as the institution of principles that have the capacity to sanctify the members themselves and thus bring about the millennium. "Building Zion," then, has ambiguous meaning in LDS culture. It can mean the strengthening of the church and its community—but it also implies a proactive stance vis à vis the Lord's second coming, the recognition, in other words, of a principle espoused by apostle Bruce R. McConkie: "We have been commanded to lay the foundations of Zion and to get all things ready for the return of Him who shall again crown the Holy City with his presence and glory."[18] The LDS people are still millennialists, in other words. But millennialists with a twist. As LDS President Spencer W. Kimball has said, "The Lord's timetable is directed a good deal by us. We speed up the clock or we slow down the hands and we turn them back by our activities or by our procrastinations."[19]

The LDS welfare system's roots extend beyond the Ohio period and into the pioneering days of the early Utah experience. The need to create successful mechanisms for poor relief among the early Mormons, precipitated initially by the transient existence of a gathered and displaced people, was intensified by their increasing isolation from an often hostile environment, physical as well as human. As prominent Mormon leader George Q. Cannon said years after plagues of crickets and federal soldiers alike had dogged the Mormon people: "We have abundantly proved by our experience that if we do not sustain ourselves no other people will sustain us, and that we must be united . . . in our temporal as well as in our spiritual affairs; and that if we would build up and strengthen ourselves in the earth, it must be by union of effort."[20] Soon after arriving in the Salt Lake Valley, Brigham Young organized a committee "empowered to receive donations, buy, sell, and make all exchanges and distributions" relative to the destitute.[21]

The harshness of the Utah environment, the doctrinal support for and institutional experiments with cooperative economics, and the feisty independence spawned by decades of opposition and conflict, combined to produce in the Mormon case a view of poor relief that emphasized brotherly responsibility combined with dignity and self-reliance. At a time when public charities generally practiced the dole, Brigham Young emphasized an early version of public works projects:

> Some have wished me to explain why we built an adobe wall around this city. Are there any Saints who stumble at such things? Oh, slow of heart to understand [and] believe. I build walls, dig ditches, make bridges, and do a great amount and variety of labor that is of but little consequence only to provide ways and means for sustaining and preserving the destitute. I annually expend hundreds and thousands of dollars almost solely to furnish employment to those in want of labor. Why? I have potatoes, flour, beef, and other articles of food, which I wish my brethren to have; and it is better for them to labour for those articles, so far as they are able and have opportunity, than to have them given to them. They work, and I deal out provisions, often when the work does not profit me.[22]

In the succeeding decades, the spirit of communitarianism and isolationism faded. Statehood, the coming of the railroad, the dispersal of Latter-day Saints throughout the intermountain west, and the Mormons' growing participation and success in a capitalist economy all engendered more accommodation and less peculiarity in Mormon culture. These changes were most deplorably evident, perhaps, in the fact that by 1933, one out of every four Utah families was on federal relief—almost double the national average.[23] In a return to original principles, and consonant with President Franklin Roosevelt's call for localities to assume the burden of welfare relief, church leaders began reestablishing the foundations of the economic self-sufficiency for which they are famous today. In 1936, LDS headquarters centralized a churchwide program, and began acquiring farms and processing facilities. Bishops' storehouses were created to serve as storage and distribution centers for the needy.

Centerpiece of the church's humanitarian and welfare operations is the complex of buildings known as Welfare Square, in Salt Lake City. Originally situated on 10 downtown acres in 1937, the complex was revamped in recent years, and now sprawls over 13 acres of modernized facilities. A new bakery was finished in August 1997, a 50,000-square-foot milk-processing plant in 1999, and a 22,000-square-foot cannery was completed in June 2000. The church welcomes visitors who watch through observation windows as volunteers produce bread and cheese, bundle relief packages, or sort clothes.

By 1990, the church held 172,000 acres of farmland, 199 agricultural production projects, 51 canneries, and 63 grain storage facilities feeding into 113 central, regional, and branch storehouses.[24] The distribution process itself is streamlined and efficient. Relief Society leaders assess member needs, the bishop signs a commodity order, and the family picks up the food and other items at the storehouse or a delivery point. In the late 1980s, orders were being filled at the rate of almost 1,000 per day, churchwide.[25]

Following the devastation of the Second World War, the church first extended welfare assistance to members outside the United States in a major way. Ezra Taft Benson, later secretary of agriculture under Eisenhower and later yet president of the church, led relief efforts to supply Europeans with food and clothing, eventually totaling 133 boxcars of

LDS welfare projects
Mormon men contributing labor on this cellar in 1938 were issued work slips by the church, redeemable for food from their local bishops if they were in need. (Courtesy of the Church Archives, The Church of Jesus Christ of Latter-day Saints)

Mormon women prepare fruit at the Salt Lake Regional Canning Center
An arm of the church's welfare program, this center and others aimed to assist members in getting off federal assistance. (Courtesy of the Church Archives, The Church of Jesus Christ of Latter-day Saints)

food, clothing, and bedding, along with thousands of individual eleven-pound packages. In recent years, those relief efforts have extended far beyond the church's own membership. In 1985, for instance, Thomas S. Monson reported that the church had called two special fast days, directing members to contribute funds for worldwide relief. The money collected, together with donated labor of service missionaries, generated over a ten-year period almost $24 million in cash donations, over $72 million in assistance, 3,600 tons of distributed food, and 243 tons of distributed medical equipment, reaching 109 countries.[26]

Today, Welfare Square is the hub of the church's global welfare program, but there are over a hundred storehouses and an equal number of canneries spread throughout the globe, as well as dozens of production projects and distribution facilities. In addition, over 2,400 humanitarian missionaries serve in welfare services worldwide. Between Thomas Monson's 1985 report and 2002, the church provided humanitarian assistance to 150 countries, including shipment of over 100,000 tons of food, medical and educational supplies, and clothing, valued at a half billion dollars. In that period, the church launched 144 major disaster assistance efforts, helping victims of flooding in Mozambique, Europe, and South America, of famine in Africa, and of war in Afghanistan. Speaking to the National Press Club in 2000, President Hinckley surveyed several examples:

> Today, this very day, as they have been during previous days, two helicopters have been flying rescue and mercy missions over the flood waters of Mozambique and Zimbabwe. When governments in that part of the world said they could do no more, we rented two helicopters at great expense to fly rescue missions. . . . We have dug wells in African villages, fed people, and supplied them with clothing and shelter. We have given aid in the Mexico fire of 1990, in the Bangladesh cyclone of 1991, in the China earthquake of 1991, in the Bosnia civil conflict of 1992, in Rwanda in 1994, in North Korea in 1996–98, in Central America in 1998, and in Kosovo in 1999, and today we are assisting substantially in Venezuela, Mozambique, and Zimbabwe.[27]

Typical of more recent LDS response to a world crisis was an effort organized in May 2002. Summoned by area leaders, some two hundred humanitarian aid volunteers rallied on Welfare Square to assemble 6,750 emergency food boxes for families in drought-stricken Malawi, Zimbabwe, and Madagascar. The church supplemented those packages with 250 tons of cereal grains and substantial clothing shipments. During the Ethiopian drought of 2003, the church responded with 10 million pounds of food assistance, much of it in the form of a nourishing porridge called Atmit produced at the Deseret Dairy powdered products facility at Welfare Square. The first emergency shipment of 80,000 pounds was flown to Addis Ababa in a church-chartered cargo plane.

One of the church's operative principles guiding their welfare program is the emphasis on self-sufficiency. And since economic viability is so largely tied to educational and vocational training, it is only natural that the church would mount a major effort to avert economic dependency by fostering more educational opportunities for its members. To this end, the church launched the Perpetual Education Fund in 2001.

In the first generation of LDS history, converts were encouraged to "gather to Zion," making a journey that often included a dangerous and costly transatlantic voyage followed by overland travel across half a continent. To provide resources for the (mostly poor and mostly British and

European) immigrants to Utah, the church initiated in 1849 a Perpetual Emigrating Fund (PEF). Converts could borrow travel expenses to get them to the Salt Lake Valley. PEF agents throughout Europe and at American points of transit chartered ships and organized overland conveyance. After establishing themselves in Utah, immigrant members were expected to repay the fund, so future converts could similarly benefit from the program. Although not all who took advantage of the program were able or willing to repay the loans, the program was a tremendously effective tool in facilitating transportation and resettlement of immigrant converts. In the thirty-eight years of its existence, the fund had dispensed millions of dollars, and assisted in the immigration of over thirty thousand Latter-day Saints.

In April 2001, President Gordon B. Hinckley announced the creation of the new PEF, modeled on its historic predecessor. Under this program, young LDS men and women from around the world may borrow money to finance their education, with returned missionaries having priority. Upon employment, they are expected to repay the fund with modest interest. Targeting underdeveloped areas especially, the fund is a powerful resource to elevate the educational and economic levels of church members. As President Hinckley said in his announcement,

> with good employment skills, these young men and women can rise out of the poverty they and generations before them have known. . . . It will not be a welfare effort, commendable as those efforts are, but rather an education opportunity. The beneficiaries will repay the money, and when they do so, they will enjoy a wonderful sense of freedom because they have improved their lives not through a grant or gift, but through borrowing and then repaying. They can hold their heads high in a spirit of independence.

To keep the focus on strengthening localities among less-advantaged members, Hinckley stipulated that "this training must be done where they live. It will then be suited to the opportunities of those areas."[28] Over $100 million was raised in the first two years, with six thousand beneficiaries. The enthusiasm of the LDS response suggests that the fund will grow consistently in the years ahead.

American Saints have long been recognized for their success-driven work ethic, embodied by the fantastic wealth of prosperous businessmen like the Mariotts, Steven Covey, and Jon Huntsman. And their ability to care for their own—in America, at least—is legendary. Mormons proudly noted President Ronald Reagan's public observation that "if, during the period of the Great Depression, every church had come forth with a wel-

Humanitarian relief in Ethiopia, 2000
In recent decades, the church has greatly expanded its international relief efforts in third world countries. (Courtesy of the Church Archives, The Church of Jesus Christ of Latter-day Saints)

fare program founded on correct principles as [the LDS] church did, we would not be in the difficulty in which we find ourselves today."[29]

But as the church internationalizes, it encounters humanitarian challenges—and economic disparities—of an entirely different order. An LDS revelation stipulates that "it is not given that one man should possess that which is above another, wherefore the world lieth in sin" (DC 49:20). As the church continues to assume an increasingly third world composition, the contrast between domestic affluence and international poverty will grow more acute. And the church will likely continue the trend of instituting more—and more innovative—programs, in order to redress the disparities condemned by LDS scripture.

Notes

1. Joseph Smith-History 1:20, 25, *Pearl of Great Price.*
2. The revelation is recorded in DC 27. The only explanation given by a heavenly messenger was that the beverage used for the sacrament was inconsequential, and that

"you shall not purchase wine neither strong drink of your enemies." The revelation forbidding the use of alcoholic drinks in general would not come until 1833 (DC 89). Water has therefore been used by custom but not express revelation.

3. Jeffrey R. Holland, "This Do in Remembrance of Me," *Ensign* 25, no. 11 (November 1995): 67, citing Joseph Fielding Smith, *Doctrines of Salvation*, comp. Bruce R. McConkie, 3 vols. (Salt Lake City: Bookcraft, 1954–56), 2:340.

4. Spencer W. Kimball, *The Teachings of Spencer W. Kimball*, ed. Edward L. Kimball (Salt Lake City: Bookcraft, 1982), 452.

5. First Presidency, 27 April 1915, in *Improvement Era* 18(1915):733–34.

6. Ezra Taft Benson, "Flooding the Earth with the Book of Mormon," *Ensign* 18, no. 11 (November 1988): 4. Quoting Joseph Smith Jr., *History of the Church of Jesus Christ of Latter-day Saints*, 7 vols., ed. James Mulholland et al. (Salt Lake City: Deseret, 1951), 4:461.

7. Boyd K. Packer, address delivered at Regional Representatives Seminar, 3 April 1987.

8. Joseph Smith, *Discourses of the Prophet Joseph Smith,* comp. Alma P. Burton (Salt Lake City: Deseret, 1977), 147.

9. Senator Aaron Harrison Cragin (N.H.), *Congressional Globe,* 41st Cong., 2nd sess. (18 May 1870): 3576–77.

10. Leonard J. Arrington, "Religion and Economics in Mormon History," *BYU Studies* 3, no. 3/4 (spring 1960–summer 1961): 15.

11. Joseph F. Smith, "The Truth About Mormonism," *Out West,* 23 (1905): 242.

12. Dean D. McBrien, "The Economic Content of Early Mormon Doctrine," *Southwestern Political and Social Science Quarterly* 6 (1925): 180. In Arrington, "Religion and Economics," 16.

13. "Religious groups joined forces to help Andrew's victims," *Sun-Sentinel,* 24 August 2002.

14. "Members Rally to Help Hurricane Victims," *LDS Church News,* 12 August 1995. The scripture President Kenneth Holbert referred to is DC 136:3, wherein Brigham Young organizes the Camp of Israel at Winter Quarters, Iowa.

15. Garth L. Mangum, "Welfare Projects," in *Historical Atlas of Mormonism* (New York: Simon and Schuster, 1994), 140.

16. Quoted in Dean L. May, "The Economics of Zion," *Sunstone* 14, no. 4 (August 1990): 22.

17. Hugh Nibley, in *Approaching Zion,* in *The Collected Works of Hugh Nibley,* 15 vols. (Provo, Utah: Deseret and FARMS, 1986–), 9:388.

18. Bruce R. McConkie, "Come: Let Israel Build Zion," *Ensign* 7 (May 1977): 116.

19. Edward L. Kimball, ed., *Teachings of Spencer W. Kimball* (Salt Lake City: Deseret, 1982), 441–42.

20. George Q. Cannon, *Journal of Discourses,* 26 vols. (London: Latter-day Saints Book Depot, 1854–86), 18:13.

21. *Manuscript History of the Church,* Brigham Young Period 1844–77 (April 1848), 27. Cited in Betty L Barton, "Mormon Poor Relief: A Social Welfare Interlude," *BYU Studies* 18 (1977–78): 68.

22. Journal History of Brigham Young, 4 March 1860. Cited in Barton, "Mormon Poor Relief," 69.

23. The national average also showed that one out of every seven families was on relief. *Salt Lake Tribune,* 5 April 1933. Cited in ibid., 86.

24. Mangum, "Welfare Projects," 140.

25. Garth L. Mangum, "Welfare Services," in Daniel H. Ludlow, ed., *Encyclopedia of Mormonism: The History, Scripture, Doctrine, and Procedures of the Church of Jesus Christ of Latter-day Saints* (New York: Macmillan, 1992), 4:1556.

26. Thomas S. Monson, "My Brother's Keeper," *Ensign* 24, no. 11 (November 1994): 43.

27. *Deseret News*, 9 March 2000.

28. Gordon B. Hinckley, *Ensign* 31, no. 5 (May 2001): 80.

29. "Lord Decreed Spirit of Welfare Work," *LDS Church News*, 29 March 1997.

Chapter 6

"All Things Are Spiritual": The Church, Politics, and Society

Jo goes on prophesying, preaching, and building the temple, and regulating his empire, as if nothing had happened. They are busy all the time establishing factories to make saints and crockery ware, also prophets and white paint.
—*New York Herald*, 1842

The Constitution "has not been a reliable friend" of the Mormons, writes one legal scholar.[1] The Saints were first disappointed in the government when Joseph Smith had petitioned President Martin Van Buren in 1839–40 for redress of the Mormon expulsions from Missouri. Van Buren considered it a state matter, and refused to intervene. Subsequent pleas for federal relief also fell on deaf ears. By the end of 1843, as political storm clouds gathered once again over the Mormon city of Nauvoo, Illinois, Smith for a time considered "petitioning Congress to receive the City Nauvoo under the protection of the United States Government."[2] As the election of 1844 approached, Smith decided to ask the five major candidates—John Calhoun, Henry Clay, Martin Van Buren, Lewis Cass, and Richard M. Johnson—how they would deal with the Mormon problem. Ignored by the last three and answered dismissively by Calhoun and Clay, Smith convened a political convention in Nauvoo to discuss Mormon options. Thus it was that on 29 January 1844, Joseph Smith announced his candidacy for president of the United States.

Martyrdom in Carthage cut short the prophet's campaign, but not before Smith had articulated positions on a full range of pressing issues of the day. Among these were slavery (sell public lands to fund complete abolition by 1850), the bloated federal government (reduce Congress by two-thirds), the Oregon question (it should belong to the United States, "with the consent of the Indians"), and penal reform ("turn the prisons into seminaries of learning").

As they feared, the Mormons in Nauvoo were again left without federal protection from hostile citizens, and were invaded by a federal army in Utah a decade after their flight there. When the crusade against polygamy went from the pressroom to the courts, judges found nothing in the Constitution to allow Mormon freedom of religious practice to trump social policy based on a general interpretation of Christian morality. Mormons continued their retreat from the political mainstream by shunning established political parties and creating their own—the People's Party. Even after the battle for statehood was won in 1896, Mormon leader B. H. Roberts was denied his seat in the House of Representatives. Unlike Roberts, Apostle Reed Smoot, elected to the Senate in 1903, was a monogamist. Nonetheless, his election provoked a repeat of attempts to deny him his seat. Prolonged hearings followed, and it would be 1907 before Smoot began in earnest his career as a distinguished U.S. senator.

In the twentieth century, exclusion became gradual acceptance, and political isolation has been transformed into enthusiastic participation. The irony of this wholesale reversal is best captured in the alarm expressed by one contemporary critic that America at the end of the twentieth century found itself "on the verge of being governed (with the complicity of the Mormons and Baptists) by a nationally established religion."[3] That is doubtless an exaggeration. But it is noteworthy that the proportion of Latter-day Saints in Congress exceeds their proportion of the general population.[4]

As the relationship of the church to national politics has changed, so has the influence of the church in the political lives of its members. As we have seen, some of the earliest dissension within the Mormon Church concerned the extent to which Joseph's spiritual leadership was seen as intruding into the personal or political sphere. The revelation designating him prophet of the newly organized church admonished his flock to "give heed unto *all* his words and commandments" (DC 21:4); that counsel required a new paradigm of spiritual leadership, one that provoked a mixed response that continues to this day in the faith. Brigham Young, most stalwart of Joseph Smith's supporters, provided a model of "sustaining the brethren" that typifies "iron-rod Mormons," those most prone to unquestioning obedience to church leaders: at a time when Smith was making questionable financial decisions, Young recalled, he found himself criticizing the prophet. Even though his reservations lasted less than a minute, he said, the "spirit of revelation manifested to me that if I was to harbor a thought in my heart that Joseph could be wrong in anything, I would begin to lose confidence in him. . . . ; Though I know that Joseph was a human being and subject to err, still it was none of my business to look after his faults. . . . It was not my prerogative to call him in question with regard to any act of his life. He was God's servant, and not mine."[5]

The "iron-rod" designation derives from Lehi's dream recorded in the Book of Mormon. There, only those who cling to a rod of iron avoid the perils of "mists of darkness" and find their way to the Tree of Life (1 Nephi 8:23–24).[6] The iron rod is a metaphorical representation for the word of God, Nephi explains. In a church led by a living prophet, whose pronouncements members are commanded to "receive, as if from mine own mouth" (DC 21:5), clinging to the iron rod means for some an uncompromising acceptance of the counsel and teachings of church authorities. Some Latter-day Saints cite in this regard the precedent of Abraham in his willingness even to sacrifice Isaac in response to an unfathomable, faith-testing command. Accordingly, most Latter-day Saints are willing to acknowledge the prophet's prerogative to counsel upon a wide variety of issues and areas. They subscribe to the counsel of Apostle Neal Maxwell, in other words, that the "orthodox Latter-day Saint scholar should remember that his citizenship is in the Kingdom and that his professional passport takes him abroad into his specialty. It is not the other way around. That fact is true not only for the professor but also for the plumber in his relationships with his union."[7]

Of course, not all Mormons march in lockstep to the call of their leaders, and never have. When the states were debating Prohibition's repeal, LDS leaders were emphatic in urging Mormons in Utah not to relinquish the proscription of alcohol. Nevertheless, a Mormon-dominated populace handily repealed the amendment. In Mormon culture, members who tend to show more independence vis à vis official church positions on doctrine and politics are sometimes called "Liahona Mormons," after the compass-like instrument in the Book of Mormon that provided general guidance to its users, according to "their faith and diligence." These members tend to emphasize a different Brigham Young than the one quoted above: the one who said "I exhort you to think for yourselves, and read your Bibles for yourselves, get the Holy Spirit for yourselves."[8] Both positions are, of course, oversimplifications. But they represent the tensions inherent in a religious culture that places a high premium on both spiritual self-reliance and on an Old Testament model of prophetic leadership. The tension between the two interpretations of discipleship is likely to grow as the church becomes increasingly global, multicultural, and subject to the forces of secularism and modernity.

At present, however, Mormons do tend toward a high degree of political solidarity and moral conformity. In particular, on the issues of abortion, homosexuality, feminism, race, the environment, and militarism, Mormon belief and practice confirm some stereotypes while challenging others. In the first of these cases in particular, LDS positions follow necessarily from a specific theology of the family, rather than allegiance to political conservatism per se.

Birth Control and Abortion

Given Mormonism's unique teachings about the premortal existence of all the human family, it is inevitable that procreation would carry special implications. Since all spirits will find incarnation eventually, the decision to conceive is simultaneously a decision to house a spirit that would otherwise go elsewhere. Brigham Young was the first to explicitly connect this belief to family planning: "There are multitudes of pure and holy spirits waiting to take tabernacles, now what is our duty?—To prepare tabernacles for them; to take a course that will not tend to drive those spirits into the families of the wicked. . . . It is the duty of every righteous man and woman to prepare tabernacles for all the spirits they can."[9] Even in twenty-first-century Mormon culture, it is almost a commonplace to hear of mothers who felt impressed to conceive again, in order to accommodate one more spirit they sensed was waiting to join the family.

Allied to this concern to provide suitable families for waiting spirits is the LDS Church's emphasis on family life itself as the foundation of both earthly existence and eternal life. Considering that the earthly family unit is not just the prototype, but also the actual nucleus and precursor to a celestialized family, any avoidance of offspring and parenthood would be rejection of one of the primary purposes behind our sojourn here on earth. From that perspective, birth control could represent a confusion of priorities and weighty obligations. As recently as 1969, the First Presidency was continuing to assert: "Where husband and wife enjoy health and vigour and are free from impurities that would be entailed upon their posterity, it is contrary to the teachings of the Church artificially to curtail or prevent the birth of children." At the same time, the statement continued, "men must be considerate of their wives who bear the greater responsibility not only of bearing children, but of caring for them through childhood. To this end the mother's health and strength should be conserved and the husband's consideration for his wife is his first duty, and self-control a dominant factor in all their relationships."[10]

The caveat that tempered fatherly obligations with common sense and respect for women had become by 1998 a decision to relinquish all family planning decision to individual couples. Thus, the current handbook states: "the decision as to how many children to have and when to have them is extremely intimate and private and should be left between the couple and the Lord. Church members should not judge one another in this matter."[11]

Considered as a strategy for family planning rather than family avoidance, artificial birth control would appear to carry no necessary theological implications. That is apparently at last recognized both in current church policy that refuses to condemn birth control and in current Mormon practice: Mormons have larger than average family size. But even in the context of larger fertility rates, Mormon women employ birth control at the same rate as the national average.[12]

It is not clear what bearing, if any, Mormon doctrine of premortal existence has on their official abortion position. Belief in the eternal existence of human souls, before and after birth, does not extend to any belief as to when that preexisting spirit enters its earthly tabernacle. But certain it is that Mormons remain among the staunchest of opponents to the practice of abortion. In 1991, the church reaffirmed its long-standing position:

> In view of the widespread public interest in the issue of abortion, we reaffirm that The Church of Jesus Christ of Latter-day Saints has consistently opposed elective abortion. More than a century ago, the First Presidency of the church warned against this evil. We have repeatedly counseled people everywhere to turn from the devastating practice of abortion for personal or social convenience. The church recognizes that there may be rare cases in which abortion may be justified—cases involving pregnancy by incest or rape; when the life or health of the woman is adjudged by competent medical authority to be in serious jeopardy; or when the fetus is known by competent medical authority to have severe defects that will not allow the baby to survive beyond birth. But these are not automatic reasons for abortion. Even in these cases, the couple should consider an abortion only after consulting with each other, and their bishop, and receiving divine confirmation through prayer.[13]

This moral opposition to the practice does not necessarily translate into an endorsement of legislation prohibiting the practice. Most people would infer support for pro-life initiatives from the church's consistent, forceful, and public denunciation of abortion. Some liberals in the church have argued that because of LDS emphasis on moral agency, members should condemn the practice but defend the freedom to choose. That rationale has little credibility in light of the scriptural basis on which Mormon leaders condemn abortion. Writing in response to *Roe v. Wade* in 1973, the First Presidency quoted *Doctrine and Covenants* 59:6: "Thou shalt not steal; neither commit adultery, *nor kill, nor anything like unto it*" (emphasis added). It is hardly plausible that the church countenances even the legal right to an act that they believe God has likened to—though not equated with—murder.

In a 1999 speech, Mormon apostle and former Utah Supreme Court Justice Dallin Oakes explicitly lamented the "seduction" of Latter-day Saints by pro-choice rhetoric, criticizing the logic of Latter-day Saints who consider themselves "anti-abortion in . . . personal life but pro-choice in public policy," and deploring as ill-conceived those arguments against "legislating morality."[14] While opposing abortion, the Mormon leadership has shown a willingness to address the crisis of unwanted pregnancy. The church has an extensive social services network that provides counseling and crisis management, and administers an extensive adoption service. While respecting the mother's right to choose adoption or single parenthood, the church believes that every child is entitled to a two-parent home and encourages expectant, single women to decide accordingly.

Homosexuality

In discussing homosexuality and religion, it is useful to distinguish between sexual practice and sexual orientation. At least, that is a distinction increasingly emphasized by Mormon leaders in recent years, in attempting to maintain an inflexible opposition to homosexual activity while avoiding the shrill condemnation and intolerance of homosexuals that is at times associated with conservative religious leaders. For example, a Letter of the First Presidency asserts, "there is a distinction between [1] immoral thoughts and feelings and [2] participating in either immoral heterosexual or any homosexual behavior."[15] That distinction also allows for certain accommodations. First, the distinction partially circumvents the troubling question of homosexuality's origins by shifting the focus, and the locus of accountability, to actions rather than propensities. Homosexual Latter-day Saints, accordingly, can qualify as members in good standing and even receive temple recommends, if they are chaste. Second, it allows for a moral posture predicated, at least in part, on a universal standard that makes any sexual relations outside of marriage, hetero- or homosexual, a sin. People of all sexual orientations, in other words, are expected to control their sexual appetites until they can find proper expression in (heterosexual) marriage. Obviously that is small comfort to homosexuals who have no hope of marital satisfaction in this life. To them, the church can only insist that "through the merciful plan of our Father in Heaven, persons who desire to do what is right but through no fault of their own are unable to have an eternal marriage in mortal life will have an opportunity to qualify for eternal life in a period following mortality, if they keep the commandments of God and are true to their baptismal and other covenants."[16]

Regarding the question of accountability for homosexual attraction, the apostle Dallin H. Oaks has made the most comprehensive attempt to find a middle ground between condoning what Mormon theology holds to be sin and condemning what increasing numbers of people believe is a genetic predisposition:

> Some kinds of feelings seem to be inborn. Others are traceable to mortal experiences. Still other feelings seem to be acquired from a complex interaction of "nature and nurture." All of us have some feelings we did not choose, but the gospel of Jesus Christ teaches us that we still have the power to resist and reform our feelings. . . . In each case . . . the feelings or other characteristics that increase susceptibility to certain behavior may have some relationship to inheritance. But the relationship is probably very complex. . . . Regardless of our different susceptibilities or vulnerabilities, . . . we remain responsible for the exercise of our agency in the thoughts we entertain and the behavior we choose.[17]

Elder Oaks cites recent scholarship by Columbia University researchers in support of this model that accommodates both genetic factors and moral agency:

> It is imperative that clinicians and behavioral scientists begin to appreciate the complexities of sexual orientation and resist the urge to search for simplistic explanations, either psychosocial or biologic. Conspicuously absent from most theorizing on the origins of sexual orientation is an

active role of the individual in constructing his or her identity. . . . We propose an interactional model in which genes or hormones do not specify sexual orientation per se, but instead bias particular personality traits and thereby influence the manner in which an individual and his or her environment interact as sexual orientation and other personality characteristics unfold developmentally.[18]

Given the church's teachings about the eternal nature of both gender and the family, it is perhaps inevitable that homosexuality could find no place in Latter-day Saint conception of the gospel. Marriage is seen as a divine pattern engaged in by gods and the inheritors of salvation, rather than a product of social evolution or even a divinely condoned expedient for the populating of a fallen world. "Marriage between man and woman is essential to His eternal plan," the First Presidency stated in a 1995 Proclamation to the World; "children are entitled to birth within the bonds of matrimony, to be reared by a father and a mother."[19] The heterosexual union of the sexes is thus the only pattern of sexuality that is consistent with a doctrine of the family. It is not really conceivable that social pressures or liberalizing forces within the church will exact further concessions or accommodations from the church on this issue, beyond the expressions of love and acceptance into the fold that church officials have already proffered.

Race

To outsiders, the Mormon record on race is a study in contradictions. As mentioned previously, studies reveal Mormons to be more politically liberal than other Americans on issues from mixed marriages to racial justice.[20] That was true as well in the 1800s. Joseph Smith campaigned for president on a platform that included emancipation, and Mormons found themselves reviled in Missouri for a perceived hostility to the institution of slavery. And indeed, in 1833, Joseph Smith had declared with prophetic authority that "it is not right that any man should be in bondage one to another" (DC 101:79). The Book of Mormon itself, translated before the church was even organized, likewise depicted the laws of the righteous Nephites as expressly decreeing that "there should [not] be any slaves among them" (Alma 27:9). As for contemporary slaves, Smith wrote, "change their situation with the whites, and they would be like them." Joseph Smith put this into religious practice by authorizing the ordination of Elijah Abel, a free black, to the priesthood and office of elder in March 1836.[21]

On the other hand, at some point in the early years of Mormonism, the pattern was initiated of excluding blacks from the priesthood, and thus from the full blessings of the restored gospel. Brigham Young announced such a policy in 1852, during meetings of Utah's first territorial legislature. He did not articulate a rationale at the time, beyond declaring that members of the African race could not bear the priesthood, and attributing such denial to the curse of Cain.[22] Associating black skin with Cain's posterity, and slavery with Ham's, was commonplace in nineteenth-century religious thinking (to be "a servant of servants," was the destiny decreed for Canaan, Ham's son of Noah in Gen. 9:25).

In popular Mormon thinking, two other elements entered into the mythology of racial distinctions. In 1835, Smith had produced the Book of Abraham, a document that declared some individuals were the recipients of blessings in mortality, because of premortal faithfulness. Writing in 1845, Apostle Orson Hyde opined that in a similar way, some spirits in the premortal realm had been neutral in the "war in heaven," and as a consequence "were required . . . to take bodies in the accursed lineage of Canaan; hence the Negro or African race."[23] At a later time, some Mormon writers would begin to invoke other portions of the Abraham text, according to which a descendent of Ham was declared to be "of that lineage by which he could not have right of Priesthood" (Abr. 1:27). Although it is likely that the lineage in question would refer to gender rather than race, generations of Latter-day Saints believed that those passages, in tandem, provided an adequate theological basis for the continued exclusion of blacks from the priesthood.[24]

Because Brigham Young never supported his policy statement with doctrinal elaboration or any claim to special revelation, the practice met increasing resistance and discomfort on the part of many members and leaders in the twentieth century. True, the First Presidency had in 1949 reaffirmed the church's position, insisting it was "not a matter of the declaration of a policy but of direct commandment from the Lord."[25] Still, since there was no official, published scriptural or doctrinal explanation for the commandment, some insisted the LDS position in this regard was more of a culturally conditioned practice than revealed principle and therefore, presumably, amenable to change.

Subtle shifts in the policy began to emerge in the 1950s. As the church expanded internationally, President David O. McKay realized the difficulties posed by the requirement that lineage purity be demonstrated, especially in racially mixed areas with a growing church presence like South

Africa and Latin America. McKay made the priesthood available to all worthy men unless African ancestry was specifically known (the burden of proof had been the reverse previously). Political pressures against the church mounted in the 1960s, with prominent Mormon dissidents like Sterling McMurrin (Kennedy's commissioner of education) publicly condemning the practice. Mormon governor of Michigan, George Romney, ran for the presidential nomination, suffering a barrage of questions and criticisms about the racial issue. A number of athletic teams staged highly publicized boycotts against Brigham Young University's teams in protest.

The church had issued a public statement in 1963, affirming its support for civil rights and insisting that priesthood doctrines had no bearing on those rights. Sociologist Armand Mauss produced studies indicating that, in spite of their loyalty to a policy of priesthood denial, Mormons were "remarkably similar to other Americans in their beliefs and attitudes about blacks and civil rights."[26] Clearly, these gestures and statistical studies were not going to be sufficient palliatives in the face of the enormous changes afoot in American racial politics of that era.

At the same time, important developments were unfolding in Africa. Without an official missionary presence, the church was nonetheless attracting widespread interest. Congregations of thousands had taken shape, all without any recognition from Salt Lake City. In Nigeria, for instance, the government denied Mormons the necessary visas to respond to local requests for contact, although fifteen thousand names and addresses were on waiting lists.[27] Over the next decade, the church made no alterations to its policy, but did engage in strenuous outreach efforts to the black community within and outside the Church, especially through recruitment of black students and speakers at Brigham Young University and the establishment of a black LDS support group called Genesis.

By 1978, the church was enjoying a relative respite from the political fires of the previous decade. But that year, a temple in São Paulo, Brazil, was nearing dedication. Work in that country, where extensive racial mixing had followed nineteenth-century emancipation, was especially fruitful. The prospect of a burgeoning national membership denied access to both the priesthood and their own temple was apparently the stimulus that prompted President Spencer W. Kimball to revisit the race proscription with his counselors and the other apostles. In June of that year, he announced to a surprised public that he felt divinely directed to lift the priesthood ban. The proclamation, subsequently canonized as scriptural revelation, pronounced that henceforth, "all worthy males" were eligible for priesthood ordination, "regardless of race or color."[28] The momentous shift represented the most dramatic revelation pronounced by an LDS prophet since the ban on plural marriage over a century earlier. Skeptics saw in the change, as they had at the time of Wilford Woodruff's antipolygamy manifesto, a concession to political pressures. Believers simply rejoiced that a living prophet was finally empowered to lift a ban that was increasingly embarrassing to the church and difficult to justify in an increasingly liberal, secular atmosphere.

The new policy has had little impact domestically, where missionary work in the inner city and among black populations still bears little fruit. The church does not maintain race-based statistics, but indications are that progress and retention are difficult. In recent years, relations between the church and the American black community have shown some remarkable developments. Commemorations of black history, sponsorship of LDS African American symposia, and outreach (especially in the aftermath of the 1992 L.A. riots) have done much to alleviate the frictions of the past. Two developments in particular are striking. In April 1988, church President Gordon B. Hinckley received the NAACP Distinguished Service Award from Julian Bond. And in 2001, the church with great fanfare made public the records of the Freedman's Bank. The extensive records from this Reconstruction-era institution, systematized under church sponsorship during an eleven-year period, make it possible for millions of African Americans to connect their family histories to the half-million names indexed in the collections. The church thereby furthered its sense of mission to connect the human family through genealogical research, while providing a service of enormous benefit to the African American community.

Internationally, the picture is different. After the 1978 policy shift, missionaries arrived in Ghana, Nigeria, and other African countries, and convert numbers grew rapidly, from fewer than two hundred to over 14,000 by 1988. In Brazil, membership quintupled in the decade after 1978. And then in 1990, Helvecio Martins, a Brazilian of black ancestry, was sustained as the first black General Authority of the Church of Jesus Christ of Latter-day Saints. In 2004, the first temple in black Africa was dedicated in Accra, Ghana. Africa and racially mixed regions of Brazil continue to be among the very most fruitful areas of church growth.

Another ethnicity that figures prominently in LDS theology and history is Native American. The title page of the Book of Mormon characterizes the sacred record as being "written to the Lamanites, who are a remnant of the

House of Israel" ("and also to Jew and Gentile"). As we have seen, Joseph Smith understood the descendents of those Lamanites to be the American Indians, and in fulfillment of scriptural command to take the gospel to them sent a proselytizing mission to Native Americans on the western border of Missouri in 1830. These feelings of spiritual stewardship and kinship that early Mormons had toward Native Americans were a frequent source of friction, especially among old settlers in antebellum Missouri that felt both outrage and alarm at the Mormons' fraternal overtures.

After LDS settlement in Utah, the reality of the cultural chasm that separated Mormon and Native American cultures settled in, and the Latter-day Saint engagement with indigenous peoples lost much of its evangelical zeal. Renewed missionary efforts in the American Southwest began again in the 1930s, and by the 1970s, over 150 wards and branches had been organized among American Indians of the region.[29] In addition, the church began to recruit Native Americans to Brigham Young University, and initiated in 1954, with the support of both federal and tribal governments, the Indian Student Placement Program in order to provide young Native Americans with improved educational opportunities during the school year. (The program was abandoned in the 1990s, largely because of criticisms that it was paternalistic and disruptive of Native American culture and family life.)

However, it was the phenomenal results of missionary work in Latin America that seemed to fulfill Book of Mormon promises about the "gentiles" restoring the "seed" of Laman and Lemuel to a knowledge of both the gospel and their own role in history (1 Nephi 13). Early explorations in South and Central America by a series of British and European explorers, but especially John Lloyd Stephens, had convinced Joseph Smith that Book of Mormon peoples were centered in that region, and an archaeological expedition made tentative but unsuccessful efforts to establish that fact at the turn of the century. Interest in the region as the locale of Book of Mormon history was rekindled in the 1940s, and about the same time missionary efforts in Latin America increased rapidly. The church entered a new phase of activity directed at connecting the origins and the destinies of those peoples to the Book of Mormon. "Lamanite" became the standard LDS term to refer to modern-day Native Americans throughout the Western Hemisphere, and even to encompass the islanders of Polynesia and the Maoris of New Zealand (the latter being, presumably, descendents of one Hagoth, a Book of Mormon character who disappears after leading several seaward migrations "northward" from the Nephite lands [Alma 63:3–8]).

Recently, critical attention to the Book of Mormon has produced the recognition that the record is better characterized as a lineage history than as the chronicle of a hemispheric empire. Accordingly, most LDS Book of Mormon scholars now argue, Mormon doctrine does not entail the belief that all Native Americans and the mixed ethnicities of Latin America have a literal connection to Israelite forbears. Lehi's family were not the solitary inhabitants of the New World, and intermarriage with indigenous populations doubtless occurred in the view of Book of Mormon scholars. In addition, they rightly point out, "Lamanite" has by the end of the Book of Mormon narrative come to denote unbelief rather than ethnic identity. This view is corroborated by an 1829 revelation referring to ancient peoples who "had become Lamanites because of their dissensions" (DC 19:48).

All this makes recent attempts to use DNA to prove the Book of Mormon inauthentic difficult, since this historical shift in definition means that neither descendents of Lehi in general, nor of the Lamanites in particular, can be connected to any particular genetic line.[30] But these controversies also leave some in the Mormon mainstream perplexed. "I am Peruvian. I grew up believing that I was a Lamanite," a member said. "I am now overwhelmed with the surprise coming from science, coming from the archaeological evidence. We don't know where the Book of Mormon took place. We don't know where the Lamanites are. If we don't know who the Lamanites are how can the Book of Mormon promise to bring them back? It's an identity crisis for many of us."[31]

For the foreseeable future, however, convert rates indicate that the appeal of the Book of Mormon and the gospel it heralds are undiminished among the peoples of Latin America—whether their relationship to Father Lehi is seen as genetic, metaphorical, spiritual, or a powerful religious mythology.

Feminism

> People wonder what we do for our women. I will tell you what we do. We get out of their way, and look with wonder at what they are accomplishing.
> —Gordon B. Hinckley

The role of women in the LDS Church is something of a paradox. Historically, Mormons have been remarkably progressive in some areas of women's issues, even while remaining one of few Christian denominations to preserve church leadership and the priesthood as exclusively male domains. For example, women exercised the vote in Utah before they did in any other state in the Union.[32] As a territory, Utah granted women suffrage in 1870, and Mormon women served on the executive committees of the church's political party at both the local and territorial levels. When, contrary to all non-Mormon expectations, LDS women did not use their new political power to oppose polygamy, the U.S. Congress rescinded that right.

Polygamy represents an instance of comparable irony. To outsiders, the institution seemed prima facie evidence of an oppressive inequality. In popular fiction of the era, as we saw, polygamous brides were frequently the victims of raiding parties or kidnappers coercing female victims into a version of white slavery. Literary heroes were often defined by virtue of their daring exploits in saving Mormon women from this version of "oriental despotism." American demagogues and preachers launched a public campaign of denunciation whose moral fervor, scope, and resources matched abolition itself.

At one point in the late 1880s, the federal government even funded the construction of a huge Industrial Christian Home as a sanctuary for escaped plural wives. The waves of refugees never materialized, and the home closed down a few years later. The public should not have been surprised. In 1870, in response to proposed antipolygamy legislation, thousands of Mormon women gathered in Salt Lake to demonstrate in support of the practice. With eloquence and surprising solidarity, they passionately attacked federal intervention in their supposed behalf. None of this is to say that LDS women found plural marriage especially amenable or emotionally satisfying. But if it was a trial, it was a trial they believed they were called by God to endure, and many prided themselves in the higher spiritual qualities of selflessness and sacrifice that such a practice required.

And in actual practice, plural marriage turned out to be far from the degrading institution of fiction and *Punch* cartoons. The social reality, unexpectedly, was that polygamy by its very nature engendered great independence and resilience on the part of women necessarily deprived of the presence of a constant companion. One historian has commented that "Mormon women in pioneer Utah had social power that was unavailable to other women throughout the United States and Europe. Polygamous wives often had sole responsibility for months or years to manage their households, farms, or family businesses. Monogamous wives did likewise whenever their husbands were called on two-year proselytizing missions (a very common practice until the 1900s)."[33] And it was not just the plural or missionary wives that Mormonism provoked to independence. Brigham Young encouraged Mormon women in general to secure an education and develop careers not typically open to women in the nineteenth century, including business, accounting, medicine, and law. "They should stand behind the counter," he urged, "study law or physic, or become good book-keepers and be able to do the business in any counting house, and all this to enlarge their sphere of usefulness for the benefit of society at large."[34] Outside Utah, few women received such encouragement in this era.

The church had inaugurated a women's organization, the Relief Society, in Nauvoo in 1842, which was disbanded in the turmoil that followed. Young reestablished it in 1867 under the leadership of the dynamic Eliza R. Snow. Soon, the organization spread to every LDS community, making valuable contributions to the economic self-sufficiency of the Saints. LDS women soon launched a grain storage program, began an ambitious silk-worm industry, and in 1872 inaugurated their own journal, the *Woman's Exponent*, unabashedly feminist in its orientation. Anticipating much of the twentieth-century feminist agenda, the *Exponent* proclaimed sexual equality and lobbied for gender equity in pay. After 1890, when the church stand against fiction had softened, LDS women published fiction in three LDS youth magazines as well as their own novels and short stories.[35] Editing and producing their own journal and literature was but one indication of the independent mentality of LDS women. In the educational realm, the LDS people had already shown themselves unusually progressive with regard to women.

As early as 1842 in the Mormon capital of Nauvoo, a Lyceum was held on the question, "Should Females be educated to the same extent as Males?" The verdict was not recorded, but evidence of the consensus reached is pretty strong. According to county records, over half the students enrolled in Nauvoo's schools were female. Slightly earlier, a witness to the migration of Mormons into Illinois had observed that "the women were generally well educated and as a rule were quite intelligent." In fact, it has been suggested that the Mormons' liberal views on the equality of the sexes were in part responsible for hostility to the church in Illinois.[36]

Shortly after the Saints entered the Salt Lake Valley, they founded the University of Deseret (now the University of Utah). After a brief existence in the 1850s, it reopened in 1868, with women comprising almost 50 percent of the class.[37] After Brigham Young advised women to attend medical schools, the Relief Society supported a number of sisters in going east to obtain training. With Relief Society support, Romania B. Pratt Penrose, Ellis Shipp and Margaret Shipp Roberts (sister wives), together with Martha Hughes Cannon and many others, returned with degree in hand to establish practices and teach classes. Eliza Snow even attempted to establish a Female Medical College so Utah could train its own women doctors.[38] By the turn of the century, more female American medical students hailed from Utah than from any other state in the Union.[39] The dual emphasis on family responsibilities and educational achievement for women continues to the present day in Mormonism. Recent studies affirm that "education . . . is more consistent with marriage, childbearing, and church activity for Mormons than is the case nationally."[40]

Suffragist leaders of the nineteenth century deplored plural marriage, but found unlikely allies among Mormon women just the same. For while it was easy to see polygamy and political equality as incompatible, Mormon women actually found in their religion a basis for aspirations to full equality and self-realization. One reason for this can be found in Mormonism's radical reinterpretation of the fall. As we have seen, Latter-day Saints see in this primordial transgression a cause for celebration and not lament. And since it was Eve whose initiative set the whole process in motion, Eve is venerated rather than reviled in Mormon thought. Church leaders have consistently taught that "Mother Eve bestowed upon her daughters and sons a heritage of honor, for she acted with wisdom, love, and unselfish sacrifice."[41] At one blow, then, Mormonism circumvents a historical tradition that sees Eve as the prototype of vulnerable, fallen woman, as Milton's weaker vessel and the universal temptress.

And finally, in what is undoubtedly the most radically feminist gesture in Christian theology, Mormon leaders have insisted that we worship God the Father, but recognize as well a Heavenly Mother. This teaching appears to have been first officially promulgated by President Wilford Woodruff in an 1893 church conference, when he said, "with regard to our position before we came here, I will say that we dwelt with the Father and with the Son, as expressed in the hymn, 'O my Father,' that has been sung here. That hymn is a revelation, though it was given unto us by a woman—Sister Snow."[42]

The verse in the hymn to which he referred asks "in the heavens, are parents single?" and continues, "no the thought makes reason stare: truth is wisdom, truth eternal tells me I've a mother there." Eliza R. Snow, Mormon poetess and author of that hymn, was a plural wife of Joseph Smith, and sources indicate that it was from Joseph she first received the idea.

In spite of the potential this doctrine bodes for a radical challenge to patriarchal theology, it remains undeveloped and unheralded, as we saw earlier. Some Mormon feminists have used the belief as a justification for praying to a Heavenly Mother, and criticize the church for its failure to celebrate and worship two deities. In actual fact, no Mormon scripture or revelation addresses the subject, and in the absence of a tradition of speculative theology, Mormon leaders generally refrain from elaboration. As one LDS scholar notes, "The widening 'theology' [concerning Heavenly Mother] which is developing is more of a 'folk,' or at least speculative, theology than a systematic development by theologians or a set of definitive pronouncements from ecclesiastical leaders. For the moment, Mother in Heaven can be almost whatever an individual Mormon envisions her to be."[43] That may be true, but in the 1990s, the church acted to discipline some whose continued public pronouncements or advocacy of their views were deemed unacceptable.[44]

In the contemporary church, Mormon stereotypes are vindicated in some regards and upset in others. Not surprisingly, given their emphasis on marriage and family, LDS women giving birth are more likely to be married than their counterparts. Mormon mothers are also more likely to be professionally employed; they graduate from college, and have postgraduate training at a higher rate than Protestant and Catholic counterparts.[45] Another stereotype has cast Utah LDS women as unusually prone to depression. The most recent research in this area, however, discovered that "LDS women report levels of life satisfaction similar to other women, have higher levels of global happiness, and . . . their levels of mental depression are significantly below those reported by other women throughout the United States."[46]

The American feminist movement of the 1960s had some impact on Mormon culture, registering on the pages of some of the independent Mormon journals (like *Dialogue*), and more particularly in the founding in 1974 of *Exponent II*, a quarterly magazine targeting readers who share "a connection to the Mormon Church and a commitment to women" (the original publication ceased in 1914).[47] But the LDS Church first confronted feminism directly and dramatically in 1976, when the First Presidency issued a statement opposing passage of the Equal Rights Amendment (ERA). The document cited the amendment's encouragement of a "unisex society," and its potential to threaten the family as an institution, by failing to recognize traditional gender roles and differences. Negative reaction to the church's position increased with the excommunication of ERA proponent Sonia Johnson in 1979, who parleyed the event into a public relations success by insisting her beliefs, rather than her public attacks on church leaders and church missionary work, were the basis for church sanctions. Ultimately, the church's ability to mobilize member opposition to the amendment was seen as decisive in its 1982 defeat, though widespread support for passage was by then waning nationally.

The most pressing questions about the church and women, of course, ultimately come down to the exclusion of women from the priesthood. Women may pray and preach in LDS worship meetings, they may give counsel in the worldwide General Conferences of the church, and they may preside over local or global auxiliaries of the church. But they cannot sit in the leading councils with apostles and prophets, or administer baptism and sit at the sacrament table to administer the Lord's Supper.

The LDS explanation for a gender-restricted priesthood is that the privileges and obligations of motherhood balance the obligations and privileges of priesthood. As Joseph Fielding Smith wrote, "A woman's calling is in a different direction. The most noble, exalting calling of all is that which has been given to women as the mothers of men. Women do not hold the priesthood, but if they are faithful and true, they will become priestesses and queens in the kingdom of God, and that implies that they will be given authority."[48] "Our roles and assignments differ," was how President Spencer W. Kimball put it more simply.[49]

That rationale may sound unsatisfactory to the childless, or those who want equal access to authority on this side of the River Jordan. Studies indicate that LDS women would like to be more involved with decision making in the church,[50] and in recent years, especially at the local level, "ward councils," leadership meetings in which women are represented, have played an increasingly emphasized role in ward governance. Most LDS women appear satisfied with the status quo regarding access to the priesthood itself. This is probably a result of several of the factors mentioned above, but most likely is a reflection of a theology that is, at its heart's core, radically egalitarian and marriage-centered. For as we have seen, marriage in Mormon thought need not be of merely temporal duration. That the marriage relationship can be of eternal duration may itself be unique among Christian belief systems. But the LDS scriptures also affirm that marriage is in fact indispensable—not just permissible—as a prelude to eternal life. As Joseph Fielding Smith put it succinctly, "a man cannot be exalted singly and alone."[51] Perhaps this explains the response typical of rank-and-file Mormon women. "To tell you the truth, the whole issue of women and the priesthood really isn't very high on my spiritual 'worry list,'" writes one woman (herself a world-renowned radiologist and wife of a General Authority). "I think no religion holding as one of its fundamental tenets that the seed of godhood is in every man and every woman and that neither can achieve it without the other could by any reasonable, fair definition be called sexist."[52]

Mormons certainly realize the potential for abuse in a patriarchal system. Joseph spoke feelingly of having learned "by sad experience that it is the nature and disposition of almost all men, as soon as they get a little authority, as they suppose, they will immediately begin to exercise unrighteous dominion." Thus the scriptural injunction to men, that "No power or influence can or ought to be maintained by virtue of the priesthood, only by persuasion, by long-suffering, by gentleness and meekness, and by love unfeigned"; as for those who undertake to "exercise control or dominion or compulsion upon the souls of the children of men, in any degree of unrighteousness, behold, the heavens withdraw themselves; the Spirit of the Lord is grieved; and when it is withdrawn, Amen to the priesthood or the authority of that man" (DC 121:39, 41, 37).

That it will continue to be a priesthood of men for a long while to come—or permanently—seems likely. President Howard W. Hunter said in 1994 that "there isn't an avenue of ever changing. It's too well defined by revelation, by Scripture. . . . I see nothing that will lead to a change of direction at the present time—or in the future."[53] There is nothing in LDS scripture that explicitly precludes such a possibility; President Hunter was apparently referring to the scriptural pattern of a male-only priesthood. Such tradition, however, does not trump revelatory novelty in Mormon thought. In theory, at least, the possibility is always there of a change that could take everyone—Mormon and non-Mormon—by surprise.

Environment

In 1798, Thomas Malthus published his highly influential *Essay on the Principle of Population* in which he argued that "the power of population is indefinitely greater than the power in the earth to produce subsistence for man." Therefore, he gloomily concluded, "I see no way by which man can escape from the weight of this law which pervades all animated nature. No fancied equality, no agrarian regulations in their utmost extent, could remove the pressure of it even for a single century. And it appears, therefore, to be decisive against the possible existence of a society, all the members of which should live in ease, happiness, and comparative leisure; and feel no anxiety about providing the means of subsistence for themselves and families."[54]

Thirty-six years later, Joseph Smith asserted rather more optimistically, God would insist that "the earth is full, and there is enough and to spare; yea, I prepared all things" (DC 104:17). This is not to say the LDS view of earthly abundance is a license to squander those assets. On the contrary, as Brigham Young insisted to the Utah Saints:

> There is only so much property in the world. There are the elements that belong to this globe, and no more. We do not go to the moon to borrow; neither send to the sun or any of the planets; all our commercial transactions must be confined to this little earth and its wealth cannot be increased or diminished; and though the improvements in the arts of life which have taken place within the memory of many now living are very wonderful, there is no question that extravagance has more than kept pace with them.[55]

Mormons have abundant reason to be especially zealous in their appreciation for the world and its resources. First, God explicitly charged mankind with accountability for his care of an abundant creation. As Joseph recorded, "it is expedient that I, the Lord, should make every man accountable, as a steward over earthly blessings, which I have made and prepared for my creatures" (DC 104:13). This idea of stewardship is deeply ingrained in Mormon religious thought. Priesthood holders make regular accountability reports, called Personal Priesthood Interviews. The Mormon temple teaches the principle through a modeled pattern of assignment and reporting. Echoing the Great Intercessory Prayer of Jesus (John 17), where he gave an accounting for the disciples entrusted to his care, Mormons are frequently reminded that their children are "on loan" to them, until they prove worthy of an eternal union. Stewardship for the earth, therefore, has special resonance in the Mormon mind, and is part of a larger pattern of probationary responsibilities with eternal repercussions.

Second, Joseph F. Smith taught that "Heaven was the prototype of this beautiful creation when it came from the hand of the Creator, and was pronounced 'good.'"[56] Darwin may have believed that it was impossible for one species to exist "for the exclusive good of another species."[57] But Joseph taught a creation whose variety and beauty were, apparently, primarily calculated to elicit human delight and rejoicing. "The fulness of the earth is yours," he wrote by way of revelation,

> the beasts of the field and the fowls of the air, and that which climbeth upon the trees and walketh upon the earth; Yea, and the herb, and the good things which come of the earth, whether for food or for raiment, or for houses, or for barns, or for orchards, or for gardens, or for vineyards, Yea all things which come of the earth, in the season thereof, are made for the benefit and use of man, both to please the eye and to gladden the heart; Yea, for food and for raiment, for taste and for smell, to strengthen the body and to enliven the soul. And it pleaseth God that he hath given all these things unto man; for unto this end were they to be used. (DC 59:16–20)

Third, the church espouses as an article of faith the belief that at the time of Christ's second advent, this earth will "be renewed and receive its paradisiacal glory." This future state of the earth involves more than a temporary cleansing preparatory to millennial glory. For it is this same earth that will eventually become the abode of the righteous. "After it has filled the measure of its creation," an LDS scripture declares, "it shall be crowned with glory, even with the presence of God the Father; That bodies who are of the celestial kingdom may possess it forever and ever" (DC 88:19–20). Presumably, seeing this realm as a prospective heaven rather than as a god-forsaken wilderness and place of exile conditions the LDS relationship to our surroundings. In that regard, Brigham Young was of the opinion that any future paradise would be the product of diligent stewardship, not miraculous transformation. "Who placed the dark stain of sin upon this fair creation? Man. Who but man shall remove the foul blot, and restore all things to their primeval purity and innocence?"[58]

Accordingly, some LDS writers see Malachi's prophecy that the hearts of the fathers would be turned to their children (Mal. 4:6) as a prediction of a more environmentally conscientious age.[59] Recent LDS prophets have emphasized the principles of earthly stewardship first enunciated by Smith and Young. President Spencer W. Kimball counseled members that "there be no undue pollution, that the land be taken care of and kept clean, productive, and beautiful."[60] And President Ezra Taft Benson asserted that "physical and spiritual laws are interrelated. Pollution of one's environment and moral impurity both rest on a life-style which partakes of a philosophy of 'eat, drink, and be merry'—gouge and grab now, without regard to the consequences. Both violate the spirit of stewardship for which we will stand accountable. . . . The Church has urged its members to be efficient users of our resources, to avoid waste and pollution, and to clean up their own immediate environment or that over which they have control."[61]

Initially, the Mormons were bound by necessity to zealously shepherd their scanty resources, eking a precarious existence out of the barren Salt Lake desert. Bringing mountain water into the valley, planting crops, and beautifying their spartan homesteads, they made the desert "blossom as a rose." Nurture rather than exploitation characterized their relationship to their environment. When the first gold and silver deposits were discovered in Bingham canyon in 1863, Young vigorously resisted pressures to develop a mining industry. The commanding officer of nearby Fort Douglas saw the mineral potential of Utah as holding the key to solving the Mormon Problem. Writing to a fellow officer, he explained:

> My policy in this territory has been to invite hither a large gentile and loyal population, sufficient by peaceful means, and through the ballot box, to overwhelm the Mormons by mere force of numbers, and thus wrest from the Church—disloyal and traitorous to the core—the absolute and tyrannical control of temporal and civic affairs . . . I have bent every energy and means of which I was possessed, both personal and official, towards the discovery and development of the mining resources of the Territory, using without stint the soldiers at my command, wherever and whenever it could be done.[62]

Young felt that the frenzied pursuit of the world's mineral wealth, epitomized in the California Gold Rush, was anathema to a Zion society and a corruption of more provident economic principles. As he protested to the Saints months after the discovery of the deposits:

> it is a fearful deception which all the world labors under, and many of this people, too, who profess to be not of the world, that gold is wealth. . . . Can you not see that gold and silver rank among the things that we are the least in want of? We want an abundance of wheat and fine flour, of wine and oil, and every choice fruit that will grow in our climate; we want silk, wool, cotton, flax and other textile substances of which cloth can be made; we want vegetables . . . The colossal wealth of the world is founded upon and sustained by the common staples of life.[63]

It is also true, as Lowell Bennion has written, that "motives more important than material interest led Brigham Young to develop agriculture rather than mining in the West."[64] Young had long expressed his fear that greed and worldliness would contaminate the spiritual character of a people long inured to hardship and frugal lifestyles. His approach was both spiritually and economically prescient. "Cooperation and planning caused the desert to bloom," writes one historian, "in marked contrast to the exploitive patterns of agriculture which on other frontiers exhausted natural resources and left the land a smoking waste."[65]

With the completion of the transcontinental railroad in 1869, Young's efforts to insulate Utah from the lure of mammon was dealt a devastating blow. Soon, in the words of one historian, "it became one of the nation's most active mining centers, and, by 1919, Salt Lake Valley had become the largest smelter district in North America. These smelters added their disgusting and unhealthy fumes to the coal-generated smoke from railroads, homes, and businesses. All of these noxious vapors turned Salt Lake City into a sinkhole that rivaled Pittsburgh, Cincinnati, Chicago, and St. Louis in airborne filth."[66]

At the present day, there are clearly discrepancies between prophetic priorities and the Utah record. President Kimball expressed great concerns in this regard, when he decried pollution of mind and body, but also of the environment. "When I review the performance of this people in comparison of what is expected," he told his people, "I am appalled and frightened."[67] Avid environmentalist and the gadfly of Mormonism Hugh Nibley points out that in recent years critics have declared the congressional delegation from Utah the most antienvironmentalist in the nation. "Ecology and environment are dirty words in Utah," he laments.[68] That may be an overstatement. But the League of Conservation Voters consistently rank the state's legislators near the bottom on environmental issues. For the 107th Congress (2001–2), both senators scored 4 percent, and its two Republican congressmen scored 5 percent and 9 percent. (The lone Democrat, Jim Matheson, scored 68 percent.) An earlier 1991 report ranked the environmental policies of the thirty largest Christian denominations in the United States; the LDS Church placed in the fifth and lowest category.[69]

The image of environmentalism was not enhanced for Mormons when in 1996 President Bill Clinton invoked the 1906 Antiquities Act to declare 1.7 million acres of southern Utah lands as the new Grand Staircase-Escalante National Monument, a move widely interpreted as vindictive and autocratic. In any case, the incident certainly echoed a legacy of federal intervention and antagonism that has made Utah culture more resistant than most to government oversight of personal and local property rights. In fact, William B. Smart, former editor of the church-owned *Deseret News*, has written that "in the past half century, no issue has torn apart my state as the use of the land that once seemed so limitless."[70] Acclaimed environmental author (and Mormon) Terry Tempest Williams has teamed with other Mormon writers to urge fellow Saints to "change our behavior of inactivity toward the earth, personally and collectively," reminding readers of how inconsistent with the heritage of Brigham Young and Joseph Smith are the affluent lifestyles and environmental apathy of today's Latter-day Saint community.[71]

During the march of Zion's Camp, an expedition mounted by Ohio Saints to assist their persecuted brethren in Missouri, someone noticed several rattlesnakes at a resting spot. A man was about to kill the reptiles when Joseph Smith reprimanded him: "How do you expect enmity to cease between man and beast," he asked, "if men continually seek to kill the animals?" He went on to say that if man "would banish from our hearts this spirit to destroy and murder, the day would soon come when the lion and the lamb would lie down together."[72] A century and a half later, Mormon President Spencer W. Kimball caused consternation among Utah sport hunters when he admonished members to heed the words of the children's song Mormons used to sing, "Don't kill the little birds."[73]

Given the strictures of the Word of Wisdom, which admonished Latter-day Saints to eat meat sparingly, and the pronouncements of Joseph Smith, one might expect Mormons to espouse a quasi-vegetarianism. The beasts John saw in his Revelation, Joseph wrote, were actual individual creatures, that represented "the glory of the classes of beings in their destined order or sphere of creation, in the enjoyment of their eternal felicity" (DC 77:3). "Always keep in view," Brigham Young concluded, "that the animal, vegetable, and mineral kingdoms—the earth and its fulness—will all, except the children of man, abide their creation—the law by which they were made, and will receive their exaltation."[74] More recently, LDS scriptorian and future prophet Joseph Fielding Smith affirmed clearly that "animals do have spirits and that through the redemption made by our Savior they will come forth in the resurrection to enjoy the blessing of immortal life."[75]

In LDS thought, it is clear that human dominion over the earth should be a call to reverence, not a license to exploit. In Mormon culture, the conflict between a tradition of frontier individualism and wilderness-taming on the one hand and environmental progressivism on the other have not found full resolution. As one observer has written, "it should be of the greatest interest and importance to see if the LDS Church is able to incorporate in any formal sense the enormous, revitalizing energy which is being generated by ecologically-minded Mormons in Utah and elsewhere today."[76]

War and Peace

In the early history of the Mormon Church, violent opposition repeatedly forced the leadership to choose between the path of armed resistance or sacrifice of personal rights. Mormons usually chose the latter as a simple matter of self-preservation. In 1833, Mormon numbers were insufficient to resist their forcible expulsion from Jackson County, Missouri. Smith mounted a paramilitary relief expedition from Ohio, called Zion's Camp, but weakened by sickness and internal dissention, and faced with overwhelming opposition from Missourians, the Saints returned to the east without waging battle. Again in 1836, the Saints submitted to removal from Clay County, Missouri. In 1838, they fought limited battles against opponents in Caldwell County, but were quickly overwhelmed and exiled once more. Established in Nauvoo, Smith commanded a militia of three to five thousand trained Mormons under arms. But even this impressive force never engaged in major conflict. Joseph submitted to an imprisonment he sensed would lead to his death, rather than ignite a civil war by summoning the Legion to defend him.

During the Civil War, the Mormons kept themselves mostly aloof from military involvement. But this was not a studied pacifism. Near neutrality (Mormons did protect Union mail routes) came more from an unwillingness to involve themselves in a quarrel between slave-holding Rebels, with whom they would have had little affinity, and a federal government that had recently invaded their own territory, and who could therefore make little claim upon their allegiance. A generation later, however, Utah had achieved statehood, and the church responded to the next conflict with patriotic zeal: once war was declared against Spain in 1898, the First Presidency issued a statement urging youth of the church to support the national cause. In the war's aftermath, and as a global conflict neared, Elder Anthony W. Ivins explained the church's position at a General Conference: "We do not hasten into war, because we do not believe in it; we believe it to be unnecessary; but, nevertheless, if it shall come, we believe it to be our duty to defend those principles of liberty and right and equality which were established by the Father."[77]

With the outbreak of World War I, Latter-day Saints were still anxious to prove their loyalty to a still dubious American public. More than twenty thousand members served in Allied armies, and about 650 died.[78] At the same time, church leaders urged respect for both conscientious objectors and enemy combatants who, as subjects of their leaders, were themselves innocent. As American involvement in World War II approached, church leaders urged caution, with prominent member of the First Presidency J. Reuben Clark especially outspoken against U.S. involvement. Even as church leaders expressed misgivings about the prospect of large standing armies on American soil, they once again clearly exonerated individual members of bloodshed committed in response to obligations imposed even by unrighteous governments or those opposed to American forces: "God . . . will not hold the innocent instrumentalities of the war, our brethren in arms, responsible for the conflict."[79] Clark would continue to espouse a pacifist position to the end of his life, but it never became the majority stand of LDS leaders. The official LDS position espoused at the time of the Vietnam conflict was that "membership in the Church of Jesus Christ of Latter-day Saints does not make one a conscientious objector. . . . [But] there would seem to be no objection . . . to a man availing himself on a personal basis of the exemption provided by law."[80]

In practice, U.S. Mormons tend to serve *less* in the armed forces than their counterparts do.[81] This is probably a result of the fact that most active LDS young men commit two years of their lives to full-time missionary service, and additional service in the military would be inordinately burdensome. Nevertheless, patriotism continues to run high among Latter-day Saints, and Mormons have served honorably in every major American war.

In an age when some Christian churches are moving toward military isolationism and even embracing pacifism, Mormon leaders have repudiated militarism while continuing to defend the concept of "just war." Spencer W. Kimball surprised the public—and much of his own constituency—when he spoke out in emphatic opposition to the Reagan administration's plan to base an MX missile system in Utah. "We are a warlike people, easily distracted from our assignment of preparing for the coming of the Lord. When enemies rise up, we commit vast resources to the fabrications of gods of stone and steel—ships, planes, missiles, fortifications," he wrote. "When threatened, we become antienemy instead of pro-kingdom of God, we train a man in the art of war and call him a patriot, thus, in the manner of Satan's counterfeit of true patriotism, perverting the Savior's teachings."[82] Still, with rare exceptions, LDS leaders have been firm supporters of American military involvements, believing, as Gordon B. Hinckley said, that "until the Prince of Peace comes to reign, there always will be tyrants and bullies, empire builders, slave seekers, and despots who would destroy every shred of human liberty if they were not opposed by force of arms."[83]

Several factors probably account for these leanings. First, Latter-day Saints see the War for American Independence as a divinely ordained prelude to the restoration of the gospel. The Founding Fathers, they believe, were foreordained by God to frame the Constitution, and the prophet Nephi saw the revolutionaries in vision, and that "the power of God was with them" (1 Nephi 13:18). The roots of the church itself, therefore, are integrally connected with a just war.

Second, the Book of Mormon, a record replete with catastrophic conflicts, validates defensive warfare while condemning a certain form of passivity in the face of evil. At a time of national crisis, Captain Moroni erects a battle standard to rally his people, "the title of liberty," on which he writes "in memory of our God, our religion, and freedom, and our peace, our wives, and our children." The record's editor later says of this Nephite freedom fighter that "if all men had been, and were, and ever would be, like unto Moroni, behold, the very powers of hell would have been shaken forever" (Alma 48:17).

When Lamanite armies threaten to overwhelm the land, Nephite dissenters who sympathize with the invaders refuse to take up arms. Moroni obtains permission to "compel those dissenters to defend their country or to put them to death" (Alma 51:15). Time and again Book of Mormon prophets remind us that the spirit of liberty is wedded to principles of righteousness. More recently, during the controversies surrounding American involvement in the second Persian Gulf War, President Hinckley spoke in muted, subtle terms, nonetheless reminiscent of Moroni's impatience with opponents of freedom. "There are times and circumstances when nations are justified, in fact have an obligation, to fight for family, for liberty, and against tyranny, threat, and oppression," he said, warning further that "it may even be that He will hold us responsible if we try to impede or hedge up the way of those who are involved in a contest with forces of evil and repression."[84]

At the same time, as Hinckley and other church leaders have urged, Latter-day Saints are commanded by revelation to "renounce war and proclaim peace" (DC 98:16). The Book of Mormon also describes a group of Lamanites who convert to righteousness and repudiate every form of violence, even taking an oath to that effect. When they are attacked by their former brethren, they submit passively, like Gandhi's benign resisters, and are hewn down by the hundreds. Their pacifism is lauded and their salvation affirmed by the admiring chronicler of the wars. In this case, however, the slain individuals had earlier made a covenant binding themselves to nonviolence. So it would appear to be their integrity more than principled passivity that accounts for this approbation. For the children of these same pacifists, not bound by the covenants of their parents, become a mighty army of "stripling warriors" themselves.

Finally, one foundation of Mormon belief is what members commonly refer to as "the war in Heaven." The oblique reference from the book of Revelation, according to which Michael and his angels fight the dragon and his angels (12:6–8), is for Mormons a key episode in the ongoing battle for human souls. Following God's announcement of a high-stakes plan involving human embodiment in this earthly sphere of mortal probation, Christ was put forward as the redeemer of the human family, with power to save the penitent. Lucifer, Mormons believe, opposed the plan, and proposed himself as a savior who would redeem all the human family, but at the cost of their moral agency. The warfare that ensued, then, culminating in the expulsion of Lucifer and his followers from Heaven, was a conflict in which defenders of the principle of moral agency contended against the proponents of spiritual tyranny. Deeply ingrained in the Latter-day Saint psyche, in other words, is a collective memory of premortal war in which Christ's valiant supporters fought for liberty. So a tradition of American patriotism combines in Mormon culture with a theology of preexistent battles over moral agency and a Book of Mormon rhetoric of righteous freedom-fighters to produce a generally widespread support for the American military and its actions.

Notes

1. Sarah Barringer Gordon, *The Mormon Question: Polygamy and Constitutional Conflict in the Nineteenth Century* (Chapel Hill: University of North Carolina Press, 2002), 231.

2. Joseph Fielding Smith, *Church History and Modern Revelation*, 4 vols. (Salt Lake City: The Church of Jesus Christ of Latter-day Saints, 1946–49), 4.

3. Harold Bloom, *The American Religion: The Emergence of a Post-Christian Nation* (New York: Simon and Schuster, 1992), 270.

4. "Latter-day Saints in the United States are somewhat more likely than other Americans to be elected to Congress." James T. Duke, "Cultural Continuity and Tension: A Test of Stark's Theory of Church Growth," in James T. Duke, ed., *Latter-day Saint Social Life: Social Research on the LDS Church and its Members* (Provo, Utah: Religious Studies Center, Brigham Young University, 1998), 84.

5. *Journal of Discourses*, 26 vols., reported by G. D. Watt et al. (Liverpool: F. D. and S. W. Richards et al., 1851–86; reprint, Salt Lake City: n.p., 1974), 4:297–98.

6. This distinction was first elaborated by Richard D. Poll, "What the Church Means to People Like Me," *Dialogue* 2 (winter 1967): 107–18.

7. Neal A. Maxwell, *Deposition of a Disciple* (Salt Lake City: Deseret, 1976), 15.

8. *Journal of Discourses,* 11:127.

9. Ibid., 4:56.

10. First Presidency Statement of David O. McKay, Hugh B. Brown, and N. Eldon Tanner, 14 April 1969.

11. *Church Handbook of Instructions* (Salt Lake City: Church of Jesus Christ of Latter-day Saints, 1998), 158.

12. See Tim B. Heaton and S. Calkins, "Family Size and Contraceptive Use among Mormons: 1965–75," *Review of Religious Research* 25, no. 2 (1983): 103–14. Calvin Goldscheider and William D. Mosher also find negligible differences in "Patterns of Contraceptive Use in the United States: The Importance of Religious Factors," *Studies in Family Planning* 22, no. 2 (March–April 1991): 102–15.

13. "LDS Position on Abortion," *Deseret News,* 12 January 1991, B6.

14. Dallin H. Oakes, "Weightier Matters," BYU Devotional Address, 9 February 1999.

15. Letter of the First Presidency, 14 November 1991.

16. Dallin H. Oaks, "Same-Gender Attraction," *Ensign* 25, no. 10 (October 1995): 7.

17. Ibid., 9.

18. W. Byne and B. Parsons, "Human Sexual Orientation: The Biologic Theories Reappraised," *Archives of General Psychiatry* 50 (1993): 236–37. Cited in Oaks, "Same-Gender," 12.

19. "The Family: A Proclamation to the World," by the First Presidency and Council of the Twelve Apostles of the Church of Jesus Christ of Latter-day Saints, first read in the General Relief Society Meeting, 23 September 1995.

20. Armand Mauss, *All Abraham's Children: Changing Mormon Conceptions of Race and Lineage* (Urbana: University of Illinois Press, 2003), 252–55.

21. D. Michael Quinn, "LDS 'Headquarters Culture' and the Rest of Mormonism: Past and Present," *Dialogue* 34, nos. 3–4 (fall–winter 2001): 141.

22. The closest thing to an authoritative declaration from a church leader would be Young's comment recorded by Wilford Woodruff on 16 January 1852: "Any man having one drop of the seed of [Cain] . . . in him cannot hold the priesthood, and if no other prophet ever spake it before I will say it now." Matthias Cowley, *Wilford Woodruff* (Salt Lake City: Deseret, 1909), 351.

23. Orson Hyde, "Speech Given Before the High Priests Quorum in Nauvoo," 25 April 1845 Liverpool, 1845, 30.

24. Hugh Nibley, most notably, argues that the passage in Abraham is about a matriarchal versus a patriarchal claim to priesthood rights. See his *Abraham in Egypt,* in *The Collected Works of Hugh Nibley,* 15 vols. (Provo, Utah: Deseret and FARMS, 1986–), 14:528.

25. First Presidency Statement, 17 August 1949. Quoted in *"Neither White Nor Black": Mormon Scholars Confront the Race Issue in a Universal Church,* ed. Lester Bush and Armand Mauss (Midvale, Utah: Signature, 1984), 221.

26. Mauss, *All Abraham's Children,* 219.

27. E. Dale LeBaron, "Mormonism in Black Africa," in Douglas J. Davies, ed., *Mormon Identities in Transition* (London: Cassell, 1996), 81.

28. "Official Declaration-2," DC.

29. Mauss, *All Abraham's Children,* 81. Mauss's is the most comprehensive treatment of the history of racial attitudes in Mormon thought.

30. In addition to the genetic imprecision of the term *Lamanite,* and the possibility of cultural interbreeding with indigenous populations, uncertainties about the exact genetic composition of the source population make DNA analysis a poor tool for assessing Book of Mormon historicity.

31. Question and Answer Session following "Does DNA Evidence Refute the Authenticity of the Book of Mormon: A Response to the Critics," January 29, 2003 (Brigham Young University). Transcript at www.salamandersociety.org/news/.

32. Wyoming extended the vote to women a few months before the Utah legislature, but held no elections where women could exercise their franchise until after Utah had.

33. Quinn, "LDS 'Headquarters Culture,'" 148.

34. *Journal of Discourses,* 13:62.

35. Rebecca de Schweinitz, "Preaching the Gospel of Church and Sex: Mormon Women's Fiction in the *Young Woman's Journal,* 1889–1910," *Dialogue* 33, no. 4 (winter 2000): 29.

36. George Givens, *In Old Nauvoo: Everyday Life in the City of Joseph* (Salt Lake City: Deseret, 1990), 227–36.

37. Leonard J. Arrington and Davis Bitton, *The Mormon Experience* (New York: Random House, 1979), 337.

38. Jill Mulvay Derr, Janath Russell Cannon, and Maureen Ursenbach Beecher, *Women of Covenant: The Story of the Relief Society* (Salt Lake City: Deseret, 1992), 107.

39. Claudia L. Bushman, *Mormon Sisters: Women in Early Utah* (Logan: Utah State University Press, 1997), 58–59.

40. Tim B. Heaton, "Familial, Socioeconomic, and Religious Behavior: A Comparison of LDS and Non-LDS Women," *Dialogue* 27, no. 2 (summer 1994): 177.

41. Beverly Campbell, "Eve," in Daniel Ludlow, ed., *Encyclopedia of Mormonism,* 4 vols. (New York: Macmillan, 1992), 2:476.

42. *Millennial Star* 56 (9 April 1894): 229.

43. Linda P. Wilcox in Maureen Ursenbach Beecher and Lavina Fielding Anderson, eds., *Sisters in Spirit: Mormon Women in Historical and Cultural Perspective* (Urbana: University of Illinois Press, 1987), 74.

44. Maxine Hanks, for example, who wrote and lectured on the subject of a Heavenly Mother, was excommunicated in September 1993. In 1997, BYU refused to grant continuing status to Gail Turley Houston, citing her "advocacy" on the issue of "praying to Heavenly Mother." Kristin Moulton, "Profs Say BYU Short on Academic Freedom," *Denver Post,* 15 September 1997.

45. Merlin B. Brinkerhoff and Marlene MacKie, "Religion and Gender: A Comparison of Canadian and American Student Attitudes," *Journal of Marriage and the Family* 47 (1985): 415–29.

46. Sherrie Mills Johnson, "Religiosity and Life Satisfaction of LDS Women" (Ph.D. diss., Brigham Young University, 2003), 97.

47. From the homepage of *Exponent II* : www.exponentii.org.

48. Joseph Fielding Smith, *Doctrines of Salvation,* 3 vols., ed. Bruce R. McConkie (Salt Lake City: Bookcraft, 1954–56), 3: 178.

49. *Ensign* 29, no. 11 (November 1979): 102.

50. Studies to this effect have been referred to by Mormon apostle Melvin J. Ballard. Cited in Lynn Matthew Anderson, "Issues in Contemporary Mormon Feminism," in Davies, *Mormon Identities,* 165.

51. Smith, *Doctrines of Salvation,* 2:65.

52. Anne Osborn Poelman, *The Simeon Solution: One Woman's Spiritual Odyssey* (Salt Lake City: Deseret, 1995), 4.

53. *Los Angeles Times,* 22 October 1994.

54. Thomas Malthus, *Population: The First Essay* (Ann Arbor: University of Michigan Press, 1959), 6.

55. *Journal of Discourses,* 13:304.

56. Ibid., 23:175.

57. "If it could be proved that any part of the structure of any one species had been formed for the exclusive good of another species, it would annihilate my theory," Darwin wrote. Thomas F. Glick and David Kohn, eds., *Darwin on Evolution* (Indianapolis: Hackett, 1996), 208.

58. *Journal of Discourses,* 10:301.

59. Alan J. Hawkins, David C. Dollahite, and Clifford J. Rhoades, "Turning the Hearts of the Fathers to the Children: Nurturing the Next Generation," *BYU Studies* 33, no. 2 (1993): 273–92.

60. Spencer W. Kimball, "Why Call Me Lord, Lord, and Do Not the Things Which I Say?" *Ensign* 5, no. 5 (May 1975): 5.

61. Ezra Taft Benson, *Teachings of Ezra Taft Benson* (Salt Lake City: Bookcraft, 1988), 644–45.

62. General Conner's report, from which this portion comes, is excerpted in B. H. Roberts, *A Comprehensive History of The Church of Jesus Christ of Latter-day Saints,* 6 vols. (Salt Lake City: Deseret, 1930), 5.

63. Discourse of 25 October, 1863, in *Deseret News* (18 November 1863).

64. Lowell L. Bennion, *The Best of Lowell L. Bennion: Selected Writings 1928– 1988,* ed. Eugene England (Salt Lake City: Deseret, 1988), 132.

65. Christopher Lasch, *The World of Nations; Reflections on American History, Politics, and Culture* (New York, Vintage, 1974), 66.

66. Thomas G. Alexander, "Cooperation, Conflict, and Compromise: Women, Men, and the Environment in Salt Lake City, 1890–1930," *BYU Studies* 35 (1995): 8.

67. Spencer W. Kimball, "The False Gods We Worship," *Ensign* 6, no. 6 (June 1976): 3–4.

68. Hugh Nibley, in *Approaching Zion,* in *Collected Works,* 9:480.

69. Terry Tempest Williams, William B. Smart, and Gibbs M. Smith, *New Genesis: A Mormon Reader on Land and Community* (Salt Lake City: Gibbs Smith, 1998), ix.

70. William B. Smart, "The Making of an Activist," in Williams et al., *New Genesis,* 1.

71. Williams et al., *New Genesis,* ix.

72. Joseph Fielding Smith, ed., *Teachings of the Prophet Joseph Smith* (Salt Lake City: Desert, 1947), 71.

73. Spencer W. Kimball, "Strengthening the Family—the Basic Unit of the Church," *Ensign* 8 (May 1978): 45.

74. *Journal of Discourses,* 8:191.

75. Joseph Fielding Smith, *Answers to Gospel Questions,* 5 vols. (Salt Lake City: Deseret, 1957–66), 2:48.

76. Richard C. Foltz, "Mormon Values and the Utah Environment," *Worldviews* 4 (2000): 16. Foltz's is an excellent overview of the political and theological dimensions of the issue.

77. Anthony W. Ivins, *Conference Report* (April 1911): 118–19.

78. D. Michael Quinn, "Conscientious Objectors or Christian Soldiers? The Latter-day Saint Position on Militarism," *Sunstone* 10, no. 2 (March 1985): 19.

79. James R. Clark, ed., *Messages of the First Presidency* (Salt Lake City: Bookcraft, 1965), 6:159.

80. Quinn, "Conscientious Objectors," 21; in 1981, LDS spokesman Don LeFevre declared "there is no place in Mormon philosophy for the conscientious objector." However, LDS history, scriptures, and First Presidency statements clearly contradict his idiosyncratic assertion, and no official declaration of the church leadership has ever supplanted their Vietnam-era posture of respect for conscientious objectors. LeFevre's statement was published in *Deseret News*, 7 May 1981, and cited in ibid., 23.

81. James T. Duke, "Latter-day Saint Exceptionalism and Membership Growth," in Davies, *Mormon Identities*, 51.

82. First Presidency Statement on Basing of the MX Missile, The Church of Jesus Christ of Latter-day Saints, Salt Lake City, Utah, 5 May 1981. Reprinted in *Ensign* 11, no. 6 (June 1981): 76.

83. Gordon B. Hinckley, "In Grateful Remembrance," *Ensign* 1, no. 3 (March 1971): 20.

84. Gordon B. Hinckley, "War and Peace," *Ensign* 33, no. 5 (May 2003): 80.

Chapter 7

"If There Is Anything Lovely or Praiseworthy": Intellectual and Cultural Life of the Latter-day Saints

> Every accomplishment, every polished grace, every useful attainment in mathematics, music, in all science and art belong to the Saints. . . . All the knowledge, wisdom, power, and glory that have been bestowed upon the nations of the earth, from the days of Adam till now, must be gathered home to Zion.
> —Brigham Young, *Journal of Discourses*

> The story of Mormonism has never yet been written nor painted nor sculptured nor spoken. It remains for inspired hearts and talented fingers yet to reveal themselves.
> —Spencer W. Kimball, *Teachings*

Building the kingdom of God was for the Mormons more than a metaphor, more than a call to a life of private, religious devotion. It involved laying out cities and streets, building temples, and creating economically self-sufficient, cohesive communities. Besides fleeing Babylon for the hope of an earthly Zion, consolidation into a Mormon community had another purpose as well. It was the necessary condition for an ambitious program of educating the Saints. "Intelligence is the great object of our holy religion," Joseph declared. And intelligence, he continued, "is the result of education, and education can only be obtained by living in compact society; One of the principal objects, then, of our coming together, is to obtain the advantages of education; and in order to do this, compact society is absolutely necessary."[1] Indeed, seven years earlier, as the gathering in Missouri began, the Saints laid the first log of a schoolhouse in Jackson County "as a foundation of Zion," even as Sidney Rigdon consecrated that land of Zion by prayer.[2]

Mormonism and the Life of the Mind

According to Latter-day Saint scripture, the life of the mind and the life of the spirit are interdependent. Through a revelation received in 1833, Joseph Smith said, "the glory of God is intelligence, or, in other words, light and truth" (DC 93:36). Smith also taught that a "man is saved no faster than he gains knowledge,"[3] and that "it is impossible for a man to be saved in ignorance" (DC 131:6). Some church leaders have interpreted these latter statements to refer to knowledge of a uniquely "spiritual nature." Bruce R. McConkie, for example, wrote that "we believe that man is saved no faster than he gains knowledge, meaning knowledge of God and of his laws, as these things are revealed by the Holy Ghost. We believe that no man can be saved in ignorance, meaning in ignorance of God and his laws, of Jesus Christ, and the truths of the gospel, as these things are made manifest by the power of the Holy Ghost."[4] Both Smith and Brigham Young, however, resisted such dichotomies that disparaged secular learning as necessarily of a lower order.

"Wherefore, verily I say unto you that all things unto me are spiritual," affirmed the Lord to Joseph Smith (DC 29:34) in the year of the church's founding, and the prophet later declared, "one of the grand fundamental principles of 'Mormonism' is to receive truth, let it come from whence it may."[5] "Were you to ask me how it was that I embraced 'Mormonism,'" declared Brigham Young, "I should answer, for the simple reason that it embraces all truth in heaven and on earth, in the earth, under the earth, and in hell, if there be any truth there. There is no truth outside of it."[6]

Smith himself was unfailingly consistent in seeing both the mysteries of godliness and the wisdom of the ancients as worth tapping into, and to do so he consistently merged the gift of prophecy with the gritty work of language study. "Seek . . . for wisdom, and behold, the mysteries of God shall be unfolded to you," promised the Lord in one of the very first revelations recorded by the prophet (DC 6:7). But the form such seeking was to take, in the prophet's case, was more demanding than the pattern of his initial epiphanies suggested. True enough, he had learned to "ask of God," as James directed, and found the heavens opened to his view. But subsequently, he was enjoined to "seek . . . out of the best books words of wisdom; [to] seek learning, even by study and also by faith" (DC 88:118).

The counsel came as part of a revelation decreeing the establishment of a "school of the prophets," wherein students would study "things both in heaven and in the earth, and under the earth; things which have been, things which are, things which must shortly come to pass; things which are at home, things which are abroad; the wars and perplexities of the nations, and the judgments which are on the land; and a knowledge also of the countries and of kingdoms." To this list of subjects was shortly added the injunction to "become acquainted with all good books, and with languages, tongues, and people." So in the School of the Prophets, Joseph and other men studied the scriptures and theology—but also German and Hebrew.

The school actually commenced operation in January 1833, in Kirtland, with fourteen elders and high priests in attendance on the second floor of the Newel K. Whitney store, and ran successfully only until April. In November 1834, the school reopened as the School of Elders, with a more general membership, and lasted until March 1835. The session was repeated the next year, when the winter gave respite from farmwork and missionary labors. Soon after, it was reorganized again as the School of the Prophets. During these years of Smith's intense efforts to educate himself and the Saints, the study of languages would feature prominently in his journal entries. "Attended school during school hours," he recorded 13 November 1835.[7]

A few days later, he noted that Oliver Cowdery had returned from New York, "bringing with him a quantity of Hebrew books, for the benefit of the school. He presented me with a Hebrew Bible, Lexicon, and Grammar, also a Greek Lexicon, and Webster's English Dictionary." The next day, Smith recorded, he "spent the day at home, in examining my books, and studying the Hebrew alphabet." That night, he attended Hebrew class and made arrangements to replace their Hebrew teacher, one Dr. Piexotto, with an experienced scholar named Joshua Seixas, apparently more reliable and better qualified to instruct the elders in that language.[8] In January, Smith accordingly organized what he called the Hebrew School, which would comprise well over a hundred eager but older students. "Spent the day reading," "spent the day studying German," and "spent the day studying Hebrew" became common entries. Eventually, Smith would add the study of Egyptian to his goals, working to fashion an "Egyptian grammar" when the study of that ancient language was still in its infancy. The wonder is that, having already demonstrated to his followers' satisfaction his power to translate an unknown language ("Reformed Egyptian") by "the gift and power of God," he would feel it necessary to add linguistic credentials to his already heralded prophetic gifts. But that was all part of a growing pattern, whereby spiritual truth and secular study were to be mutually reinforcing.

These schools catered to the elders and leaders of the church, but the youth were not neglected, nor were females in general. The Kirtland School opened in 1834, accepting students of all ages. Diaries of Kirtland residents refer to a wide variety of coursework, including evening geography classes and a writing school, and Eliza R. Snow taught a "select school" for young ladies in Kirtland.

Joseph's intellectual agenda, according to a visiting elder from Missouri, inspired the members with "an extravagant thirst after knowledge."[9] Even an anti-Mormon acknowledged that

> the Mormons appear to be very eager to acquire education. Men, women and children lately attended school, and they are now employing Mr. Seixas, the Hebrew teacher, to instruct them in Hebrew; and about seventy men in middle life, from twenty to forty years of age, are most eagerly engaged in the study. They pursue their studies alone until twelve o'clock at night, and attend to nothing else. Of course many make rapid progress. I noticed some fine looking and intelligent men among them. . . . They are by no means, as a class, men of weak minds.[10]

A few years later, an artillery officer observed with alarm the growing presence in Illinois of thousands of "warlike fanatics." Even so, he felt to exclaim that "ecclesiastical history presents no parallel to this people, inasmuch as they are establishing their religion on a learned footing. All the sciences are taught, and to be taught in their colleges, with Latin, Greek, Hebrew, French, Italian, Spanish, &c., &c. The mathematical sciences, pure and mixed, are now in successful operation, under an extremely able professor of the name of Pratt, and a graduate of Trinity College, Dublin, is president of their University."[11]

Though Joseph's lack of formal schooling has been often emphasized (in part to support the unlikelihood of his authorship of the Book of Mormon), many among the first generation of church leaders were no strangers to the schoolroom. Joseph's father Joseph Sr., his scribe Oliver Cowdery, as well as Orson Hyde, Sidney Rigdon, William E. McLellin, and others all taught school before learning about the restoration. So it was not a stretch when in June 1831, Cowdery, along with William W. Phelps, was commanded by revelation not just to select but to actually write books that could be used in the schools.

In addition to a theology linking intelligence to spiritual growth, Joseph was motivated in his zeal for learning by his belief in the service that antiquities could render the cause of Book of Mormon historicity. This hope found expression in a city newspaper announcement during the Nauvoo years: "According to a Revelation, received not long since, it appears to be the duty of the members of the Church of Jesus Christ of Latter Day Saints to bring to Nauvoo their precious things, such as antiquities, . . . as well as inscriptions and hieroglyphics, for the purpose of establishing a Museum of the great things of God, and the inventions of men, at Nauvoo." The collection of "ancient records, manuscripts, paintings and hieroglyphics," like the city library, was to be housed in the Seventies Hall.[12] Designs for the library's museum were ambitious:

> Among the improvements going forward in this city, none merit higher praise, than the Seventies' Library. The concern has been commenced on a footing and scale, broad enough to embrace the arts and sciences, every where: so that the Seventies' while traveling over the face of the globe, as the Lord's "Regular Soldiers," can gather all the curious things, both natural and artificial, with all the knowledge, inventions, and wonderful specimens of genius that have been gracing the world for almost six thousand years. Ten years ago but one seventy, and now "fourteen seventies" and the foundation for the best library in the world! It looks like old times when they had "Kirjath Sapher," the city of books.[13]

Studying classical languages and aspiring to fashion a university in the midst of Illinois swampland in the 1840s seems a striking incongruity—especially in light of the Yankee pragmatism that informed the backgrounds of most first-generation Mormons. Josiah Quincy, later mayor of Boston, visited the prophet at Kirtland and dryly remarked that "no association with the sacred phrases of Scripture could keep the inspirations of this man from getting down upon the hard pan of practical affairs."[14] Even had Joseph not been absorbed in building settlements in Ohio, Missouri, and Illinois, founding a gospel kingdom, and contending with lawsuits, incarcerations, and forced exiles—his hardscrabble upbringing and Puritan heritage would not suggest the basis for a theology of intellectual aspirations such as noted by outside observers. Rodney Stark has remarked that "LDS theology places a premium on rationality and intellectual growth."[15] And Thomas O'Dea has written that "the Mormon definition of life makes the earthly sojourn basically an educative process. Knowledge is necessary to mastery, and the way to deification is through mastery, for not only does education aid man in fulfilling the present tasks, it advances him in his eternal progress."[16]

As the Saints traded residence in the City of Joseph for life in the Territory of Deseret, Brigham Young's passion for the practical, and his blurring of spiritual and temporal kingdoms, eclipsed even Joseph Smith's. Scratching out an existence in the Utah wilderness, the Saints had respite—for a few years—from hostile neighbors, but not from the Herculean task of making a desert yield a scanty sustenance, let alone "blossom like a rose." In such a climate, devotion was measured by the establishment of material steps toward an earthly Zion, not by psalms and canticles or saintly study. As one historian of Mormonism notes, the religious imperative "was building up the kingdom and inhabiting it," and the most "expressive worship signs were irrigation canals, or neatly built and nicely decorated houses, or good crops of sugar beets."[17]

In such a light, writes one scholar, the lack of a stronger pioneer intellectual subculture "seems less a cause for wonder than that there *was* a strong intellectual thrust" in spite of "the exigencies of pioneer necessity" and other factors.[18] From their way station in Winter Quarters, the Illinois exiles established a press and produced what may have been the first printing west of the Mississippi (an epistle to the scattered saints). Then, in 1850, only three years after settlement in the Valley, the Saints opened a University of Deseret (later the University of Utah), the first university west of the Missouri. Shortly thereafter, the Saints requested $5,000 in federal funds for a public library. It opened in 1852 with three thousand volumes, about the same time that Boston's first public library opened, and before Chicago had one of its own.[19]

In 1854, the Saints had been in the Valley less than seven years. That winter, at Lorenzo Snow's large and spacious house, several men and women met to participate in the newly organized Polysophical Society. They played instruments (from the piano to bagpipes), sang, recited original poetry, and discoursed extemporaneously. The small group swelled with members anxious to enrich their minds and souls with a healthy dose of refinement in the midst of a cultural and agricultural desert. Outgrowing the private home of Snow, they soon occupied the public Seventies Hall and occasionally the capacious Social Hall. Less than two years later, the organization had been dissolved in response to ecclesiastical pressures, and replaced by a Deseret Theological Class under Brigham Young's direction.[20]

Part of the problem was timing. The years 1856–57 saw the spread of a "Mormon reformation," a period of puritan retrenchment in which Mormon fire-breathers barnstormed Utah, railing against complacency and backsliding. In the absence of exterminating orders and pogroms, LDS leaders seemed to think, Mormons were losing their spiritual focus; bluestocking diversions suggested too much longing for the refinements of a Babylon they had fled. But other societies flourished. In February 1855, sixty men met in the Salt Lake City Council House and formed the Universal Scientific Society with Wilford Woodruff as president. Woodruff expressed the society's goals in a presidential address: "We are desirous of learning and possessing every truth which will exact and benefit mankind. . . . We wish to be made acquainted . . . with art, science, or any other subject which has ever proved of benefit to God, angels or men." The society went on to establish their own library, reading room, and museum.[21]

From such pioneer beginnings, Mormon educational efforts in Utah have gone on to foster a religious culture of unusual academic achievement. At the present time, Mormons in general obtain a higher level of education than other Americans, having higher rates of high school graduation, college graduation, and doctoral degrees.[22] In a famous study of the 1940s, E. L. Thorndike found Utah ranked number one as the birthplace of people listed in *American Men of Science*, number two as the state producing people listed in *Leaders in Education*, and the fourth most prolific state in producing men and women listed in *Who's Who in America*.[23] Another researcher analyzing the origins of American scientists and scholars found in his 1974 study that

> the most productive state is Utah, which is first in productivity for all fields combined in all time periods. It is first in biological and social sciences, second in education, third in physical sciences, and sixth in arts and professions. Compared to other states in its region, it is defiantly productive. This result seems clearly to be due to the influence of Mormon values, because Mormon youth predominate in the colleges of the state, and because other variables, such as climate, geography, natural resources, and social class, do not appear to explain the exceptional record of this state.[24]

Brigham Young University
The church-owned and -operated school in Provo, Utah, is the largest private university in America, enrolling some 34,000 students from well over one hundred countries. (Photo credit: Mark A. Philbrick/BYU. Used by permission)

The Mormon alliance of the life of the mind and a rigid orthodoxy has not always been a placid one. As we have seen, LDS faith in prophetic leaders who receive divine revelation, a literalist bent in their scriptural exegesis, and a founding story that opposes a fullness of gospel truth to apostate traditions and the philosophies of men do not always make for a church especially trusting of the faculties of human wisdom. Brigham Young was hostile to the very term *philosophy*, and the Book of Mormon warns of those who, beguiled by "the cunning plan of the evil one . . . think they are wise" when they are merely learned (2 Nephi 9:28).

Like many Christian institutions, Mormonism suffered the spasms of Darwin's disruption of the classical creationist paradigm, and the church even dismissed four evolutionists from the BYU faculty in 1911. Today, by contrast, there is a small dinosaur museum and a top evolutionary biology program at BYU. But other stresses clearly persist. For example, Brigham

Young University, founded in 1875, is the largest private, church-sponsored university in the country, enrolling nearly thirty thousand full-time students, with thousands more at its campuses in Idaho and Hawaii. It has nationally ranked programs across a whole spectrum of fields, and it ranks among the top twenty in National Merit scholars enrolled. But ironically, its graduates are not eligible for the national honorary Phi Beta Kappa, because of criticisms about academic freedom at the church-run school. Pressures on faculty to remain faithful to LDS teachings have produced some discontent and a handful of excommunications in recent years.

It would be tempting to see in this regard an unavoidable conflict between traditional canons of belief in a conservative church, and secular standards of the scientific and intellectual communities. But here the Mormon case presents us with a significant sociological anomaly. Studies have found that in general, educational attainment correlates negatively with religious belief. The better educated Christians become, the less committed to religious belief and practice they are. In the case of Latter-day Saints, however, "no evidence was found to indicate that college education is detrimental to the religiosity of Mormons." In fact, those "with post-bachelor's degrees are, on the average, more religious than those who never attended college. In short, college-educated Latter-day Saints . . . both as a group and by specific level of education, were, on the average, more religiously involved than noncollege-educated Latter-day Saints." In particular, "college-educated Mormons are *more* apt to attend church and to exhibit other manifestations of 'high' religiosity than are less-educated Mormons."[25] Alluding to the way in which LDS belief incorporates education into "the total religious milieu," the researcher concludes that "Latter-day Saint theology appears to negate the secularizing impact of education by sacralizing it."[26]

Much that is true of the LDS intellectual tradition is also true of their artistic heritage. The same forces that militated against an early indulgence in intellectual pursuits were obstacles to participation in or production of the trappings of high culture. In fact, while Joseph produced several revelations encouraging a life of intellectual pursuit, the LDS theology of the beautiful rests on slimmer foundations. The church's near creedal Thirteen Articles of Faith conclude with an injunction to seek after "anything virtuous, lovely, or of good report, or praiseworthy," and that admonition is generally invoked as a mandate for artistic engagement. As historian Richard Bushman dryly acknowledges, the relevant words "could refer to the Red Cross as easily as to painting."[27] Still, the fact remains that the Mormon people have displayed a persistent striving for the beautiful, and have sought for ways to represent their faith and their heritage through various artistic media.

Theater

When the Puritans closed the English theaters in 1642, they initiated a tradition of suspicion and hostility toward the dramatic arts that would resurface persistently in the American religious tradition through the nineteenth century (and beyond). Even a man of letters like Joseph Smith's contemporary Ralph Waldo Emerson, according to his biographer, "expressed a vigorous puritan disapproval of theater and drama" as a Harvard undergraduate."[28] It was against this tide of moralism that Brigham Young protested: "Now understand it—when parents whip their children for

Salt Lake Theatre
Dedicated in 1862, the Greek-style interior was influenced by the Drury Lane and Boston Theatres. An ardent supporter of theater, Brigham Young himself became the president of the Deseret Dramatic Association.

reading novels, and never let them go to the theater, or to any place of recreation and amusement, but bind them to the moral law, until duty becomes loathsome to them; when they are freed by age from the rigorous training of their parents, they are more fit for companions to devils, than to be the children of such religious parents."[29]

Joseph Smith apparently shared Brigham's views on the theater, although there is no record that he, like Brigham, enjoyed drama enough to take a role in an actual production. (Brigham played in the Nauvoo production of Thomas Lyne's *Pizarro*, a popular melodrama.) Nauvoo boasted at least two locales where the Saints staged their plays—a small hall called the "Fun House" and the lower room of the Masonic hall. Within fifteen years of settling the Valley, the Saints had constructed the elegant Salt Lake Theatre. Performers were initially all homegrown, but eventually national figures would headline there. (The nationally renowned Edwin Booth played Hamlet in 1887 and the famous Madame Albani sang there two years later.) It would be the setting not only for dramatic and musical productions, but for benefit lectures, inaugural balls and ceremonies for governors, political debates and mass meetings and, on one occasion, a two thousand strong anti-anti-polygamy demonstration by Utah women.

In fact, it would appear that when the theater functioned as the locus of high culture, it attracted considerably fewer patrons. A local editor complained in 1907 that "the proneness of the present age . . . toward the frivolous, the obscene and the low" accounted for low turnout for a series of Shakespeare productions.[30] At least one production of local origin was more successful. A story from the Book of Mormon (of Alma's son Corianton) was written by B. H. Roberts and adapted by O. U. Bean for the stage. It was apparently enthusiastically received, and eventually played on Broadway. Mormon engagement with drama persisted late into the twentieth century through the practice of "road show" competitions. Beginning in the 1930s, local units produced their own short musicals or theatricals and presented them locally and in stake or regional competitions. In that same era, the church also staged an outdoor spectacle that has since grown to become Mormonism's equivalent of Germany's Oberammergau. Combining theater on the grand scale with a missionary thrust, the Hill Cumorah Pageant, staged annually in Upstate New York, may be the country's largest and oldest outdoor drama. The extravagant performance features volcanoes, earthquakes, hundreds of armored warriors, priests, court dancers, kings, and peasants, a seven-level stage, ten light towers, digitally

Hill Cumorah pageant
Based on the Book of Mormon, this pageant is one of America's largest outdoor spectacles, drawing a hundred thousand people annually to its upstate New York locale. (Courtesy of the Church Archives, The Church of Jesus Christ of Latter-day Saints)

recorded music, water curtains, and a spectacular descent of Christ from heaven. It is not high art, but it does attract one hundred thousand visitors yearly, and is a further instance of the church's efforts to make the Book of Mormon a significant source of artistic expression.

Few if any dramatic works by LDS authors have achieved greatness, though a modern piece by Thomas Rogers does an admirable job of confronting some of the tensions and tragedy implicit in a faith that will increasingly experience conflict between spiritual idealism and political pragmatism. *Huebener*, written in 1976, chronicles the true saga of Helmuth Huebener, a seventeen-year-old Latter-day Saint who worked covertly to oppose the Nazi regime. The dilemma of opposing evil while "being subject to rulers" and "honoring, obeying, and sustaining the law" is not only as timeless as Antigone, but increasingly vexing for a church trying to gain political legitimacy and the freedom to proselytize in a number of undemocratic societies. At the present, however, it may be that Mormons will more frequently appear as the subject than the authors of celebrated dramas (as in Tony Kushner's biting treatment of Mormons and Mormonism in his Pulitzer Prize-winning *Angels in America*).

Music

Of all the forms of art, music is probably least problematic in its utility for religious purposes. It is therefore no surprise that it had the earliest explicit sanction and devotional attention of the early Latter-day Saints. (Although Brigham Young reminisced that he "never heard the enchanting tones of the violin, until I was eleven years of age; and then I thought I was on the highway to hell."[31]) "The song of the righteous is a prayer unto me," declared the Lord to Joseph Smith in revelation, at the same time calling upon the prophet's wife Emma "to make a selection of sacred hymns . . . to be had in my church" (DC 25:12, 11). Five years later, the first collection of ninety hymns was published. Establishing a pattern that continues to the present day, Protestant standards alternated with hymns of LDS composition. The current edition, for example, contains Luther's "A Mighty Fortress" and Charles Wesley's "Rejoice, the Lord Is King!" as well as W. W. Phelps's "Praise to the Man who Communed with Jehovah!" and George Manwaring's "Joseph Smith's First Prayer," two stirring hymns that celebrate Joseph Smith and his First Vision. Many other hymns also rehearse a unique Mormon heritage and doctrines. William Clayton's "Come, Come Ye Saints" is the closest thing Mormons have to a national anthem (although Phelps' "The Spirit of God Like a Fire is Burning" and William Fowler's "We Thank Thee O God For a Prophet" are close competitors); other hymns celebrate modern temples, vicarious work for the dead, and the Latter-day gathering,

It was in that same year, 1835, that the prophet formed a singing school in Kirtland. Nauvoo had its choirs as well, but inhabitants were more prone to recollect the distinctive sounds of the Nauvoo Brass Band. Tradition held that its members had been converted in England, and migrated to the City of Joseph as a group.[32] Even after the prophet's death, as persecutions mounted, the city persisted in its quest for a haven of artistic solace. In March 1845, a large music and concert hall was dedicated that housed a one hundred-voice choir and band. Audiences of up to one thousand enjoyed marathon (five-hour!) performances until the time of the forced exodus approached.[33]

It would be in Utah that the Mormons established their most world-renowned musical institution, the Salt Lake Tabernacle Choir. According to tradition, Brigham Young heard a quartet of Welsh converts singing in their native tongue, and remarked that they should become the nucleus of a great church choir. Two years after entering the Valley, the forerunner of the Tabernacle Choir was formed; by 1893, conductor Evan Stephens had

Mormon Tabernacle Choir
Beginning with their 1893 performance at the Chicago World's Fair, the choir began to serve as effective goodwill ambassadors of a church striving for greater public acceptance. (Courtesy of the Church Archives, The Church of Jesus Christ of Latter-day Saints)

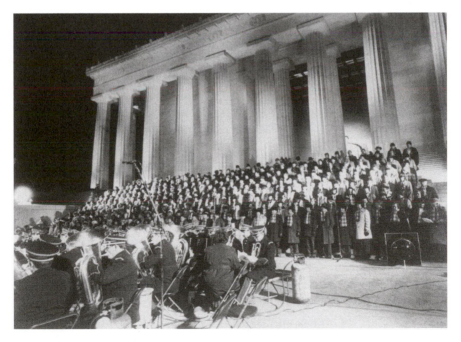

Mormon Tabernacle Choir
Now a beloved, solidly American institution, the choir has sung at four presidential inaugurations, including Reagan's in 1981. (Courtesy of the Church Archives, The Church of Jesus Christ of Latter-day Saints)

enlarged their numbers to three hundred, and led them on their first out-of-state tour culminating at the Chicago Columbian Exposition. The choir's role as an ambassador of the church was enhanced in 1929, when they commenced a three-month series of radio broadcasts. Popular response converted the series into what is now the oldest continuous radio program in America.

It is perhaps ironic that the Tabernacle Choir, established by a church in exile, achieved its greatest popularity upon releasing "The Battle Hymn of the Republic"; as an ambassador of the church, the choir now sings everything from American and ethnic folksongs to elaborate choral works of classical composers, and has performed at thirteen world fairs and four U.S. presidential inaugurations. Meanwhile, a number of LDS composers have worked to fashion musical works that relate the unique claims and message of their faith, such as the *Restoration* oratorios of Merrill Bradshaw and B. Cecil Gates, and Leroy Robertson's *Oratorio for the Book of Mormon.*

Literature

"What are you reading?" asks a character of a young lady in Jane Austen's *Northanger Abbey*. "Only a novel," she replies. "Only some work in which the greatest powers of the mind are displayed, in which the most thorough knowledge of human nature, the happiest delineation of its varieties, the liveliest effusions of wit and humour, are conveyed to the world in the best-chosen language."[34] Austen's description was half wry self-mockery, but half self-justification as well, since novels in the age of Romanticism were almost universally disparaged as silly, self-indulgent, or dangerous forays into melodrama and immorality. Of course, most unbelievers would classify Joseph Smith's Book of Mormon as a work of fiction. If so, he authored the most influential, widely published and read book ever written by an American (over 100 million published as of the new millennium). But as for works of fiction consciously created by LDS members, little incentive existed within the Latter-day Saint community for their production. With the publication of Frederick Marryat's *Travels and Adventures of Monsieur Violet* in 1843, Mormons would begin to figure with increasing frequency as lampooned villains in a stream of British and American novels. Their ill-treatment by popular novelists, nickel weekly hacks, and moral crusaders, would only reinforce their culturally imbibed notion that novels were an instrument for the corruption of young and old alike.

Once settled in the City of Joseph (Nauvoo), the Saints would establish a modestly stocked Library and Literary Institute. Records indicate that biographies of Napoleon, works by John Locke and other philosophers, and religious works and European history were popular—but novels were seldom read.[35] "Falsehoods got up expressly to excite the minds of youth," Brigham called them, though he grudgingly conceded on several occasions that he would rather have them read novels than nothing, or be deprived the opportunity for aesthetic exploration by puritanical parents.[36] As late as 1889, church President Wilford Woodruff was still admonishing youth that there was "no time to waste in reading novels."[37] True, Joseph had encouraged his Saints to "seek ye out of the best books words of wisdom" (DC 88:118), but good books were generally understood by his contemporaries to exclude works of fiction.[38]

Poetry, however, was different. In 1856 European Mission President Franklin Richards told members that it was "the duty and privilege of the Saints . . . to procure and study the poetical works of the Church, that their authors may be encouraged and the spirit of poetry [may be] cultivated in the bosoms of the readers."[39] The church even subsidized the publication of five thousand copies of *The Harp of Zion*, a collection of poems by Scottish convert John Lyon, in 1853. A few years later, the church produced *Poems: Religious, Political, Historical* by the brilliant Eliza R. Snow, who had been publishing her poems in LDS periodicals since 1840. Sales of both, however, were disappointing.

In 1888, the cause of a Mormon literary tradition received powerful endorsement when apostle Orson F. Whitney issued a call for a "home literature," and prophesied that "we will yet have Miltons and Shakespeares of our own."[40] For two decades, in the words of one critic, Mormon writers "borrowed the techniques of popular sentimental fiction and the values of the genteel tradition with a superficial adaptation to Mormon themes."[41] Nephi Anderson's *Added Upon* (1898), for example, succeeded in blending conventions of the sentimental novel with LDS conceptions of premortality so successfully that it was reprinted fifty times. The first real flowering of an authentic Mormon literary tradition commenced with the 1939 publication of Vardis Fisher's Harper Prize novel, *Children of God: An American Epic*. Maurine Whipple won a Houghton Mifflin literary fellowship in 1938 to write the acclaimed *The Giant Joshua* (1941). Together with Elinor Pryor's *And Never Yield*, Lorene Pearson's

The Harvest Waits (both 1941), and Virginia Sorenson's *A Little Lower than the Angels* (1942) and *The Evening and the Morning* (1949), these books constitute the most accomplished Mormon novels of the era.

Some LDS authors have responded to the enduring Mormon absorption with their own history by producing works of historical fiction. One series in particular, *The Work and the Glory*, by Gerald N. Lund, has probably outsold any work of fiction every written by a Mormon on Mormon themes. The eight-volume series is a novelized, but well-researched, retelling of early church history. Works like Lund's, and publications of Deseret in general, which operates under a mandate to publish "faith-promoting" literature, are not likely to receive many critical plaudits for their uncompromising celebration of Mormon history and doctrine. But they are the mainstay of the larger Mormon reading public.

Artistically speaking, the best Mormon literature in recent years has been in the short story genre. Levi Peterson, Douglas Thayer, and Don Marshall, to name only three authors, have produced masterful slices of authentic Mormon experience with poignancy, wit, and a fine sense of ironic understatement. Science fiction bestseller Orson Scott Card has experimented with Mormon themes in some of his work, most notably his *Seventh Son* (first in the Alvin Maker series), a fantasy based very loosely on the life of Joseph Smith. An early form of the work won the World Fantasy Award for best novella, thus demonstrating again that Mormon themes can be successfully incorporated into mainstream fiction. Similarly, in the *Homecoming* series, he transposes Book of Mormon characters and plotting into a science fiction context.

In the genre of the personal essay, Eugene England's probing dissent from Mormon cultural orthodoxy earned him both suspicion and respect. Terry Tempest Williams, mentioned earlier, has won national respect for her writing, which blends an idiosyncratic Mormon spirituality with the nature-ethos of one of America's premiere environmentalists. In recent years, it has been the case that essay and short story writers, when they operate independently of church publishers and BYU-sponsored journals, are more likely to explore the complexities and ambiguities of Mormonism, in ways that range from genuinely provocative to unabashedly cynical. It is at these contested boundaries between faithfulness and artistic irreverence, that the most aesthetically sophisticated work is being produced in Mormon literature. The independent Association for Mormon Letters (that conducts conferences and competitions), and journals like *Exponent II*, *Dialogue*, and *Sunstone*, all of which publish fiction and poetry, provide a forum for a small but thriving literary subculture. What remains to be seen is whether the two cultures of Mormon literature will remain relatively polarized.

Painting

Conversion in a foreign land, immigration to America, and a trek across the plains to Utah pulling a handcart, was as authentic an embodiment of the Mormon experience as one could hope to find. Carl C. A. Christensen (1831–1912), a Danish convert, combined his training in the Royal Academy of Fine Art with his pioneer handcart experience and religious zeal to become the most effective and celebrated visual chronicler of early Mormon history.[42] After stints at farming and scene-painting, he began work in 1878 on his "Mormon Panorama," a series of twenty-three paintings that chronicled Mormon history from the First Vision of 1820 to the westward trek of 1847. The tempera paintings were a majestic 6 × 10 feet each, and were stitched together in a scroll, which was unrolled in a traveling exhibition to the accompaniment of a lecture on church history that Christensen delivered in scattered western communities. His paintings, in their homespun, quasi-primitive style, powerfully document the harrowing, the triumphant, and the quotidian episodes of Mormonism's early history.

In the year 1890, the Salt Lake temple, under construction since 1853, was at last nearing completion. As the physical embodiment of ultimate devotion and sacrifice, the temple demanded the finest materials and workmanship the Saints could muster. Knowing that several interior rooms would require extensive murals, two local artists, John Hafen and Lorus Pratt, approached George Q. Cannon of the First Presidency with a proposal. If the church would provide financial support for them to study in France, they would use their improved art to adorn the temple walls. So it was that the pair of "art missionaries"—and eventually three other local talents—soon enrolled as students in the Julian Academy in Paris. There they focused their formal education on academic figure drawing, but informally imbibed influences of both the Impressionism that had by then peaked, and the Barbizon School of landscape realism. Returning to Utah, the artists fulfilled their commission to prepare the temple murals, and taught a new generation of Utah artists, sending some of the best—including the gifted Mahonri Young—to Paris in a second wave.

After the turn of the century, Mormon artists would find their training a little closer to home. Minerva Teichert (1888–1976), who studied at the

Lamanite Maidens, by Minerva Teichert (oil, ca. 1935)
An acclaimed artist, Teichert made the Book of Mormon a principal source for artistic treatment. (Courtesy of Brigham Young University Museum of Art. All Rights Reserved)

Art Institute in Chicago and the New York Art Students League, was also an accomplished painter of historical genre who favored murals. To Latter-day Saints, she is most renowned for her series of works on the Book of Mormon, rendered in her distinctive, broad brush strokes influenced by the bold style of her mentor Robert Henri. Achieving even greater national recognition in this era was Arnold Friberg (1913–), perhaps the only Utahn to be appointed to the Royal Society of Arts and receive a commission to do portraits of British royalty (Prince Charles and Elizabeth II). The LDS Church commissioned Friberg to produce a series illustrating the Book of Mormon, and his scenes of heavily muscled Nephites and Lamanites have adorned most editions to the present day. It was, in fact, those illustrations that prompted Cecil B. DeMille to enlist Friberg to work on the monumental *Ten Commandments*, for which work Friberg was nominated for an Academy Award.

Several Utah artists have found success among their Mormon audience in attempting to merge their faith and art. James C. Christensen stands out as one who has achieved international popularity for his work

Alma the Younger Called to Repentance, by James Christensen (stained glass, 1980) Phenomenally popular as a contemporary artist of the whimsical and fantastical, Christensen has also produced notable work on both Christian and, in particular, LDS themes. (By Permission, James Christensen)

of striking visual intensity that celebrates the whimsical and the fantastical. Most of his religious forays stop short of acquiring the particular features of an LDS faith perspective or Mormon subjects, thus maintaining a more universal appeal to his work.

If Mormonism is indeed somewhere between a denomination and a full-blown cultural or ethnic entity, then the status of its cultural tradition is of great moment. One scholar has observed the connection between the flowering of a uniquely Mormon literature, and the establishment of "a clear cultural identity," the expression of a genuine "Mormon ethnicity."[43] Judaism and Islam have had millennia and fourteen hundred years, respectively, to amass sufficient aesthetic and intellectual achievements to make Jewish culture and Islamic tradition credible monikers. If Rodney Stark is correct that we have, in the case of Mormonism, a faith group in the process of becoming a world religion, then its corresponding cultural identity will take shape as it is informed by such factors as a shared canon of artistic achievement, a developing aesthetic sensibility, the adumbration of a core mythology of origins, the elaboration of distinctive intellectual dimensions to the faith, and the development of a unique cultural grammar and cultural vocabulary. The above sketch is meant to suggest the beginnings of such a process. But perhaps former LDS President Spencer W. Kimball was right, and the real story of Mormonism is a subject for "inspired hearts and talented fingers yet to reveal themselves."

Notes

1. *Elders Journal* 1 (October 1837–August 1838): 54.

2. "Chronology of Church History," Appendix 2, in Daniel H. Ludlow, ed., *Encyclopedia of Mormonism*, 4 vols. (New York: Macmillan, 1992), 4:1653.

3. Joseph Smith Jr., *History of the Church of Jesus Christ of Latter-day Saints*, 7 vols., ed. James Mulholland et al. (Salt Lake City: Deseret, 1951), 4:588.

4. Bruce R. McConkie, *Conference Report* (April 1953): 75.

5. Smith, *History*, 5:499.

6. *Journal of Discourses*, 26 vols., reported by G. D. Watt et al. (Liverpool: F. D. and S. W. Richards et al., 1851–1886; reprint, Salt Lake City: n.p., 1974), 5:73.

7. Smith, *History*, 2:311.

8. Ibid., 2:318.

9. John Corrill, in William Mulder and Russell Mortensen, eds., *Among the Mormons: Historic Accounts by Contemporary Observers* (Lincoln: University of Nebraska Press, 1958), 87.

10. James H. Eells to Br. Leavitt, Kirtland, Ohio (1 April 1835), in Mulder, 88.

11. *New York Herald*, 17 June 1842.

12. *Times and Seasons* 4, no. 13 (15 May 1843): 201. Little progress in the collection occurred during Joseph's lifetime.

13. "Seventies' Library," *Times and Seasons* 5, no. 24 (1 January 1844): 763.

14. Josiah Quincy, *Figures of the Past* (Boston: Little, Brown, 1926), 326.

15. Rodney Stark, "The Basis of Mormon Success: A Theoretical Application," in James T. Duke, ed., *Latter-day Saint Social Life: Social Research on the LDS Church and its Members* (Provo, Utah: Religious Studies Center, Brigham Young University, 1998), 58.

16. Thomas O'Dea, *The Mormons* (Chicago: University of Chicago Press, 1957), 147–48.

17. Jan Shipps, *Mormonism: A New Religious Tradition* (Urbana: University of Illinois Press, 1985), 125.

18. Maureen Ursenbach, "Three Women and the Life of the Mind," *Utah Historical Quarterly* 43 (winter 1975): 40.

19. Details of Territorial and other libraries from an address of Leonard H. Kirkpatrick, 2 October 1961, *BYU Speeches of the Year* (Provo, Utah: Brigham Young University Press, 1961), 5.

20. Ursenbach, "Three Women," 26–40.

21. T. Edgar Lyon Jr., *John Lyon: The Life of a Pioneer Poet* (Provo, Utah: Brigham Young University Religious Studies Center, 1989), 225.

22. Ibid.; James T. Duke, "Cultural Continuity and Tension," in Duke, *Latter-day Saint Social Life*, 83.

23. E. L. Thorndike, "The Origin of Superior Men," *Scientific Monthly* 56 (1943): 426.

24. Kenneth R. Hardy, "Social Origins of American Scientists and Scholars," *Science* 185 (1974): 500.

25. Howard M. Bahr and Renata Tonks Forste, "Toward a Social Science of Contemporary Mormondom," in James T. Duke, *Latter-day Saint Social Life*, 157.

26. Gerald Stott, "Effects of College Education on the Religious Involvement of Latter-Day Saints," *BYU Studies* 24, no. 1 (winter 1984): 52.

27. Richard L. Bushman, "Would Joseph Smith Attend the New York Stake Arts Festival?" *Dialogue* 35, no. 3 (fall 2002): 212.

28. Robert D. Richardson Jr., *Emerson: The Mind on Fire* (Berkeley: University of California Press, 1995), 9.

29. *Journal of Discourses*, 2:94.

30. Editor's Table, *Improvement Era* 11, no. 9 (July 1908).

31. *Journal of Discourses*, 2:94.

32. George W. Givens, *In Old Nauvoo: Everyday Life in the City of Joseph* (Salt Lake City: Deseret, 1990), 177.

33. Givens, *Old Nauvoo*, 177.

34. Jane Austen, *Northanger Abbey* (Bonn: Koneman, 1999), 29–30.

35. Kenneth W. Godfrey, "A Note on the Nauvoo Library and Literary Institute," *BYU Studies* 14 (spring 1974): 386–89.

36. *Journal of Discourses*, 2:94; 9:173.

37. Brigham Young (9 October 1872), *Journal of Discourses,* 15:222; Wilford Woodruff (29 July 1889), in Brian H. Stuy, ed., *Collected Discourses*, 5 vols. (Burbank, Calif., and Woodland Hills, Utah: B.H.S., 1987–92), 1:326.

38. "Good books" implicitly excluded "foolish trash and novels" in the admonition of one Latter-day Saint writing to her children a few decades later. See Sarah

Dearmon Pea Rich, Autobiography, BYU Special Collections, Writings of Early Latter-day Saints, 21.

39. Thomas E. Lyon, "Publishing a Book of Mormon Poetry: *The Harp of Zion*," *BYU Studies* 27, no. 1 (winter 1987): 85.

40. Orson F. Whitney, "Home Literature," *Contributor* (July 1888).

41. Edward Geary, "The Poetics of Provincialism: Mormon Regional Fiction," *Dialogue* 11 (summer 1978): 15.

42. Now housed in the BYU Museum of Art, these paintings have been published (*Art in America* 58 [May–June 1970]: 52–65) and exhibited in the Whitney Museum of American Art, also in 1970.

43. Patricia Nelson Limerick, "Peace Initiative: Using the Mormons to Rethink Ethnicity in American Life," *Journal of Mormon History* 21, no. 2 (fall 1995): 1–30.

Chapter 8

Schisms, Secularism, and a Global Church

It is probable that the Mormons are the forerunners of the coming real America.
—D. H. Lawrence, *Studies in Classic American Literature*

If Mormonism is able to endure, unmodified, until it reaches the third and fourth generation, it is destined to become the greatest power the world has ever known.
—Leo Tolstoy in 1892

One of the great strengths and appeals of Mormonism would also prove to be its bane. The emphasis on a kind of spiritual egalitarianism, with every member entitled to the gift of revelation, attracted those disposed to consider themselves seekers, and those resentful or wary of professional clergy and elitist religion. As one writer of the era protested, "The teachers of religion of all denominations assume an arrogant, dictatorial style, in order to convince their followers that they are in possession of the secrets of Heaven."[1] When Joseph Smith declared that "no man can receive the Holy Ghost without receiving revelations. The Holy Ghost is a revelator,"[2] he was opening the door to a church filled with prophets. That abiding sense of personal entitlement to revelation has worked to fashion a vibrant faith of deeply committed members. But it has also worked, in the early years especially, to invite challenges to Joseph Smith's leadership by competing would-be prophets.

First Crises

Hiram Page was one of the eight men who saw and handled the gold plates, and his name is appended to an affidavit so testifying. Some months after the church's organization, he began to make use of a seerstone, through which he claimed to receive revelations for the church. Many members, including Smith's own scribe Oliver Cowdery, were persuaded by them, prompting Smith to produce a revelation that established for all time the principle of the supreme spiritual authority in the church. The revelation, by declaring that "no one shall be appointed to receive revelations and commandments [for] this church excepting my servant Joseph Smith, . . . until I shall appoint . . . another in his stead" (DC 28:2, 7), effectively transformed the role of a prophet into the office of prophet.

After Smith was martyred in 1844, uncertainty about the succession caused a temporary crisis, prompting the emergence of several claimants to the mantle of Joseph. Aggravating the confusion was the fact that at one time or another, Smith had intimated more than half a dozen principles by which to determine a successor.[3] On 6 August Brigham Young, senior apostle in the Quorum, returned from a mission he had been serving in England with most of the other apostles. They convened a public meeting in Nauvoo, where the members overwhelmingly sustained the Quorum of the Twelve as the governing body.

Although the majority of Saints acknowledged the leadership of the Quorum of the Twelve Apostles, with Brigham Young at the head, some thousands rejected his leadership and remained behind. A significant number threw in their lot with one James Strang, a recent convert baptized by Joseph Smith. Asked to scout a possible refuge for the Saints in Wisconsin, he produced a letter allegedly written by Smith appointing him successor. Most Mormons then and since have believed the letter a forgery, but many flocked to the new "prophet and king." In 1845, Strang claimed to find a set of brass plates buried beneath a tree, and translated them with a Urim and Thummim given him by an angel—thus reenacting the seminal episodes of Joseph's own early career.

Persecution and conflict led Strang's group to find refuge on Beaver Island in Lake Michigan a few years later, by which time Strang had attracted to his cause a number of prominent Mormon leaders. These included former apostles John Page and William McLellin, as well as Smith's brother William and William E. Marks, erstwhile president of the Nauvoo Stake. Popular fiction writer James Oliver Curwood wrote a fanciful—and rather hostile—account of the island kingdom (*The Courage of Captain Plum,* 1903), which had in fact grown to a few thousand by the time Strang was assassinated in 1856 by disaffected followers. His church survived him, although members believe that Joseph Smith and James Strang were the only prophets necessary for a restoration. It is hard to know how many Strangites (who call themselves members of the Church of Jesus Christ of Latter Day Saints) exist today. Their official Web site claims their members are "few, but stable in size for 145 years." It is not likely that more than a few hundred—if that many—remain.

The Reorganized Church of Jesus Christ of Latter-day Saints

The most formidable challenge—numerically—to Young's leadership would not coalesce until 1860. Like the Utah Saints, Strang's group practiced plural marriage. Many Saints who rejected Young and polygamy, therefore, found Strang an unattractive alternative. In a portentous 1832 revelation, Joseph Smith had prophesied that "the Lord God will send one mighty and strong, holding the scepter of power in his hand, clothed with light for a covering, whose mouth shall utter words, eternal words; while his bowels shall be a fountain of truth, to set in order the house of God" (DC 85:7). After Smith's death, Jason W. Briggs and Zenas Gurley thought they had found the mighty and strong one in James Strang, but abandoned him when he, too, turned to plural marriage. They switched their loyalty to Joseph's brother, William Smith. When Smith also turned out to be an advocate of polygamy, Briggs and Gurley left his fold as well. In 1851, Briggs became convinced that the predicted figure would come "through the seed of Joseph Smith."

The young son of the slain prophet, Joseph Smith III, was the logical candidate. Not yet twelve at the time of his father's martyrdom, he had remained in Illinois with his mother Emma at the time of the exodus. Many contemporaries were adamant in their belief that the prophet had ordained the child as his successor. As early as 1844, one contemporary historian noted that "'The Prophet,' it is said, has left a will or revelation, appointing a successor; and, among other things, it is stated that his son, a lad of twelve years, is named therein as his successor."[4]

By 1856, an agglomeration of groups had united in their hope that Joseph Smith III would assume his place as his father's heir to the prophetic mantle, and sent a delegation to formally invite him to do so. He declined, but by 1860 he felt directed by God to step forward, and assumed the role of prophet and president in Amboy, Illinois, the first in a line of lineal descendents of Joseph Smith to occupy that position. Not only did the young leader repudiate polygamy, but he in fact rejected most of his father's final doctrinal innovations during the Nauvoo years and some earlier ones as well. The plurality of gods, temple ordinances for the living and the dead, a literal gathering, and Joseph's translation of the Book of Abraham also disappeared from the theological landscape in the new Reorganized Church of Jesus Christ of Latter Day Saints.

The RLDS Church drew large numbers of defectors from the Utah church, and engaged in successful missionary labors as well. By 1890, the group numbered twenty-five thousand or so, with the population now centered in Iowa rather than Illinois. LDS numbers by that point approached two hundred thousand, so the RLDS constituted perhaps 10 percent of all persons tracing a religious tie to Joseph Smith. In the years since, the RLDS Church continued the pattern initiated by Joseph III, of tempering the founding prophet's radical restorationism with a more traditionally Protestant sensibility. They have acted decisively to shed those elements of distinctness, exclusiveness, and exceptionalism that outsiders might interpret as elitist or discriminatory. Beginning in 1966, RLDS leaders emphasized the building of Zion as a worldwide work of spiritual transformation, rather than a more literal process rooted in a discourse about the House of Israel and chosen remnants. Spiritual leaven rather than spiritual separateness, seems to be the theme.

In 1968, the church announced plans for a temple at church headquarters in Independence, Missouri. When it was completed in the 1990s, it was dedicated to world peace, and made a place of prayer and contemplation open to all comers. No sacred ordinances, member-only weddings, or ceremonies hid from public eyes were to take place there.

In 1984, RLDS President Wallace B. Smith revealed that henceforth, women would be ordained to the priesthood. Conservative factions challenged the policy change, but it was instituted nonetheless. Recent years have also witnessed a conspicuous deemphasis on the Book of Mormon and on Joseph Smith's revelatory experiences. In one notable instance, an RLDS pastor was removed in 1991 for repeatedly "emphasizing the Book of Mormon in his worship meetings" and "mentioning Joseph Smith's name over the pulpit," in spite of warnings to desist.[5] The church's expository pamphlet, "Faith and Beliefs," does not mention the name of Joseph

Smith, and the official Web site mentions neither Smith nor the Book of Mormon. In fact, the brochure explicitly moves away from one of Joseph Smith's most salient teachings—the full distinctness of God the Father, Christ, and the Holy Ghost. Although "no official church creed . . . must be accepted" by members, the RLDS church does affirm its belief that the "living God is triune: one God in three persons."[6]

Finally, in 1996, one of the last and most distinctly RLDS connections to Joseph Smith was severed when Grant McMurray was ordained the church's president—the first leader to have no direct blood connection to the Mormon prophet. McMurray has consistently insisted that being "a prophetic people is more important than being a people with a prophet." Accordingly, as the church's office of president becomes less and less associated with the title of prophet and its connotations of a literal link between God and a "peculiar people," vestiges of historic Mormonism will be exceedingly difficult to discern in this descendent of the nineteenth-century church. As if to speed that process, the RLDS voted in 2000 to change their official name to the Community of Christ.

Although to all appearances, the Community of Christ is no longer positioned as radically hostile to or distinct from mainstream Protestantism—or perhaps because it has lost its hard contours of difference—the church has suffered a substantial decline in numbers in recent decades. From a peak of perhaps 350,000 members, membership has declined to 250,000 or less.

Other Offshoots of the Restoration

Besides the colony of Strang and followers of Joseph Smith III, many other splinter groups flared briefly, usually to expire within months or a generation or two at most. Sidney Rigdon, erratic first counselor to Joseph, was the first claimant to the succession; he was rejected by the general membership at a mass meeting weeks after the martyrdom, when the Twelve Apostles won public support. He gathered a group of supporters, but lost their confidence by 1846, when a number of his prophecies failed to materialize and he endorsed plural marriage. (One of his followers, William Bickerton, organized a group in Pennsylvania in 1862, later moving with a few loyal supporters to Kansas.) In the years immediately after the martyrdom, other figures tried to reestablish a church in Kirtland, trying to galvanize supporters and a few dozen Mormon families who had not moved West. McLellin attempted to do so in 1847 after a brief flirtation with Strang's group, but his effort fizzled out by 1849. About the same time McLellin was recruiting, James C. Brewster and Hazen Aldrich also made Kirtland the center of a succession effort. They reclaimed the Kirtland temple for their place of worship, named their movement the Church of Christ, and even briefly published a newspaper before falling out with each other and fading from the scene a few years later.

Other efforts occurred farther afield. Lyman Wight, a former apostle, led a band of Saints to Texas, where he claimed Joseph had directed him to establish a colony. His followers numbered a few hundred, but the group dissolved upon Wight's death in 1858. Another leader who followed Strang briefly before striking out on his own was Charles B. Thompson, who in 1841 had published the first major work defending the Book of Mormon (*Evidences in Proof of the Book of Mormon*). Thompson recruited to his cause four or five dozen families from the Council Bluffs, Iowa area where Saints gathered in preparation for the trek to Utah. He settled with them in a successful communitarian society on the banks of the Soldier River in northern Iowa. A concerned Orson Pratt brought them to Brigham Young's attention in 1852, but the Utah leader's unconcern seemed justified when the group broke up three years later.

Alpheus Cutler had participated in leading councils of the church during Joseph's life, and claimed that he had received a private ordination to assume Joseph's position upon the prophet's death. He established his followers in Iowa, but never gathered as many as two hundred loyalists. The prophet's brother William Smith, Book of Mormon witness David Whitmer, ex-apostle and clerk to the Quorum of the Twelve William McLellin— all became associated with schismatic efforts, but left no enduring legacy.

Like Joseph Smith, Brigham Young provoked his share of disillusioned or disaffected followers. The most significant challenge to his leadership was organized in 1868 under the leadership of William S. Godbe, a powerful businessman in Utah. Brigham Young's resistance to precious-metal mining in Utah aroused the anger and eventual opposition of Godbe and several colleagues, who resisted Young's whole vision of a self-sufficient, highly structured, autonomous economy. As in Kirtland, a prophet was claiming the prerogative to counsel and even dictate in matters extending beyond the doctrinal and into the realm of economic policy. And also as in Kirtland, those claims were seen by some members as evidence of autocracy and cause for disaffection.

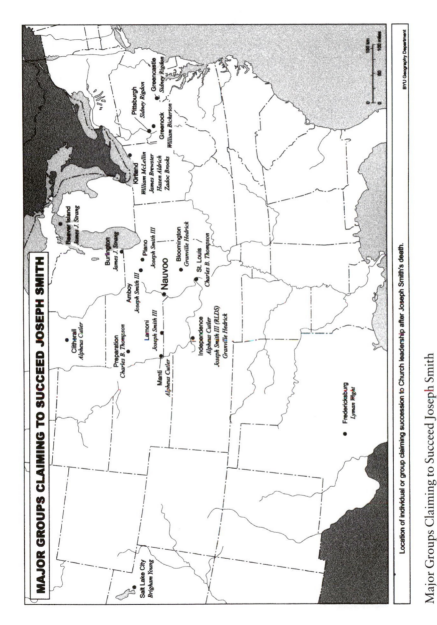

MAJOR GROUPS CLAIMING TO SUCCEED JOSEPH SMITH

Salt Lake City
Brigham Young

Beaver Island
James J. Strang

Burlington
James J. Strang

Clitherall
Alpheus Cutler

Preparation
Charles B. Thompson

Manti
Alpheus Cutler

Amboy
Joseph Smith III

Lamoni
Joseph Smith III

Plano
Joseph Smith III

Nauvoo

Bloomington
Granville Hedrick

St. Louis
Charles B. Thompson

Independence
Alpheus Cutler
Joseph Smith III (RLDS)
Granville Hedrick

Fredericksburg
Lyman Wight

Kirtland
William McLellin
James Brewster
Hazen Aldrich
Zadoc Brooks

Pittsburgh
Sidney Rigdon

Greenock
William Bickerton

Greencastle
Sidney Rigdon

Location of individual or group claiming succession to Church leadership after Joseph Smith's death.

100 km
100 miles

BYU Geography Department

Major Groups Claiming to Succeed Joseph Smith
(From *Historical Atlas of Mormonism*, by S. Kent Brown, Donald Q. Cannon, Richard Jackson. Gale Group,
© 1994, Gale Group. Reprinted by permission of the Gale Group.)

Godbe's search for a doctrinal and institutional alternative to Mormonism led him to found a Church of Zion in 1870. The movement's leaders eventually turned to spiritualism, and claimed to be in contact with a number of deceased Mormon leaders. As a vehicle for their criticisms of the LDS leadership, the Godbeites initiated a paper (later called the *Salt Lake Tribune*), which for decades served as a powerful medium for Utahns opposed to Mormon hegemony. Godbe's movement espoused ideals of universal brotherhood and theological liberalism, which for a while attracted considerable support among Utah intellectuals. By 1880, however, the movement had largely dissolved.

Modern Polygamists

Another category of religionists tracing their roots back to Joseph Smith's teachings—modern polygamists—emerged not upon his martyrdom, but five decades after. By 1886, the church was under excruciating pressure to cease the practice of plural marriage. In 1882 the Edmunds Law had disenfranchised polygamists and attached fines and imprisonment to the practice. Federal authorities were imprisoning convicted polygamists, church leaders had fled underground, and more drastic legislative sanctions would soon threaten to destroy the church itself as an institution. It was in the midst of this crucible of persecution that President John Taylor allegedly received a revelation about the status of the "New and Everlasting Covenant," or plural marriage. According to the text of this disputed document, the Lord insisted that "I the Lord am everlasting and my covenants cannot be abrogated nor done away with; but they stand forever. Have I not given my word in great plainness on this subject? . . . I have not revoked this law nor will I for it is everlasting."[7]

The church has denied that such a revelation exists,[8] and for revelations to be binding to Latter-day Saints they must be presented to the church publicly according to the Law of Common Consent, where members are entitled to vote to sustain their canonization (DC 26:2). In any event, when the church officially abandoned the practice in 1890, a period of some uncertainty followed; several secret polygamous marriages were countenanced over the next decade or more, leading some members to believe that the official announcement ending the practice was for public consumption only.

By 1904, church President Joseph F. Smith reaffirmed the Manifesto forbidding plural marriage, and announced future participants in the practice would be excommunicated. Over the next few decades, scattered groups and individuals rejected the Woodruff Manifesto and Smith's reaffirmation of it, and invoked the purported Taylor revelation as a basis for unflagging devotion to polygamy. Formal organizations emerged in the 1930s, centered in northern Utah and along the Utah–Arizona border, who soon claimed for themselves the designation of Mormon fundamentalists. By the 1950s, competing factions had emerged, and today the major groups are led by the Allred clan (the Apostolic United Brethren) and by Rulon Jeffs (the Fundamentalist Church of Jesus Christ). Several smaller groups as well as countless independent fundamentalists are scattered across the west, to the number of several tens of thousands.

Although plural marriage was officially practiced by the LDS Church for barely a fourth of its history by a small percentage of its members, it is hard to separate the practice from the religion in the popular imagination. The enduring visibility of modern polygamists who call themselves Mormon fundamentalists, although they are entirely repudiated by the official church, only aggravates the problem of perception. The Church of Jesus Christ of Latter-day Saints affirms an unbroken line of authority, much as the Catholic Church does, from its first leader to the present. "As to any danger of your leaders leading you astray," assured Brigham Young, "if they should try to do so the Lord would quickly sweep them from the earth." Wilford Woodruff was equally confident: "I say to Israel, the Lord will never permit me or any other man who stands as president of this Church to lead you astray."[9] In addition, Woodruff reaffirmed in the Manifesto the principle first enunciated by Joseph Smith, that "there is never but one on the earth at a time on whom this power and the keys of this priesthood are conferred" (DC 132:7). A contrary perspective by polygamous dissenters has led to a proliferation of groups claiming independent authority. And once freed from the constraints of the centralized supervision and institutional sanction that characterized early Mormon practice of polygamy, its modern counterparts have spawned an endlessly splintering range of legally and morally problematic versions.

Twenty-First-Century Tensions

The Church of Jesus Christ of Latter-day Saints is at present on a trajectory to far outstrip other restoration groups in both numbers and rate of growth. No significant LDS schisms over doctrine or practice seem likely to emerge in the foreseeable future; if anything, the church in recent years has increasingly reaffirmed many of its core, distinctive doctrines, in what a prominent Mormon sociologist designates a period of "retrenchment" since the 1960s. Armand Mauss sees emphatic reaffirmation of five core values: the principle of continuous revelation through modern prophets, genealogy and temple work, the missionary program, family renewal, and religious education.[10] It was as if Latter-day Saints had succeeded only too well at assimilating to American society after early years of alienation and antagonism—so successfully one critic marvels at "how American [Joseph Smith's church] proved to be."[11] So the church at present is caught in a paradox: it has gone from being "the Great American Abomination" depicted in nineteenth-century screeds, to characterizations as a quintessential American religion. Latter-day Saints obviously appreciate the respect and status they have achieved; at the same time, media persistence in linking them with a polygamous past and renegade polygamists today, and limited acceptance by fellow Christians, can be stinging indicators that Mormonism still persists in the minds of many as something more exotic than kindred. That would make Brigham Young happy. "I am satisfied that it will not do for the Lord to make this people popular," said the ever pugnacious Brigham Young. "Why? Because all hell would want to be in the church. The people must be kept where the finger of scorn can be pointed at them."[12]

The primary reason for Mormonism's resistance to liberalization and doctrinal compromise is its doctrine of prophetic inspiration. Believing as members do that the current, living prophet literally receives the mind and will of the Lord to direct the church, external criticism is irrelevant and internal criticism inconsistent with the principle of priesthood stewardship: the prophet and only the prophet is entitled to receive revelation for the good of the collective church. Even constructive criticism is generally likened to the well-intentioned but catastrophic meddling of Uzza in the Old Testament. As a Levite, he was not authorized to touch the ark of the covenant. But upon seeing the oxen stumble that pulled the sacred object, he instinctively reached out to steady it. "And the anger of the LORD was kindled against Uzza, and he smote him" (1 Chron. 13:10).

Observers are prone to attribute another cause to Mormonism's steadfast conservatism: a leadership that is much more aged than the average Mormon. At the turn of the twenty-first century, the average age of the First Presidency and Quorum of the Twelve was older than at any time in the church's history. Until the recent presidency of Howard W. Hunter, no LDS prophet had been born in the twentieth century. Neither has any church president had—nor is any likely to have—training in a seminary or school of theology. This elderly leadership, indifference or even hostility to formal theology, and abiding faith in prophetic revelation after the pattern of Moses, have created a culture more than commonly resistant to the influences of secularism and liberalism. Still, a number of voices have appeared calling for changes in various areas. Notable examples include the efforts of some intellectuals to liberalize historiography and feminist dissenters.

In 1965, LDS historian Leonard Arrington and a group of scholars expressed the desire for a Mormon history executed in more "human or naturalistic terms."[13] Since the organization that year of the Mormon History Association the study of the Mormon past has become thoroughly professionalized. The group first headed by Arrington, the Mormon History Association now boasts more than a thousand members. Several journals in the field of Mormon history are published, and several Utah presses as well as an increasing number of national presses publish monographs in the field. Some members and leaders of the church, however, feel that the secular academy with its standards cannot do justice to the history of an institution rooted in divine origins, and that the effort to "recognize... the human side of Church history"[14] has been carried too far. At the same time, the church over the years has been reluctant to grant full access to its massive archival collections, heightening suspicion and ill-will on the part of some non-Mormon historians without and some dissident LDS historians within the church. As a result, the field is sometimes polarized between those perceived to be doing "faithful history" that is blemish free and inaccurate, and dissidents and disaffected Mormon scholars seen to be undermining the faith. In the same way, publishing outlets are increasingly categorized as orthodox (FARMS, BYU Studies, BYU Press) or liberal (Signature Books, Sunstone, Dialogue).

By 1983, even outside observers were referring to the "Crisis in Mormon historiography." Martin Marty, a prominent religious scholar, then asserted that "Mormon thought is experiencing a crisis comparable to but more profound than that which Roman Catholicism recognized around the time of the Second Vatican Council (1962–5). Whatever other changes were occurring in the Catholic church, there was a dramatic, sometimes traumatic shift in ways of regarding the tradition." The Catholic response, the observer continued, was to move away from the position that "Catholic teaching has come intact, as it were, protected from contingency, from a revealing God."[15]

In the case of Mormon Studies, "ways of regarding the tradition" are certainly contested. Specifically, the debates have grown more intense and focused as some practitioners of the "new Mormon history" critique the accuracy of orthodox church history and the historical plausibility of the Book of Mormon, and propose a simple solution: sever the connection between history and theology. "History as theology is perilous," said President Grant McMurray of the Community of Christ (the former Reorganized Church of Jesus Christ of Latter Day Saints), a church that has moved ever farther away from accepting Joseph Smith's visions and the scripture he produced as literally rooted in historical events.[16] No Mormon would dispute that theology's reliance upon a particular history can make for peril. When master forger Mark Hoffman passed off as authentic a series of fabricated letters and documents that dramatically challenged normative accounts of early Mormonism, critics celebrated and apologists scrambled to assimilate the difficult discoveries.[17] When the forgeries were revealed, many Mormons breathed a collective sigh of relief—but the perils of history-based theology do not make that history any more expendable in the minds of mainstream Mormons.

On the contrary, the Latter-day Saint leadership appears steadfastly committed to the assertion of Schopenhauer: "Christianity, he wrote, "has this peculiar disadvantage of not being, like other religions, a pure doctrine, but is essentially and mainly a narrative or history, a series of events . . . ; and this very history constitutes the dogma, belief in which leads to salvation."[18] If this is true of Christianity in general, it is doubly true of Mormonism in particular.

We have seen how this principle operates in the case of the Book of Mormon especially. But LDS doctrine as a whole is rooted inescapably in history; its claims to divine authority and restored truth are entirely dependent on the narratives of LDS origins. Without an uncompromising belief in Joseph Smith's literal visitation by God and heavenly angels, verbally communicating and physically transmitting to him ancient records and priesthood keys, and without verifiable evidence of a continuing conduit linking Joseph's successors to God—a God who personally directs the continuing work of the Restoration—Mormonism would utterly lose its claim to be the unique institutional form of the one true gospel.

What this means in practice is that challenges to orthodox accounts of the church's past strike at the very heart of the faith. For most of its history, Mormonism was chronicled by its own faithful members. Early Saints were prodigious journal writers and record keepers. The very first injunction given the new church decreed that a record should be kept, and Joseph's scribe Oliver Cowdery was appointed. Shortly thereafter, the office of church historian was created, and John Whitmer was commanded to make "a history of all the important things which he shall observe concerning my church" (DC 69:3). From that day until 1972, church leaders filled the role. That was the year the first professionally trained historian, the nationally respected Leonard Arrington, was appointed, ushering in an era of the professionalization of Mormon Studies, greater access to LDS archival materials, and a proliferation of research and publications in the field. But the New Mormon History was at times more frank about—and frankly critical of—the Mormon past than some church leaders were comfortable with. A period of retrenchment began with the closer supervision of writing projects and the curtailing of many others. In 1981, Apostle Boyd K. Packer gave an address to church educators, in which he expressed concern that LDS historians were making a virtue out of "sympathetic detachment." He cautioned against putting secular standards above personal testimony, and admonished teachers and scholars to "build faith rather than destroy it."[19] Some LDS scholars bristled at his suggestion that church loyalty required an ostensible faith-based perspective. Relations between church intellectuals and the church leadership were further strained the next year, when the office of church historian reverted to ecclesiastical control. Elder G. Homer Durham of the First Quorum of Seventy became the new church historian.

While the church archives remain strictly controlled, with many documents unavailable to professional scholars, other signs are promising. The church recently published on seventy-four DVDs a collection of four hundred thousand images from its historical archives, making that trove of documents instantly available to the public. The church is also in the process of publishing a comprehensive collection of Joseph Smith's papers, whose dozen or so volumes dwarf previous collections. A third initiative, the Book of Mormon critical text project, began publication in 2001. The project includes an analytical transcription of the printer's and extant original Book of Mormon manuscript, a history of textual changes, and an analysis of textual variants. Mormon historical scholarship, in other words, continues at a high pitch in spite of persisting tensions.

The place of women in Mormonism has been a further—though limited—source of conflict. As we saw, the feminist movement has never appeared to garner great support among LDS women—presumably because Mormons accept as a premise of their faith a model of prophetic leadership that precludes social agitation and consensus building as avenues to doctrinal change. Nevertheless, a few Mormons continue to be vocal in condemning the patriarchal model of church government and the Mormon failure to elaborate and celebrate a belief in a Heavenly Mother. But with the passing of feminism as a front-burner political issue, any burgeoning Mormon feminism has lost most of its steam.

In the fall of 1993, responding to a spate of activism by dissenting historians and feminists, LDS church courts disciplined six scholars and writers.[20] Five were excommunicated—which is the harshest penalty imposed by the church, resulting in revocation of church membership and cancellation of all ordinances performed. One was disfellowshiped, a slightly lesser sanction. The practice of excommunication has a long history in the church, with Smith first defending the practice in 1835. He wrote in a declaration of belief that "all religious societies have a right to deal with their members . . . according to the rules and regulations of such societies; provided that such dealings be for fellowship and good standing . . . They can only excommunicate them from their society, and withdraw from them their fellowship" (DC 134:10).

Church discipline has been practiced by several denominations throughout religious history. The LDS faith is one of few to continue the practice into the twenty-first century. In most cases, disciplinary councils, as they are called, are convened for cases of moral transgression (sexual sin is the most common reason), and have as their stated purpose the facilitation of repentance. But leaders may call members in as well when their criticism of the church becomes public, and is seen as both intentional and de facto impediment to its work and ministry. Since the early 1990s, few high-profile excommunications have occurred.

Predictably, the church has defended its right to discipline its own members in recent years. In response to the negative publicity surrounding the ouster of the "September Six," the church issued this statement:

> We have the responsibility to preserve the doctrinal purity of the Church. . . . Faithful members of the Church can distinguish between mere differences of opinion and those activities formally defined as apostasy. Apostasy refers to Church members who "(1) repeatedly act in clear, open, and deliberate public opposition to the Church or its leaders; or (2) persist in teaching as Church doctrine information that is not Church doctrine after being corrected by their bishops or higher authority; or (3) continue to follow the teachings of apostate cults (such as those that advocate plural marriage) after being corrected by their bishops or higher authority."[21]

Certainly this right is generally acknowledged, but the practice has enhanced public perceptions of the church as hostile to intellectual freedom and dissent. It is certainly common in the secular press to portray Mormonism as hostile to free inquiry and the life of the mind, and the church-owned Brigham Young University has been sanctioned by the American Association of University Professors for infringements on academic freedom.

Charges that the Mormon church is overly authoritarian of course go back to the Joseph Smith era. As we have seen, some of the earliest internal dissentions arose from the extent to which Joseph's spiritual leadership was seen as intruding into the personal or political sphere. Most Latter-day Saints are willing to acknowledge the prophet's prerogative both to speak authoritatively upon doctrine and to counsel upon a much wider variety of issues and areas than religious leaders typically address. And the resulting conformity among Mormons in matters of doctrine and behavioral patterns strikes many as anomalous in an increasingly modern, secular society—and especially unusual in a culture as typically individualistic as the American.

There are those who argue that the successful globalization of religion requires some accommodation to modernity—including more tolerance of dissent and difference. Historically, as one writer points out, "Christian orthodoxy has proven remarkably durable and adaptable through two millennia and is developing new forms even today throughout the world."[22] Some religious scholars see that as a sign of a mature church with a secure sense of itself. But from a Mormon perspective, greater ideological toleration may be seen as coming at the cost of a diminished commitment of church members to an inspired church leadership. To cite one example, the Catholic Church maintains an official opposition to abortion at least as emphatic as Mormonism's. Yet statistics reveal no discernible influence of that position on the numbers of Catholic persons having abortions; they obtain them at a rate even higher than that of their Protestant counterparts. Mormons, on the other hand, experience abortions at a rate dramatically lower than the national average.[23] (The category of mothers who work outside the home is another area where "the influence of prophetic instruction . . . is substantial." Over 70 percent of married American women with children are in the labor force, compared to only 49 percent of Mormon women.[24]) Many complicating factors cloud the analogy. But the example suggests two very different perceptions that may follow when religious homogeneity is evident: either Mormonism has somehow managed, against the tides of modernity, to preserve an abiding conception of the prophet as a literal spokesperson for God, whose words and counsel command a remarkable degree of compliance among rank-and-file members; or institutional safeguards against dissent and a suspicion of intellectualism have produced a religious body in which conformity itself has positive value, and diversity of expression and practice is culturally suppressed.

Certainly the LDS leadership has labored hard to preserve a cohesive and committed membership, even in the absence of a physical gathering that insulates Saints from worldly influences. Apostle Neal Maxwell, for instance, has counseled the Latter-day Saint scholar to "remember that his citizenship is in the Kingdom and that his professional passport takes him abroad into his specialty. It is not the other way around."[25] In the nineteenth century, Brigham Young and the Mormons were a curiosity as attractive to notable visitors as any exhibit of P. T. Barnum. In the twenty-first, it is Mormons that have become the comfortable travelers. And so far, Mormon culture, even as it becomes ever more geographically diffuse, continues to demonstrate remarkable solidarity and resilience to schism.

The Next World Religion?

Twice a year, several dozen men and women fluent in any of fifty-six languages assemble on the second floor of the world's largest conference hall dedicated to religious purposes. As the annual or semi-annual world conference of the Church of Jesus Christ of Latter-day Saints gets under way, proceedings are simultaneously beamed in a panoply of languages to rival a United Nations conference, from the LDS Conference Center in Salt Lake City to an LDS membership of more than a dozen million members scattered in a hundred countries throughout the globe.

Brigham Young University, the church's flagship educational institution, offers instruction in some 35 languages, several more than its nearest American competitor in linguistic diversity, Yale. Walking across its sprawling campus in Provo, Utah, one is likely to encounter more linguistic and cultural variety in 30 minutes than in any locale of comparable size in the world. It is not just the 1,600 students from 110 countries that contribute to the polyglot mosaic; 2,000 other students participate annually in study abroad (the largest participation of any American college) and several times that many have lived in foreign nations as missionaries for

The LDS Conference Center
Completed in 2000, this building seats 21,333—more than Madison Square Garden's
main arena. The building and grounds cover almost 10 acres. (Courtesy of the Church
Archives, The Church of Jesus Christ of Latter-day Saints)

periods of 18 to 24 months. As a consequence, three-quarters of its students are fluent in two or more languages.

Cultural diversity is one consequence of a church that increasingly sees itself—and is seen by sociologists—as a possible candidate for the status of the next world religion. "Mormonism: the Next World Religion?" was the question posed by a conference of scholars convened in Durham, England, in April 1999, who met to assess the implications of that development. Rodney Stark framed the possibility in dramatic terms in 1984, when he claimed on the basis of statistical projections that "some now living may see it grow from its 11 million in the year 2000 to the neighborhood of two hundred sixty seven million by the year 2080." Criticized as extravagant by some sociologists, Stark revisited his forecast fifteen years later, and indicated that interim developments had only convinced him that his earlier estimate may have been too conservative. As of 1999, "membership is substantially higher than my most optimistic projection," he said.[26]

Wilford Woodruff recalled as an aged man an episode that transpired in a tiny log schoolhouse near Kirtland, Ohio, in the church's infancy. All the priesthood holders in the vicinity convened in the fourteen-foot-square structure, and were challenged by Joseph to testify of the church and its future. Responding to their feeble attempts to grasp its destiny, he issued a prophecy: "I want to say to you before the Lord, that you know no more concerning the destinies of this Church and kingdom than a babe upon its mother's lap. You don't comprehend it. It is only a little handful of Priesthood you see here tonight, but this Church will fill North and South America—it will fill the world."[27]

Whether Stark's projection or Smith's prediction is fulfilled, the church is currently in the throes of a tremendous surge in numbers. The newly converted and the newly born are at present increasing church rolls by one million every three years, aided in great measure by 62,000 full-time missionaries. The rate of increase is not without accompanying challenges. "As the Church moves out across the world and into the future we face two very serious problems," President Hinckley said to the Los Angeles World Affairs Council.

> The first is the training of local leadership. All of our local congregations are headed by local people, volunteers who work at their regular vocations and carry on as they are called—as bishops, for instance—serving those around them. Of course, we not only have converts who are poor and less educated but also people of means and skills and influence. We take people of all kinds as we find them and then we train them and make of them effective and wonderful leaders. . . . The second problem we face is providing places of worship as we grow so rapidly in these areas. We are constructing nearly 400 new houses of worship each year. It is a phenomenal task.[28]

But as the church assumes the dimensions of a world religion, it also acquires a membership of increasing cultural diversity. And it may be that the greatest challenge—and the greatest changes—facing Mormonism will be ethnic and cultural, not numeric and financial. In some ways, Mormonism's beginnings did not portend a successful internationalization of the membership. First, Joseph Smith established a dramatic series of connections between the restored gospel, and a very particular idea of place—American place. Moroni, he related, was an angel who had inhabited *this* hemisphere. And the artifacts of Nephite civilization, and the icons of God's reemerging covenant, were emphatically local. The Book of Mormon was uncovered in upstate New York. Its contents chronicled three ancient civilizations that inhabited the American continent. And the most quoted Book of Mormon passage in early church publications was Ether 13:4–8, which predicts "a New Jerusalem upon *this* land." Even the abode of Adam, Smith revealed, was in the land of Daviess County, Missouri.

What this means, of course, is that the Book of Mormon was physically connected as an actual artifact and ancient history, in the mind and in the tactile experience of early saints, with this land. And the history in the Book of Mormon was explicated in terms of that very physical terrain over which the Saints themselves trekked and camped. America was the abode of Adam and Moroni, the cradle of American independence and the restoration, and the future home of the inhabitants of Zion. Certainly, Harold Bloom's identification of Mormonism with "the American Religion" finds ample validation in the intensely American complexion of Mormonism's early elaboration.

Of course, locale was not the only American feature of Mormonism. Historians have long construed the church as an expression of a particular American cultural climate and Joseph Smith as a quintessentially American prophet. Indeed, many of Mormonism's features were especially appealing in light of an ethos that worked to democratize religious experience in the postrevolutionary period. "The disintegration of older structures of authority," writes historian Gordon Wood, was part of a "democratic revolution" that profoundly affected American culture. "Countless numbers of people were involved in a simultaneous search for individual autonomy," and "people were given personal responsibility for their salvation as never before."[29]

"To the honorable men of the world," Smith began one of his open letters, "we . . . say unto you, Search the Scriptures search the revelations which we publish, and ask your heavenly Father . . . to manifest the truth unto you. . . . You will then know for yourselves and not for another: You will not then be dependent on man for the knowledge of God; . . . Every man lives for himself."[30]

Mormonism, in other words, may be seen as the religious anticipation of Emerson's 1837 "American Scholar speech," wherein the sage admonished his Harvard audience to establish an authentically American expression of culture. Mormonism represented such an original, indigenous expression of American piety that claimed direct authorization from God, without the need of mediating Old World customs, traditions, authority, or scriptures. Nevertheless, it was to the Old World that Joseph quickly turned, in his quest for receptive converts. The first missionaries to sally abroad went out from Kirtland, Ohio, in 1837. Six months later, they had recorded six hundred baptisms, and for the next two decades, the rate would only increase, until there were over thirty thousand British Mormons—more than the entire Territory of Utah boasted.[31] As these converts poured into Illinois and later Utah by the thousands, the first cultural amalgamation of the church began—though the common ancestry of most members made the process virtually seamless. But over the next generation, missionary work would expand to other nations as well. Scandinavia was opened for missionary work in 1850, and would prove second only to Britain as a source of converts. The same year, missionary work commenced in France and Italy, followed by Germany. By the turn of the century, over a hundred thousand converts would stream across the ocean to New Orleans, sail the Mississippi to Iowa, and outfit with wagons or handcarts before the last leg of the trek across the prairies and mountains to Salt Lake City. Some sailed to New York first, and others directly to California.

The heritage of gathering is evident today in the communities scattered throughout Utah, where descendents of Scots, Welsh, German, Scandinavian, and Italian immigrants carry on family businesses and distinctive ethnic surnames. By the end of the nineteenth century, gathering was effectively at an end. Nevertheless the practice of culling fruit from foreign vineyards rather than emphasizing new plantings would shape the church's demographics for generations to come. As late as 1960, more than a half century after converts ceased to gather to Utah, over 90 percent of all Mormons were members who had been born in, converted in, or drawn to America (with a portion in Canada). Those members who lived abroad were not organized in wards and stakes like their American counterparts, but organized in branches and districts, a scheme that reflected the church's provisional or immature status in those areas. Almost a century after Brigham Young's death, it was still for all intents and purposes a Utah church.

Internationalization

When the era of transformation began, change occurred at a rate that has sociologists sitting up and taking notice. At the turn of the century (1900), 90 percent of the LDS membership resided in the United States. By 1960, that percentage was unchanged. Over the next thirty years, South America's share went from one to 16 percent, Mexico and Central America from one to 11, and Asia from virtually none to 5 percent.[32] In 1961, the first non-English-speaking stake of the church was organized in the Netherlands, and a few months later, the first Spanish-speaking stake was organized in Mexico City. In three short decades, the church was totally transformed. By 1990, there were 1,700 stakes, with more than three-quarters outside Utah. Active in fifty nations in 1950, the church was now organized in 128, and over a third of church members lived in those foreign countries. By the year 2000, a watershed demographic shift had occurred—over half of church members were now foreign-language speakers.

At the same time, it is important to point out that the internationalization of the church has not unfolded evenly throughout the globe. The vast majority (85 percent in 1995) reside in the Western Hemisphere,[33] where the phenomenal growth rate continues to be centered. In that sense, it may be more accurate to refer to Mormonism as a "New World" religion, rather than a New "World Religion." The reasons for the success of the church in Latin America and Africa, and its more labored growth in Europe and Asia, have not been fully explored, but at least in part derive from the fact that, as Mauss reminds us, the United States and increasingly Latin America have more of an open religious-market mentality than is the case in Europe, Asia, and elsewhere.[34] It also appears to be the case, as Rodney Stark has noted, that for a new religious movement to succeed, it must maintain a balance between cultural continuity with its host societies, and a certain degree of tension with those societies. Cultural factors like a Christian heritage and strong family ties, for example, seem especially relevant to the church's success in Latin America. The church has long been justly noted not for its family-centered doctrines alone, but for providing an unusually powerful community that is, essentially, a vastly enlarged family.

Elaine Pagels has recently written that the great appeal of first-generation Christianity was the feeling of entering into an extended family community.[35] We have the unique historical circumstances and organizational principles that allowed nineteenth-century Mormonism to foster such cultural cohesiveness and intragroup loyalty. In the transition to the twenty-first century, Mormonism has so far proved resilient in that regard, even as a number of factors have worked to challenge Mormon distinctness. Initially, Mormonism was an extended clan. Latter-day Saints carried communalism to an extreme only seen in rare Utopian experiments. Cultural, political, and religious isolation in Utah continued the trend of entrenchment and clannishness provoked by years of persecution in New York,

Ohio, Missouri, and Illinois. But with the cessation of formal gathering at the dawn of the twentieth century, literal community became increasingly metaphorical.

At about the same time, the elimination of Utah's distinct political parties and the church's abandonment of polygamy erased major political and religious boundaries of separation. A lifestyle of frequent meetings scattered throughout the week, collaborative work on welfare projects—farms and orchards and canneries—at the local levels, as well as the frequent construction of new chapels in which all members participated—continued a tradition of communalism well into the next century.

But since the 1980s, most meetings have been brought together into a Sunday block, the church's sprawling complex of welfare projects has been centralized and consolidated, and building projects have been entirely relegated to contractors. In addition, the infiltration of "gentiles" into Utah and the proliferation of church units outside the intermountain west mean that Mormons are increasingly likely to rub shoulders with fellow Mormons in fewer contexts outside Sunday services. The high public profiles of respected Mormon athletes, businessmen, and politicians, like Steve Young, the Marriotts, and Mitt Romney or Orrin Hatch, further diminish the sense of Mormons as a people apart, peculiar and alien. What all this means is that the very identity of Mormonism may be changing as the sharp contours of difference fade. Caught between a desire for full accommodation and respect on the one hand, and a mission to stand as a "peculiar people" with a claim to an utterly unique message on the other, Mormonism will continue to aspire to the status envisioned by President Spencer W. Kimball, of a respected people "seen as distinct and different—in happy ways—from the [people] of the world."[36]

Other pressures will operate as well to reshape the Mormon cultural identity—and one is the process of internationalization. It is not just that the actual ethnic composition of the church is rapidly changing. It is also the fact that cross-cultural contact and assimilation requires a sharpened, introspective attention to what is essential and fundamental to the faith and what is contingent and cultural. But it is not a simple matter to ascertain where the line separating doctrine and cultural baggage lies. And the resultant dangers can cut two ways.

On the one hand, it is clear that some cultural practices are incompatible with LDS—and Christian—teachings. Apostle Dallin H. Oaks implied as much in a General Conference address, warning that "the traditions or culture or way of life of a people inevitably include some practices that must be changed by those who wish to qualify for God's choicest blessings."[37] In some cases this is obvious. Female circumcision and cannibalism come to mind. But Elder Dallin Oaks has more subtle forms of behavior and attitudes in mind. For example, he has said, "the [LDS] doctrine and practice of personal responsibility and personal effort collide with individual traditions and local cultures in many lands." In other words, the principle of economic self-reliance so central to the church's welfare program is construed here as an essential dimension of the gospel that may require converts to abandon a "culture of dependency." The difficulty comes in recognizing what more subtle departures from American cultural experience are hostile to an essential Mormonism, and, more challenging still, just what aspects of Mormon cultural experience are incompatible with or extraneous to, the essential Mormon religion.

For some foreign observers, there is fear that an "American" religion will threaten to efface or disparage their own cultural identity altogether. Seeking to allay such concern, Apostle Dallin Oaks has said, "the present-day servants of the Lord do not attempt to make Filipinos or Asians or Africans into Americans. . . . His servants seek to persuade all—including Americans—to become Latter-day Saints."[38] But in the eyes of some, American missionaries are representatives of America, not of Mormonism. Accordingly, rebels in Colombia, Peru, and Chile bombed LDS chapels in the 1980s, 1990s, and into 2000, apparently seeing them as emblems of Yankee imperialism. (Leftists also murdered Mormon missionaries during those years in both Bolivia and Peru.) Part of the problem may result from a common missionary practice of offering free English classes to local residents as a way of eliciting good will and providing a popular service. (Indeed, when the church entered postcommunist Bulgaria in 1990, the first thing the government asked the church to do was to send English teachers.[39])

Converts from other lands, in other words, may need to abandon cultural practices and conditioning that is incompatible with the gospel as taught by Mormons. But at the same time, Mormons will increasingly be challenged to consider what aspects of their religion are themselves mere cultural inheritance. In the case of Oaks's example, promotion of economic self-reliance, a revealed eternal principle, can in Utah Mormon culture merge imperceptibly into an aggressive entrepreneurial spirit, economic ambitiousness, and rampant materialism that by any fair measure are not only separate from but antithetical to the teachings of Mormonism's founders and present leaders.

Elder Edwin Cannon baptizing converts in Nigeria
Since the 1978 declaration opening the priesthood to all worthy males, the church's
presence in black Africa has accelerated rapidly. Missionary work in Latin America has
also proved fruitful, much more so than in Europe or in the United States itself. In the
present century, the church will grow increasingly internationalized. (Courtesy of
Janeth Cannon)

Brigham Young was emphatic on the dangers here: "The worst fear
that I have about this people," he said, "is that they will get rich in this
country, forget God and His people, wax fat, and kick themselves out of
the Church and go to hell. This people will stand mobbing, robbing,
poverty, and all manner of persecution, and be true. But my greater fear for
them is that they cannot stand wealth; and yet they have to be tried with
riches, for they will become the richest people on this earth."[40] In more
recent years, church President Spencer W. Kimball questioned the propen-
sity for corporate acquisitiveness among the Saints: "Why another plant,
another office, another service, another business? Why another of anything if one has that already which provides the necessities and reasonable
luxuries? Why continue to expand and increase holdings, especially when

those increased responsibilities draw one's interests away from proper family and spiritual commitments."[41]

But a Protestant—or Mormon—work ethic is not the only area where moral principles and culturally conditioned values can become confused. Sacred music, modes of social interaction and displays of affection, dress and grooming, expressions of reverence, gender roles and relations, conceptions of patriotism—all these have moral implications, but are nonetheless culturally negotiated behaviors and concepts. They are but a sampling of the myriad dimensions to religious experience that Mormons will be provoked to reconsider in their growing engagement with other cultures. In the process, they will necessarily be required to reconsider what it means to be a Latter-day Saint, and to articulate in a considered way the essential features of the gospel they espouse, shed of all its ambient paraphernalia deposited by the accidents of history and geography, the Puritan inheritance, by the good and bad in American culture, and by all other "traditions of the fathers" so condemned in Mormon scripture.

Doubtless the resulting interpenetration of Mormonism with other cultures will enrich and deepen the meaning of Latter-day Saint identity, as it continues to unfold in a larger context than the Utah valley that dominated its first century, or the American culture that defined its second phase. Mormonism, wrote Rodney Stark, stands "on the threshold of becoming the first major faith to appear on earth since the Prophet Mohammed rode out of the desert."[42] If he is right, then the third phase in Mormonism's self-definition is about to be revealed.

Notes

1. *Theophilanthropist* (1810), 278, 338, cited in G. Adolph Koch, *Religion of the American Enlightenment* (New York: Crowell, 1968), 181, 183.

2. Joseph Fielding Smith, comp., *Teachings of the Prophet Joseph Smith* (Salt Lake City: Deseret, 1976), 328.

3. D. Michael Quinn details eight: (1) by a counselor in the First Presidency, (2) by a special appointment, (3) through the office of associate president, (4) by the presiding patriarch, (5) by the Council of Fifty, (6) by the Quorum of the Twelve Apostles, (7) by three priesthood councils, (8) by a descendent of Joseph Smith Jr. His is the most detailed account of the claimants to succession authority. See "The Mormon Succession Crisis of 1844," *BYU Studies* 16, no. 1 (autumn 1975): 224–33.

4. Henry Brown, *The History of Illinois, from its first discovery and settlement to the present time* (New York: Winchester, 1844), 489.

5. Diane Butler Christensen, "Disillusioned RLDS Faithful Form New Flock," *Utah County Journal*, 15 September 1991.

6. "Community of Christ: Faith and Beliefs" (n.p.: Community of Christ, n.d.).

7. Douglas M. Todd Journal, 1 September 1934, [no author], *The Most Holy Principle,* 3 vols. (Murray, Utah: GEMS, 1970), 442–43.

8. "From the personal knowledge of some of us, from the uniform and common recollection of the presiding quorums of the Church, from the absence in the Church Archives of any evidence whatsoever justifying any belief that such a revelation was given, we are justified in affirming that no such revelation exists." Official Statement, *Deseret News,* Church Section, 18 June 1933.

9. *Journal of Discourses,* 26 vols., reported by G. D. Watt et al. (Liverpool: F. D. and S. W. Richards et al., 1851–86; reprint, Salt Lake City: n.p., 1974), 9:289; G. Homer Durham, ed., *The Discourses of Wilford Woodruff* (Salt Lake City: Bookcraft, 1946), 212.

10. Armand Mauss, *The Angel and the Beehive: The Mormon Struggle with Assimilation* (Urbana: University of Illinois Press, 1984).

11. Harold Bloom, *The American Religion: The Emergence of a Post-Christian Nation* (New York: Simon and Schuster, 1992), 43, 127.

12. *Journal of Discourses,* 12:272.

13. Leonard J. Arrington, "Scholarly Studies of Mormonism in the Twentieth Century," *Dialogue* 1 (1966): 28.

14. James B. Allen and Leonard J. Arrington, "Mormon Origins in New York: An Introductory Analysis," *BYU Studies* 9, no. 3 (spring 1969): 241.

15. Martin E. Marty, "Two Integrities: An Address to the Crisis in Mormon Historiography," *Journal of Mormon History* 10 (1983): 3.

16. Grant McMurray made this statement in his keynote address at the Mormon History Association annual meeting, Kirtland, Ohio, 22 May 2003.

17. Hoffman's forgeries spurred a series of major revisionist histories whose influence persists, even though the main catalyst—a letter signed by Martin Harris in which he quotes Joseph Smith describing a salamander that transformed into an angel—was revealed as fraudulent.

18. Arthur Schopenhauer, *Parerga and Paralipomena: Short Philosophical Essays,* trans. E.F.J. Payne (Oxford: Clarendon, 1974), 2:369.

19. Boyd K. Packer's remarks were presented at the Fifth Annual Church Educational Systems Religious Educators' Symposium, 22 August 1981, Brigham Young University, Provo, Utah. They were published as "The Mantle Is Far, Far Greater Than the Intellect," *BYU Studies* 21, no. 2 (spring 1981).

20. The six were D. Michael Quinn, historian; Avraham Gileadi, Isaiah scholar; Paul Toscano, attorney; Lavina Fielding Anderson, editor and writer; Maxine Hanks, editor and writer; and Lynne Kanavel Whitesides, president of the Mormon Women's Forum.

21. Statement by the First Presidency and the Quorum of the Twelve, 17 October 1993. The definition of apostasy is from *General Handbook of Instructions* (Salt Lake City: Church of Jesus Christ of Latter-day Saints, 1989), 10–13.

22. Elaine Pagels, *Beyond Belief: The Secret Gospel of Thomas* (New York: Random House, 2003), 181.

23. "Catholics are as likely as women in the general population to have an abortion. . . . Catholic women of childbearing age are 29% more likely than their Protestant counterparts to have abortions. The rate is even higher—33%—if Hispanics are factored in" *Family Planning Perspectives* 28, no. 4 (July–August 1996). Among 15–19-year-old women, the abortion rate in 1999 was 8 per 1,000 in Utah, 52 per 1,000

in New York, and 120 per 1,000 in Washington, D.C. "Abortion and Pregnancy Rates by State," Guttmacher Institute, www.agi-usa.org/pubs/state_facts99.html.

24. Bruce A. Chadwick and H. Dean Garrett, "'Choose Ye This Day Whom Ye Will Serve,'" in Douglas Davies, ed., *Mormon Identities in Transition* (London: Cassell, 1996), 173.

25. Neal A. Maxwell, *Deposition of a Disciple* (Salt Lake City: Deseret, 1976), 15.

26. The Rise of a New World Faith," *Review of Religious Research* 26, no. 1 (September 1984): 19, 22–23; "Extracting Social Scientific Models from Mormon History," *Journal of Mormon History* 25, no. 1 (spring 1999): 176.

27. *Conference Report* (8 April 1898): 57.

28. Address of President Gordon B. Hinckley to the Los Angeles World Affairs Council, 13 May 1999.

29. Gordon S. Wood, "Evangelical America and Early Mormonism," *New York History* 61 (October 1980): 368, 367, 361.

30. *The Evening and the Morning Star* 1, no. 3 (August 1832): 22.

31. The numbers were 34,299 for 1840–49 and 43,304 for 1850–59. Tim B. Heaton, Stan L. Albrecht, and J. Randal Johnson, "The Making of British Saints in Historical Perspective." *BYU Studies* 27, no. 2 (spring 1987): 119.

32. Tim B. Heaton, "Vital Statistics," in Daniel H. Ludlow, ed., *Encyclopedia of Mormonism*, 4 vols. (New York: Macmillan, 1992), 4:1520.

33. Armand L. Mauss, "Identity and Boundary Maintenance: International Prospects for Mormonism at the Dawn of the Twenty-first Century," in *Mormon Identities in Transition* (London: Cassell, 1996), 13.

34. Mauss, *Angel and Beehive*, 14.

35. Elaine Pagels, *Beyond Belief: The Secret Gospel of Thomas* (New York: Random House, 2003), 6–10.

36. Spencer W. Kimball, "The Role of Righteous Women," *Ensign* 10 (November 1979): 104.

37. Dallin H. Oaks, "Repentance and Change," *Ensign* 33 (November 2003): 38.

38. Oaks, "Repentance," 39.

39. Kahlile Mehr, "Keeping Promises: The LDS Church Enters Bulgaria, 1990–1994," *BYU Studies* 36, no. 4 (1996–97): 72.

40. Reported in James S. Brown, *Life of a Pioneer*, 122–23 [1900]; quoted in Bryant S. Hinckley, *The Faith of Our Pioneer Fathers* (Salt Lake City: Deseret, 1956), 13.

41. Spencer W. Kimball, *The Teachings of Spencer W. Kimball*, ed. Edward L. Kimball (Salt Lake City: Bookcraft, 1982), 354.

42. Rodney Stark, "The Rise of a New World Faith," *Review of Religious Research* 26, no. 1 (September 1984): 19.

Appendix A

The Prophets and Other Notables

Presidents of the Church of Jesus Christ of Latter-day Saints

Joseph Smith	6 April 1830–27 June 1844
Brigham Young	5 December 1847–29 August 1877
John Taylor	10 October 1880–25 July 1887
Wilford Woodruff	7 April 1889–2 September 1898
Lorenzo Snow	13 September 1898–10 October 1901
Joseph F. Smith	17 October 1901–19 November 1918
Heber J. Grant	23 November 1918–14 May 1945
George Albert Smith	21 May 1945–4 April 1951
David O. McKay	9 April 1951–18 January 1970
Joseph Fielding Smith	23 January 1970–2 July 1972
Harold B. Lee	7 July 1972–26 December 1973
Spencer W. Kimball	30 December 1973–5 November 1985
Ezra Taft Benson	10 November 1985–30 May 1994
Howard W. Hunter	5 June 1994–3 March 1995
Gordon B. Hinckley	12 March 1995–

Joseph Smith (6 April 1830–27 June 1844)

"The early Mormon leaders possessed a singular and fascinating power, which they practiced on all that came within their influence, by which they pretended to cure diseases and work miracles. . . ."

The mystery of it is, how Smith came to possess the knowledge of that magnetic influence, several years anterior to its general circulation throughout the country."

"That is no mystery to me," she replied. "Smith obtained his information, and learned all the strokes, and passes, and manipulations, from a German peddler. . . . Smith paid him handsomely, and the German promised to keep the secret."[1]

Few figures in American history have provoked the range and intensity of emotions that Joseph Smith, founder of the Church of Jesus Christ of Latter-day Saints has. Many attempts have been made to account for the tremendous influence of what John Greenleaf Whittier called "the master-spirit of this extraordinary religious movement."[2] Maria Ward's fanciful account of the Mormon prophet bartering with a German peddler for the secret of mesmerism was echoed in a number of nineteenth-century novels that ascribed to the prophet uncanny powers of attraction and persuasion.

Smith had his own explanation for his hold over his people: "Sectarian priests cry out concerning me, and ask, 'Why is it this babbler gains so many followers, and retains them?' I answer, It is because I possess the principle of love. All I can offer the world is a good heart and a good hand. The Saints can testify whether I am willing to lay down my life for my brethren."[3] As arrest and probable death closed in on the prophet following the *Nauvoo Expositor*'s destruction, Joseph fled with his brother across the Mississippi into Iowa, planning to go from there to the west. Word came to him that the Saints felt his flight was a betrayal, and close associates accused him of cowardice. Smith replied, "If my life is of no value to my friends it is of none to myself." His brother Hyrum counseled return as well. "We shall be butchered," Smith said prophetically.[4] Then he and Hyrum turned back.

The loyalty of Joseph for his people was clearly reciprocated. On the eve of Smith's martyrdom, the prophet turned to Dr. Willard Richards and said, "If we go into the cell, will you go in with us?" Without hesitation the answer came: "Brother Joseph, you did not ask me to cross the river with you—you did not ask me to come to Carthage—you did not ask me to come to jail with you—and do you think I would forsake you now? But I will tell you what I will do; If you are condemned to be hung for treason, I will be hung in your stead, and you shall go free." Joseph exclaimed, "You cannot." And the doctor replied, "I will."[5]

Many attested to the personal appeal of the prophet's personality—but his attraction was no less powerful in public forums. Even in an age of great oratory, his gifts as a public speaker were remarkable. Early Saint and apostle Parley P. Pratt said of Smith, "I have known him to retain a congregation of willing listeners for many hours together in the midst of cold, sunshine, rain or wind while they were laughing at one moment and weeping at the next. Even his most bitter enemies were generally overcome, if he could once get their ears." His effect seemed to be not so much the product of rhetorical skill per se (as was true of Sidney Rigdon, for instance), but of an ability to convey sincerity of character and emotional honesty. Peter H. Burnett, who would become the first governor of California, said of him that "his manner was so earnest, and apparently so candid, that you could not but be interested. . . . In the short space of five days (at Gallatin [scene of the election day riot]) he had so managed to mollify his enemies that he could go unprotected among them without the slightest danger."[6]

Joe Smith was not a very good name for a prophet, detractors remarked. But Joseph himself both protested and aggravated the familiarity such a name implied. He reproved a Methodist minister for a public use of such a nickname (in a Sunday sermon), but it is hard to know if his reproach was entirely serious. "Considering only the day and the place, it would have been more respectful to have said Lieutenant-General Joseph Smith," he chided.[7] But he was more generally concerned to disdain the image of sanctimoniousness and false pride, often to his own detriment. On one famous occasion, he concluded a scriptural debate with visiting ministers by accompanying them out the door. But before bidding farewell, he unexpectedly drew a line in the sand, and jumped. Turning to the surprised clergymen, he then said, "which one of you can beat that?" They were not impressed.[8] Though he insisted that "a prophet was a prophet only when he was acting as such,"[9] his lack of piousness was an affront to many.

As remarkable as Smith's ability to elicit loyalty, of course, was his capacity to arouse hostility. "The envy and wrath of man have been my common lot all the days of my life," he lamented to his fellow Saints, "and for what cause it seems mysterious, unless I was ordained from before the foundation of the world for some good end, or bad. . . . But nevertheless, deep water is what I am wont to swim in" (DC 127:2). His self-characterization was no exaggeration. He was the subject of numerous lawsuits in his lifetime—many of them frivolous or vexatious, and suffered several imprisonments of up to five months. He was shot at, assaulted, tarred and feathered, illegally sentenced to be executed, and finally murdered by an armed mob of over a hundred. In the midst of one incarceration, he found comfort in his belief that such trials were not without a sanctifying effect:

And if thou shouldst be cast into the pit, or into the hands of murderers, and the sentence of death passed upon thee; if thou be cast into the deep; if the billowing surge conspire against thee; if fierce winds become thine enemy; if the heavens gather blackness, and all the elements combine to hedge up the way; and above all, if the very jaws of hell shall gape open the mouth wide after thee, know thou, my son, that all these things shall give thee experience, and shall be for thy good. (DC 122:2, 6–7)

What seems beyond doubt is Joseph's own certainty that he was called of God to reshape the Christian world, and this certainty was easily construed by doubters as unpardonable hubris. "I stood alone," he wrote to editor John Gordon Bennett, "an unlearned youth, to combat the worldly wisdom and multiplied ignorance of eighteen centuries, with a new revelation." But with Cromwellian confidence, he added that "one man empowered from Jehovah has more influence with the children of the kingdom than eight hundred millions led by the precepts of men."[10]

In his thirty-nine years, he saw the church he founded grow from six to more than twenty-five thousand members. He founded a city that within five years rivaled Chicago in size, and established a faith group resilient enough to weather mobbings and expulsions. He translated and published the Book of Mormon and a book of revelations. He claimed to bring back to earth priesthood authority, the keys possessed by prophets of past generations, and temple ordinances and rituals lost in the mists of ancient history.

As bold as his theological and empire building gestures were, his vision was even more ambitious. His campaign for the presidency of the United States was aborted only by his murder. His designs to re-erect Zion in the midst of Missouri, to implement a Utopian economic order, were halted by opposition from without and listless support within. His increasingly daring theological expositions had not yet crescendoed, and his self-revelation was only beginning, when the bullets at Carthage cut short his life. He hinted tantalizingly of revelations still to come, both from heaven and from his personal spiritual odyssey: "No man knows my history," he claimed. "I cannot lie down until my work is finished ... When I am called at the trump and weighed in the balance, you will know me then."[11]

Brigham Young (5 December 1847–29 August 1877)

It is tempting to summarize the character and contributions of Brigham Young by contrasting him with his predecessor. Joseph was over six feet tall and weighed more than two hundred pounds. Like George Washington, much of Smith's charisma was a function of his commanding physical presence and dignified carriage. Brigham Young, on the other hand, was somewhat shorter, about 5′10″, and generally described by words like stocky, compact, and solid, befitting his background as a carpenter. The famous explorer Richard Burton described Young as he appeared in 1860, at the height of his powers:

> fifty-nine years of age: he looks about forty five. . . . Scarcely a grey thread appears in his hair, which is parted on the side, light colored, rather thick. . . . The forehead is somewhat narrow, the eyebrows are thin, the eyes between grey and blue, with a calm, composed, and somewhat reserved expression. . . .
>
> His manner is at once affable and impressive, simple and courteous. . . . He shows no signs of dogmatism, bigotry, or fanaticism, and never once entered—with me at least—upon the subject of religion. He impresses a stranger with a certain sense of power.[12]

Joseph is generally credited as the towering spiritual innovator, revealing new doctrines up to the moment of his death. Young achieved fame as the city builder, great colonizer, organizer, and practical implementer of the gospel program. Both Mormons and outsiders have tended to emphasize these stark differences. A hostile Senator Thomas Kearns, for instance, reported to his colleagues in a much publicized speech that

> the Mormons have been taught to revere Joseph Smith as a direct prophet from God. He saw the face of the All Father. He held communion with the Son. The Holy Ghost was his constant companion. He settled every question, however trivial, by revelation from Almighty God. But Brigham was different. While claiming a divine right of leadership, he worked out his great mission by palpable and material means. I do not know that he ever pretended to have received a revelation from the time that he left Nauvoo until he reached the shores of the Dead Sea, nor through all the thirty years of his leadership there.[13]

Young's lifelong friend Heber C. Kimball pointedly denied such distinction in their spiritual vocations: "You need not ask who administer to brother Brigham; for I will tell you: They are Moses and Aaron, Elijah, Jesus, Peter, James, and John, brother Joseph, Michael the Archangel, and the hosts of the righteous behind the veil."[14] In other ways as well, Smith had set the pattern. It was Smith, for example, who orchestrated the city planning of Nauvoo, and led a well-organized relief expedition of hundreds of men called "Zion's Camp" over a thousand miles from Kirtland to Missouri. In his role as the American Moses, Young was but extending the lead of Joseph, gathering not thousands, but tens of thousands to a new Zion in the west. And of course Young did not merely found Salt Lake City, but directed the colonization of more than a hundred settlements throughout the west, making him the greatest colonizer in American history, and perhaps the world.

Still, the difference between Joseph as the creator of a new faith tradition, and Young as the empire builder, cannot be denied. As one Mormon historian has put the case, "Brigham Young was first a great disciple and student of Joseph Smith and only secondly a great leader in his own right. He saw himself as the master-builder—not the architect—of the Kingdom and of Zion."[15]

Under Young, the Saints continued the experiment in theocracy begun by Joseph Smith. In his roles as territorial governor (1850–57), trustee-in-trust, and prophet of the church, he combined political, economic, and religious authority in one man. Certainly the blurring of lines was disturbing to American sensibilities. But as he insisted, "I know no difference between spiritual and temporal labors. God has seen fit to bless me with means, and as a faithful steward I use them to benefit my fellow men—to promote their happiness in this world in preparing them for the great hereafter."[16]

Young served as prophet and president thirty years, the longest in LDS Church history and more than twice as long as Joseph Smith. He led a people on the longest and most massive recolonization effort in American history. He established over a hundred communities, and pioneered successful, large-scale irrigation techniques, to tame a wilderness thought to be largely uninhabitable and incapable of crop production. He supervised the immigration of tens of thousands of converts, and the building of railroads, canals, roads, a theater, and two universities. His longtime friend and counselor, George Q. Cannon, summarized the prodigious scope of Young's contributions: "From the organization of the Church, and the construction of the Temples, the building of Tabernacles; from the creation of a provisional state of government and a Territorial government, down to the small matter of directing the shape of these seats upon which we sit this day; upon all these things, as well as upon the settlements of the Territory, the impress of his genius is apparent."[17]

John Taylor (10 October 1880–25 July 1887)

John Taylor was thirty-five when a mob broke in and fired indiscriminately into the room holding Joseph and Hyrum Smith, Willard Richards, and himself. He took four bullets, but recovered to travel westward with the Saints. He assumed leadership of the church following Brigham Young's death in 1877.

Taylor was English by birth, and joined the church in 1836 after emigrating to Canada; he was ordained an apostle two years later. Once a Methodist preacher himself, Taylor would spend many years performing and directing missionary work of the church in England, Scotland, France, Germany, Belgium, and much of the United States. A talented writer, he edited the official LDS newspaper, *Times and Seasons*, as well as the *Nauvoo Neighbor*, and wrote the church's first major work of Christology, *The Mediation and Atonement of Our Lord and Savior Jesus Christ* (1882). At the time of the great exodus, he assisted in organizing the Mormon Battalion, led a company of Saints to Salt Lake City, and served many years in the territorial legislature.

Taylor inherited the mantle of leadership at a time of crisis. The first prosecution under federal antipolygamy laws was finally resolved on 6 January 1879, when a verdict against George Reynolds was upheld by the Supreme Court.[18] Taylor was at the time acting president of the church, and would be ordained prophet in October 1880. In 1882, Congress passed the Edmunds Bill, which made prosecution of polygamists vastly easier than previous legislation. As prosecutions and imprisonments quickly followed, Taylor found it necessary to disappear into the polygamous underground in 1885. In 1887, while Taylor was in hiding, the corporation of the church was formally dissolved and its assets confiscated by a new act, the Edmunds–Tucker Law. Five days before a federal marshal took charge of the church's property, John Taylor died at the age of seventy-eight.

Wilford Woodruff (7 April 1889–2 September 1898)

One of the most assiduous record-keepers in the history of the church, Wilford Woodruff is renowned today as the most effective missionary of his era as well, baptizing six hundred English converts in a matter of weeks. Like other prominent leaders, Woodruff had gone into hiding to avoid prosecution for polygamy in 1885. He watched the funeral of his predecessor from the veiled windows of an office in Salt Lake City. He was still in hiding when he was formally sustained as the new prophet and president in April 1889. In one of the most momentous decisions in church history, Woodruff issued the "Manifesto," announcing the cessation of plural marriage, to a shocked church and incredulous public in September of the next year.

Financially crippled, its leaders imprisoned or in hiding, its members stripped of political rights and all means of redress exhausted, the Mormon Church was in desperate circumstances. Latter-day Saints were individually committed enough to "the principle" and resilient enough in the face of over a half century of persecution that they would probably have persisted in their civil disobedience indefinitely. Skeptics saw the "Manifesto" as a "revelation" of convenience, a capitulation masquerading as divine command. But Woodruff insisted that "The Lord showed me by vision and revelation exactly what would take place if we did not stop this practice. . . . I saw exactly what would come to pass if there was not something done. I have had this spirit upon me for a long time. But I want to say this: I should have let all the temples go out of our hands; I should have gone to prison myself, and let every other man go there, had not the God of heaven commanded me to do what I did do; and when the hour came that I was commanded to do that, it was all clear to me. I went before the Lord, and I wrote what the Lord told me to write" (DC Official Declaration-1).

Aftershocks from the polygamy earthquake made the era of transition difficult—but it had begun. Woodruff would wait another year before appearing in public with the First Presidency. And in 1893, Mormonism was denied any meaningful participation in the World's Parliament of Religion, held at the Chicago World Fair, although the purpose of the Congress was "to promote and deepen the spirit of human brotherhood among religious men of diverse faiths."[19] Mormonism, in the eyes of the parliament's organizers, was still a little too diverse. But under Woodruff's leadership, the church was turning a corner, and before he died in 1898, the fourth president of the Mormon Church saw Utah admitted as the forty-fifth state in the Union.

Lorenzo Snow (13 September 1898–10 October 1901)

Lorenzo Snow was the last prophet of the church's founding generation. He knew Joseph Smith, attended the school of prophets, and, like three of his predecessors, assisted in the great migration westward. Snow was also the only prophet who actually served prison time—almost a year when he was in his seventies—for the practice of plural marriage.

Although Lorenzo Snow held the office of president for only three years, he oversaw major policy changes that profoundly affected the future of the church. First was his decision to emphasize the principle of tithing as a key to both the financial recovery of the church and the spiritual wholeness of its members. After the economic ravages wrought by Edmunds–Tucker, Snow was able to put the church back on the road to solvency. At the same time he was putting the financial house in order, Snow reversed the policy (as old as the church itself) of gathering the Saints to Zion. This change he coupled with a renewed emphasis on taking the gospel into all the world. During the first years of his administration, apostles dedicated Japan, Palestine, Russia, and several countries in Europe for missionary work. By stimulating worldwide missionary work, while encouraging converts to build Zion in their homelands, he heralded the era of the worldwide church.

Joseph F. Smith (17 October 1901–19 November 1918)

Joseph F. Smith was born in Far West, Missouri, only weeks after nineteen Mormons were massacred at the nearby settlement of Haun's Mill. He was a boy of five when his father Hyrum, brother of the prophet, was killed in Carthage Jail. A few years later he was driving an ox team across the plains with his widowed mother, and two years after being orphaned at age thirteen, he was sailing for Hawaii as a missionary. By the time he was twenty-seven, he was ordained an apostle by Brigham Young.

Soon after he succeeded Lorenzo Snow to the presidency in 1901, the Senate hearings on seating Reed Smoot were playing out, a kind of last gasp of national intolerance of Mormonism. Smith's grueling experiences with Illinois persecutors, driving his mother's wagon across the plains as a nine-year-old, and presiding over mission work while in his teens steeled him for the harrowing attacks and interrogations he endured as the church's representative at the Smoot hearings and in the media. With Smoot's successful seating in 1907, and then the coming of World War I, a period of toleration and church prosperity began.

In the midst of the Smoot affair, Smith gave impetus to a Mormon historical consciousness and stewardship that has flourished ever since. In 1905, at Sharon, Vermont, the church erected a monument noting the centennial anniversary of the birth of the prophet Joseph Smith, and in 1907 the church purchased historic sites associated with the prophet's early life. The reconstructed city of Nauvoo, Illinois, and historic preservation and rebuilding in Kirtland, Ohio, are late twentieth- and early twenty-first-century extensions of those initiatives.

Smith's other enduring legacy was his exposition of LDS doctrine, represented in the collection *Gospel Doctrine* (1919). Most important in this regard was his "Vision of the Dead," which he received just weeks before his own death in 1918. The most comprehensive account in Mormon doctrine of life after death, Smith's vision describes Christ's visit to Paradise (as intimated to the thief on the cross) and the manner in which the gospel is preached to spirits who had no knowledge of Christ in this life. In 1981 his account was canonized as section 138 of the *Doctrine and Covenants*, one of a small handful of revelations canonized after the death of Joseph Smith.

Heber J. Grant (23 November 1918–14 May 1945)

Heber J. Grant was cut from a different bolt of cloth than his predecessors. An avid businessman and entrepreneur, Grant was financially prosperous and deeply drawn to a life of commerce. Called as an apostle in 1882 at the age of twenty-five, Grant was soon called upon to use his financial acumen to help steer the church successfully through the national financial crisis of 1893.

At the relatively youthful age of sixty-two, Grant succeeded Joseph F. Smith, in 1918. The coming Depression years again made his background especially relevant to his church service. With Mormonism finally reaching more general American acceptance, the controversies of polygamy buried, and the distraction of war over, Grant became an effective ambassador of the church. His travels approached a half-million miles, as he spoke to civic and professional organizations throughout the country, fostering a new era of respect for and more accurate understanding of the LDS faith. Through personal charisma, public lectures, business contacts, and the promotion of national tours by the Tabernacle Choir, he worked successfully to encourage more favorable media depictions of the church and its history.

Grant headed two initiatives with far-reaching consequences for the modern church. First, he established an extensive seminary and institute program that supplemented the secular education of LDS youth with spiritual training through the high school and college years. In 2001, over seven hundred thousand students were enrolled in the program Grant introduced. At least equally significant was the establishment in 1936 of the Church Security Program, later renamed the Church Welfare Program.

Having served in the church's leading councils through two World Wars, a financial panic, and the Great Depression, Grant died after one of the longest church leadership careers ever—almost sixty-five years.

George Albert Smith (21 May 1945–4 April 1951)

George Albert Smith assumed the presidency just in time to oversee relief efforts directed at succoring European Saints devastated by years of war. Church growth was steady and consistent under his administration, as the church reestablished a missionary program long crippled by the war years. Before his years as president, Smith was instrumental in getting the church to incorporate Boy Scouting into its youth program. The Church has long since been the major sponsor of scouting as a result. In his relatively short term as president, Smith gained renown principally as a man of Christ-like attributes, well suited to guide the church through a period of postwar healing and reconciliation.

David O. McKay (9 April 1951–18 January 1970)

It was during the administration of David O. McKay that the internationalization of the church began in earnest. As church membership trebled from one million to almost three, President McKay encouraged foreign converts to cease their migration to Utah, and "build up Zion" in their native lands. He traveled over 2 million miles as president, and was the first prophet to visit Saints in Asia, South and Central America, Africa, and Australia. In fact, he considered turning the Church into a worldwide organization his greatest accomplishment as a leader.

Possessed of great personal charisma, McKay was renowned for his measured judgment, his political moderation and tolerance, and his gentleness of character. A teacher by background and a lover of Robert Burns and Shakespeare, McKay may have been the most humanistically inclined of the Mormon prophets. Education became a focus of his administration, and under his guidance Brigham Young University became the largest church-affiliated college in America.

Much of McKay's influence was the product of sheer longevity. No Mormon before him had served as long in the presiding councils of the church—sixty-four years. By the time of his death in 1970, well over half the membership of the church had known no other prophet in their lifetimes. Even today, his legacy is frequently invoked by Mormons who cite his famous slogans, "Every member a missionary," and "No other success can compensate for failure in the home." Of the sixteen Mormon temples operating or announced during his lifetime, he dedicated or planned half of them.

Joseph Fielding Smith (23 January 1970–2 July 1972)

Born when Brigham Young was leading the Mormons, Joseph Fielding Smith assumed the presidency a year after men had landed on the moon. Ninety-three at the time, he served for only two and a half years before his death. But his impact on the church was considerable, effected primarily through his extensive writings. He produced twenty-five books on gospel subjects, and probably did more than any leader to shape the modern development of Mormon doctrine. Though not officially sanctioned or canonical, works such as *Essentials in Church History*, *Answers to Gospel Questions* (5 vols.), and *Doctrines of Salvation* (3 vols.) spoke authoritatively across a spectrum of historical and doctrinal issues. Like his similarly prolific son-in-law apostle Bruce R. McConkie, Smith was more rigid in his orthodoxy than many church leaders, but his writings continue to carry significant weight with members even today.

Harold B. Lee (7 July 1972–26 December 1973)

When Harold B. Lee was ordained prophet in 1972 at the relatively young age of seventy-three, it was expected he would serve a long and vigorous term. His unexpected death eighteen months later left him the youngest LDS prophet to die since Joseph Smith's martyrdom. His major contributions to the church were in the areas of church correlation and the welfare program. The former was an initiative dating to the 1960s to streamline, simplify, and better coordinate church programs and objectives. All church activities and programs were organized around the three areas of children, youth, and adults. Subsequently, all church materials, activities, organizations, curricula, and periodicals were placed under the centralized direction of the priesthood.

Spencer W. Kimball (30 December 1973–5 November 1985)

Spencer Wooley Kimball assumed the church presidency in 1973 at the age of seventy-eight. With his distinctive raspy voice (the consequence of surgery for throat cancer), his gentle wit, and his energetic pace that left younger colleagues dazed, President Kimball was one of the most beloved leaders of modern times. Though he led the church less than a dozen years, and only seven or eight before he was incapacitated, he oversaw a dynamic period of institutional and doctrinal changes.

As an apostle, he had been assigned to work with Native Americans, and he was instrumental in creating the Indian Student Placement Program in 1954, wherein children of the Navajo and other tribes boarded with members during the school year, to improve their educational opportunities. As prophet, Kimball quickly established a dramatic vision for a more ambitious missionary effort. Under his leadership, the number of missionaries grew by 50 percent, and work spread to communist countries and sub-Saharan Africa.

His ministry registered an enormous impact on the lives of millions for several reasons. First, he initiated dramatic institutional changes. He consolidated worship services into a three-hour Sunday block, thus transforming the order and experience of Sabbath worship in the church. In 1978, he announced that the priesthood would henceforth be available to all worthy males, thus making leadership roles possible and membership more attractive to members of black ethnicity. This was the most profound announcement in church doctrine and practice since the revocation of polygamy as a practice in 1890. He increased the number of temples operating or planned from sixteen to forty-two, organized the First Quorum of Seventy, divided the world into Areas with General Authorities assigned to each, and drew heavily from the international church for new leadership. These doctrinal and administrative changes, together with his practice of holding frequent regional conferences, had the effect of making the church leadership—and temple worship—more accessible to members spread across the globe.

In addition, Kimball's ministry was an exercise in returning to the basics. Though simple to the point of understatement, his messages were influential precisely because they were so practical and easy to implement. He admonished members to beautify their yards, plant gardens, keep journals and family histories, and be better neighbors. At the same time, Kimball's response to the political upheavals of the 1970s and 1980s demonstrated a striking blend of progressivism and conservatism, emphasizing the church's capacity for dynamic change and innovation as well as steadfast commitment to what it perceived as eternal principles. So even as the church restructured administratively and extended full equality to members of black ancestry, it reiterated emphatic opposition to abortion, homosexual practices, and the Equal Rights Amendment, in the latter case applauding the goal of political equality, but disapproving the means as a threat to family structure.

Ezra Taft Benson (10 November 1985–30 May 1994)

Ezra Taft Benson was the highest political official to succeed to church leadership. Before his call as prophet, Benson's most notable church service had come in his call to preside over the European mission of the church in the aftermath of World War II. He supervised the distribution of relief supplies to the suffering Saints there, and reorganized missionary work across Europe. His experiences there galvanized both his sensitivity to suffering and his commitment to the values that he felt had made victory and generosity in victory possible—democracy and free enterprise. Under Eisenhower, Benson served as secretary of agriculture a full eight years, while he was simultaneously serving as an LDS apostle. He was a passionate advocate of the nation's farmers and a staunch political conservative. A committed anticommunist, his outspokenness on the subject led to some concerns about the prospect of a politicized Benson presidency. However, upon his succession after the death of Spencer W. Kimball, Benson chose to make increased attention to the Book of Mormon the theme of his tenure. He was convinced, and publicly testified, that he had been commanded of God to do just that. "He has revealed to me," he would say, "the absolute need for us to move the Book of Mormon forward now in a marvelous manner."[20] And indeed, he did more than any LDS prophet to make that book the "keystone of Mormonism," spurring a greater role for that scripture in members' daily devotion and in church teaching that it retains today.

Fittingly, Benson presided over the church in the years when the Berlin Wall fell and the Soviet Union disintegrated, preparing the way for missionaries to spread throughout communist Europe.

Howard W. Hunter (5 June 1994–3 March 1995)

On 7 February 1993, Howard W. Hunter was speaking at Brigham Young University in his capacity as president of the Quorum of the Twelve Apostles. A man approached the podium and threatened to detonate a bomb unless the apostle read a statement. The senior apostle refused, and a few minutes later some students subdued the man. An unfazed President Hunter simply resumed his address. As he did in 1988, when before a world audience, he fell at the podium and broke three ribs.

Those episodes reveal the steadfast, understated record of a man whose consistent service as apostle for three and a half decades contrasts ironically with the shortest presidency of any prophet in church history— less than nine months. Yet even today, Hunter is remembered for making temple worship the focus of his presidency, prophetically establishing a theme that would be acted upon by his successor Gordon B. Hinckley in dramatic fashion.

Gordon B. Hinckley (12 March 1995–)

Gordon B. Hinckley has reaped one accomplishment even Joseph Smith might envy. He tied Michael Jordan as the fifth most highly admired man in the world, according to a Gallup poll.[21] The fifteenth president of the LDS Church, Gordon B. Hinckley was the first since President Kimball in the early years of his ministry to bring unbounded energy and (relatively) youthful vitality to the position (he was eighty-four at his sustaining). Long schooled in the public relations area of church administration, Hinckley has been the most effective and successful leader to date in exploiting the potential of the media to shine a positive light on Mormonism.

During his presidency, he has held major news conferences in New York City, Japan, Korea, Mexico, England, and Germany; was interviewed by reporters from the *New York Times*, *Wall Street Journal*, BBC, and London News Radio; and appeared with Mike Wallace and Larry King, making him the most recognizable LDS Church leader of the modern era and one of its most articulate spokesmen. His book *Stand for Something*, a New York Times bestseller, has brought his words to more Americans than any predecessor since Joseph Smith.

"I do not anticipate any dramatic change in course," President Hinckley told the media the day after his designation as the church's fifteenth prophet. "Procedures and programs may be altered from time to time, but the doctrine remains constant. We are dedicated, as have been those before us, to teaching the gospel of peace, to the promotion of civility and mutual respect among people everywhere, to bearing witness to the living reality of our Lord Jesus Christ, and to the practice of His teachings in our daily lives."[22] If he has not changed the church's direction, he has certainly accelerated one of its programs. The most conspicuous achievement of President

Hinckley as church leader has been the burgeoning number of temples over which he has presided. Church presidents from Joseph F. Smith to Ezra Taft Benson had predicted a coming day when temples would "dot the earth."[23] In 1995, when Benson died, forty-nine temples had been constructed. In just two years of his presidency (1999–2000), Hinckley oversaw the dedication of that exact same number, as many as all fourteen of his predecessors combined. He is well on the way to tripling the total (128 as of March 2003).

President Hinckley's influence on the course of the church preceded his formal call to the presidency, since he was counselor to both Spencer W. Kimball and Ezra Taft Benson during those years when they were ailing and hindered from exerting vigorous leadership.

Other Notables

Eliza R. Snow (1804–87)

It would be tempting, but mistaken, to connect Eliza Roxey Snow's importance to her close connections to three Mormon prophets. Sister to fifth church president Lorenzo Snow, she also had the interesting distinction of being married to Joseph Smith as a plural wife (1842) and then, subsequent to his death, as a plural wife of Brigham Young (1844). Her well-deserved fame, however, is traceable to her remarkable gifts as a poet, stature as an intellectual, and influence as a leader and role model for Mormon women. In 1842 she participated in the founding of the Relief Society (the LDS women's organization) in Nauvoo; in 1867, under Brigham Young's direction, she reorganized the auxiliary and served as its president until her death.

She was especially effective in carving out important roles for pioneer Mormon women, influencing their participation in Utah's political process, their dispatch to eastern medical schools, their positions of responsibility in Utah's substantial Home Production effort, and the establishment of a women's journal (*The Woman's Exponent*). Best known perhaps as the author of the Mormon hymn (and virtual scripture) "Oh My Father," which poignantly tells of man's premortal estate, she authored two volumes of poetry and seven other books.

Parley P. Pratt (1807–57)

Converted immediately upon reading the Book of Mormon, Parley Parker Pratt was an indefatigable missionary and influential shaper of early Mormon doctrines and institutions. One of the original twelve apostles called by Joseph Smith, he worked closely with the prophet, experiencing mobbings, imprisonment, and the trek to Utah. Pratt was a prolific and skilled writer, and his *Voice of Warning* (1837) was the first sustained exposition of Mormon teachings. After the Book of Mormon, it was the primary proselytizing tool used by missionaries into the twentieth century. He was himself one of the most traveled missionaries of his era, and answered more than twenty calls, serving throughout the states from California to New York, and in Canada, South America, and England. While in the latter assignment, he founded one of the church's longest-running periodicals, the *Millennial Star*.

In Utah, Pratt was active in territorial politics, and helped write the constitution for what would be the Utah Territory. Hoping to ease the learning of English for foreign converts, Brigham Young appointed him to devise a Mormon phonetic system called the Deseret alphabet. (Initially the result was so successful that Deseret News articles appeared in the new alphabet, two elementary readers were produced, and the entire Book of Mormon was published in Deseret text. In spite of its popularity with many immigrants, it faded from use by the 1870s.)

In addition to several works of theology, Pratt wrote many hymns still sung by Mormon congregations, poetry, a history of the Missouri persecutions, and the most colorful and literary autobiography of early Mormonism (not published until 1874). He was murdered while serving yet another mission to the eastern states.

Emmeline B. Wells (1828–1921)

Emmeline Wells, along with Eliza R. Snow, was the church's staunchest advocate of women's rights. Utah women had been granted the vote in 1870, but Congress soon revoked it in 1877. Wells campaigned for its restoration, which occurred in 1896. She was also active on the national scene, working with prominent suffragists Susan B. Anthony and Elizabeth Cady Stanton. Her work as a liaison with non-Mormon women did much to further respect and recognition for Utah's women.

An accomplished writer, Wells was also, from 1877 on, editor of the *Woman's Exponent*, whose slogan typified her life's work: "The Rights of the Women of Zion and the Rights of the Women of All Nations." Incongruously, in the minds of outsiders, Wells was also a powerful proponent of polygamy, defending the practice before three U.S. presidents and congressional committees.

As president of the Relief Society, she oversaw ambitious grain distribution projects, providing relief to victims of drought in Utah, of famine in China, and of earthquake in San Francisco. In 1891 she joined with others to found the Women's Press Club, devoted to the encouragement of women's writing.

She was the first Utah woman to receive an honorary degree, and the only woman recognized with a bust in the State Capitol Rotunda.

Orson Pratt (1811–81)

Converted by his brother Parley, Orson Pratt joined the church in 1830, and like him was appointed a member of the first Quorum of the Twelve Apostles of the new organization. Like Parley, Orson published important early treatises and tracts, including the first public account of Joseph Smith's first vision (*An Interesting Account of Several Remarkable Visions*, Edinburgh, 1840). Also like Parley, Orson served numerous missions, continued to write prolifically, administered church affairs in England and domestically, and was involved in territorial politics. He was a true pioneer (the first Mormon to enter the Salt Lake Valley) and a durable veteran, being the last surviving of the original twelve apostles. When Brigham Young wanted a respected voice making the public announcement on polygamy in 1852, he chose Pratt. It may have helped that Pratt had himself been initially so opposed to the principle that he was excommunicated for a brief period. His eventual, hard-won conversion to the principle made him one of its most vigorous defenders. His twelve-part exposition of polygamy, published as *The Seer* in 1853, is the most extensive apologetics for the principle in Mormon literature.

Even though he was essentially self-taught, Pratt became an accomplished mathematician and astronomer, and was known as the leading scientific mind among the early Saints. He played a key role in organizing the university established by Joseph Smith in Nauvoo, continued as an active public lecturer and promoter of science in Utah, and wrote on both scientific and mathematical subjects. An experienced editor, Pratt was also responsible for the first modern edition of the Book of Mormon, dividing it into chapters and verses and including references.

B. H. Roberts (1857–1933)

Considered by most LDS scholars as the outstanding Mormon intellectual of his era, B. H. Roberts was "the best theologian and historian that Mormonism had in its first century."[24] Roberts was a prolific writer, a dominant orator, an impassioned defender of the faith, an influential church leader (a seventy and mission president), and always a fiercely independent force to be reckoned with, both by enemies of the church and by his fellow brethren in the church. As a historian, he edited the official *History of the Church* (1902–32), drawn largely from the papers of Joseph Smith and his scribes. He also authored a *Comprehensive History of the Church* (1930), which relied on contemporary historical documents, and brought church history into the twentieth century. In spite of over thirty published works, he considered his greatest contribution to be his *The Truth, The Way, The Life*, a three-volume masterwork on Mormon doctrine that was finished in 1928 but was never published in his lifetime (he was unwilling to make minor changes to accommodate a church committee that reviewed it).

Active in territorial politics, he was elected to the U.S. House of Representatives in 1898, but was never seated because of opposition to his practice of polygamy (for which offense he served time in the Utah penitentiary). The most sophisticated scholar of the Book of Mormon of his time, he was unorthodoxly frank in acknowledging the weight of challenges to the scripture raised by critics, even as he continued in his position as most visible and relied-upon apologist for the church. His most enduring legacy was the independence of the intellect that he manifested, even at the occasional cost of personal tranquility and harmonious relations with colleagues.

James E. Talmage (1862–1933)

James Talmage was a brilliant scholar and internationally recognized scientist, and served as president of the University of Utah (1894–97). Even before his calling as an apostle in 1911, Talmage served in a number of important capacities, such as advising leaders during the Reed Smoot congressional hearings and revising the *Pearl of Great Price*. (He would later head a committee to issue a new edition of the Book of Mormon.) But his lasting impact as one of Mormonism's most important theologians came through the publication of three of his books in particular (he authored several). *The Articles of Faith: Being a Consideration of the Principal Doctrines of The Church of Jesus Christ of Latter-day Saints* (1899) is a systematic exposition of the thirteen tenets listed by Joseph Smith as a summary of LDS teachings, which he wrote at the request of the First Presidency. Though many church doctrines fall outside the purview of the thirteen articles, Talmage's study is a comprehensive treatment of basic tenets. *Jesus the Christ: A Study of the Messiah and his Mission*, which he published in 1915 (also at the request of church leaders), provides a detailed study of Jesus' premortal status, his earthly life and ministry, and manifestations of Christ in modern times. It is the most authoritative treatment of Christology in the church.

The Great Apostasy (1909), a scholarly overview of ecclesiastical history from New Testament times to the nineteenth century, shaped the Mormon conception of the Christian tradition as constituting a systematic corruption of the primitive gospel, necessitating its full restoration by a modern prophet.

Hugh Nibley (1910–)

Hugh Nibley is the dominant intellect of modern Mormonism. His erudition, productivity, and eloquently provocative denunciations of the foibles of contemporary culture—Mormon and non-Mormon—have won him widespread respect, even as his Dickensian idiosyncrasies have won him affection. Two roles in particular have fallen to Nibley's particular province. He was the first, and is still the most eminent, scholar to convincingly defend the Book of Mormon against the modern attacks—or studied indifference—of non-Mormon intellectuals. His polemical zeal can at times intrude upon his scholarly rigor, but even evangelical scholars have acknowledged that "whatever flaws may exist in his methodology, Nibley is a scholar of high caliber," noting that his work has appeared in world-class journals, and been praised by non-LDS scholars such as Jacob Neusner, James Charlesworth, Cyrus Gordon, Raphael Patai, and Jacob Milgrom.[25]

Even as he has done more than any other Latter-day Saints to endow Mormons with confidence in the intellectual viability of their faith system, Nibley has been a most vociferous critic of contemporary Mormon culture. Perhaps no leader or contemporary intellectual has so pointedly and eloquently indicted Mormon offenses in the areas of militarism, materialism, antienvironmentalism, and intellectual malaise—tendencies that, he insistently demonstrates, betray the Mormon doctrinal heritage. An uncompromising idealist, he insists that "a Zion that makes concessions is no longer Zion."[26]

Notes

1. Maria Ward, *Female Life Among the Mormons. A Narrative of Many Years' Experience Among the Mormons* . . . (London: Routledge, 1855).

2. William Mulder and Russell Mortensen, eds., *Among the Mormons: Historic Accounts by Contemporary Observers* (Lincoln: University of Nebraska Press, 1958), 158.

3. Joseph Smith Jr., *History of the Church of Jesus Christ of Latter-day Saints*, 7 vols., ed. James Mulholland et al. (Salt Lake City: Deseret, 1951), 5:498.

4. Smith, *History of the Church*, 6:549–50.

5. Ibid., 6:616.

6. James B. Allen and Glen M. Leonard, *The Story of the Latter-day Saints* (Salt Lake: Deseret, 1976), 132–33.

7. Mulder, *Among the Mormons*, 140.

8. Truman Madsen, *Joseph Smith the Prophet* (Salt Lake City: Bookcraft, 1989), 25.

9. Smith, *History of the Church*, 5:265.

10. Ibid., 6:74.

11. Ibid., 6:317.

12. Richard F. Burton, *The City of the Saints and Across the Rocky Mountains to California* (1861; New York: Knopf, 1963), 262–64.

13. B. H. Roberts, *Defense of the Faith and the Saints*, 2 vols. (Salt Lake City: Deseret, 1907), 1:178.

14. *Journal of Discourses*, 26 vols., reported by G. D. Watt et al. (Liverpool: F. D. and S. W. Richards et al., 1851–86; reprint, Salt Lake City: n.p., 1974), 5:205.

15. Ron Esplin, "Brigham Young and Priesthood Denial to Blacks: An Alternate View," in "Historian's Quarter," *BYU Studies* 19 (1978–79): 396.

16. *New York Herald*, 10 April 1873.

17. George Q. Cannon, quoted in Preston Nibley, *Brigham Young: The Man and His Work*, 4th ed. (Salt Lake City: Deseret, 1960), 534, 537.

18. Early prosecutions against Brigham Young and others for adulterous relations with polygamous wives had been unsuccessful.

19. Initially denied any participation at all, officials eventually agreed to allow a church representative to read a paper in a small conference room. Denied the right, accorded all other faiths, to address the full conference, the LDS Church declined the compromise. See B. H. Roberts, *The Comprehensive History of the Church of Jesus Christ of Latter-day Saints*, 6 vols. (Provo, Utah: Church of Jesus Christ of Latter-day Saints, 1957), 6:236–41.

20. *Ensign* 28, no. 11 (November 1988): 4–6.

21. Gallup Poll, 29 December 2000, reported in *Deseret News*, 4 January 2001.

22. Statement to the media, 13 March 1995, in *Church News*, 18 March 1995.

23. "In 1906 I heard President Joseph F. Smith make this statement in Rotterdam, Holland: 'The day will come when temples of the Lord will dot this whole land of Europe,'" LeGrand Richards, *Conference Report*, October 1959, 35; "Our predecessors have prophesied that temples will dot the landscape of North and South America, the isles of the Pacific, Europe, and elsewhere. If this redemptive work is to be done on the scale it must be, hundreds of temples will be needed." *Teachings of Ezra Taft Benson*, 247.

24. Sterling McMurrin, "Brigham H. Roberts: A Biographical Essay," in B. H. Roberts, *Studies of the Book of Mormon*, ed. Brigham D. Madsen (Salt Lake City: Signature, 1992), xxvi.

25. Carl Mosser and Paul Owen, "Mormon Apologetic, Scholarship and Evangelical Neglect: Losing the Battle and Not Knowing It?" *Trinity Journal* (1998): 182.

26. Hugh Nibley, *Approaching Zion*, in *The Collected Works of Hugh Nibley*, 15 vols. (Provo, Utah: Deseret and FARMS, 1986–), 9:30.

Appendix B

The Articles of Faith

1 We believe in God, the Eternal Father, and in His Son, Jesus Christ, and in the Holy Ghost.

2 We believe that men will be punished for their own sins, and not for Adam's transgression.

3 We believe that through the Atonement of Christ, all mankind may be saved, by obedience to the laws and ordinances of the Gospel.

4 We believe that the first principles and ordinances of the Gospel are: first, Faith in the Lord Jesus Christ; second, Repentance; third, Baptism by immersion for the remission of sins; fourth, Laying on of hands for the gift of the Holy Ghost.

5 We believe that a man must be called of God, by prophecy, and by the laying on of hands by those who are in authority, to preach the Gospel and administer in the ordinances thereof.

6 We believe in the same organization that existed in the Primitive Church, namely, apostles, prophets, pastors, teachers, evangelists, and so forth.

7 We believe in the gift of tongues, prophecy, revelation, visions, healing, interpretation of tongues, and so forth.

8 We believe the Bible to be the word of God as far as it is translated correctly; we also believe the Book of Mormon to be the word of God.

9 We believe all that God has revealed, all that He does now reveal, and we believe that He will yet reveal many great and important things pertaining to the Kingdom of God.

10 We believe in the literal gathering of Israel and in the restoration of the Ten Tribes; that Zion (the New Jerusalem) will be built upon the American continent; that Christ will reign personally upon the earth; and, that the earth will be renewed and receive its paradisiacal glory.

11 We claim the privilege of worshiping Almighty God according to the dictates of our own conscience, and allow all men the same privilege, let them worship how, where, or what they may.

12 We believe in being subject to kings, presidents, rulers, and magistrates, in obeying, honoring, and sustaining the law.

13 We believe in being honest, true, chaste, benevolent, virtuous, and in doing good to all men; indeed, we may say that we follow the admonition of Paul—We believe all things, we hope all things, we have endured many things, and hope to be able to endure all things. If there is anything virtuous, lovely, or of good report or praiseworthy, we seek after these things.

JOSEPH SMITH

Appendix C

Creeds, Confessions, and Mormonism: A Comparison

Apostles' Creed

I believe in the God, All Governing; And in Christ Jesus His only begotten Son, our Lord, who was begotten of the Holy Spirit and the Virgin Mary, who was crucified under Pontius Pilate and buried, who rose from the dead on the third day, ascending to the heavens, and taking His seat at the Father's right hand, whence He shall come to judge both living and dead;

And I believe in the Holy Spirit, the holy Church, the forgiveness of sins, the resurrection of the body, life everlasting.[1]

This is the most widely accepted statement of the fundamentals of Christian belief, originating in the first Christian centuries. With caveats about an apostasy of the original church and God's literal fatherhood of Christ, Mormonism embraces the principles here outlined.

Nicene Creed (excerpt)

We believe in one God, the Father All Governing, creator of all things visible and invisible; And in one Lord Jesus Christ, the Son of God, begotten of the Father as only begotten, that is, from the essence of the Father, God from God, Light from Light, true God from true God, begotten and not created, of the same essence [reality] as the Father [*homoousion to patri*], through whom all things came into being....

First formulated at the Council of Nicaea in 325, this influential creed sorted out the controversies of the era regarding the nature of God and of

Jesus Christ. Contrary to the theologically contentious concept of "one essence" (homoousion), Mormonism asserts a unity of Godhead persons in purpose only.

Chalcedonian Creed (excerpt)

Following, then, the holy fathers, we unite in teaching all men to confess the one and only Son, our Lord Jesus Christ. This selfsame one is perfect both in deity and also in human-ness; this selfsame one is also actually God and actually man, with a rational soul and a body. He is of the same reality as God [*homoousion to patri*] as far as his deity is concerned and of the same reality as we are ourselves as far as his human-ness is concerned; thus like us in all respects, sin excepted. . . .

[We also teach] that we apprehend this one and only Christ-Son, Lord, only-begotten in two natures; [and we do this] without confusing the two natures, . . . without dividing them into separate categories, without contrasting them according to area or function. The distinctiveness of each nature is not nullified by the union. Instead the "properties" of each nature are conserved and both natures concur in one "person." . . .

Formulated in 451, this is the most important creedal statement setting out the doctrine of the Trinity as it would be embraced by most Christians. Mormons likewise acknowledge Christ's dual nature. They believe he possessed full humanity, as son of an earthly mother, and divinity, as son of a Heavenly Father and insofar as Christ is the mortal incarnation of Jehovah himself. But this dual nature is understood without reference to any form of consubstantiality, and as a condescension without mystery. The quandary to which the Chalcedonian formula (and the concept of homoousion) is a response is largely circumvented in Mormonism by the premise that God and Christ are wholly distinct beings, with Christ receiving the attributes of both a divine Father and an earthly mother.

Athanasian Creed (excerpt)

Whoever desires to be saved must above all things hold the Catholic faith. . . . We worship one God in Trinity, and Trinity in unity, without either confusing the persons or dividing the substance. For the Father's person is one, the Son's another, the Holy Spirit's another; but the Godhead of the Father, the Son, and the Holy Ghost is one, their glory is equal, their majesty coeternal. . . .

And in this trinity there is nothing before or after, nothing greater or less, but all three persons are coeternal with each other and coequal.

Originally ascribed to Athanasius (fourth century), now believed to have been written between the fourth and eighth centuries, this creed is a hugely influential statement of Trinitarian thought. Not only, as we have seen, does Mormonism accept the distinct personhood of the Father and Son, but it considers the Father to have clear precedence in the heavenly hierarchy. The designation of Christ as the "firstborn of every creature" (Col. 1:15) has reference, Mormons believe, not just to his resurrection (as Col. 1:18 suggests), but to his precedence among God's spirit progeny.

Augsburg Confession (excerpts)

We unanimously hold and teach, in accordance with the decree of the Council of Nicaea, that there is one divine essence, which is called and which truly is God, and that there are three persons in this one divine essence, equal in power and alike eternal. . . . It is also taught among us that since the fall of Adam all men who are born according to the course of nature are full of evil lust and inclinations. . . . Moreover, this inborn sickness and hereditary sin is truly sin . . . . We must do all such good works as God has commanded, but we should do them for God's sake and not place our trust in them as if thereby to merit favor before God. For we receive forgiveness of sin and righteousness through faith in Christ, as Christ himself says, . . . "when you have done all that is commanded of you, say, 'We are unworthy servants.'"

It is ordained of God that whoever believes in Christ shall be saved, and he shall have forgiveness of sins, not through works but through faith alone without merit.

Formulated in 1530 by Philip Melanchthon, this is the first of the great Protestant confessions and the basis of Lutheran teachings. The Book of Mormon similarly teaches that "it is by grace that we are saved" (2 Nephi 25:23) and that "if ye should serve him with all your whole souls yet ye would be unprofitable servants" (Mosiah 2:21). However, LDS believe that since God cannot contravene our agency, our compliance with law is both

necessary as an expression of our choice, and to subject us to the sanctify-
ing influence of God's laws. ("That which breaketh a law, . . . and willeth to
abide in sin, cannot be sanctified by law, neither by mercy" [DC 88:35].)

The Westminster Confession (excerpts)

. . . There is but one only living and true God, who is infinite in being and
perfection, a most pure spirit, invisible, without body, parts, or passions; . . .

By this sin [our first parents] fell from their original righteousness and
communion, with God, and so became dead in sin, and wholly defiled in
all the parts and faculties of soul and body. They being the root of all
mankind, the guilt of this sin was imputed; and the same death in sin, and
corrupted nature, conveyed to all their posterity descending from them by
ordinary generation. . . .

Man, by his fall into a state of sin, has wholly lost all ability of will to
any spiritual good accompanying salvation: so as, a natural man, being
altogether averse from that good, and dead in sin, is not able, by his own
strength, to convert himself, or to prepare himself thereunto. . . .

These angels and men, thus predestinated and foreordained, are particularly and unchangeably designed; and their number is so certain and
definite that it can not be either increased or diminished.

Approved by the English Parliament in 1648, this document establishes the
basis of Reformed theology (of Calvinist or Zwinglian descent), embraced
by the Puritans in England and the American colonies, as well as by the Pres-
byterians. It also served as basis for the Baptist creeds and, with minor mod-
ifications, was adopted by the Congregationalists. Latter-day Saints, as we
have seen, believe in a God who has a glorified body, with parts and passions.
They believe man does not inherit the sin or guilt of Adam, and is not inher-
ently good or evil, but rather innocent (DC 93:38). Though grace makes pos-
sible man's repentance and salvation, men and women are "free to choose
liberty and eternal life . . . or to choose captivity and death" (2 Nephi 2:27).

Note

1. All versions of the creeds and confessions in this section are from John H. Leith,
ed., *Creeds of the Churchs: A Reader in Christian Doctrine from the Bible to the Pres-*
ent, 3d ed. (Atlanta: John Knox, 1982).

Appendix D

LDS Membership Growth

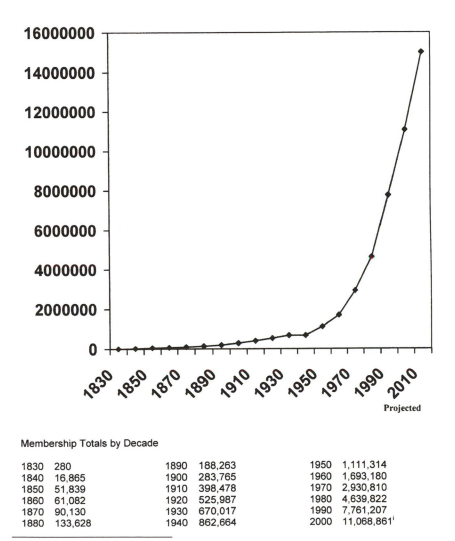

Projected

Membership Totals by Decade

1830	280	1890	188,263	1950	1,111,314
1840	16,865	1900	283,765	1960	1,693,180
1850	51,839	1910	398,478	1970	2,930,810
1860	61,082	1920	525,987	1980	4,639,822
1870	90,130	1930	670,017	1990	7,761,207
1880	133,628	1940	862,664	2000	11,068,861[i]

[i] Figures from Deseret News 2003 Church Almanac (Salt Lake City: Deseret News, 2003).

Timeline

23 December 1805	Joseph Smith born in Sharon, Vermont
1818	Smith family buys a farm in Manchester, near Palmyra
spring 1820	Smith's First Vision
21 September 1823	First visitation of Moroni
22 September 1827	Smith obtains gold plates
February 1828	Martin Harris takes partial translation of Book of Mormon to Prof. Charles Anthon of Columbia for authentication
June 1838	Harris borrows and loses 116 MS pages of Book of Mormon
July 1828	Angel Moroni temporarily takes plates and interpreters from Joseph
22 September 1828	Plates and seerstone restored to Joseph Smith
7 April 1829	Oliver Cowdery begins work as Joseph's scribe
15 May 1829	Smith and Oliver Cowdery ordained to Aaronic priesthood by John the Baptist
May or June 1829	Peter, James, and John appear to Smith and confer the Melchizedek priesthood
June 1829	Joseph and Emma relocate to Whitmer farm in Fayette, New York
June 1829	Three witnesses (Oliver Cowdery, Martin Harris, David Whitmer) are shown the gold plates by an angel. Smith shows them to eight others soon after

end of June 1829	Book of Mormon fully translated
11 July 1829	Copyright secured for Book of Mormon
August 1829	Printing of Book of Mormon begins by E. B. Grandin
26 March 1830	Book of Mormon offered for sale in the Palmyra bookstore of E. B. Grandin
6 April 1830	Official organization of the church
11 April 1830	Oliver Cowdery preaches first public discourse in the church
June 1830	"Vision of Moses" revealed to Joseph Smith
December 1830	Smith receives first revelation on principle of gathering
February 1831	Smith and core of saints move to Kirtland, Ohio
6 April 1831	Fourth conference of church held in Kirtland, membership about two thousand
summer 1831	Saints begin settling Jackson County, Missouri
16 February 1832	The "Vision" (DC 76) received
24 March 1832	Joseph Smith and Sidney Rigdon assaulted by mob in Hiram, Ohio
1 June 1832	First issue of Mormon periodical, *The Evening and the Morning Star*, published in Independence, Missouri
June 1832	First missionaries travel outside United States, to preach in Canada
27 February 1833	Revelation known as the Word of Wisdom given to Joseph Smith
18 March 1833	First Presidency of the church organized with Sidney Rigdon and F. G. Williams as Smith's counselors
20 July 1833	Mob destroys Mormon printing press and assaults Mormon leaders in Independence, Jackson County. (Incomplete) copies of Book of Commandments published nonetheless
23 July 1833	Saints agree to leave Jackson County; construction of Kirtland temple begins

5 November 1833	Remaining Saints forcibly evicted from Jackson County; most move to Clay County
17 February 1834	First stake and first high council of the church organized at Kirtland, Ohio
3 May 1834	Official name of church becomes Church of Jesus Christ of Latter-day Saints
8 May–30 June 1834	March of Zion's Camp—paramilitary body led by Joseph Smith to assist Missouri saints against mob depredations
14 February 1835	The Quorum of the Twelve Apostles organized in Kirtland, Ohio
28 February 1835	Organization of the First Quorum of the Seventy begins in Kirtland, Ohio
17 August 1835	*Doctrine and Covenants* accepted as third standard work of church
27 March 1836	First temple dedicated in Kirtland, Ohio
3 April 1836	Jesus, Moses, Elijah, and Elias appear to Joseph Smith in Kirtland temple
29 June 1836	Saints asked to leave Clay County, Missouri
fall 1836	Saints begin remove to specially created Caldwell County
13 June 1837	Heber C. Kimball and companions leave Ohio on first foreign mission (to England)
12 January 1838	Joseph flees violence in Kirtland for Missouri
14 March 1838	Joseph arrives in Far West, Caldwell Company, and establishes new church headquarters
4 July 1838	Sidney Rigdon delivers inflammatory address in Far West, Missouri
6 July 1838	515 Ohio Saints depart for Missouri
8 July 1838	Revelation on tithing given to Joseph Smith
6 August 1838	Violence against Saints erupts at polling in Gallatin, Daviess County, Missouri
11 October 1838	Mormons driven from DeWitt, Missouri; go to Far West, Caldwell County

25 October 1838	Battle of Crooked River in Caldwell County results in several casualties and death of apostle David Patten
27 October 1838	Missouri Governor Lilburn Boggs issues extermination order
30 October 1838	Haun's Mill Massacre in Caldwell County
31 October 1838	Joseph Smith and other leaders betrayed into militia custody
1 November 1838	Smith and others sentenced to be shot by court martial; General Alexander Doniphan refuses order; disarmed Saints in Far West are pillaged
10 November 1838	Saints in Daviess County, Missouri, evicted by militia
1 December 1838	Joseph Smith begins long incarceration in Liberty Jail, Missouri
23 February 1839	In Quincy, Illinois, citizens adopt measures for the relief of the Saints expelled from Missouri
25 April 1839	Commerce, Illinois, selected as new gathering place
10 May 1839	Joseph Smith arrives in Commerce, soon to become Nauvoo, Illinois
29 November 1839	Smith denied redress for Missouri depredations by President Van Buren
6 April 1840	Brigham Young and fellow missionaries arrive in Liverpool, England
20 July 1840	First immigrant converts arrive from England in New York City
15 August 1840	Joseph Smith publicly announces principle of baptisms for dead
16 December 1840	Nauvoo granted city charter with extraordinary rights
31 December 1840	Church membership at 17,000
4 February 1841	Nauvoo Legion organized with Joseph Smith as lieutenant-general
6 April 1841	Cornerstones of Nauvoo temple laid
21 November 1841	Baptisms for dead commence in basement of Nauvoo temple

24 October 1841	Elder Orson Hyde dedicates Palestine for return of the Jews
1 March 1842	Joseph Smith begins publishing Book of Abraham
1 March 1842	Smith publishes Articles of Faith in response to an editor's request
17 March 1842	Relief Society organized
4 May 1842	Joseph introduces temple endowment
6 August 1842	Joseph prophesies Saints will be driven to refuge in Rocky Mountains
6 April 1843	Balance of Kirtland Saints decide on removal to Nauvoo
12 July 1843	Revelation on plural marriage recorded
29 January 1844	Smith announces candidacy for president of the United States
7 April 1844	Smith delivers "King Follett" discourse, containing most radical of LDS doctrine
11 May 1844	Smith organizes the secret political body, Council of Fifty
7 June 1844	First and only issue of inflammatory *Nauvoo Expositor* published
10 June 1844	Nauvoo press destroyed as "public nuisance" by court order
11–12 June 1844	Smith arrested and acquitted by Nauvoo municipal court for action against the *Nauvoo Expositor*
17 June 1844	Smith and others arrested and acquitted a second time on charges of riot related to *Expositor* episode
25 June 1844	Smith and fellow accused surrender to Carthage constable and are remanded to prison
27 June 1844	Smith brothers murdered by mob in Carthage, Illinois
8 August 1844	Most Mormons accede to the twelve apostles' assumption of church leadership
January 1845	Illinois legislature repeals the Nauvoo Charter
30 May 1845	Murderers of Joseph and Hyrum Smith acquitted by jury in Carthage, Illinois

15 February 1846	Brigham Young and other leaders cross Mississippi, leading exodus west
30 April 1846	Joseph Young dedicates Nauvoo temple
1 May 1846	Orson Hyde dedicates Nauvoo temple
30 June 1846	U.S. Army solicits five hundred Mormon volunteers for Mexican War
13 July 1846	Four companies of the Mormon Battalion raised from Saints encamped along Missouri River
10 September 1846	Bombardment of Nauvoo against few remaining Saints begins by force of 1,800 men
29 January 1847	Mormon Battalion arrives in San Diego, completing historic trek
7 April 1847	Pioneer Camp leaves Winter Quarters to find permanent settlement site
28 June 1847	En route to Salt Lake valley, pioneers meet Jim Bridger
22 July 1847	Advance company of pioneers enters Great Salt Lake Valley
24 July 1847	Brigham Young enters the Salt Lake Valley
28 July 1847	Young picks temple site, and surveyors begin to lay out city
December 1847	Young calls upon all members worldwide to gather to Great Basin of the Rocky Mountains
June 1848	"Miracle of Seagulls," as birds devour devastating crickets
14 February 1849	Salt Lake City divided into nineteen wards of nine blocks each
5 March 1849	Provisional State of Deseret established
October 1849	Perpetual Emigrating Fund established to assist pioneer immigrants
9 September 1850	Utah Territory organized by Congress
20 September 1850	President Millard Fillmore appoints Brigham Young Utah governor
31 December 1850	Church membership at 52,000

11 November 1851	University of State of Deseret (now University of Utah) begins operation
29 August 1852	Church practice of polygamy first publicly acknowledged
3 September 1852	First emigrants from Europe funded by Perpetual Emigration Fund arrive in Great Salt Lake City
14 February 1853	Brigham Young breaks ground for Salt Lake City Temple
5 May 1855	Fast day inaugurated, first Thursday of each month
6 April 1853	Salt Lake temple cornerstones laid
19 January 1854	Deseret alphabet adoption announced
9 June 1856	First handcart company of pioneers leaves Iowa City, Iowa
13 May 1857	Parley P. Pratt murdered near Van Buren, Arkansas
26 September 1856	First company of "handcart Saints" arrive in Salt Lake Valley
24 July 1857	During Utah Pioneer Day celebrations, word arrives of impending invasion by federal army
7–11 September 1857	Fancher wagon train members massacred at Mountain Meadows, Utah
15 September 1857	Brigham Young declares martial law, forbids federal troops to enter the Salt Lake Valley
26 June 1858	Col. Johnston's army passes through Great Salt Lake City
6 April 1860	Joseph Smith III becomes president of Reorganized Church of Jesus Christ of Latter Day Saints
31 December 1860	Church membership at 61,000
6 March 1862	The Salt Lake Theatre dedicated
8 July 1862	Morrill antibigamy law passed making plural marriage illegal
10 March 1863	Brigham Young arrested for bigamy (never brought to trial)
6 October 1867	First church conference held in newly constructed historic tabernacle on Temple Square
10 May 1869	Transcontinental railroad completed at Promontory Summit, Utah

28 November 1869	Young Ladies' Retrenchment Association, forerunner of today's young women program, organized
10 January 1870	The last rail of the Utah Central Railway laid in Salt Lake City
February 1870	Liberal Party of Utah formed in opposition to (Mormon-dominated) People's Party
12 February 1870	Utah women receive the elective franchise
31 December 1870	Church membership at 90,000
June 1872	*Woman's Exponent*, a paper run by Mormon women, founded
9 May 1874	General Conference discussions of "United Order" lead to establishment of several cooperative economic ventures
23 June 1874	Poland Bill, limiting jurisdiction of Utah probate courts, becomes law
10 April 1875	George Reynolds sentenced to a year in prison, and $300 fine for polygamy
10 June 1875	First Young Men's Mutual Improvement Association, forerunner of today's young men's program, organized
3 October 1875	President Ulysses Grant visits Salt Lake City
9 October 1875	The Tabernacle of Mormon Choir fame dedicated in Salt Lake City
16 October 1875	Brigham Young Academy (later University) established in Provo, Utah
23 March 1876	Mormon colonization of Arizona begins at the Little Colorado
6 April 1877	First Utah temple dedicated in St. George
29 August 1877	Brigham Young dies
19 May 1878	Mormon settlement in Colorado begins
6 January 1879	Supreme Court confirms verdict against George Reynolds for polygamy
30 April 1879	Emma Hale Bidamon, Joseph Smith's widow, dies
19 June 1880	Primary established as worldwide organization for Mormon children

10 October 1880	*Pearl of Great Price* becomes fourth standard work of church
31 December 1880	Church membership at 134,000
22 March 1882	Edmunds Bill signed by President Chester A. Arthur, mandating five years' imprisonment, $500 fine, and disfranchisement for polygamy
20 April 1882	George Q. Cannon denied his seat in Congress because of polygamy
1884–90	Underground develops to protect polygamists from federal prosecution
18 February 1887	Edmunds–Tucker Law disincorporates church, abolishes female suffrage, dissolves Perpetual Emigrating Fund, and confiscates most church property
25 July 1887	President John Taylor dies while in Mormon underground
24 September 1890	President Wilford Woodruff's Manifesto ending practice of plural marriage accepted at General Conference of church
31 December 1890	Church membership at 188,000
1891	Mormon political party, the People's Party, disbanded
4 January 1893	Voting restrictions in Utah removed
6 April 1893	Salt Lake Temple dedicated by President Wilford Woodruff
8 September 1893	Mormon Tabernacle Choir takes second place in Chicago World Fair competition
9 June 1895	First stake outside United States created in Cardston, Alberta, Canada
4 January 1896	Utah becomes forty-fifth state
5 November 1896	Fast Day moved to first Sunday of month
8 May 1899	President Lorenzo Snow establishes a new emphasis on tithing (that continues to present day)
25 January 1900	B. H. Roberts, representative from Utah, denied seat by U.S. House

31 December 1900	Church membership at 284,000
15 October 1903	Brigham Young Academy becomes Brigham Young University
February 1907	U.S. Senate seats Reed Smoot, after years of acrimonious hearings and debate
10 January 1907	Church declared free from debt, brought on by crippling antipolygamy legislation
summer 1907	Joseph F. Smith becomes first church president to visit European Saints
31 December 1910	Church membership at 400,000
27 April 1915	Church inaugurates a Home Evening program
27 November 1919	Dedication of first temple outside continental United States (Laie, Hawaii)
31 December 1920	Church membership at 526,000
6 December 1925	South American missionary work begins in Argentina
July 1929	Mormon Tabernacle Choir has first weekly radio broadcast, beginning run as longest continuing radio broadcast in history
31 December 1930	Church membership at 670,000
7 April 1936	Church security program (later church welfare program) instituted
July 1937	First Hill Cumorah pageant held in New York
November 1938	Church begins microfilming genealogical records
31 December 1940	Church membership at 863,000
1947	Church membership reaches one million
25 November 1952	Apostle Ezra Taft Benson appointed President Dwight D. Eisenhower's secretary of agriculture
31 December 1950	Church membership at 1,111,000
11 September 1955	First European temple (near Bern, Switzerland)
31 December 1960	Church membership at 1,700,000
12 March 1961	First non-English-speaking stake organized, in The Hague, Netherlands
3 December 1961	First Spanish-speaking stake created, in Mexico City
1963	Church membership reaches 2 million

January 1964	New program of home teaching replaces ward teaching
26 April 1964	First Asian meetinghouse dedicated, in Tokyo
January 1965	Modern Family Home Evening program launched; Monday designated Family Home Evening night in October 1970
1 May 1966	First South American stake established in São Paolo, Brazil
31 December 1970	Church membership at 2,930,000
1971	Church membership reaches 3 million
1 October 1975	First Quorum of Seventy organized by Spencer W. Kimball
25 June 1975	Missouri Governor Christopher Bond rescinds LDS extermination order of 1838
21 February– 11 March 1977	President Kimball meets with state heads in Mexico, Bolivia, Chile, and Guatemala, and with U.S. President Jimmy Carter
3 April 1976	Two revelations added to Mormon canon
1978	Church membership reaches 4 million
8 June 1978	Priesthood extended, by revelation, to "all worthy males"
22 July 1978	Senate passes bill making Mormon Trail a national historic trail
9 November 1978	Missionary work in black Africa begins in Nigeria
18 February 1979	The one thousandth stake of the church organized
31 December 1980	Church membership at 4,640,000
3 October 1982	Book of Mormon officially subtitled, "Another Testament of Jesus Christ"
1 April 1982	Announcement of church membership reaching 5 million
2 January 1985	Brigham Young University's football team declared national champions
28 October 1984	The 1,500th stake of the church organized
4 October 1986	Stake Seventies Quorums dissolved

23 January 1987	Forger Mark Hoffman begins prison term for "Mormon bombings"
15 May 1988	First stake organized in black Africa in Aba, Nigeria
August 1988	Church completes 100 million temple endowments for the dead
19 January 1989	Mormon Tabernacle Choir performs at inauguration of President George H. Bush, as they did for Presidents Johnson (1965), Nixon (1969 and 1973), and Reagan (1981).
31 December 1990	Church membership at 7,761,000
1 May 1991	Church calls its 500,000th full-time missionary since 1830
24 June 1991	Russian Republic grants church official recognition
6 August 1994	Church announces one-third of American public contacted by Mormon missionaries
23 September 1995	First Presidency issues "Proclamation on the Family"
28 February 1996	Proportion of Mormons outside United States surpasses 50 percent
November 1997	Church membership reaches 10 million
4 October 1997	New policy announced of smaller temples in remote areas of low LDS density
15 January 1999	Last surviving granddaughter of Brigham Young (Marian Morgan) celebrates hundredth birthday
24 May 1999	Church launches a Web-based genealogical database with hundreds of millions of names, that records 3 billion hits in first eighteen months
1 April 2000	First conference in the new 21,000-seat Conference Center convenes in Salt Lake City
22 April 2000	One hundred-millionth Book of Mormon printed (100th language version printed this year also)
September 2000	Church membership reaches 11 million; proportion of non-English speakers surpasses 50 percent
1 October 2000	Boston temple, one hundredth in church, dedicated by President Hinckley
Winter 2002	Olympics held in Salt Lake City, giving unprecedented media exposure to church

Glossary

Aaronic priesthood: The Aaronic, or lesser, priesthood, which pertains to the "outward ordinances," was restored to Joseph Smith by John the Baptist. It embodies, for example, the authority to baptize and to administer the sacrament of bread and water. Considered a preparatory priesthood, its possessors are generally youth between the ages of twelve and eighteen or nineteen.

apostasy: As applied to individuals, the term refers to a change from faithfulness to disaffection and opposition to the church and its teachings (as opposed to "inactive," which refers to those who have merely lapsed into indifference). As applied to a historic era, the term designates the process by which the original authority and true teachings of Christ's church were either lost or deliberately perverted, necessitating a restoration of the gospel by a prophet called of God.

apostle: An office in the Melchizedek priesthood. Called to be "special witnesses of Christ," men ordained as apostles are also set apart as members of the Quorum of the Twelve Apostles, the governing body in Mormonism second in authority only to the First Presidency (the prophet/president and his counselors).

area authority: An office announced in April 1995, these leaders serve under the direction of an area presidency. As of 1997, area authorities are assigned to be members of Quorums of the Seventy (other than the First and Second Quorums, which are comprised of General Authorities only).

area presidency: In June 1984, the Church organized thirteen "areas," the largest geographical administrative unit of the church, and called area presidents to preside over them. Area presidents and their counselors are called from the Quorums of Seventy. Many areas have been added since 1984.

atonement: The cardinal theological principle of Mormonism refers to the vicarious suffering of Christ in Gethsemane, whereby he took upon himself the sins of all mankind, making possible man's physical resurrection and eternal salvation.

baptism for the dead: Considering baptism an essential ordinance for salvation, and believing all individuals throughout human history are entitled to the opportunity, Latter-day Saints baptize living proxies in their temples on behalf of deceased persons. They cite 1 Corinthians 15:29 as precedent ("else what shall they do which are baptized for the dead, if the dead rise not at all: why are they then baptized for the dead?").

bishop: The presiding authority in a ward. He is responsible for the temporal and spiritual welfare of all members in his congregation. He conducts both leadership meetings and worship services, provides counseling, oversees all staffing and physical facilities, supervises care of the needy, and coordinates missionary work.

Book of Mormon: One of the four books of scripture of the Church of Jesus Christ of Latter-day Saints. Translated by Joseph Smith from gold plates he retrieved from a hillside in 1827 as directed by the angel Moroni, the record contains the history and teachings of two groups who emigrated to the New World, one at the time of the Tower of Babel, the other around 600 B.C.

branch: A local unit generally smaller in size than a ward, and presided over by a "branch president" rather than a bishop.

brass plates: According to the Book of Mormon, Lehi's sons retrieved and carried to the New World a set of records from one Laban of Jerusalem, containing the five books of Moses, "a record of the Jews from the beginning even down to the reign of Zedekiah," and the writings of Isaiah and other prophets.

brethren: While Latter-day Saints address each other as "brother" or "sister," "the brethren" refers to the General Authorities of the church, though they are usually addressed as "Elder" so-and-so, as are full-time missionaries.

calling: A position in the church that a person is formally invited to fulfill by a bishop or other priesthood leader.

celestial: Joined to marriage, the term denotes an eternal union solemnized in the temple and enduring into the eternities. Also denotes the highest kingdom of glory in Mormonism's multitiered heaven. Subdivided into three "heavens or degrees," only the highest one allows of eternal increase, or the privilege of having posterity.

chapel: Strictly speaking, the sanctuary within the meetinghouse, but generally refers to the local meetinghouse itself, where worship services, auxiliary meetings, and social events are held. Often features a full-size gymnasium and stage in addition to chapel and classrooms.

Conference: Usually refers to one of the semi-annual, two-day world conferences of the church, transmitted to millions of members worldwide, where the prophet and General Authorities of the church present addresses on a variety of topics during four general sessions and one special Priesthood Session. Historically originating from the Tabernacle on Temple Square, the proceedings now occur in the LDS Conference Center, the world's largest religious-purpose auditorium. Stakes also hold their own conferences semi-annually, and wards annually.

confirmation: The priesthood ordinance, following baptism, by which one is declared a member of the Church of Jesus Christ of Latter-day Saints and is given the gift of the Holy Ghost by the laying on of hands (those performing the ordinance place their hands upon the member's head as they pronounce the words of the ordinance).

deacon: The first office in the Aaronic priesthood, to which all boys are ordained at the age of twelve if worthy. Their duties include passing the bread and water in the Sacrament Service.

disciplinary council: Called church courts in earlier years, disciplinary councils are conceived by Mormons as an essential part of the repentance process in cases of serious transgression, though it is understandable that outsiders would often construe them as punitive in nature. They are presided over by a bishop and counselors, or by a stake president and high councilmen. Verdicts rendered in these councils may range from no action taken, to disfellowshipment or, in most serious cases, excommunication.

disfellowshipment: A sanction that imposes on a member certain restrictions on church activity (such as participation in ordinances or church callings), but does not rescind his or her membership. It is imposed as a result of a disciplinary council, usually for several months or a year.

Doctrine and Covenants: A scriptural compilation of revelations received principally by Joseph Smith but also by subsequent prophets. They establish church doctrine, organization, procedure, and government, and include particular commands and directions of primarily historical interest as well.

elder: The office to which, in most cases, Melchizedek priesthood holders are initially ordained. It entails the authority to confer the gift of the Holy Ghost, to give priesthood blessings, and to "administer in spiritual things." As a title, the term is applied to full-time male missionaries, and to the General Authorities of the church other than the First Presidency or the presiding bishop.

endowment: A ceremony in a Mormon temple, consisting of certain covenants and promises, and deemed essential preparation for entering the celestial kingdom and receiving one's exaltation.

***Ensign*:** The official church magazine for adults, containing a monthly message from the First Presidency, news, and inspirational articles.

eternal life: Virtually synonymous with exaltation. Eternal life means the kind of existence or life God enjoys, as distinct from immortality, which means endless life.

exaltation: Salvation in the highest order of the celestial kingdom, where marriage and family relationships persist eternally and candidates preside over their own worlds and spirit progeny.

excommunication: The most severe sanction a church disciplinary council can impose, excommunication revokes a member's church membership and any blessings or rights associated with such membership. Usually imposed on those who actively work to undermine the church and its teachings, or those who persist in a pattern of serious sexual or moral transgression.

Family Home Evening: A weekly gathering of an LDS family, usually on Monday, involving some combination of prayer, hymns, a gospel lesson, games, and refreshments.

fast offering: A monthly offering, in addition to tithing, that is paid in conjunction with foregoing two meals on the first Sunday of the month (called "Fast Sunday").

fireside: A meeting held in a home or church, outside regular services, to hear an inspirational or educational speaker.

First Presidency: The governing body of the Church of Jesus Christ of Latter-day Saints, comprising the prophet and president of the church, together with his counselors. These are usually two in number, but some presidents have chosen additional counselors.

First Vision: The appearance of the Father and Son to Joseph Smith in the "Sacred Grove" near his home, which he recorded as occurring in the spring of 1820. Though he understood the episode as giving direction to his personal quest for truth, it was heralded in retrospect as the ushering in of the restoration of the gospel and of the dispensation of fullness of times.

Friend: The official church magazine for children, issued monthly, and containing activities, stories, and inspirational messages.

garments: Sacred undergarments worn by Mormons who have received their temple endowments, and worn to serve as a reminder of particular covenants.

gathering: From December 1830 until the turn of the century, Latter-day Saints were commanded to physically gather together. From that time, the work of the gathering has been construed as primarily spiritual— that converts to the gospel in whatever land they reside represent the gathering of Israel. At the same time, Latter-day Saints understand the return of the Jews to Palestine as literal fulfillment of the gathering prophesied by Old Testament prophets.

General Authority: Any leader of the church whose jurisdiction is church-wide. The title refers to members of the First Presidency, Quorum of the Twelve, the First and Second Quorums of Seventy, presiding bishopric, and patriarch to the church. Unlike other church leaders, General Authorities serve full-time and are compensated from church funds.

gentile: In the Book of Mormon, gentile usually refers to one not of the House of Israel. In Mormon culture, the term designates a non-Mormon.

godhead: God the Father, his Son Jesus Christ, and the Holy Ghost. The three constitute what has been characterized as "social trinitarianism," a trinity composed of three separate and distinct beings.

grace: The unearned benevolence toward man that God manifested in the gift of his son and that Christ manifested in his personal suffering to make immortality universal and salvation possible, upon conditions of obedience to his laws.

heaven: Characterized in Mormon thought as comprising three kingdoms (the celestial, terrestrial, and telestial). Virtually every person will inherit one of the heavenly spheres. Latter-day Saints aspire to exaltation, attained by those who are valiant in their faith and obey the laws and ordinances of the gospel in this life or vicariously. It entails the blessing of eternal marriage and eternal posterity.

hell: Refers to the state in the spirit world between death and resurrection, suffered by the wicked and rebellious. Also called "spirit prison" and "outer darkness." After the resurrection, only the "sons of perdition" return to such a condition. Their fate, said Joseph Smith, is to suffer "eternal punishment," but in the sense of eternal punishment being God's punishment. Therefore, "the end thereof, neither the place thereof, nor their torment, no man knows."

high council: A group of twelve high priests chosen to assist the stake president in administering a stake. They advise on ecclesiastical callings at the stake level, supervise areas from music to employment to family history, and serve as advisors to wards and branches.

high priest: An office in the Melchizedek priesthood, and to which bishops and their counselors, stake presidents and their counselors, and administrators of larger units must be ordained. Senior male members of the church are generally ordained high priests as well, regardless of ecclesiastical calling.

Holy Ghost: The third member of the godhead, a personage of spirit whose influence is accessible to all truth-seekers, and whose personal ministrations or right to companionship is called the Gift of the Holy Ghost.

home teaching: The program or activity wherein priesthood holders fourteen years and older visit assigned families in their ward to present an uplifting message, ascertain family needs, serve as a liaison to ward leaders, and generally be friends to and resources for the family.

immortality: The condition of endless life in a resurrected body, a universal right assured through the atonement and resurrection of Jesus Christ.

institute: The church educational program that provides religious instruction to college age youth, generally in a weekly meeting. Usually established on or near college campuses.

investigator: Any nonmember who demonstrates sufficient interest in Mormonism to take the missionary lessons as a possible prelude to baptism.

Korihor: A character in the Book of Mormon who uses sophistry to lead people away from Christ. By extension, Latter-day Saints use the term to refer to modern-day intellectualizers or sophists who undermine— generally from within the church—what their critics perceive to be church orthodoxy.

Lamanite: In the Book of Mormon, a descendent of Laman, Nephi's rebellious brother. Later, the designation lost its ethnic value, and meant any person aligned with the enemies of ancient American followers of Christ. Today, the term is loosely, and inaccurately, used by Mormons to refer to Native Americans (since the Book of Mormon connects some, but certainly not all, of the continent's aborigines with the ancient Lamanite peoples).

Law of Consecration: Variously implemented with varying degrees of success by early Saints in Missouri, Ohio, and Utah, this principle requires the member to "consecrate" personal property to the church, retaining or receiving back only what is sufficient for one's needs. Though not an actual economic program at present, the vow to live the principle is still made as part of the temple endowment.

Liahona: According to the Book of Mormon, a brass, spherical object that functions like a compass, but only according to "faith and diligence and heed." In Mormon culture, a "Liahona Mormon" is one whose approach to gospel living is more flexible and liberal than the "iron rod" Mormon, who is more strict and orthodox.

Manifesto: The declaration issued by President Wilford Woodruff on 6 October 1890, suspending the practice of plural marriage.

Melchizedek priesthood: The actual authority given by God to act in his name as relating to all things necessary for salvation. Possessed by the prophets of old, conferred by the laying on of hands by Christ to his apostles during his ministry, by the resurrected Peter, James, and John to Joseph Smith in 1829, and lineally passed on through successive generations to all eligible members ever since. (This group did not include members of African descent until 1978.)

millennium: A thousand-year era of peace when, according to the tenth article of faith, "Christ will reign personally upon the earth; and . . . the earth will be renewed and receive its paradisiacal glory."

Mormon: A prophet and Nephite general of the late fourth century who led his people in their final and self-destructive war against the Lamanites. Mormon abridged the thousand-year history of his predecessor record-keepers and engraved his account upon gold plates. Moroni finished off the abridgment after Mormon's death, and gave it the name Book of Mormon. Early critics referred derisively to Latter-day Saints who preached the Book of Mormon as Mormonites or, later, simply Mormons. Eventually the Saints themselves embraced the pejorative term, in spite of official efforts to discourage its use that continue to the present day.

Mutual: The combined young women's and young men's program of the Church, involving youth from twelve to eighteen. Youth meet Sunday for an hour of instruction, and one weeknight for additional lessons and activities.

Nephi: Fashioner of the gold plates and first keeper of the record that will become the Book of Mormon. Son of Lehi, leader of the clan that leaves Jerusalem for the New World (ca. 590 B.C.), Nephi becomes leader of his people when they split from the Lamanites, a clan faction led by two of his brothers who rebel against Nephi and seek to destroy his followers.

Nephite: Originally in the Book of Mormon, a descendent of Nephi. Not always more righteous as a people than their enemies the Lamanites, the Nephites were nonetheless keepers of the gold plates, generally accepting of the gospel (which they taught before Christ's coming), and led by righteous prophets. Soon the designation comes to mean any individual "friendly to Nephi," and centuries later the term denotes "true believers in Christ."

New Era: The official church monthly magazine for youth.

ordinance: A ceremony performed by authority of the priesthood. Those essential for salvation would include baptism, confirmation and bestowal of the Holy Ghost, ordination to the Melchizedek priesthood (for males), washings, anointings, endowment, and sealing (temple marriage). Other ordinances include ordination to the Aaronic priesthood, blessing of children, blessing of the sick, and other forms of priesthood blessings.

paradise: According to the Book of Mormon, "a state of happiness, rest, and peace" where the righteous go upon death to await the resurrection. Those unfamiliar with the gospel of Christ are taught there, as Mormons believe Jesus suggested to the thief on the cross whom he promised to see in Paradise (Luke 23:43).

patriarch: An office in the Melchizedek priesthood. Their primary responsibility is to bestow patriarchal blessings, which worthy members receive once in their lifetime, usually in their teens.

patriarchal blessing: A formal pronouncement, given by inspiration, that declares the lineage of the recipient—that is, the tribe of Israel with which he or she is identified. The blessing includes a prophetic statement of the person's life mission, counsel and admonitions, and promises and blessings that are conditioned upon the individual's faithfulness.

Pearl of Great Price: A scriptural work that includes writings of Moses (largely an emended version of Genesis 1–5 but with additional materials), writings of Abraham, parts of Joseph Smith's personal history, and Smith's reworking of Matthew 24.

Plan of Salvation: A plan proposed by God in a premortal council, that envisioned the creation of the earth, man's embodiment and earthly probation, an atoning sacrifice to be wrought by a savior, and the possibility of man's resurrection and exaltation to be predicated upon obedience to prescribed laws and gospel ordinances.

polygamy: Technically the taking of more than one spouse. Mormons practiced polygyny, or the taking of plural wives, in very limited numbers in the 1830s and 1840s, then openly and more commonly from 1852 until the practice was gradually abandoned beginning with President Wilford Woodruff's Manifesto barring the practice in 1890. No polygamous groups are recognized by the church today, and any member who practices plural marriage is subject to excommunication.

priest: Office in the Aaronic priesthood to which worthy males of sixteen are ordained. Priests may bless the sacrament as well as baptize.

priesthood: The power to act in the name and with the authority of God. Consists of the Aaronic, or lesser, priesthood, and the Melchizedek, or higher, priesthood. The former was possessed by John the Baptist, and was closely related to the Levitical priesthood of the Old Testament. The latter was bestowed by Christ upon his twelve apostles. Both were restored to Joseph Smith by resurrected beings, and passed on by the laying on of hands through subsequent generations of the church.

Primary: The organization for children ages three to twelve, generally held during the second and third hours of the LDS worship services. Presided over by a president and her two counselors.

prophet: The designation applies to the president and spiritual leader of the church. The president, his counselors, and the twelve apostles are all sustained as "prophets, seers, and revelators," but as *the* prophet, the church president is the only leader able to speak with absolute authority as God's mouthpiece.

quorum: An organized body of men or boys possessing the same priesthood office and generally operating at the ward level, as a deacons quorum or the elders quorum.

Quorum of the Twelve: The twelve apostles who are called as special witnesses of Christ and preside over the church, second in authority only to the First Presidency. Modeled after the body of twelve ordained by Jesus Christ in the New Testament.

Relief Society: The organization to which all active LDS women belong was founded by Joseph Smith in 1842. Members conduct their own Sunday meeting, minister to each other through monthly visits, meet one evening a month for special activities or lessons, and attempt to put into practice their motto, "Charity never faileth."

revelation: Through Joseph Smith and other prophets, Mormons believe, God restored gospel truths as actual communicated content. By teaching that the Holy Ghost is a revelator, Smith emphasized that all the faithful are entitled to revelation. LDS conceptions of revelation, related as they are to anthropomorphic conceptions of God, are more literal, more "dialogic," than traditional theologies of revelation.

rm: Returned missionary, meaning a young man or young woman who has completed twenty-four or eighteen months of service, respectively, and is thus a prime candidate for a member of the opposite sex interested in pursuing courtship and a temple marriage.

sacrament: In Mormonism, the administration of the Lord's Supper, which entails the blessing by prescribed prayer of broken bread and water, which are then passed to all members of the church in commemoration of the Lord's atonement and by way of personally renewing baptismal covenants. Also short for "Sacrament Meeting," the worship service where this ordinance is administered. Mormons use the word *ordinance* where other Christians would use *sacrament*.

saint: Term used by Paul in his epistles to refer to members of the early church, as in "the saints at Ephesus," or "the saints at Philippi." It is in this sense that Mormons call themselves Latter-day Saints, as distinct from ancient-day saints or primitive Christians.

salvation: In one sense, salvation for Mormons encompasses all who are not heirs of final damnation (i.e., who are not "sons of perdition"). Inheritors, accordingly, of the celestial, terrestrial, and telestial kingdoms. In another sense, salvation refers only to those who inherit the highest level of celestial glory, comparable in this sense to "exaltation."

Satan: In Mormon belief, Satan, or the devil, is a real personage who was known as Lucifer in his original position as an archangel in the presence of God. He rebelled against God's plan for human salvation, was cast out with a third of heaven's hosts, and now seeks to oppose and confound the work of Christ.

second coming: Latter-day Saints are millennialists, that is, they believe that Christ will literally return to earth at some point in the not too distant future (hence *Latter-day* Saints) in power and glory to sit in judgment on the nations.

seminary: The course of instruction in the LDS scriptures and church history and doctrine that high school age members of the church take during the school year. It generally is held in the very early morning before school, but in some areas is held weekly or—in areas of high LDS concentration—during the school day itself.

set apart: To authorize an individual, by the laying on of hands, to act in a particular calling. Generally occurs following the sustaining of the individual by the congregation, and is usually accompanied by words of blessing and counsel.

seventy: An office in the Melchizedek priesthood, traditionally entailing responsibilities in the area of missionary work. Since 1986, the office has been reserved for General and Area Authorities who assist the First Presidency and Quorum of the Twelve in church administration. Seventies are organized into Quorums of Seventy, and are presided over by a presidency of seven all chosen from the First Quorum of Seventy. This First Quorum of Seventy, after the First Presidency and the Quorum of the Twelve, comprises the third presiding quorum over the church. Members of the First Quorum are generally called until age seventy. Members of the Second Quorum, as well as Area Authority Seventies making up the other quorums, are called for five-year terms.

sons of perdition: The only individuals to suffer eternal torment, those who "den[y] the Holy Spirit after having received it" (DC 76:35). In Joseph Smith's teachings, this means to betray a perfect knowledge of the truth, in a manner comparable to denying the sun is shining while one sees it.

spirit prison: Figurative expression to refer to the spiritual darkness known by those who await the resurrection in a state of suspense, wickedness, or anxiety. Called "outer darkness" in the Book of Mormon, this state is temporary except for those who commit the unpardonable sin against the Holy Ghost and become "sons of perdition," consigned to hell or outer darkness indefinitely.

standard works: The four works that are part of the Mormon scriptural canon, comprising the Holy Bible (King James Version for English speakers), the *Doctrine and Covenants*, the Book of Mormon, and the *Pearl of Great Price*.

stake: The unit of church organization comprised of five to twelve wards and branches, generally totaling anywhere from two thousand to seven thousand members, and presided over by a stake president, assisted by a high council.

stewardship: The area of responsibility pertaining to an individual in his or her calling or parental role. Church government emphasizes a pattern of assignment of responsibility followed by regular reporting to file leaders, often referred to as stewardship and accountability. Stewardship can also refer to material resources, talents, or even family members, that one is responsible to care for, shepherd, nurture, or wisely employ.

sustaining: Latter-day Saints are called to positions—at all levels—by revelation, not by a democratic process. Nevertheless, members are given the opportunity at the time callings are made, and again in church conferences, to formally signify their willingness to support their leaders from the local level to the prophet himself, by raised hands. That formal show of support is a "sustaining." The term also refers to the general principle of supporting one's leaders.

tabernacle: The historic, oblong structure on Temple Square in Salt Lake City and venue for practices and performances of the world famous Tabernacle Choir has a capacity of over 12,000. Completed in 1867, semi-annual world conferences of the church were held there every year until 2000, when the new 21,000-seat Conference Center was completed.

teacher: The second office in the Aaronic priesthood, to which worthy boys of fourteen years are ordained. Their principal duty is preparation of the sacrament.

telestial: The lowest kingdom of glory, the abode of those who persist in refusing the gospel of Christ, but are not guilty of "denying the Holy Spirit" (the unpardonable sin). Likened to the glory of the stars, and often compared by Mormons to the conditions of the present world. Nevertheless, Joseph Smith declared its glory "surpasses all understanding."

temple: Unlike chapels or meetinghouses, LDS temples are holy sanctuaries that are not open to the public except during pre-dedication open houses. Only those members who have special recommends, indicating a certain level of devotion to church teachings, are allowed to enter. Inside, members participate in ordinances such as washings, anointings, and sealings, considered necessary for exaltation. These ordinances are performed for those who participate as well as vicariously for the deceased. Well over a hundred temples are in operation worldwide.

temple marriage: A marriage performed in a temple by priesthood authority, and thus not subject to dissolution upon the death of the individuals. A requirement for exaltation.

Temple Square: The 10-acre parcel in downtown Salt Lake City on which the Salt Lake Temple, famed Tabernacle, Visitors' Centers, and other buildings are located.

temple work: Refers to the performing of ordinance work done by proxies on behalf of the deceased. Considered by Mormons to be an important duty and one of the highest forms of service.

terrestrial: The middle kingdom of the saved, inherited by "the honorable" people of the world, "they who are not valiant in the testimony of Jesus." Compared to the glory of the moon.

testimony: To Latter-day Saints, a testimony is a knowledge of eternally significant truths imparted by the Spirit. Those truths are generally understood to include the divine sonship and resurrection of Jesus Christ, the prophetic calling of Joseph Smith and subsequent Mormon prophets, and the veracity of the Book of Mormon and other scriptures. Members also use the term to refer to conviction regarding particular principles, such as tithing, eternal families, etc.

three witnesses: The three men, Martin Harris, David Whitmer, and Oliver Cowdery, who testified that an angel displayed to them the gold plates, and that the voice of God declared Smith's translation of them to be true. All three became alienated from Joseph Smith, but affirmed their testimonies throughout their lives.

tithing: A contribution amounting to 10 percent of a member's income (usually paid on the gross), and one of the requirements for a temple recommend. Monies collected locally are sent to Salt Lake and administered from church headquarters.

United Order: As used in the *Doctrine and Covenants*, the term refers to the envisioned implementation of the laws of consecration and stewardship in a functioning, economically communal organization. In actual fact, while brief communitarian experiments were attempted in the Ohio and Missouri in the 1830s, United Orders were organized under that name primarily in Utah, Mexico, and Canada, during the late 1800s, most notably at St. George and Orderville, Utah.

Urim and Thummim: "Lights and perfections" in Hebrew, refers to a priestly device of mysterious workings in the Old Testament. Joseph Smith came to use the terms to refer to the interpreters he found with the gold plates, described as comprising two stones set in a large, figure-8 frame. He also used the term at times to refer to the seerstone he used.

visiting teaching: The program administered by the Relief Society in which pairs of adult women are assigned to visit particular women of the ward on a monthly basis, to deliver a message of spiritual uplift and serve as friend and resource. Roughly analogous to the men's home teaching program.

ward: The standard unit of the church, geographically defined and roughly analogous to a Catholic parish. It is presided over by a bishop, and holds from two hundred to eight hundred members of record.

Word of Wisdom: The Mormon code of health, received by Joseph Smith in 1833. It proscribes alcohol, tobacco, and "hot drinks" (interpreted by Hyrum Smith and ever since to mean tea and coffee), and enjoins the use of fruits and grains "in their season," general prudence in diet, and sparing use of meat. Originally conceived as counsel only, the code now has the force of a commandment and is a requirement for temple admission.

year's supply: A stock of food and essential items that Mormons are encouraged to lay up against contingencies ranging from unemployment to natural disaster or other emergencies. Though associated in the popular understanding (and in many LDS opinions) with apocalyptic events, the food storage program is increasingly touted by leaders as part of "provident living."

Zion: In one sense, Zion is held to be another name for the New Jerusalem of prophecy that will be built, Saints believe, in Jackson County, Missouri. Zion also refers to his people generally, or as a revelation to Joseph Smith declared, "This is Zion—the pure in heart" (DC 97:21). In a related sense, Zion is taken to refer to the church as the earthly incarnation of the kingdom of God. Finally, Mormons often refer to Utah as Zion, though nonresidents at least take that usage to be ironic.

Select Annotated Bibliography

General

Arrington, Leonard, and Davis Bitton. *The Mormon Experience*. New York: Random House, 1979. The best one-volume account of Mormon history available, but also includes sections on Mormon doctrine, organization, and culture.

Davies, Douglas. *An Introduction to Mormonism*. Cambridge, U.K.; New York: Cambridge University Press, 2003. Excellent introduction by a non-LDS sociologist, with a focus on temple rituals and theology.

Eliason, Eric, ed. *Mormons and Mormonism: An Introduction to an American Religion*. Urbana: University of Illinois Press, 2001. Excellent collection of essays on Mormonism and American culture by a variety of religious scholars and historians.

Newell, Coke. *Latter Days: A Guided Tour Through Six Billion Years of Mormonism*. New York: St. Martin's, 2000. A lively, quirky overview of Mormonism, written as an introduction for the nonmember.

History

Alexander, Thomas. *Mormonism in Transition: A History of the Latter-day Saints, 1890–1930*. Urbana: University of Illinois Press, 1986. Focuses on those years of greatest Mormon accommodation to American society.

Allen, James B., and Glen M. Leonard. *The Story of the Latter-day Saints*, 2d ed. revised and enlarged. Salt Lake City: Deseret, 1992. A general, narrative overview with special emphasis on twentieth-century developments. Sympathetic and reliable.

Arrington, Leonard. *Great Basin Kingdom: Economic History of the Latter-day Saints, 1830–1900*. Cambridge, Mass.: Harvard University Press, 1958.

Ground-breaking study by the dean of Mormon studies that set a new standard for works on Mormon history.

Backman, Milton V., Jr. *The Heavens Resound: A History of the Latter-day Saints in Ohio, 1830–1838*. Salt Lake City: Deseret, 1983. Best account of the formative Ohio years of the church.

Brown, S. Kent, Donald Q. Cannon, and Richard H. Jackson, eds. *Historical Atlas of Mormonism*. New York: Simon and Schuster, 1994. Authoritative, concise essays arranged chronologically with useful maps and graphs.

Bullock, Thomas. *The Pioneer Camp of the Saints*. Ed. Will Bagley. Invaluable record of the westward trek of Brigham Young's pioneer company, based on the journal of the official "clerk of the camp of Israel."

Bushman, Richard. *Joseph Smith and the Beginnings of Mormonism*. Urbana: University of Illinois Press, 1984. The most detailed account to date of the formative years of Mormonism.

Flanders, Robert B. *Nauvoo: Kingdom on the Mississippi*. Urbana: University of Illinois Press, 1965. This classic study of Nauvoo attempts to interpret its history as a tragedy precipitated by a complex of economic, political, and cultural factors, without falling into blame or apologetics.

Givens, Terryl L. *The Viper on the Hearth: Mormons, Myths, and the Construction of Heresy*. New York: Oxford University Press, 1997. A study of the ways fiction both reflected and exacerbated the Mormon conflict, emphasizing the religious roots of anti-Mormon hostility.

LeSueur, Stephen C. *The 1838 Mormon War in Missouri*. Columbia: University of Missouri Press, 1987. Thorough, scholarly treatment of the Missouri conflict.

Mulder, William, and Russell Mortensen, eds. *Among the Mormons: Historic Accounts by Contemporary Observers*. Lincoln: University of Nebraska Press, 1958. A rich treasury of foundational material by Joseph Smith, Brigham Young, and Sidney Rigdon, and reactions by Twain, Emerson, Dickens, and a host of contemporaries.

Shipps, Jan. *Mormonism: The Story of a New Religious Tradition*. Urbana: University of Illinois Press, 1985. An important study that established Mormonism as an entity that transcended a mere denominational category.

Biography

Alexander, Thomas G. *Things in Heaven and Earth: The Life and Times of Wilford Woodruff, a Mormon Prophet*. Salt Lake City: Signature, 1991. A scholarly interpretation of a dynamic missionary and leader, whose extensive journals make possible an unusually penetrating examination of his life in the context of early LDS history.

Arrington, Leonard. *Brigham Young: American Moses*. New York: Knopf, 1985. Sympathetic treatment of the Mormon leader, with attention to the range of roles he played in Western as well as Mormon history.

Brodie, Fawn. *No Man Knows My History: The Life of Joseph Smith, the Mormon Prophet*. New York: Knopf, 1945. Tremendously influential psycho-biography by a Mormon dissenter.

Dew, Sheri. *Go Forward with Faith: The Biography of Gordon B. Hinckley*. Salt Lake City: Deseret, 1996. An unabashedly admiring portrait of modern Mormonism's most well-traveled, publicly visible prophet.

Hill, Donna. *Joseph Smith, the First Mormon*. Garden City, N.J.: Doubleday, 1977. Most balanced one-volume biography available.

Kimball, Edward L., and Andrew E. Kimball. *Biography of Spencer W. Kimball*. Salt Lake City: Bookcraft, 1977. A well-written biography of one of late twentieth-century Mormonism's most dynamic and beloved prophets.

Pratt, Parley P. *The Autobiography of Parley P. Pratt*. Rev. ed., Scot F. Proctor and Maurine J. Proctor. Salt Lake City: Deseret, 2000. An especially eloquent and readable account of the life of one of early Mormonism's leading lights and theologians.

Schindler, Harold. *Orrin Porter Rockwell: Man of God, Son of Thunder*. Salt Lake City: University of Utah Press, 1966. Able and exciting biography of the gunslinger bodyguard of Joseph Smith and Brigham Young, and one of Mormonism's most colorful and controversial figures.

Smith, Lucy Mack. *History of Joseph Smith by his Mother*. Revised and enhanced edition. Ed. Scot Facer Proctor and Maurine Jensen Proctor. Salt Lake City: Bookcraft, 1996. One of few sympathetic sources of information on Joseph's early life. Inaccurate in many details, but indispensable nonetheless.

Plural Marriage

Daynes, Kathy. *More Wives than One: Transformation of the Mormon Marriage System, 1840–1910*. Urbana: University of Illinois Press, 2001. Perhaps the best (and most statistically based) overview of the varieties of Mormon plural marriage.

Gordon, Sarah Barringer. *The Mormon Question: Polygamy and Constitutional Conflict in the Nineteenth Century*. Chapel Hill: University of North Carolina Press, 2002. An excellent legal history of the antipolygamy crusade, with attention to the role of rhetoric in shaping the debate.

Hardy, C. Carmon. *Solemn Covenant: The Mormon Polygamous Passage*. Urbana: University of Illinois Press, 1992. The most thorough and scholarly treatment of Mormon defenses of polygamy, and of the murky years of church capitulation and transition out of the polygamous era.

Van Wagoner, Richard S. *Mormon Polygamy: A History*. Salt Lake City: Signature, 1989. A well-researched history of plural marriage from beginnings to the present.

Doctrine

Davies, Douglas J. *The Mormon Culture of Salvation: Force, Grace and Glory*. Aldershot, England: Ashgate, 2000. An insightful analysis of Mormon theology from a sociological perspective.

McConkie, Bruce R. *Mormon Doctrine*. Salt Lake City: Bookcraft, 1958. Not a compendium of official doctrine, but an enormously influential, encyclopedic volume nonetheless by one of modern Mormonism's most outspoken, theologically conservative apostles. Strongly influenced throughout by the writings of church President Joseph Fielding Smith, McConkie's father-in-law.

McMurrin, Sterling. *The Theological Foundations of the Mormon Religion*. Salt Lake City: University of Utah, 1959. Scholarly exposition of Mormon doctrine from a philosophically informed perspective.

Roberts, B. H. *The Truth, the Way, the Life: An Elementary Treatise on Theology*. Ed. John Welch. Provo, Utah: BYU Studies, 1994. An attempt at a comprehensive theology by one of the most gifted intellects among past church leaders.

Talmage, James E. *The Articles of Faith*. Salt Lake City: Deseret, 1899. Systematic, expansive treatment of the thirteen articles of Mormon belief.

Talmage, James E. *Jesus the Christ*. Salt Lake City: Deseret, 1915. A church-commissioned study of Christ by the LDS apostle that tracks his role from premortal deity to coming Messiah.

Scripture and Other Primary Sources

The Book of Mormon. Salt Lake City: The Church of Jesus Christ of Latter-day Saints, 1981. First published in 1830, the defining scripture of the LDS faith.

Clark, James R., ed. *Messages of the First Presidency of The Church of Jesus Christ of Latter-day Saints*. 5 vols. Salt Lake City: Bookcraft, 1966–71. A useful, though not current, compilation of official church letters, declarations, and pronouncements.

The Doctrine and Covenants. Salt Lake City: The Church of Jesus Christ of Latter-day Saints, 1981. Compendium of revelations received, mostly by Joseph Smith but with subsequent prophets represented as well.

Ehat, Andrew F., and Lyndon W. Cook. *The Words of Joseph Smith*. Provo, Utah: Religious Studies Center, Brigham Young University, 1980. Collection of discourses (from second-hand sources) from Smith's Nauvoo period, the era of his richest doctrinal production.

The Holy Bible Containing the Old and New Testaments. Salt Lake City: The Church of Jesus Christ of Latter-day Saints, 1979. This official LDS scripture is the King James Version, with extensive cross-references, study aids, and footnotes keyed to many emendations by Joseph Smith.

Jessee, Dean, ed. *Papers of Joseph Smith*. 2 vols. Salt Lake City: Deseret, 1989–92. Includes several versions of his "first vision," journal and letter excerpts, etc. Scholars at Brigham Young University are preparing a much more comprehensive edition of the Joseph Smith papers, to be published in 2005.

Joseph Smith's New Translation: of the Bible. Intr. F. Henry Edwards. Independence, Mo.: Herald, 1970. "A complete parallel column comparison of the Inspired Version of the Holy Scripture and the King James Authorized Version."

Journal of Discourses. 26 vols., reported by G. D. Watt et al. Liverpool: F. D. and S. W. Richards et al., 1851–86; reprint, Salt Lake City: n.p., 1974. Comprehensive collection of addresses delivered by LDS leaders in the Salt Lake tabernacle in the territorial era. Important source of teachings, although the discourses are not considered official statements of church doctrine.

Pearl of Great Price. Salt Lake City: The Church of Jesus Christ of Latter-day Saints, 1981. Fourth book of scripture, or "standard work" of the church. Includes writings attributed to Moses and Abraham, as well as revelations and writings of Joseph Smith and successors.

Smith, Joseph, Jr. *Teachings of the Prophet Joseph Smith*. Ed. Joseph Fielding Smith, Salt Lake City: Deseret, 1938. Quasi-canonical compendium of some of Smith's most important teachings.

Smith, Joseph, Jr. *History of the Church of Jesus Christ of Latter-day Saints*. 7 vols. Introduction and notes by B. H. Roberts. Salt Lake City: Deseret, 1952. Covers the first generation of Mormonism; written in first person, but based in many instances on minutes of his secretaries and scribes.

Vogel, Dan. *Early Mormon Documents*. Salt Lake City: Signature, 1996– . Extremely useful collection of primary source materials, comprising five volumes and counting.

Scriptures—Secondary

Backman, Milton V., Jr., and Richard O. Cowan. *Joseph Smith and the Doctrine and Covenants*. Salt Lake City: Deseret, 1992. Sets the revelations of the *Doctrine and Covenants* in LDS historical context.

Barlow, Philip. *Mormons and the Bible: The Place of the Latter-day Saints in American Religion*. New York: Oxford University Press, 1991. A comparative study of the place of the Bible in the LDS faith.

Gee, John. *A Guide to the Joseph Smith Papyri*. Provo: FARMS, 2000. A succinct apologetic overview of the history and controversy surrounding the Smith papyri.

Givens, Terryl L. *The Hand of Mormon: The American Scripture that Launched a New World Religion*. New York: Oxford University Press, 2002. An overview of the influence, apologetics, and reception of the Book of Mormon, with attention to the historical, theological, and institutional value attributed to the book.

Metcalfe, Brent Lee. *New Approaches to the Book of Mormon: Explorations in Critical Methodology*. Salt Lake City: Signature, 1993. Collection of essays that contest the historicity of the Book of Mormon, written mostly by dissidents and disaffected Mormons.

Nibley, Hugh. *Lehi in the Desert; the World of the Jaredites; There were Jaredites. The Collected Works of Hugh Nibley*. Vol. 4. Salt Lake City: Deseret and FARMS, 1988 (reprint of 1952 ed.). The first and hugely influential Mormon apologetics that employed cultural and textual criticism to argue for the Book of Mormon's plausibility.

Nibley, Hugh. *Since Cumorah. The Collected Works of Hugh Nibley*. Vol. 6. Salt Lake City: Deseret and FARMS, 1988 (reprint of 1967 ed.). A collection of evidence amassed by Mormonism's premiere twentieth-century scholar to defend the Book of Mormon's historicity.

Parry, Donald W., Daniel C. Patterson, and John W. Welch. *Echoes and Evidences of the Book of Mormon*. Provo, Utah: Foundation for Ancient Research and Mormon Studies, 2002. A compendium of Book of Mormon apologetics by LDS researchers.

Sorenson, John L. *An Ancient American Setting for the Book of Mormon*. Salt Lake City: Deseret and FARMS, 1996. A scholarly defense of a Mesoamerican locale for Book of Mormon history.

Sociology

Cornnwall, Marie, Tim B. Heaton, and Lawrence A. Young, eds. *Contemporary Mormonism: Social Science Perspectives*. Urbana and Chicago: University of Illinois Press, 1994.

Duke, James T., ed. *Latter-day Saint Social Life: Social Research on the LDS Church and its Members*. Provo, Utah: Religious Studies Center, Brigham Young University, 1998. Both of the above books offer a useful array of cultural and sociological studies of Mormonism.

Heaton, Tim B., Stephen J. Bahr, and Cardell K. Jacobson. *Health, Wealth, and Social Life of Mormons: Comparisons with National Trends*. Lewiston, N.Y.: Edwin Mellen, 2005. An impressive compilation of current statistics on sociological aspects of Mormonism.

Mauss, Armand. *The Angel and the Beehive: The Mormon Struggle with Assimilation*. Urbana: University of Illinois Press, 1984. A valuable study that explores post-1950 cultural changes and tensions inherent in modern Mormonism.

Mauss, Armand. "Flowers, Weeds, and Thistles: The State of Social Science Literature on the Mormons." In Ronald W. Walker, David J. Whittaker, and James B. Allen, eds. *Mormon History*. Urbana: University of Illinois Press, 2001, 153–97. This review essay surveys the strengths and shortcomings of social science research on Mormonism from its beginnings, by both Mormon and non-Mormon scholars.

Mauss, Armand, and Dynette Ivie Reynolds. "A Topical Guide to Published Social Science Literature on the Mormons." In James B. Allen, Ronald W. Walker, and David J. Whittaker, *Studies in Mormon History 1830–1997: An Indexed Bibliography*, Urbana and Chicago: University of Illinois Press, 2000. This comprehensive bibliography is the best source for recent and classic social science studies (most in journal article form) of Mormonism, on topics from health to humor to politics.

Sorenson, John. *Mormon Culture: Four Decades of Essays on Mormon Society and Personality*. Salt Lake City: New Sage, 1997. A provocative sampling of essays by an LDS anthropologist.

Reference

Allen, James B., Ronald W. Walker, and David J. Whittaker. *Studies in Mormon History, 1830–1997: An Indexed Bibliography*. Urbana and Chicago: University of Illinois Press, 2000. Comprehensive and superbly organized.

Church Almanac: The Church of Jesus Christ of Latter-day Saints. Salt Lake City: Deseret, published biannually. Terrific compendium of statistical information on all aspects of the LDS Church.

Flake, Chad J., and Larry W. Draper. *A Mormon Bibliography 1830–1930*. 2d ed. Provo, Utah: Religious Studies Center, 2003. More than 14,000 references to books, documents, and other materials relating to Mormonism.

Ludlow, Daniel H., ed. *Encyclopedia of Mormonism: The History, Scripture, Doctrine, and Procedures of the Church of Jesus Christ of Latter-day Saints.* New York: Macmillan, 1992. Highly authoritative and thorough four-volume reference work.

Whittaker, David J. *Mormon Americana: A Guide to Sources and Collections in the United States.* Provo, Utah: BYU Studies, 1995. An invaluable guide, but also includes superbly written overviews on topics from Mormon literature to historic sites.

Periodicals

BYU Studies. Published by Brigham Young University, this journal features scholarly articles in a variety of fields, including history, literature, and theology.

Church News. Weekly supplement to the *Deseret News,* including both news and feature articles from the international church. Also distributed separately.

Dialogue: A Journal of Mormon Thought. Describes itself as "an independent quarterly established to express Mormon culture and to examine the relevance of religion to secular life."

Ensign. The official monthly magazine of the church, with First Presidency messages, inspirational articles, and news of the church.

Exponent II. Founded in 1974 as "a forum for Mormon women to share their life experiences." Comprises essays, fiction, poetry, and interviews.

Journal of Book of Mormon Studies. A semi-annual journal that publishes research supporting Book of Mormon historicity and analyzing Book of Mormon doctrine and teachings. Produced by the Foundation for Ancient Research and Mormon Studies, now part of Institute for the Study and Preservation of Ancient Religious Texts, at Brigham Young University.

Journal of Mormon History. Published by the Mormon History Association, an association of more than a thousand Mormon and non-Mormon scholars and nonprofessionals.

Meridian. An on-line magazine catering to LDS members, with news, feature articles, and resources for teaching. (www.meridianmagazine.com)

Sunstone. An independent journal that at times has an edge to its contributions on "Mormon experience, scholarship, issues, and art." Increasingly associated with the dissident and liberal strains of Mormon thought.

Web Sites

www.lds.org   The official Web site of the Church of Jesus Christ of Latter-day Saints. Comprehensive treatment of history, doctrine, publications, etc.

www.mormon.org   Also an official LDS Web site, with basic information and viewable videos.

www.familysearch.org   The official Web site for genealogical research, listing hundreds of millions of names.

www.farms.byu.edu   The Web site of the Brigham Young University-related Foundation for Ancient Research and Mormon Studies (FARMS), which is primarily devoted to Book of Mormon scholarship. Articles by credentialed scholars, though clearly apologetic in nature.

www.famousmormons.net   A fun site that has sections from "famous people rumored to be Mormon but not" to LDS inventors, businessmen, and celebrities.

www.cofchrist.org   The official Web site of the Community of Christ, formerly the Reorganized Church of Jesus Christ of Latter Day Saints. Overview of beliefs and current ministry, with little emphasis on their history.

www.churchofjesuschristoflatterdaysaints.org   Web site of "the true Mormon church" that recognizes James Strang as Joseph Smith's successor. Wealth of historical and biographical material, with links to an assortment of doctrine, photographs, and material relevant to Mormonism generally but the Strangite movement in particular.

www.utlm.org   Web site of Utah Lighthouse Ministry, run by the couple most famous for their lifelong commitment to refuting the claims of Mormonism, Jerald and Sandra Tanner. Like other Web sites viewing Mormonism as a cult or dangerous deception, this site expressly attempts to "document problems with the claims of Mormonism."

www.religioustolerance.org/lds.htm   While clearly devoted to a critique of the LDS faith rather than neutrality, this site is more restrained than most of its kind. Unfortunately, the site often selects as representative of Mormon thought those quotations that are extreme or atypical, and consequently can lack accuracy as well as balance.

www.Inephi.com   An on-line version of the first edition of the Book of Mormon, accessible by page number or by modern chapter and verse designations.

Databases

Gospelink 2001. Deseret Book, 2000. A collection of several hundred books and both historical and scholarly periodicals on the subject of Mormonism, virtually all written by Mormon authors. Excellent source of both doctrinal and historical backgrounds and commentary, though lacking in any negative or critical treatments.

New Mormon Studies CD-ROM. Smith Research Associates/Signature Books, 1998. From an independent publisher, contains 970 works, including primary and secondary source materials in Mormon studies.

Selected Collections from the Archives of the Church of Jesus Christ of Latter-day Saints. Provo: Brigham Young University Press, 2002. This massive collection of seventy-four DVDs contains over four hundred thousand images of manuscripts from LDS history.

Index

About the Author

TERRYL L. GIVENS is Professor of Religion and Literature at the University of Richmond, Virginia. He is the author of *By the Hand of Mormon: The American Scripture that Launched a New World Religion* (2002) and *The Viper on the Hearth: Mormons, Myths, and the Construction of Heresy* (1997).